STUDIES IN NAVAL HISTORY

General Editor
N. A. M. RODGER

PIRACY AND THE ENGLISH GOVERNMENT, 1616–1642

PIRACY AND THE ENGLISH GOVERNMENT, 1616–1642

David Delison Hebb

Scolar Press

© David Delison Hebb, 1994

All rights reserved. No part of this publication may be reproduced, stored in a retrieval system, or transmitted in any form or by any means, electronic, mechanical, photocopying, recording, or otherwise without the prior permission of the publisher.

Published by
SCOLAR PRESS
Gower House
Croft Road
Aldershot
Hants GU11 3HR
England

Ashgate Publishing Company
Old Post Road
Brookfield
Vermont 05036
USA

British Library Cataloguing-in-Publication data.
Hebb, David Delison
  Piracy and the English Government,
  1603–42. – (Studies in Naval History)
  I. Title II. Series
  359.00941

ISBN 0–85967–949–7

Library of Congress Cataloging-in-Publication data
Hebb, David Delison
    Piracy and the English goverment, 1616–1642 / David Delison Hebb.
      p. cm. — (Studies in naval history)
    Based on the author's thesis (Ph.D.).
    Includes bibliographical references and index.
    ISBN 0–85967–949–7
    1. Great Britain—History, Naval—Stuarts, 1603–1714. 2. Great Britain—Politics and government—1603–1649. 3. Pirates—
—History—17th century. I. Title. II. Series.
DA86.H43 1994
941.06—dc20   93–8651
                 CIP

Typeset in 10 point Times by Photoprint, Torquay, Devon and printed in Great Britain at the University Press, Cambridge.

CONTENTS

List of Tables, Plates and Maps vii

List of Abbreviations xii

Conventions xiii

Acknowledgements xiv

Introduction 1

PART 1   JAMES I AND THE PIRATE SCOURGE

    1   James I and the suppression of piracy 7

    2   Naval finance: the Algiers expedition 21

    3   The Algiers expedition: diplomatic background 43

    4   Anglo-Spanish negotiations 60

PART 2   THE ALGIERS EXPEDITION AND THE COST OF PIRACY

    5   The Algiers expedition 77

    6   The Algiers expedition: assessments, aims and accomplishments 105

		7 Captivity and redemption	136
PART 3		POLITICS, APPEASEMENT, SHIP MONEY AND THE SALLEE EXPEDITION	
	8	Diplomatic initiative: Sir Thomas Roe's embassy	173
	9	Piracy, parliament and personal rule	198
	10	Piracy and the origins of Caroline Ship Money	219
	11	The Sallee expedition of 1637	237
	12	Epilogue and conclusion	266

Sources and Bibliography — 277

Index — 293

TABLES, PLATES AND MAPS

Table 1	Customs records comparing assessments with size of towns' trade	40
Table 2	The chief characteristics of the royal warships	82
Table 3	Merchant ships in Mansell's fleet	83
Table 4	English losses to the Barbary pirates, 18 May 1639 to 15 January 1640	141
Plate 1	Algiers in the 17th century, showing the 'mole' fortifications in the centre foreground	viii
Plate 2	Stern quarter view of the *Sovereign of the Seas*, 1637, showing the elaborate carving and gilt work	ix
Map 1	The Western Mediterranean in the 17th century	x
Map 2	Sally, 1637, showing Rainsborough's siege lines, from John Dunton, *A True Journal of the Sally Fleet*	xi

Plate 1 Algiers in the 17th century, showing the 'mole' fortifications in the centre foreground. Courtesy of the National Maritime Museum

Plate 2 Stern quarter view of the *Sovereign of the Seas*, 1637, showing the elaborate carving and gilt work. Courtesy of the National Maritime Museum

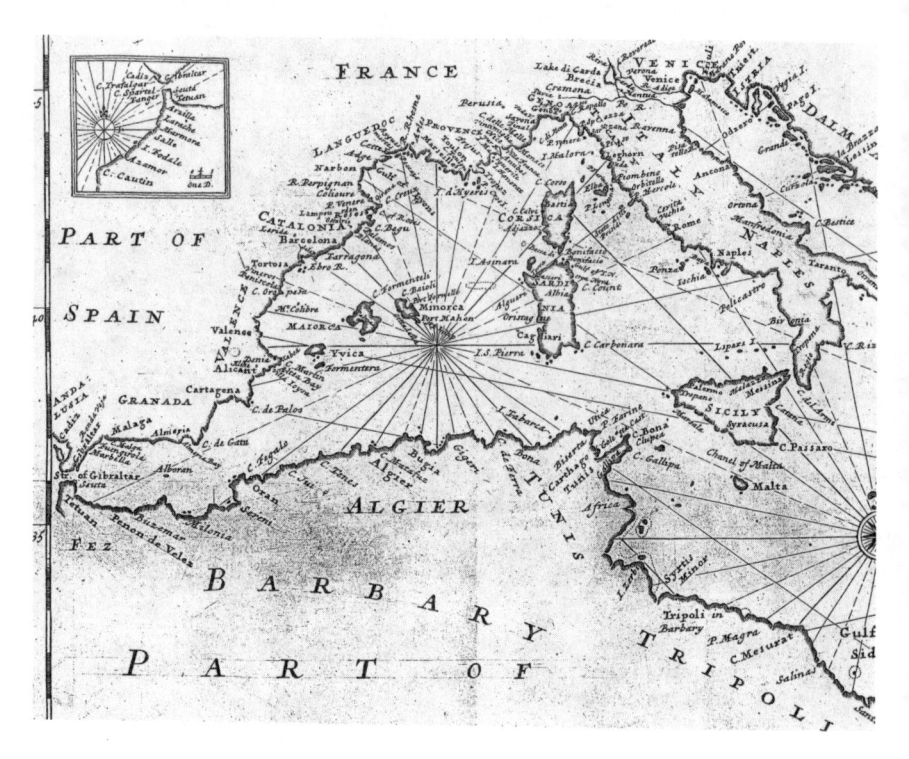

Map 1 The Western Mediterranean in the 17th century

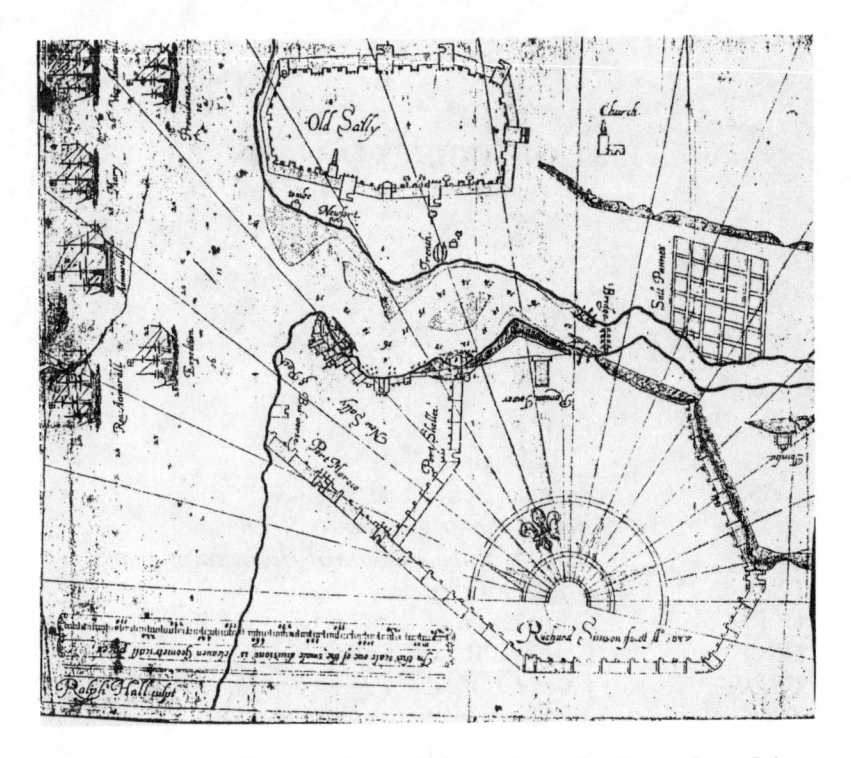

Map 2 Sally, 1637, showing Rainsborough's seige lines, from John Dunton, *A True Journal of the Sally Fleet*

LIST OF ABBREVIATIONS

AGS	Archivo General de Simancas, Spain
APC	*Acts of the Privy Council of England*
BIHR	*Bulletin of the Institute of Historical Research*
BL	British Library
CLRO	Corporation of London Record Office
CRO	Cornwall Record Office
CSPV	*Calendar of State Papers Venetian*
DNB	*Dictionary of National Biography*
EHR	*English Historical Review*
Econ. Hist. Rev.	*Economic History Review*
HLRO	House of Lords Records Office
HMC	Historical Manuscripts Commission
KAO	Kent Archives Office
MM	*The Mariner's Mirror*
PRO	Public Record Office
TRHS	*Transactions of the Royal Historical Society*

CONVENTIONS

All quotations cited in this book have been modernized, except where the original spelling or punctuation has been thought necessary to convey the style of the writer or particular sense of the document. Also, contractions have been extended except where the original form is required for reasons of style or sense.

The dates of English documents are Old Style, but with the year regarded as beginning on 1 January. Continental documents dated in the New Style have been cited this way. In any case where uncertainty may arise, both Old and New Style dates are given: for example, 1/10 January, or 7 March 1620/21.

Two forms of citations of manuscripts in the Public Record Office documents are used. So that the reader may more conveniently refer to the source, I have cited the document or item number for manuscripts which have been calendared, rather than the folio: e.g., PRO, SP 14/90/24. For uncalendared manuscripts, I have cited the document by folio number, e.g., PRO, SP 84/77/f.124.

The translations of French and Spanish documents are my own while my translations of Dutch documents have been corrected and improved by Dr A.H. Marshall.

ACKNOWLEDGEMENTS

This book has evolved from my PhD thesis which was supervised by Penelope J. Corfield and Conrad S.R. Russell. I wish to thank both for their friendly instruction, patience and assistance over the years. I would also like to thank my examiners, Gerald E. Alymer and Peter Earle for their helpful comments and suggestions.

Although historical research is a lonely activity, one works with and benefits greatly from the labour and friendship of others. Over the years, many historians have aided me with the fruits of their research and knowledge, including James Cockburn, Richard Conquest, Patricia Crawford, Richard Cust, Gregor Duncan, Peter Earle, John Fielding, Norah Fuidge, Jordan Goodman, Vanessa Harding, Graham Haslam, Alistair Hawkyard, Katrina Honeyman, Sari Hornstein, Ann Hughes, Mark Kishlansky, Peter Lake, Roger Lockyer, Joyce Lorimer, Al Marshall, Gigliola Pagano de Divitiis, Geoffrey Parker, Nicholas Rodger, Henry Rosevere, Ian Roy, Sandy Solomon, Victoria Stappels-Johnson, Victor Stater, David Thomas, Nicholas Tyacke, Sarah Tyacke, Alexandra Wigdor and Nuala Zehedieh.

I am indebted to numerous archivists and librarians for their courtesy and helpfulness. In particular I would like to thank the staff and members of the Institute of Historical Research, University of London, whose kindness and assistance has made my research a more pleasant undertaking. I would also like to thank the leaders and members of the research seminars at the Institute which I have attended and at which I have given draft versions of several of the chapters of this book. In particular, I would like to pay tribute to three historians, now deceased, who provided guidance and encouragement when I was beginning my research: Joel Hurstfield, S.T. Bindoff, and F.J. Fisher.

Finally, I would like to pay special thanks to three women without whose generous assistance, affection and encouragement I could not have written this book: Penelope Corfield, Patricia Croot, and Jane Waldfogel.

DDH

INTRODUCTION

When James I observed that piracy[1] had become 'too deeply rooted among' his English subjects he was at once both wiser and more foolish than he knew.[2] From the time of Elizabeth I, the English had been perceived as a nation of pirates. This image persisted into the reign of James I, has been sustained in literature, and has now become fixed in the popular mind.[3] The lives of famous English pirates and their exploits have been related many times, and their social and economic background analysed meticulously and well by academic historians.[4]

However, English piracy was not entrenched as deeply as James I believed. On the contrary, in the early 17th century English piracy declined sharply.[5] Indeed, at the very time James was

---

[1] Piracy is defined in the *Oxford English Dictionary*, pp. 900, 1389, as 'The practice or crime of robbery and depredation on the sea or navigable rivers, etc., or by descent from the sea upon the coast, by persons not holding a commission from an established state.' This form of predation differs from privateering which is 'by armed vessels owned and officered by private persons, and holding a commission from the government, called "letters of marque" '. Privateering in the early Stuart period has been covered carefully and well by J.C. Appleby, 'English Privateering during the Spanish and French Wars, 1625–30' (unpublished PhD thesis, University of Hull, 1983); I wish to thank Dr Appleby for the many useful comments he has made.

[2] *CSPV*, 1619–1621, p. 356.

[3] See C.M. Senior, *A Nation of Pirates: English Piracy in its Heyday*; N. Williams, *The Sea Dogs*; P. Newark, *The Crimson Book of Pirates*.

[4] R.O. Moore, 'Some Aspects of the Origin and Nature of English Piracy, 1603–25' (unpublished PhD thesis, University of Virginia, 1960); C.M. Senior, 'An Investigation of the Activities and Importance of English Pirates 1603–40' (unpublished PhD thesis, University of Bristol, 1973). I wish to thank Dr Senior for the generous advice he has given me.

[5] Senior, *Nation of Pirates*, pp. 145–52, convincingly shows that English piracy had declined in the second decade of the century, and this trend continued.

complaining about the piratical nature of his subjects, they were much more often victims of foreign pirates rather than perpetrators of piracy.

The expansion of the English merchant marine, which virtually doubled between 1582 and 1629, and the development of Atlantic and Mediterranean trade routes made English shipping much more vulnerable to piracy.[1] However, the damage to English shipping from foreign pirates has escaped the notice of historians, and the attempts of the English government to counter or suppress pirates has not been appreciated by scholars.[2] This book attempts to redress this deficiency; an assessment of English losses to piracy between the years 1616 and 1642 will be provided as well as a description of the diplomatic, political, economic, and social consequences of piracy in this period.[3]

The beginning and ending dates of this study need a word of explanation. Piracy changed dramatically in the second decade of the 17th century. Pirates from the Barbary states began to operate in the Atlantic. For example, in 1616 a fleet of pirates from Algiers raided Santa Maria in the Azores and carried away hundreds of the island's inhabitants. This expansion had consequences, and certainly from this year English shipping began to suffer and the government became aware of the pirate threat. The ending date was chosen for more familiar reasons. First, the outbreak of the Great Rebellion disrupted government policy. From 1642, king and parliament were so preoccupied with political and military matters that attempts to deal with the problem of piracy effectively ceased for several years. Second, the Civil War altered the problem of piracy. The war substantially increased naval resources available to the government, and though foreign pirates continued to be a source of trouble, they were less of a threat than formerly.

Originally, I intended to analyse the problem of piracy in terms of protection rents and costs along the lines suggested by Professor

---

[1] R. Davis, *The Rise of the English Shipping Industry: In the Seventeenth and Eighteenth Centuries*, p. 10, and by the same author, 'England and the Mediterranean, 1570–1670', in *Studies in the Economic History of Tudor and Stuart England*, ed. F.J. Fisher, pp. 117–37.
[2] Only D.G.E. Hurd, 'Some Aspects of the Attempts of the Government to Suppress Piracy During the Reign of Elizabeth I' (unpublished MA thesis, University of London, 1961), is directly concerned with this topic.
[3] Senior, *Nation of Pirates*, p. 145. E.G. Friedman, *Spanish Captives in North Africa in the Early Modern Age*, p. 13, is able to show that pirate attacks on Spanish vessels in the Atlantic increased eight-fold in the two decades after 1610.

Lane and developed by other economic historians.[1] This form of analysis identifies and calculates the amount traders have to pay directly or indirectly to protect their goods against the various forms of organized violence. Lower protection costs may give a group of traders or the traders of one nation a comparative advantage. However, greater familiarity with the source material revealed insoluble difficulties in applying this approach to the actions of pirates against English shipping in the early 17th century. The absence of a series of marine insurance records, for example, makes it impossible to calculate ship losses with the precision required by this approach. Moreover, the organization and financing of the navy make it exceedingly difficult to define and apportion protection costs rationally. For example, what portion of expenditures on a warship, like the *Sovereign of the Seas*, should be considered as a protection cost if the great size of the vessel and costly decorations were primarily a consequence of royal psychological needs or aesthetic desires?

Even were suitable evidence available, an analysis of protection costs would provide only a limited, static picture. It would not show why the government responded or how effectively. Consequently, a different and more dynamic approach to the study of piracy has been employed in this book. Estimates of economic damage caused by pirates have been made, but other costs, including the social damage and political implications of piracy are explored and evaluated so that a more comprehensive assessment of the problem can be presented.

Piracy was not the chief national or international problem faced by the Stuarts, but as Sir John Digby advised James I, it was like a thorn in the foot – painful and crippling – hurtful enough to compel one to seek a remedy.[2] The responses of the government to the problem of piracy form the second, major theme of this study. Sometimes naval force was employed while at other times diplomacy or appeasement was favoured. The reasons for the adoption of these very different policies are explored and related to broader governmental concerns. In a sense, this book is an extended essay about policy-making – an attempt to discover how

---

[1] F.C. Lane, *Venice and History: The Collected Papers of Frederic C. Lane*, pp. 383–9; also, C.G. Reed, 'Transactions Costs and Differential Growth: Seventeenth Century Western Europe', *Journal of Economic History*, XXXIII, pp. 182–90, and N. Steensgaard, *The Asian Trade Revolution of the Seventeenth Century, the East India Companies, and the Decline of the Caravan Trade*.
[2] BL, Add. MS. 1580, f.108.

information was acquired by the central government and used to formulate policy. It also serves as a case study of how local, national, and international political interests shaped government policy, and how, in turn, they were influenced by the policies of the Stuart government. In the course of research for this book, it quickly became apparent that piracy was more than a naval problem and, consequently, I have tried to put it in a wider and truer context. Also, as I began to research the responses of the English government to the problem of piracy, I became aware of how much policy was determined by political events on the Continent and England's relations with the continental powers. In my narrative and analysis of events, I have, therefore, attempted to place the problem of piracy in the diplomatic context in which English policy was made and executed.

Part 1
JAMES I AND THE PIRATE SCOURGE

1
JAMES I AND THE SUPPRESSION OF PIRACY

On 20 March 1617, James I, whilst on his way to Scotland, sent the Privy Council the following message:

> One thing there is, which we again seriously recommend unto your diligence, which is a matter of a high nature, wherein both the advancement of our honour and the welfare of our loving subjects are deeply interested: for what can be more honourable to the propagation of our name and glory, to all ensuing posterity; then when we have not only governed our own kingdoms in peace and tranquility, but established by the enterprise of our authority a settled repose in all our neighbour countries, to draw our sword against the enemies of God, and man, that is the pirates, which at this time infest the seas, to the detriment of intercourse, and commerce of all trade: or wherein can we more clearly demonstrate our affectionate care to our good subjects, then by our protection to endeavour to enable them, that they may enjoy themselves, and the continuance of their wonted trades in peace and security.[1]

This passage of the king's letter has a double significance: first of all, the king's recommendation marks the first definite step in setting out an expedition against the pirates of Algiers; but, just as importantly, it provides an indication that the expedition was, in James's words, 'a matter of a high nature' and one which interested the monarch personally.

In part, James was motivated by a desire to secure the welfare of

[1] PRO, SP 14/90/136.

his subjects and their commerce; but also, as he makes plain, the expedition was being undertaken to advance his honour. Although it is a letter of instruction, the tone is very personal; it expresses James's sentiments as well as offering guidance to his government in London. This passage also reveals the king's intense dislike of pirates. They were more than an irritation; they were enemies, not only of man but of God as well; they were deserving of the sword. In writing this piece, James also cast himself in a familiar role – that of a peacemaker of the highest order. By a stroke of the pen, the king in this letter grandly proclaimed his intention to bring order and tranquility to the seas.

From the beginning of his reign, James I termed himself *Rex Pacificus*, and gloried in this title.[1] He told his first parliament that of the many blessings he was bringing, peace was foremost and a consequence of his person: 'I have ever, I praise God, kept peace and amity with all, which hath been so far tied to my person.[2] Later he claimed that he knew 'not by what fortune the diction of *Pacificus* was added to my title at my coming to England, that of the lion, expressing true fortitude, having been my diction before. But I am not ashamed of this addition. For King Solomon was a figure of Christ in that he was a king of peace.'[3] He delighted in being portrayed as a modern Solomon. He wished to be the peacemaker of Europe, settling the quarrels that divided the peoples and princes. In the first years of his reign, James sought to bring an end to the conflict in the Low Countries, and in the last half-dozen he laboured to prevent, limit, and end the Thirty Years War.[4] Though a self-proclaimed peacemaker, he was not a pacifist and on several occasions in his reign resorted to the use of military force, as he was to do against the pirates of Algiers.

James's formative years in Scotland caused him to develop an unusually strong hatred of men of force. Separated from his mother soon after birth, he grew up a pawn in a world of power politics. The future king was at the mercy of older, stronger, ruthless men who manoeuvred to use him for their own ends.[5]

---

[1] *Journal of the House of Lords* hereafter *Lords Journals*, III, p. 250b; D.H. Willson, *King James VI and I*, pp. 271–2.
[2] Willson, *King James*, p. 271.
[3] Ibid., p. 272.
[4] Ibid., pp. 271–87; also S.R. Gardiner, *History of England: From the Accession of James I to the Outbreak of the Civil War, 1603–1642*, III, p. 361.
[5] Willson, *King James*, pp. 13–57; J.M. Brown, 'Scottish Politics 1567–1625', in *The Reign of James VI and I*, ed. A.G.R. Smith, pp. 22–7.

Advisers and friends were banished and killed as factions fought for control of the boy.[1] He was bullied, threatened, and even kidnapped before he was old enough and sufficiently skilful to gain ascendancy over the lords and ministers of state and kirk.[2]

Given such a background, it is not surprising that timidity marked James's character, so much so, that some thought him a coward.[3] As king, he showed little respect for violent forceful men, like soldiers, and he also displayed a positive loathing of pirates for they, above all others, epitomized a violent disregard for the settled, peaceful order of society.[4] 'If ever a king hated pirates it was James', observed D.H. Willson, the king's foremost biographer.[5] Pirates harmed and intimidated the king's subjects, carried them off into slavery, disrupted commerce, and damaged amicable relations between states. These were practical reasons for disliking pirates, but the king's animosity rested on fundamental, philosophical reasons as well. While objectionable in many ways, military men and privateers at least acted within the framework of a society based on state order: pirates, on the other hand, were patently contemptuous of all rulers and state authority.

From the beginning of the reign, James's hatred of pirates was very pronounced. In 1603, when the Venetian ambassador complained about some English pirates and accused the Lord High Admiral of aiding them, the king could hardly control his anger. As the ambassador spoke, James began to show 'extreme impatience, twisting his body, striking his hands together, and tapping with his feet'. Unable to contain himself any longer, he cried out at last, ' "By God I'll hang the pirates with my own hands, and my Lord Admiral as well" '.[6] Though the Lord Admiral was not hung, many pirates were. Admiralty court records attest to the activity of the government in these years.[7] On 22 December 1608, for example, 19 pirates were hung in a row from Wapping pier,[8] the traditional place of execution for pirates.[9]

---

[1] G. Donaldson, *Scotland: James V to James VII*, pp. 171–5, 178–80.
[2] J.M. Brown, 'Scottish Politics', pp. 22–39.
[3] Willson, *King James*, p. 274. Sir John Oglander thought James the 'most cowardly man that ever I knew': *A Royalist's Notebook: The Commonplace Book of Sir John Oglander, Kt., of Nunwell*, ed. F. Bamford, p. 193.
[4] Willson, *King James*, pp. 273–4.
[5] Ibid., p. 274.
[6] *CSPV*, 1603–1607, p. 100.
[7] PRO, HCA 1/5/39 to 1/6/187. Oyer and Terminer Records show that out of 260 criminal actions, 240 were for piracy or receiving or abetting pirates.
[8] PRO, SP 14/90/136.
[9] C.M. Senior, *A Nation of Pirates: English Piracy in its Heyday*, p. 121.

Years later, James liked to boast to the Spanish ambassador how great an enemy of pirates he was and that in the few years since his coming to the throne of England more pirates had been hanged than in the previous hundred years.[1] In the early years, the efforts of the Crown were aimed at a reduction of piracy in English waters or by Englishmen since this was the main source of trouble.[2] The king's prerogative powers were employed to suppress piracy. Royal commissions were established and proclamations issued to enforce the law or extend its effectiveness.[3] Royal pronouncements against pirates came almost yearly in the first decade of Stuart rule: in 1603, 'A Proclamation concerning Warlike ships at Sea' was issued, and three months later general instructions were given in 'A Proclamation to represse all Piracies and Depredations upon the Sea'; in 1604 came 'A Proclamation for the search and apprehension of certaine Pirats'; on 1 March 1605, 'A Proclamation for revocation of Mariners from forreine Services' struck at English pirates serving abroad, while a second on 8 July, 'A Proclamation with certaine Ordinances to be observed by his Majesties subjects toward the King of Spaine' further restricted English pirates; on 13 June 1606, 'A Proclamation for the search and apprehension of certaine Pirates' was published; and on 8 January 1609, 'A Proclamation against Pirats' was promulgated.[4]

In these early years, most of the Crown's measures were directed toward English pirates or those that supported them, but in the second decade of his rule a new threat emerged: pirates from North Africa began to prey upon English ships. Being 'Turks', i.e., heretics, as well as pirates, they were doubly damned in the king's eyes. Long before, when still a very young man in Scotland, James had expressed hatred of the Turks in an epic poem. Entitled *Lepanto*, it celebrated the Christian naval victory of 1571.[5] It provides an insight into the royal mind and a partial

---

[1] *Documentos Inéditos para la Historia de España*, IV, pp. 52–8.
[2] Ibid., pp. 124, 135–6, 147–8.
[3] PRO, HCA 14/39/ff.217–218.
[4] *Stuart Royal Proclamations*, vol. I, *Royal Proclamations of King James, 1603–25*, ed. J.F. Larkin and P.L. Hughes, nos 15, 28, 46, 50, 53, 67, 93, contain the proclamations referred to above. This list is only a partial indication of royal interest and the use of royal instruments to strike at piracy. Other proclamations, such as that of 27 November 1609, which prohibited English merchants from trading in ports frequented by pirates, dealt with the matter indirectly. See for example, PRO, SP 14/37/96.
[5] *New Poems of James I of England*, ed. Allen W. Westcott; *Lusus Regius, being Poems and other Pieces by King James I*, ed. R.S. Rait.

explanation of the king's motives in supporting the proposal of an expedition against the 'Turks' of Algiers. The poem begins with a confrontation between God and Satan, in which God portrays the Turks as agents of Satan who incites their attacks on Christians. God then declares that Christendom will resist the Turks and sends the Angel Gabriel to inspire the Venetians to take up arms. But Venice is too dispirited and unable to act alone. Victory comes only after the Christian states unite. Under the command of the princely hero, Don John of Austria, the united fleet sets forth to crush the Turks.

Although James's account of the defeat of the Turks was romanticized, the battle of Lepanto, of course, was very real and marked a turning point in the struggle for naval supremacy in the western Mediterranean.[1] No more great naval battles in the Mediterranean took place, but the conflict between Moslems and Christians continued for centuries with piracy becoming 'a substitute for declared war'.[2] Though referred to as 'Turks', these pirates were of several nationalities and operated not from Turkish bases but from the Barbary ports of Algiers, Tunis, Tripoli, and Sallee.[3] By the second decade of the 17th century, none of these pirate capitals was under Turkish control.[4] Sallee was often in rebellion against the Emperor of Morocco, and had long since ignored Ottoman.[5] The three North African regencies had thrown off much of the authority of the Sultan, even though they still owed allegiance to Constantinople.[6]

Nominally, the Barbary regencies were governed by a Bashaw (or Pasha), the Sultan's representative, but the real power in the Barbary states rested in the military order of janissaries. Through their governing council, the Divan, made up of senior officers, they elected their leaders, the Beys or Deys, who *de facto* ruled the

---

[1] A.C. Hess, 'The Battle of Lepanto and its Place in Mediterranean History', *Past and Present*, no. 57 (1972), pp. 53–73. Hess downgrades the long-term significance of the Turkish defeat.

[2] F. Braudel, *The Mediterranean: And the Mediterranean World in the Age of Philip II*, vol. II, p. 865.

[3] P. Earle, *Corsairs of Malta and Barbary*, pp. 29–30, 35; J. Pignon, 'La Milice des janissaires de Tunis au Temps des Deys, 1590–1630', *Les Cahiers de Tunisie*, IV (1956), p. 307; Pierre Dan, *Histoire de Barbarie et de ses corsaires*, p. 110.

[4] E.G. Friedman, *Spanish Captives in North Africa in the Early Modern Age*, pp. 9–10, indicates that Constantinople started to lose control in the early 1590s.

[5] R. Coindreau, *Les Corsaires de Salé*; see also, Friedman, op. cit., pp. 10, 12, 24–5.

[6] R. Mantran, 'L'Evolution des relations entre la Tunisie et l'Empire Ottoman du XVIe au XIXe siècle', *Les Cahiers de Tunisie*, VII (1959).

states.[1] The janissaries initially provided the Ottoman emperors with a military force to conquer and subdue the native Moorish population of the region. But as the 16th century developed, their composition changed; increasingly their recruits were drawn from the islands of the Aegean, Cyprus, and the Levant. The functions of the 'Turkish' rulers also changed over time. They still served to control the peoples of the Barbary hinterland and in times of declared war supported the Sultan, but increasingly they became integrated in the economic and piratical activities of the port towns.[2]

By the 17th century the Barbary regencies had in fact become pirate states;[3] in the words of a distinguished 17th-century jurist, Charles Molloy, they were 'pirates that have reduced themselves into a Government or State, as those of Algiers, Sally, Tunis, and the like'[4] and therefore not entitled to the rights and privileges due to privateers of civilized states. Molloy's judgement accurately reflects a political reality. They may have been highly organized and supported by a nominal, local authority, and therefore they were different from simple freebooters, but in a legal sense they were, nevertheless, pirates.[5] Their activity was never authorized by the Sultan, and, at times, it was carried out against his express wishes.[6]

The rise of Algiers, Sallee, and to a lesser extent Tunis and

---

[1] Earle, *Corsairs*, pp. 24–5; J.B. Wolf, *The Barbary Coast: Algiers under the Turks, 1500–1830*, pp. 77–8. Originally the Beys had been nominated by Constantinople: Friedman, *Spanish Captives*, p. 9.

[2] Earle, *Corsairs*, pp. 24–5.

[3] J.E.G. de Montmorency, 'Piracy and the Barbary Corsairs', *Law Quarterly Review*, XXXV (1919), pp. 133–42. The piratical nature of the Barbary states has been the subject of historical dispute. Nineteenth-century historians such as R.L. Playfair, *The Scourge of Christendom: Annals of British Relations with Algiers prior to the French Conquest* and S. Lane-Poole, *The Barbary Corsairs*, portrayed the corsairs as villainous pirates. Sir Godfrey Fisher, *The Barbary Legend: Trade and Piracy in North Africa, 1415–1830*, set out, as his title indicates, to correct the earlier view. Though stated fairly, this work goes too far in exculpating the Barbary corsairs. This is especially true for the early 17th century, and may be a consequence of the author's reliance on calendars rather than manuscripts. It must be observed that contemporaries always referred to them as pirates and treated them so at law, an unambiguous test of their status.

[4] C. Molloy, *De jure maritimo et navali: or, a treatise of affairs maritime and of commerce*, p. 61. Molloy's judgment is certainly accurate in a legal sense but it does not take into account the contribution made to the growth of piracy in the Barbary states by nominal Christians; see Earle, *Corsairs*, pp. 97–123.

[5] This was the opinion of Henry Martin, Chief Judge, High Court of Admiralty: PRO, SP 16/40/24.

[6] PRO, SP 105/110/f.87v, contains a realization by Council that the Sultan was unable to control pirates.

Tripoli, as centres of piracy can only be understood when considered in the context of the Moslem-Christian conflict.[1] Their growth owes much to the struggles that took place in the late 16th and early 17th centuries Christian world, and especially in Spain. Although conquered in the 14th and 15th centuries, the Moorish elements were never assimilated. Instead, many Moriscos retained the language and cultural traits of their Islamic heritage, until measures were taken in the mid-16th century to enforce adoption of Christian belief and Castilian customs.[2] This brought rebellion by the Moriscos in 1568–70 in Granada and the eventual destruction of the Moorish community in that province with thousands killed or forced to flee.[3] Many of the embittered survivors reached the North African ports where they found scope to take revenge on Spanish or Christian ships.[4] The final expulsion of the Moriscos occurred in the years between 1609 and 1614 when tens of thousands more were massacred or expelled.[5] In all, about 275 000 Moriscos were driven out, many fleeing to the Barbary ports, bringing with them grievances which they took out on Spanish subjects or Christian ships who fell within their grasp.[6]

The arrival of northern Europeans also contributed to the growth of the Barbary ports as pirate bases. Some came first, as merchants, to trade cloth or fish.[7] Others sought a safe port from which to continue the trade they had learned during the long wars with Spain. With peace, privateering became illegal and piracy was virtually eliminated from British waters as bases in the west country and Ireland were eliminated. Some former privateers and pirates came to Algiers or Tunis or the other havens of North Africa.[8] From these ports they could obtain supplies, refit their ships, rest, and sell their booty. Most of the famous pirates of these years – Gifford, Verney, Ward, Dansker – operated from

---

[1] Braudel, *The Mediterranean*, II, pp. 865, 872–91; Earle, *Corsairs*, pp. 3–22.
[2] J.H. Elliott, *Imperial Spain, 1469–1716*, pp. 50–1, 232–5; A.D. Ortiz, *The Golden Age of Spain, 1516–1659*, pp. 166–76.
[3] Elliott, *Imperial Spain*, pp. 235–7; Ortiz, op. cit., p. 37.
[4] Ortiz, op. cit., pp. 170–2. This point is skilfully developed by Friedman, *Spanish Captives*, pp. 12, 24–5.
[5] Ortiz, op. cit., p. 172. In 1610 the entire community (1200) of Hornachos in the Extremadura was expelled; they settled in Sallee.
[6] Elliott, *Imperial Spain*, pp. 301–3; Ortiz, op. cit., pp. 170–2.
[7] English merchants were trading with Barbary ports from the late 16th century. John Tipton was appointed consul to Tunis, Tripoli, and Algiers in 1585: A.C. Wood, *A History of the Levant Company*, p. 15; and was residing there in the 1580s: Playfair, *Scourge of Christendom*, p. 26.
[8] Senior, *Nation of Pirates*, p. 87.

the Barbary ports.[1] Though they may have come out of necessity, some of these old sea-dogs found the cities of Barbary positively attractive, not only for professional reasons but also for the degree of personal freedom that they found.[2]

These northerners were credited with making significant contributions to the growth of 'Turkish' piracy. It was claimed that they introduced local mariners and pirates to the use of northern-type sailing ships and taught the Moslems to navigate the Straits of Gibraltar.[3] Until the early 17th century the Barbary pirates relied on large, heavily-manned, oar-driven galleys to sink or capture their victims, but from the second decade of the 17th century, they began to employ not only lateen but square-rigged sailing ships in their piracy.[4] It is certainly possible that the 'Turks' adopted northern-type ships as a result of the presence of renegade Christian pirates, but it seems just as likely that the inspiration came from other sources.[5] Merchant ships from Northern Europe traded with the Barbary ports decades before the Christian pirates arrived. As a consequence, there were many opportunities for the 'Turks' to become familiar with northern-type sailing ships. The eventual adoption of northern-type ships may have come independently. It may have come as a response to the same stimuli: the heavy weather and wind system of the Atlantic made strong ships and sail power attractive, and the increasing effectiveness of heavy guns may have influenced the evolution of ship design. In a similar manner, it is possible that the 'Turks' acquired

---

[1] For an account of the famous Captain Dansker's activities by the English consul in Algiers, c. 1608/1609, see PRO, SP 71/1/f.17. Dansker was '. . . a ffleming borne . . .' and sailed in a great ship built in Lubeck; his crew consisted of about 20 Christians including some Englishmen, but the rest were mainly 'Turks'. Between 17 November and 8 December 1608, Dansker took three ships, a great argosy from Sicily with a viceroy aboard and two small English ships from Dartmouth. In the fight with the argosy, 25 Turks were killed and about 50 wounded; on the argosy between 50 to 70 were killed and 100 wounded. Both English captains surrendered without a fight; their ships returned to Algiers but not the goods.
[2] Ibid., pp. 20, 22, 25, 27, 29, 36, 38–40, 66, 89–101; *CSPV*, 1607–1610, pp. 140–1.
[3] Braudel, *The Mediterranean*, I, p. 119; J. Pignon, 'Un Document inédit sur la Tunisie au debut du XVIIe', *Les Cahiers de Tunisie*, IX (1961), pp. 141–209.
[4] Fleets at Lepanto were made up entirely of galleys; Earle, *Corsairs*, pp. 48–53; Cottington to Buckingham in, *Cabala, Sive Scrinia Sacra: Mysteries of State and Government, in Letters of Illustrious Persons and Great Ministers of State, As well Foreign as Domestick, In the Reigns of King Henry the Eighth, Queen Elizabeth, King James, and King Charles*, part I, pp. 201–2; PRO, SP 14/90/24. For more details on the fleets of the Barbary pirates, see A. Devoulx, 'La marine de la Regence d'Alger', *Revue Africaine*, XIII (1869), pp. 384–420.
[5] J.F. Guilmartin, jr, *Gunpowder and Galleys: Changing Technology and Mediterranean Warfare at Sea in the Sixteenth Century*, pp. 253–73.

navigational information and skills from renegade Christian pirates, as some claim,[1] but it seems just as likely that they gained their ability to sail the Straits and Atlantic by trial and error or from other sources, such as the refugee Moriscos, most of whom came from Granada and Andalusia, the part of Spain nearest to the Straits and the centre of the Spanish Indies trade.[2] From Seville alone, 7000 men, many of whom worked in the dockyard and port, were expelled in the great purge of the early 17th century.[3]

It is impossible to prove or disprove whether design innovations were transferred or developed independently. What is certain, however, is that by the early 17th century the character of the operations of the Barbary pirates had changed dramatically.[4] Increasingly, 'tall ships'[5] were used by Barbary pirates. With such ships, the pirates ranged the western Mediterranean and took, on average, 70 to 80 Christian vessels a year between 1592 and 1609, and in the decades that followed, at least that many ships were seized.[6] Initially, operations were confined to the Mediterranean, but then the pirates began to operate in the Atlantic, going as far as the Canaries and Azores and making their presence felt on the Spanish coast, as English diplomatic reports of the period testify.[7]

Levant Company ships fell to the pirates, as the records of the company attest, and as early as 1608 the company petitioned Salisbury for relief. In response, a government commission was set up to examine ways to bring about a reduction of piracy.[8] As the

---

[1] J. Denucé, *L'Afrique au XVIe siècle et la commerce anversois* (1937), (*Collection de documents pour l'histoire du commerce*, vol. II), p. 12.
[2] Ortiz, *Golden Age of Spain*, p. 172.
[3] Elliott, *Imperial Spain*, p. 303.
[4] Friedman's analysis, *Spanish Captives*, pp. 3–4, 13, of redeemed Spaniards gives statistical validity to this observation.
[5] See letter of Cottington, in *Cabala*, part I, p. 201.
[6] A. Tenenti, *Naufrages, corsaires et assurances maritimes à Venise (1592–1609)*, p. 27, and by the same author, *Piracy and the Decline of Venice 1580–1615*, pp. 16–32; Braudel, *The Mediterranean*, II, pp. 886–7; Senior, *Nation of Pirates*, p. 108.
[7] H.D. Grammont, 'La Course, l'esclavage et la rédemption à Alger', *Revue Historique*, XXV–XXVI (1884–5), pp. 28–9; S. Bono, *I Corsari barbareschi* (Turin, 1964), p. 178; Denucé, *L'Afrique* p. 20. For contemporary English reports of these developments, see the letters of Carew, in *Letters from George Lord Carew to Sir Thomas Roe, ambassador to the court of the Great Mogul, 1615–1617*, ed. J. Maclean (Camden Society, LXXVI, 1860), pp. 61, 67, 111, 125, 130.
[8] PRO, SP 14/37/91; HCA 14/39/ff.217–18; *APC*, 1613–1614, pp. 145–6. For a proposal to destroy the fleet of Algiers in 1610, see H[istorical] M[anuscripts] C[ommission] 9, *MSS of Marquess of Salisbury*, part XXI (1970), p. 250.

problem grew worse in the second decade of the century, the company again turned to the government for relief.

Until 1617, Crown policy against pirates had been characterized by two features: English subjects engaging in piracy (or abetting it) were prosecuted rigorously; and diplomatic efforts were regularly made to encourage foreign princes to control their piratical subjects. For example, in 1604, after the peace with Spain, James I revoked all letters of marque and prohibited English seamen from sailing under foreign colours.[1] Later, the king attempted to woo former privateers away from piracy by offering a general pardon. This measure was partially successful; at least 12 captains and pirate crews surrendered to the king's mercy.[2]

James also wrote letters to the Sultan requesting him to curb the activities of his Barbary subjects, but these efforts were to no avail.[3] The Sultan was unable to control the Barbary pirates, had he the will to do so, according to the English ambassador.[4] And so English losses continued to mount,[5] so much so that in early 1617 several of the London trading companies banded together to petition the Crown for aid in combating pirates. The origins of this petition remain obscure. The records of Trinity House, the Levant and East India Companies do not disclose its authorship, but it was not a measure without precedent: petitions about pirates and expeditions against Algiers had been proposed previously.[6]

However, unlike earlier proposals, the merchants' petition of 1617 received a positive response from the king. The Levant

---

[1] Proclamation of June 1603 making privateering illegal was issued before the Treaty of London and was signed in 1604, see *Stuart Royal Proclamations*, vol. I, p. 30.
[2] APC, 1611–1614, p. 69.
[3] For example, PRO, SP 105/143/f.19; SP 105/147/f.76.
[4] PRO, SP 105/147/ff.71v, 76; SP 105/110/f.87v.
[5] PRO, SP 105/110/ff.75, 85v, 87v–8; Cottington to Buckingham, in *Cabala*, part I, pp. 201–2. Also, Carew to Roe in *Letters from Carew to Roe*, pp. 50, 60–2, 111. On 19 March 1619, the Privy Council declared that '400 sail of the Western Ports' had been lost in the past four years: PRO, SP 14/107/40. More explicit evidence of the extent of damage done by the pirates may be found, for example, in P.V. McGrath, 'The Merchant Venturers and Bristol in the Early Seventeenth Century', *MM*, XXXVI (1950), pp. 69–80, which shows (p. 69) that from 1610 to 1620 Bristol lost 45 ships: 27 of these were taken by Barbary pirates and another three by unspecified pirates.
[6] PRO, SP 14/37/91; J.S. Corbett, *England in the Mediterranean: A study of the rise and influence of British power within the Straits, 1603–1713*, I, p. 52. As an example of an earlier petition, on 24 November 1608, Levant merchants petitioned the king for ships to suppress pirates: PRO SP 14/37/91.

JAMES I: THE SUPPRESSION OF PIRACY

company's 'Minutes of the Proceedings of the General Court' of 11 February 1617, record the first steps:

> Mr. Deputy [Nicholas Leate], Mr. Garraway, Mr. Abdy, the Husband, the Secretary & such others as the deputy shall call . . . are appointed to prepare a petition (read and approved, at this court) to the kings Majesty in behalf of the Company, for some course to be taken for suppressing the Pirates, in the Straits, who increasing daily do much disturb the general trade and Commerce into those parts and therefore to move for redress.[1]

The wording of this minute does not preclude the possibility that the company was responding to a proposal put to it by another company or by outsiders, but it does suggest that the initiative behind the proposal came from the Levant merchants.

Earlier meetings of the General Court of the company on 16 December 1616 and 9 January 1617, indicate that Abdy, Garraway, Morris Abbot, and Edward James had entreated the king to write to the Sultan calling on him to redress the wrongs done to their ships and men.[2] Also a brief note in the company's papers, dated 16 January 1617, indicates that a committee was being set up to consider what to do 'about Pirates in the Straits'.[3]

The sequence of events can be traced back to 1608 with the Levant merchants' petition 'for ships to suppress the pirates of Algiers'.[4] The Crown did not accede to this request but responded instead by first issuing a proclamation prohibiting merchants from trading with any port used by the pirates.[5] Soon thereafter James I dispatched a letter to the Sultan complaining of the pirates of Algiers and Tunis. In it he warned that the pirates had 'grown to such a multitude and strength of men and ships as no Merchants following the ordinary course of trade can avoid danger'.[6] In order to pre-empt claims by the Sultan that such

---

[1] PRO, SP 105/147/f.88.
[2] PRO, SP 105/147/ff.85, 91.
[3] PRO, SP 105/147/f.45. It may be significant that the *APC*, 9 March 1617, contain an entry which refers to a complaint about pirates made 'by Levant and East Indian merchants'. *APC*, 1616–1617, p. 181.
[4] PRO, SP 14/37/91.
[5] PRO, SP 14/37/96.
[6] PRO, SP 105/143/f.19. James I called for satisfaction and the restitution of the ships and goods belonging to his subjects.

piracies were really just acts of reprisal, a general pardon was offered to former English privateers operating in the Mediterranean.[1] These diplomatic measures accomplished little; shipping losses continued to be heavy. In 1615 the English government had reached the conclusion 'that if a careful hand [were] not held over this Nation, there is many that for recompense and revenge of their losses and wrongs would . . . overthrow all the trade in those seas, which would easily be done for you know it were a small matter to lye before Alexandria and in the Arches[2] that no ship would pass'.[3] Shortly thereafter the English ambassador advised the company that it would be prudent to use only ships 'stronger in Bulke and well manned and provide for their owne safety'.[4]

A short time later, the ambassador received another letter from James I which he presented to the Sultan. It read that, 'notwithstanding diverse former letters on the insolence of Pirates of Algiers and Tunis, we again urge you to try to resolve the problem' and that 'above 100 sail of ships for which we can show good records' had been taken by these pirates since the beginning of the reign.[5] Apparently the king's letter achieved little, for at the beginning of 1616 the ambassador once more was ordered to complain of pirates' acts, but this time the message contained a veiled threat 'that if the Grand Signor himself does not remedy it, they will in time cut off trade in the Levant, which will redound in the end as much to his damage as ours'.[6] This was not a hollow threat for ambassador Pindar was given warning at the time that 'if you see them continue their extreme course, take care of our people that a convenient time may be given them for conveying their persons, moneys, and goods out of the country, as the use of prizes is the like case'. Clearly, the patience of English government was rapidly becoming exhausted; remedies relying on force were now being given active consideration.

---

[1] PRO, SP 14/65/37. But, as Lord High Admiral Nottingham feared, this sort of action came too late to be of much good. Moreover, Nottingham thought sending a small force would also do no good.
[2] A common word among seamen of the period for 'archipelago'; in this case it is used to refer to the Aegean archipelago.
[3] PRO, SP 105/110/f.75.
[4] PRO, SP 105/147/f.65, letter of 20 May, arrived 11 August 1615. On receipt of the ambassador's letter, the General Court ordered all ships freighted by the company to sail in convoy for protection.
[5] PRO, SP 105/147/f.76. 15 August 1615.
[6] PRO, SP 105/110/f.85.

The very magnitude of the problem meant that it could no longer be ignored or treated lightly. From various sources the government was almost daily receiving word of the growing threat. Sir Francis Cottington, agent in Madrid, sent a lengthy report to the Lord High Admiral on 22 September 1616 advising that

(1) 'the strength and boldness of the pirates (or rather of the Turks) had grown to unknown heights';
(2) they now operated in the Atlantic Ocean as well as the Mediterranean;
(3) their fleet contained 40 tall ships of 200 to 400 tons, organized into two squadrons with one of 18 sail operating in the vicinity of Malaga, and the other and larger fleet in the waters between Lisbon and Seville;
(4) lately the pirates took three or four ships of the western ports of England about four leagues from Malaga, and another seven ships of London carrying pipe staves were taken near Ireland,
(5) the pirates were crewed by Moors with few or no Christians among them;
(6) the Council of War thought that the King of Spain might ask James to join him in suppressing the pirates; and
(7) Spanish shipping suffered little, in his opinion, compared to that belonging to foreign (and especially English) merchants.[1]

Shortly thereafter, George Lord Carew wrote to Sir Thomas Roe commenting upon the growing threat of the pirates and the need for the Christian princes to act in concert to effect a solution to the problem.[2] Further indication that the piracy was reaching epidemic proportions in 1616 is found in the correspondence of Sir Paul Pindar, ambassador at Constantinople. In one of his many letters on the subject, he wrote that the French had resolved to cut off all trade with Turkey because they had suffered so much at the hands of the pirates of Algiers, Tunis, and Tripoli.[3]

About the same time, other sources were also highlighting the increasing range of the Barbary pirates: seven ships of the Newfoundland fishing fleet, according to the informants of Lord Carew, had been lost (two were sunk and five captured;) more ominously, the government was advised that Turkish pirates were

[1] *Cabala*, part I, pp. 201–2.
[2] *Letters from Carew to Roe*, p. 62.
[3] PRO, SP 105/147/f.71v. Pindar's letter was dated 24 November 1615 but did not arrive until early in 1616.

now even operating in English home waters; a report was received informing Westminster of the taking of a Sallee pirate ship in the Thames, off Leigh, five miles above Southend.[1]

On 9 January 1617, James I made one final attempt to achieve a solution by diplomatic means. New letters were written to the Sultan and also to his admiral. So grave had the situation become that these letters were sent by a special express messenger at the enormous cost of over £100.[2] Another sign that a shift in government policy was forthcoming may be found in correspondence of the Levant company. Ambassador Pindar was expected to return soon, but the company was informed that the king might not replace him, unless the pirate problem were resolved.[3] The company then set out to appoint a committee to consider a future course for dealing with the 'pirates in the Straits'.[4] This committee would draw up the petition which the company soon submitted to the king; and it was in response to this petition (as stated at the beginning of this chapter) that James I gave the order which started preparations for an expedition against the pirates of Algiers.

---

[1] PRO, SP 14/90/24; *Letters from Carew to Roe*, p. 111, letter of June 1617. Though not widely reported at the time, these ships were actually taken near the Straits while heading for Italy with their catch, but this incident shows that a wide geographic range of shipping was affected by Barbary pirates. The report of the Sallee pirate in the Thames was also somewhat misleading for the crew were largely European in origin.

[2] PRO, SP 105/147/ff.85v–86, 87, 91, 93. Pindar reports the king's letters had no effect; in the ambassador's words 'the whole Nation [were] . . . as Pirates deserving to be punished'.

[3] PRO, SP 105/110/f.94v.

[4] PRO, SP 105/147/ff.45, 88.

2
NAVAL FINANCE: THE ALGIERS EXPEDITION

From a letter of the Council to Sir Thomas Smith, dated 9 March, we know that the merchants' petition was 'lately exhibited unto his Majesty . . . whereof his Majesty apprehending in his great wisdom, and careful tendering above all things the preservation of lives, goods, and the liberties of his loving subjects, hath therefore recommended the petition unto this Board . . . to assist and advise his Majesty for some remedy'. To this end the Council thought fit to prepare by conferring with the merchants, ordering Smith, 'as governor of many companies', to call representatives to meet with them.[1] Three days later Smith replied that he had met with 'such of the said several companies as be in town' and found 'a true sense and feeling in them of the losses & miseries of such who have suffered by the violence of their robberies'. But he went on to say that they felt 'unfit and unable to direct in so weighty a course' being bold only 'to present their opinions how some part of the charge may be raised from the merchants and owners of ships . . . that (with your lordships' help and assistance, twenty thousand pounds a year for the term of two years) may be collected (with some reasonable contentment from the said parties)'.[2]

When the Council wrote to Smith, they also sought advice from Sir Ferdinando Gorges, 'in regard to his good experiences and interest in the west parts, where many have suffered much in this kind, as we are informed'.[3] Letters were dispatched to Gorges and he in turn wrote to the mayors of the west country ports to

---

[1] *APC*, 1616–1617, pp. 181–2.
[2] PRO, SP 14/90/115. Smith's reply was in the name of 15 merchants drawn mainly from the Levant, Barbary, and East India companies.
[3] *APC*, 1616–1617, pp. 181–2.

send men to meet him at the next assizes in Exeter to confer 'in measures to put down and extinguish piracy on the high seas'.[1]

While the Council took these steps, the king continued to consider the matter as he progressed to Edinburgh. On 14 April, while in Lincoln,[2] he ordered the Council to include sea captains in their discussions.[3] More important was the instruction to Sir John Digby, the former ambassador to Spain and close adviser on foreign policy, directing the commissioners for the Spanish Business to consider the course to be taken against the Barbary pirates.[4] This commission advised the king on negotiations with Spain aimed at bringing about a reconciliation of the two nations (and hopefully Christendom) through the marriage of the Prince of Wales and the Infanta.[5] The commission was composed of the following:

> Lord Keeper: Sir Francis Bacon
> Lord Treasurer: Thomas, Earl of Suffolk
> Lord Privy Seal: Edward, Earl of Worcester
> Lord Steward: Ludovic, Duke of Lennox
> Bishop of Ely: Lancelot Andrewes
> Lord Chamberlain: William, Earl of Pembroke
> Earl Marshal: Thomas, Earl of Arundel
> Vice-Chamberlain: Sir John Digby
> Chancellor of the Exchequer: Sir Fulke Greville
> Secretary of State: Sir Thomas Lake
> Archbishop of Canterbury: George Abbot
> Comptroller of the Household: Edward, Lord Wootton
> Captain of the Guard: John, Lord Fenton
> Master of the Horse: George, Earl of Buckingham[6]

---

[1] HMC 8, *9th Report*, App., p. 265, 19 April 1617, letter of Sir Ferdinando Gorges to Robert Trelawny.
[2] PRO, SP 14/90/136.
[3] PRO, SP 105/147/f.89.
[4] PRO, SP 14/91/52 and inclosure.
[5] S.R. Gardiner, *History of England: From the Accession of James I to the Outbreak of the Civil War, 1603–1642*, III, p. 58; *APC*, 1616–1617, pp. 181–2; PRO SP14/90/146. The commission was appointed on 2 March to take up the pirate matter and met several times between the 14th and the 30th.
[6] PRO, SP 14/90/146. Not all members attended all the meetings which considered possible actions to be taken against the Barbary pirates; Digby, for example, missed the initial one for he was still attending James (PRO, SP 14/91/52). To the original group, Sir Ralph Winwood, Secretary of State, was added, though since he was accompanying James on the royal progress, he did not take part initially. Winwood was known for his anti-Spanish sentiments; he may have been added to assure those who feared that the proposed expedition was a pro-Spanish measure (PRO, SP 14/90/136,146).

FINANCE: THE ALGIERS EXPEDITION

Joining the commissioners in the discussions of 28 April were representatives of Trinity House, including a number of unnamed sea captains, simply described as 'experienced' men.[1] Also present were the following representatives of the merchant interest:

> East India Company: Morris Abbot, Humphrey Hardford, Thomas Mun
> Levant Company: Nicholas Leate, Jeffrey Kerby, Hugh Hammersly
> Spanish Company: Edward James, Lawrence Green, Robert Bateman, William Andrewes
> Barbary Company: Humphrey Slaney, John Dike, Robert Wright, Richard Hall
> French Company: Robert Bell, Mr Wollestone
> Muscovy Company: Richard Wiche, William Stone
> Eastland Company: Mr Greenway, Thomas Simonds
> West country: Sir Fernando Gorges, Abraham Colmer, Mr Sherwin
> Flanders Company: Rowland Backhouse[2]

Because the king was absent from London in April 1617, those present felt a need to relate in detail to James the course of discussion. We are thus provided with a rare glimpse into the type of debate or consideration that preceded the adoption of a particular government policy in the Early Stuart period.[3]

The agenda of the meeting was drawn up by the councillors or commissioners; they intended to deal in turn with the military, financial, and diplomatic aspects of the problem. The meeting was opened with an announcement that the king wished all present to know that he was willing to grant relief as requested by the merchants in the petition. The Crown's representatives, therefore, were desirous of learning how best to finance and effect such an enterprise. The merchants replied that 'they conceived that the City of London and the other Ports might be brought to contribute the sum of forty thousand pounds in two years'. This was as far as they would go, though they did say that 'they would not be backward, nor wanting' if it appeared that his majesty were

---

[1] PRO, SP 14/91/52.
[2] *APC*, 1616–1617, pp. 181–2.
[3] PRO, SP 14/91/52, includes a five-page report. The discussion here (pp. 24–6) and the quotations contained therein are from this report.

pursuing the matter earnestly. This assurance, however, was elicited by the commissioners 'only after long debate with them of all circumstances of the Business, and we letting them understand, that the forty thousand pounds were ever understood to be from the City of London, besides the Contribution which the Port Towns might be drawn into'. At this point, the councillors pressed the London merchants to volunteer more, £60 000, but to no avail.

The discussion over strategy generated considerable debate. Two approaches were put forward initially. Some favoured a surprise attack on Algiers. Others recommended a protracted campaign 'continued upon them for some years until by degrees they might be extirpated'. Doubts on the efficacy of a surprise attack quickly surfaced. All agreed that in times of trouble the pirates of Tunis and other small ports sought refuge in Algiers; thus, this strategy could not work unless Algiers were surprised, i.e., taken. But when questioned on this point, the merchants and sea captains 'with one voice judged it impossible . . . [and] demonstrated by many reasons, and by the Situation and Strength of the Place which they made appear by their Plotts which they had present'.

The strategy of protracted war was then deliberated at length. Everyone seemed to agree on the ultimate success of such a course. It was thought that 'there was no other way for the Subversion and overthrow of the Pirates, but by the keeping of a continual Strength and Power upon them for some years'. But it was also readily perceived that a protracted war was likely to prove costly. This realization prompted a long discussion on whether it would be possible to get other nations to contribute to the proposed expedition.

At first it was suggested by some merchants that the Dutch might be interested, but that the Spanish would have no desire to suppress the pirates because 'they only traded with strong fleets to the Indies; and the weakening of the English, French, and Hollanders (who chiefly suffered by the Pirates) was advantageous unto the Spaniards'. This assertion was, however, soon challenged by speakers who reminded the committee 'that some of the Ships of Genoa, carrying great quantities of moneys out of Spain . . . had been taken by Pirates . . . [and that the Spanish] Coasts were so strangely infected, as there was no passing between Port and Port; that multitudes . . . were daily Captived and made Slaves, That . . . [Philip's] Customs by reason of the interruption of

Trade, were much diminished; And that the last year his India Fleet was laid for and endangered by theirs'. These arguments proved persuasive for, after a while, it was moved that Spain might be asked to contribute 'by way of supplying Ready Money, then by Uniting or Joyning of his Forces with his Majesty's'.

At this suggestion, some of the councillors expressed concern that the expedition might be delayed were it to become the subject of formal negotiations with other states. They wondered whether it might not be better to proceed on the basis of setting out an English fleet. James need 'send only unto the king of Spain in a courteous and friendly manner to let him understand . . . that it might fall out, that his said Fleet might have cause to make use of his [i.e., Spanish] Ports, which happening his majesty would entreat from the king of Spain, all good and friendly usage, of which there was no cause to doubt, but that Princes in Amity would afford one to another'.

On hearing this, the merchants 'respectfully replied' that they would willingly honour their offer and would leave to the Crown and Council the means and course by which the enterprise might be effected. This acquiescence was, however, tempered, if not undercut, when they added that 'their Opinions were, That the fittest way, and the likeliest to work the Effect intended, was that his Majesty would be pleased, by his Ministers, to treat with other Princes, for the uniting of their Forces, or least for Joining in a contribution towards the Charges'.

The captains and seamen were asked whether they might recommend any action in the interim. They replied only that nothing should be undertaken partially or prematurely. Only when all the financial and naval resources had been assembled should the expedition go forward. Any other course, they warned, would prove wasteful and possibly undermine the eventual success of the enterprise. Each captain individually was then asked again whether a surprise attack on Algiers might succeed, but all agreed that only a protracted campaign could overthrow the pirates.

Foreign assistance was thought desirable by the naval men. French and Dutch assistance would help, but they believed that Spanish aid would be more useful and that without it 'little good was to be done against the Pirates for many Reasons'. In wartime, ships should carry not above five months' victuals; in any case, they could not carry above six months' victuals. Two months' supplies were needed for the outward voyage, and another two for the return journey. Therefore, a fleet could remain on station for only two months at most (without the use of friendly ports for resupply). The pirates would remain safely in port until the blockading force had exhausted its supplies and was compelled to retire. The pirates would then put to sea with a vengeance.

For the proposed enterprise to have a chance, they believed the fleet must have access to nearby ports to revictual, refit, or serve as a place of refuge in severe weather. The French ports were too distant, being over 600 nautical miles from Algiers. If the English fleet had to depend on French ports, it 'would neither get sudden Intelligence of the Pirates coming abroad, nor be so forward as much to keep them in'. Secondly, the naval experts indicated that if use of Spanish ports were denied, voyages to and from Algiers would become much more risky given the prevailing winds.

On this last point, discussion ended with all agreed that there was only one course of action. When James assented to their proposal, it was agreed that more thought would have to be given on the manner of execution. In the meantime, instructions should be drawn up advising Lord Digby on the need to obtain Spanish support for the expedition.

By showing how government actually worked in Stuart England this process is of historical interest. First, the central and decisive role of the Crown before, during, and after the meeting is evident. Both in tone and action the privy councillors deferred to James. The basic decisions had been the king's; e.g., James decided to take action on the merchants' petition. In his letter dated 20 March, James indicated that he favoured a course of suppression, thus the broad outline of the policy was set out before the meeting of the committee of the 28th.[1]

Second, the meeting shows the advisory function of the councillors. Discussion was guided along the lines favoured by the king, but the councillors also laboured to learn whether such a course were possible and which strategy was most likely to succeed. In this regard, the meeting of the 28th was consultative: opinions were sought, debate encouraged (although always along specified lines), and views or proposals scrutinized. It was also consultative in another sense: economic and regional interests were represented in the discussions, as well as the advice of experts.

This meeting also brings out both the effective features and weaknesses of the conciliar system of government. Policy-making benefited from the way a range of options was sought and

---

[1] PRO, SP 14/90/136.

scrutinized. The commissioners were adept and thorough examiners. In the course of these deliberations, almost all major problems were anticipated. Only the administrative difficulties were ignored by the councillors. They never considered how the levy was to be applied or collection organized and administered. As with other Early Stuart fiscal expedients, the absence of established administrative machinery meant that collection was on a haphazard basis, left to local interests and open to abuse and dispute, both of which delayed receipt, as the latter half of this chapter will illustrate.

The financial preparations for the Algiers expedition have never been examined. And yet, for a number of reasons, they are worthy of detailed consideration. First, the fiscal arrangements for the Algiers expedition serve as an indicator of the function, methods, attitudes, and effectiveness of that range of quasi-legal financial expedients employed by the Stuart regime, such as the forced-loan and the benevolence. Second, the financial preparations for the Algiers expedition underline and explain the central problem of the early modern English monarchy: its inability to finance military operations on a scale necessary to defend national interest and consequently its own position.[1] Third, many of the delays and difficulties of the expedition can be traced back to the way it was financed.[2]

In particular, the financial history of the expedition provides the missing dimension to discussions of the vexing problem of naval finance in the 1630s. Studies of Early Stuart financial measures have largely ignored the pre-history of Ship Money,[3] seeing it primarily as an innovation of (and explained by) the personal rule of Charles I. There has also been a tendency to concentrate on the constitutional aspects of Stuart naval finance.[4] While the general

---

[1] C.S.R. Russell, *Parliaments and English Politics 1621–1629*, pp. 70–84, develops this theme; M. Howard, *War in European History*, pp. 55, 67–9, sees it as a European phenomenon.
[2] *APC*, 1621–1623, e.g., *Levant Company* v *Spanish Company* dispute delayed the expedition. This point is taken up again in Chapter 4.
[3] Ship Money refers to a levy used to meet extraordinary naval needs. Originally it had been restricted to port towns and was for ships and men. In the 1630s, to meet the demands of the time, the levy was extended by the Crown (without the consent of parliament). Collections were on a national basis and money was requested rather than ships. By the late 1630s, Ship Money had become an issue of constitutional importance dividing the political nation.
[4] Even M.D. Gordon, 'The Collection of Ship-Money in the Reign of Charles I', *TRHS*, 3rd series, IV (1910), pp. 155–62, approached the topic of collection and disbursement almost exclusively from a political point of view.

structural problems of English government, long evident before the 1630s, have been closely examined,[1] naval finance has not hitherto been explored as fully. This problem will be considered in greater depth in a later chapter; here we are concerned only with describing the methods and machinery of this precursor of Ship Money.

Swales's article on the aborted Ship Money levy of 1628 implies that Ship Money may be seen as an evolutionary measure.[2] However, the extent to which the novel features of Ship Money were anticipated by the levy for the Algiers expedition has been largely overlooked. Also, as will be demonstrated below, the Algiers levy raised fiscal problems that could only be resolved by the adoption of the sort of reforms implicit in Ship Money.[3]

Naval finance was based on medieval methods and conditions. From the beginning, the king's navy led neither a continuous existence nor was it centrally organized.[4] Warfare was intermittent, and therefore warships were needed only occasionally. It was both militarily feasible and economically prudent to do without a permanent navy.[5] Because the warships of the time served mainly as transports for soldiers using swords, lances and arrows, merchant ships could be employed as men-of-war. Thus a navy could be raised to meet a temporary need simply by calling on the seaports of the realm to contribute ships and crew as the need arose. Not only was the organization of naval power decentralized in this way, cost was also transferred to the maritime communities. In turn, the burden of construction costs and maintenance was spread over all the years of peace when the ships would be used as merchantmen, and not just for the relatively brief times that ships were needed for war.

This system of organization and finance, fit for medieval conditions, was no longer suitable in the 17th century. Advances in

---

[1] For a concise description of the problems, see Russell, *Parliaments and English Politics*, pp. 64–9. The concept of functional weakness is defined by G.E. Aylmer in *The Tudors and Stuarts*, ed. W. Lamont, p. 137, and has been developed by the same author, in *The King's Servants: The Civil Service of Charles I, 1625–1642*, and 'Attempts at Administrative Reform, 1625–40', *EHR*, LXXII (1957), pp. 229–59.
[2] R.J.W. Swales, 'The Ship Money Levy of 1628', *BIHR*, L (1977), pp. 164–76.
[3] Ibid., p. 166.
[4] M. Oppenheim, *A History of the Administration of the Royal Navy and of Merchant Shipping in Relation to the Navy*, Chap. I; G.S. Marcus, *A Naval History of England*, I, *The Formative Centuries (to 1793)*, pp. 3–15.
[5] Marcus, *A Naval History*, pp. 3–4; A. Saul, 'Great Yarmouth and the Hundred Years War in the Fourteenth Century', *BIHR*, LII (1979), pp. 105–15, especially pp. 108–9.

naval technology made merchant ships less and less suitable for use in war. Cannon (at first small and light) became the principal weapons of naval engagements. In consequence, the design of warships diverged from merchantmen. Men-of-war increasingly became gun platforms. In consequence, they were heavily and expensively built with too little hull space to be operated economically in peacetime as merchantmen.[1] This specialization meant that special-purpose warships had to be built and maintained. These were very expensive, so that in times of war they still had to be supplemented with some merchantmen.[2]

The origins of the Royal Navy can be traced back to the Tudors. Henry VIII built a large fleet, consisting of some 53 ships at his death, but this was possible only because Henry was able to tap the singular source of income that became his on the dissolution of the monasteries.[3] The size of the navy was reduced following Henry's death. Only with the Spanish threat in the late Elizabethan period was the navy rebuilt, reaching a strength of 23 ships in 1587.[4] This level was maintained in the years of war but only by further expenditure of capital assets, a royal policy that could not long endure and one that was reversed in the reign of James I.[5]

By avoiding war or the need to use naval force, James was able to reduce the navy to minimal numbers and therefore costs to a tolerable level.[6] For example, when the Council recommended that two small ships be provided to protect fishermen against pirates, Winwood wrote to Lake that the king disliked the resolution because he feared it might become an expensive precedent.[7] As related earlier, James was drawn reluctantly to the use of naval force against the Barbary pirates. Only after exhausting diplomatic means did he favour setting forth his navy. The merchants' petition offering to contribute a portion of the

---

[1] A.H. Taylor, 'Carrack into Galleon', *MM*, XXXVI (1950), pp. 144–51; A.H. Taylor, 'Galleon into Ship of the Line, I', *MM*, XLIV (1958), pp. 267–85; 'Galleon into Ship of the Line, II' and 'III', *MM*, XLV (1959), pp. 14–24, 100–14.
[2] J.P. Cooper, 'Sea-Power', in *New Cambridge Modern History*, IV, *The Decline of Spain and the Thirty Years War*, ed. J.P. Cooper, p. 227.
[3] Oppenheim, *Administration of the Royal Navy*, pp. 45–99; C.S.L. Davies, 'The Administration of the Royal Navy under Henry VIII: the Origins of the Navy Board', *EHR*, LXXX (1965), pp. 268–88.
[4] Oppenheim, *Administration of the Royal Navy*, pp. 115–84.
[5] Ibid., pp. 185–216.
[6] Russell, *Parliaments and English Politics*, pp. 70–2, 81; C.S.R. Russell, *The Crisis of Parliaments: English History 1509–1660*, pp. 90–1. On costs: Oppenheim, *Administration of the Royal Navy*, pp. 185–93.
[7] PRO, SP 14/90/115.

cost probably did much to persuade James to authorize an expedition.

It is not clear whether the original petition included a specific offer of £40 000 or just some general statement about a willingness to contribute. Precisely what the merchants had in mind is also unclear. Later, when delays and increasing costs were becoming burdensome, some merchants suggested that they had originally contemplated an expedition financed and controlled entirely by the City. The king's involvement would have been limited simply to leasing royal ships.[1]

In the event, the Crown was very much in charge from the beginning. London merchants and shipowners were ordered to raise £40 000 and the outports an additional £9000.[2] London's contribution was divided up as follows:[3]

	£
Levant Company	8000
Spanish Company	9000
East India Company	8000
Merchant Adventurers	6000
Trinity House	4000
Eastland Company	2000
French Company	2000
Muscovy Company	1000

Some of the assessments were later renegotiated following complaints of unfairness to the Crown.[4] The outports were required to contribute the following amounts:[5]

	£
Bristol	2500
Plymouth	1000
Exeter	1000
Dartmouth	1000
Barnstaple	500
Hull	500

[1] PRO, SP 14/111/27.
[2] PRO, SP 14/90/136.
[3] PRO, SP 14/105/44,47; *APC*, 1616–1617, pp. 263–4.
[4] PRO, SP 14/105/91; SP 105/148/ff.36,38; *APC*, 1618–1619, pp. 360–1; 1621–1623, 1 Sep. 1621, pp. 37–8.
[5] PRO, SP 14/112/77.

Weymouth and Melcombe Regis	450
Lyme Regis	450
Southampton	300
Newcastle	300
Cinque Ports	200
Yarmouth	200
Ipswich	150
Colchester	150
Poole	100
King's Lynn	100
Chester	100

Among other things, this list certainly shows that contemporaries believed that the ports of the south and west suffered the most from pirates and had the most to gain from their suppression. It does not include all of the outports. The Welsh ports of Cardiff and Milford Haven, as well as the ancient port of Boston and the distant ones of Carlisle and Berwick were not included. No reason is given for their exclusion. The port books indicate all were active at the time, though their foreign trade may have been too small or too remote from the threat of pirates to warrant inclusion.[1]

More significant is the nature of the contribution. Cash payments were required. Unlike the later 'innovating' Ship Money levies, there was no pretence that these sums were in lieu of contributions of ships.[2]

Assessments were always referred to as 'contributions' or 'offerings' or 'levy'; but like other Stuart fiscal measures, such as the 'benevolences' or 'loans', there was little that was voluntary about them. They were in fact a tax. The money was paid into the Exchequer. 'Contributors' were given no choice as to whether they wished to give, as some would discover, nor were they able to determine the amount they wished to pay.[3]

The fiscal arrangements of the Algiers expedition are emblematic of a general feature of Jacobean government: that curious combination of compulsion allied with consultation. A charge was made, but not imposed arbitrarily. Representatives of the port towns and companies were called to meet with ministers to advise the Crown on ways and means, but the total amount was not open

---

[1] PRO, Descriptive List of Exchequer, Queen's Remembrancer, Port Books, 1960.
[2] Gardiner, *History of England*, VII, pp. 375–6.
[3] For example, *APC*, 1618–1619, p. 422; 1619–1621, p. 278.

to discussion, except when the Crown wished to suggest that more should be levied. Although decision-making was concentrated in royal hands, the Crown appreciated that, at least, it must appear to be shared with representatives of commercial and local political interests.

In these meetings, the outports were under-represented, and only a few were directly represented. The differing interests within the ports had no voice at all. The financial arrangements were made primarily by Londoners or a few London agents of the west country.[1] This fact may account for the extensive number and variety of complaints that were to come from the outports in the months ahead. Nevertheless, these meetings were not sham affairs. There is evidence that a genuine attempt was made to apportion charges on some reasonable basis. In a letter to the Council, Sir John Wolstenholme and Sir Nicholas Salter, customs farmers, wrote:

> The contribution was not laid according to the custom paid by any Company, or in any Port for then the Merchant Adventurers should have paid far greater, and diverse other companies also. But consideration was rather had, that those ports should pay most which had the amplest trade into the Levant Seas, the place of greatest danger; amongst which Bristol is the principal and far above any other port (London excepted) which we conceived was a sufficient reason, to induce the imposing of the sum, though we do not make ourselves the sole agents of that business.[2]

In general, the Crown left unspecified the detailed execution of policy. This was not unusual. Even in as important a measure as the 'Great Contract' the government was silent on the details as to how tax was to be apportioned or who would pay.[3]

The disadvantages of this approach were intimated in the letter of Wolstenholme and Salter, quoted above. The assessments had been determined on information provided by London oligarchs.

---

[1] *APC*, 1616–1617, pp. 181–3, for example, seven-eighths of representatives at meeting on 9 March were Londoners.
[2] PRO, SP 14/108/32.
[3] A.G.R. Smith, 'Crown, Parliament and Finance: the Great Contract of 1610', in *The English Commonwealth 1547–1640*, ed., P. Clark, A.G.R. Smith, N. Tyacke, pp. 111–26.

Bristol and other outports, however, felt that their assessments were unfair.[1] Also, as is brought out in this letter, the principle underlying the apportionments was never clearly defined. As a result it appeared that decisions were made on an arbitrary basis.

This process engendered uncertainty, especially at the local level. Many questions, small in the general scheme but of importance locally, were left to caprice or partisan interest.[2] No instructions were given as to how the Algiers levy was to be administered. Who was to pay and how much? Shipowners, merchants? Resident or non-resident traders? Householders, aliens? None of these questions was anticipated by government, yet each became a matter of dispute and delayed payment. Eventually, every one of these questions had to be resolved by the Privy Council.

After some dispute, Trinity House of London agreed to raise its portion by placing a levy on ships using London. The rate was on a tonnage (3d to 18d per ton) and destination basis. But only after the Privy Council had given authorization, did the customs farmers agree to restrain ships until they paid the appropriate rate.[3]

In June 1617, after instruction from the Council, the London trading companies met, to decide how to raise their contribution. They settled upon a levy on imports and exports. Goods going to or from the Levant seas, Spain, Portugal, Barbary, or the Azores, were required to pay one pound in a hundred. Those items to or from Germany, the Netherlands, France, Norway, or the Eastland countries were to pay ten shillings for every hundred pounds.[4] Again, the customs farmers were to administer the collection.[5]

Many of the outports later came to adopt a similar system. Exeter, Lyme Regis, Weymouth, and Plymouth relied on a duty on imports and exports to pay the charge.[6] But inherent in this system of rating was delay. Money could not be paid into the Exchequer until it had been received. Eventually, many ports had to borrow money, at interest, so that many delayed payment as

---

[1] PRO, SP 14/107/5,40; SP 14/108/31,32.
[2] Problems of this type were not restricted to assessments and administration of the Algiers levy: for example, see A. Hassell Smith, 'Militia Rates and Militia Statutes 1558–1663', in *The English Commonwealth*, pp. 93–110.
[3] PRO, SP 14/116/10,11: based on tonnage employed in 1616, over £1000 p.a. would be collected. PRO, SP 14/105/47 gives a breakdown of the proposed rates.
[4] *APC*, 1619–1621, pp. 70–1; 1616–1617, pp. 263–4.
[5] *APC*, 1618–1619, p. 316.
[6] Ibid., pp. 397, 452–3, 414.

long as possible. Weymouth, Lyme Regis, and Ipswich are cases in point.[1]

Some of the delays in payment were the result of official negligence. For instance, it took weeks for an outport mayor to get permission to raise the contribution by a local levy. When permission was finally received, no warrant was enclosed enabling customs officials to stay ships that refused to pay. This sort of delay happened repeatedly. Lyme Regis, Exeter, and Plymouth all had to write to the Council a second time for warrants; weeks passed before they could begin to collect money.[2] Moreover, even when the Council knew how to respond, officials were slow to reply. Barnstaple, Plymouth, and Exeter were forced to write to the Clerk of the Council, Sir Clement Edmondes, begging the courtesy of a reply to their requests.[3]

The root of the problem lay not with an individual but with the antiquated revenue system itself. This system was essentially medieval, suited for a different society and economy. In the medieval period the economy was less integrated consisting of many largely autonomous units. They could be identified with relative ease and taxed accordingly: beneficiaries could be singled out to pay their share.[4] The medieval system also accepted a large portion of contribution in kind or service, such as in ships, provisions, or crew.[5]

But by the early 17th century, basic social and economic conditions had changed; the economy was more integrated and specialization within sectors was a common feature. Both of these developments made it more difficult to employ the type of naval finance system used earlier.[6] No longer was it possible to identify easily the beneficiaries. Shipowners, sea captains and crews were an obvious choice. But should all mariners pay? Equally? Should all merchants be levied, or just those in foreign trade? What about inland manufacturers, port residents, consumers; didn't they

---

[1] PRO, SP 14/105/130; SP 14/115/57,104.
[2] PRO, SP 12/112/8; *APC*, 1618–1619, pp. 397, 414, 452–3, 446–7.
[3] PRO, SP 14/116/71; SP 14/169/120; SP 14/109/154.
[4] D.C. North and R.P. Thomas, *The Rise of the Western World*, pp. 26–9; E. Miller, 'The Economic Policies of Governments: France and England', in *Cambridge Economic History of Europe*, III, ed. M.M. Postan, E.E. Rich, E. Miller, pp. 302–6.
[5] Saul, 'Great Yarmouth and the Hundred Years War', pp. 108–9.
[6] J. de Vries, *The Economy of Europe in an Age of Crisis, 1600–1750, passim*; Howard, *War in European History*, pp. 2, 14, 41, 49, 53.

benefit as well? All stood to gain, but how much should each pay? Who should determine the rates? On what basis would the rating be done, and by whom? Even if these questions had been resolved initially, no bureaucracy existed to collect and administer the tax.

The government of James I did not possess the administrative machinery to answer these questions, nor a taxation system that could provide naval finance efficiently and fairly. Until the basis of naval finance was altered and the government expanded and improved, the Crown could only expect dispute and delay in collecting revenue.

The most serious area of contention was between the outports and the London companies. Again and again the outports complained that the size of their assessment was disproportionate to their share of the trade to the Levant seas or southern oceans. On this issue, Bristol and Southampton led the way. Their complaint was closely tied up with a growing dissatisfaction with the monopoly rights of the London trading companies.[1] At this time only the west coast of Italy, Sardinia, and Sicily were open to trade. Southampton averred that the Londoners damaged their trade as much as the pirates; the mayor wrote that 'very few of them do any Trade at all into the Straits, being (as they say) debarred by the Company of Merchants Trading in the Levant Seas from importing any of the Commodities of those countries into this kingdom'.[2]

Bristol also claimed its share was disproportionate to the port's trade, though, unlike Southampton, many Bristol merchants traded to the southern parts.[3] Such was the criticism of London, that at one point the Council had to write to Lord Zouch that the expedition against the pirates was not, as intimated in a letter of the Cinque Ports, 'for the benefit and advantage of London or any particular place alone . . . but for the security of common trade'.[4]

Disputes also took place between the London companies. For example, the Merchant Adventurers wanted the Council to reduce its assessment; it claimed its trade was local and thereby little hurt

---

[1] PRO, SP 14/107/5,40; SP 14/108/32.
[2] PRO, SP 14/107/5.
[3] PRO, SP 14/108/32. For example, when the charter of the Spanish Company was renewed, 577 merchants were named, 237 came from the outports and of these 94 were from Bristol: P.V. McGrath, *Records Relating to the Society of Merchants Venturers of the City of Bristol in the Seventeenth Century* (Bristol Record Society XVII, 1952), p. 2.
[4] PRO, SP 14/107/40.

by pirates; it believed that the merchants trading to Iberia or the Mediterranean, as the most interested parties, should pay nine-tenths of the charge.[1] Additional charges on cloth, it claimed, would be injurious to home manufacturers. In a similar fashion the Spanish Company wrote to the Council complaining about the size of its assessment and recommending that the Levant Company should pay a greater portion.[2]

Most companies questioned the amount they were assessed. The Eastland Company requested the Council reduce its share because trade was bad; in any case, it was only one-eighth that of the Merchant Adventurers, while their charge was one-third as much.[3] The Muscovy Company also requested a reduction in its charge since it claimed [accurately] that its trade had not been bothered by Algerian pirates.[4]

There were also complaints that some trading groups, such as the merchant strangers of London, had escaped assessment altogether. The resistance of the merchant strangers was feeble and soon they were ordered to pay a duty of 1% on their trade to the southern seas and ½% on goods to or from northern Europe.[5] So widespread were the complaints by various interest groups in London that in the end the Council ordered a general meeting of the companies so that they could reconcile their differences over the assessments.[6]

Similar disputes arose within and between the outports, often because of the differing nature of their trades. The merchant adventurers of Dorchester (a member port of Weymouth and Melcombe Regis) complained that they were assessed unfairly because the rate on those trading to France (Dorchester's market) and Spain (Weymouth's market) was the same, but the value of the Spanish trade was four times that of the French.[7] After considering Dorchester's case, the Council wrote to Weymouth explaining that London and most of the western ports were charging according to the origin or destination of the goods. Trade to Spain and the Levant should bear a greater portion since this

---

[1] PRO, SP 14/105/91.
[2] PRO, SP 105/148/f.36.
[3] PRO, SP 14/105/42,43.
[4] PRO, SP 14/111/27.
[5] *APC*, 1618–1619, pp. 383–4.
[6] Ibid., pp. 360–1.
[7] APC, 1619–1621, p. 87. Also *APC*, 1618–1619, p. 453: 18 May, the dispute between Dartmouth and Totnes was to be settled at a meeting chaired by Wolstenholme.

trade suffered more from piracy. Weymouth was ordered to change its rates; those trading with France were to pay half that contributed by the Spanish and Mediterranean traders.[1] Along the same lines, Poole sought relief because 'their town hath not in it above one neer merchant adventurer, the adventurer of this town being not in any staple trading but in fishing voyages for Newfoundland . . . as by his Majesty's Customs Books of this Poole may plainly appear.'[2] Similarly, Exeter and Lyme Regis wrote that they traded only with Brittany and should therefore pay less.[3]

Head ports and their member ports fought vigorously over assessments. Typical was the conflict between Dartmouth, a head port, and Totnes, a member port. When the mayor of Dartmouth tried to get the merchants of Totnes to contribute, the latter stated that since they had not been explicitly named in the order of the Council, they were not obliged to pay.[4] Even after officials of Dartmouth obtained specific authority from the Council to assess Totnes, the member port still refused to pay because (according to town officials) their share of the port's charge was too large.[5] This dispute could not be resolved locally. Totnes sent a delegation to the Council to challenge Dartmouth's claim that its trade was three times that of the head port. This dispute dragged on for several months and ended only when the Council ordered Totnes to pay half the charge.[6] Even then Totnes did not give up. Officials of the port wrote that they would pledge themselves to pay their half-share on condition that they were freed from the interference of Dartmouth or any other place.[7]

Yarmouth had similar trouble with Lowestoft, Orford, and Aldeburgh.[8] Like Totnes, Liverpool refused to pay because it had not been named in the Council's order, and went on to inform the Council that they were ready to go to law to establish the town's independence from Chester,[9] whose other member ports, Beaumaris and Carnarvon, also refused to contribute though on different grounds. They were too poor, they claimed, to pay the

[1] *APC*, 1619–1621, pp. 389–90.
[2] PRO, SP 14/107/39.
[3] PRO, SP 14/107/45; *APC*, 1618–1619, pp. 389–90.
[4] PRO, SP 14/107/10.
[5] *APC*, 1618–1619, p. 394.
[6] Ibid., pp. 453, 456.
[7] PRO, SP 14/109/95.
[8] PRO, SP 14/107/26; SP 14/108/81; *APC*, 1618–1619, pp. 410–11.
[9] PRO, SP 14/107/33; SP 14/108/22.

£20 which Chester officials had assessed.[1] In this case the Council requested the customs farmers to furnish records on the trade of these ports so that the Council might determine the validity of contesting claims.[2]

Port towns also came into conflict with inland areas. For example, Weymouth complained that most of the trade passing through the port belonged to merchants of inland towns; consequently, the port wished to put a levy on this trade.[3] Colchester wrote to the Council that merchants of the port were only factors, and, therefore, that they had insufficient means to pay the assessment. The money could be raised, officials claimed, only by putting a levy on the whole of Colchester.[4] The merchants of Exeter tried to get the entire county to be assessed but were overruled.[5]

Because ports used different methods of assessments, merchants began to move trade to where they could pay less or avoid taxation altogether. For example, the Eastland Company started using Ipswich for its cloth shipments. In this case, the other London companies complained to the Council and, eventually, the Eastland Company was forced to pay its share of the London assessment.[6] Weymouth informed the Council that inland merchants were moving trade to Poole to avoid duty.[7] And Lyme Regis stated that merchants of Taunton were threatening to use another port if Lyme Regis officials tried to compel them to pay a share of the port's assessment.[8] From Barnstaple came requests that the town be spared further payment because they had contributed £250 voluntarily in the first year without resorting to a levy, but now the town's merchants were also being forced to pay duty on their goods at Exeter, Plymouth, and Dartmouth.[9]

Finally, additional delays came from a series of disputes within

---

[1] PRO, SP 14/107/33; SP 14/111/87.
[2] PRO, SP 14/109/9 and inclosure. Beaumaris was found to have only two barques, one of 17 tons, another of 12; Carnarvon had three, one of 16 tons and two of 10 tons each.
[3] PRO, SP 14/107/18. Similar cases exist for Exeter: SP 14/107/45; Hull: SP 14/107/13; and Lyme Regis: SP 14/108/36.
[4] PRO, SP 14/105/114.
[5] PRO, SP 14/107/45.
[6] *APC*, 1618–1619, p. 323.
[7] PRO, SP 14/109/81.
[8] PRO, SP 14/115/105.
[9] PRO, SP 14/111/82; SP 14/115/88.

the port towns. Both Plymouth and Weymouth requested and were granted the authority to tax 'others as inhabit and reside there' as well as shipowners and merchants.[1] To Poole, the Council wrote that though earlier instructions indicated that the assessment was aimed primarily at merchants and shipowners, 'yet it is in no way meant that other traders of ability residing there and taking benefit of that port should be exempted from a charge so much concerning the common security of trade and intercourse'.[2]

However, when Woodbridge received a similar licence and extended its levy, it was informed by the council that 'our meaning was not that such gentlemen or others that live upon their lands and whose condition and course of life hath no relation at all to merchandising or trade should be charged in this service further then what of their own free motion and will should offer for the advancement of so public and worthy a work'.[3]

Most of these disputes resulted from the Council's abdication of responsibility for the detailed implementation of the policy. Without specific instructions from the Council, disputes were inevitable. Because of these disputes and the time spent resolving them, contributions from the ports were late arriving. The piecemeal method used by the Council in dealing with complaints also contributed to the delays. For example, after hearing and resolving between one port and a member outport, no attempt was made by the Council to give similar orders or advice to other ports. As a consequence, complaints of a similar nature were sent successively to the Council. Each dispute was treated individually, but after each case had been examined (and each examination took time), similar orders would be sent out.[4]

Some complaints appear to be contrived, but the basis for others seems genuine. For instance, the amount assessed for the Spanish Company was disproportionate to the financial strength of the company. It was required to pay more than the much richer Levant Company whose trade was threatened as much by the pirates and who had been the chief instigator of the project.[5]

---

[1] *APC*, 1619–1621, p. 92.
[2] *APC*, 1618–1619, p. 409.
[3] *APC*, 1619–1621, p. 126.
[4] For example, PRO, SP 14/107/10, 108/22, 112/8, (Liverpool, Chester, Plymouth, Fowey, Dartmouth and Totnes).
[5] A.C. Wood, *A History of the Levant Company*, pp. 23–4; R. Ashton, *The City and the Court 1603–1643*, pp. 14–15; PRO, SP 14/105/44; SP 14/121/33. Nicholas Leate claimed the Spanish merchants had procured action by corrupting the Clerk of the Council, Sir Clement Edmonds, by bribing him with £50.

Table 1
Customs records comparing assessments with size of towns' trade

Town	Assessment (£)	Inwards and Outwards Amount (£)		
		1613	1614	1615
Exeter	1000	4086	3708	3716
Barnstaple	500	844	959	1182
Weymouth	450	1903	2151	1882
Lyme Regis	450	–	3031	2780
Bristol	2500	–	3519	3885

Although many complaints were concerned with the relative amounts assessed, others were over the absolute size of the assessment. The sums required of several outports were very substantial. For example, the mayor of Lyme Regis pointed out that the amount assessed for the port was equal to 20 subsidies.[1] Several west country ports complained about the level of the assessments. In response, the Council examined the customs records to see if the assessments were out of line with the size of the towns' trade (see Table 1).[2]

While these figures provide a general indication of the value of the trade of these ports, it should also be noted that the figures were for earlier, more prosperous years. The years of the Algiers assessments, 1617–1621, were ones of economic depression.[3] Even so, the figures show how heavy a burden the Algiers' duty was for these towns. The list also shows that it fell very unevenly. Bristol, for example, was assessed two and a half times the amount of Exeter, even though the customs payments of each port were approximately the same.

Although there was great dissatisfaction with the way the tax was levied, the need for such an expedition was accepted by all. Nor did any port or company question the constitutional authority of the Crown to impose such a tax. At one point the Spanish Company did suggest that the levy might infringe upon its liberties, but when the Council replied that the king would take legal counsel on the matter, the Company chose to pay rather than

---

[1] PRO, SP 14/105/141.
[2] PRO, SP 14/108/31: Bristol was the port complaining.
[3] B.E. Supple, *Commercial Crisis and Change in England, 1600–1642: A study in the instability of a mercantile economy*, pp. 52–72.

go to law.[1] Also, in view of the legal and political disputes over Ship Money in the 1630s, it is worth noting that nobody objected that they were asked for money, rather than ships, as was the common practice.

Not all towns or individuals paid willingly. Woodbridge ignored the Council's order – even after it had been read out formally in church.[2] In such cases, the Council had to apply further pressure on the recalcitrants before they would pay up. Usually it was enough for the Council to ask for the names of the offenders. On the rare occasion when that was not enough, bonds were called for and the offenders asked 'to make their immediate repair unto us where they shall further understand our pleasure'.[3] At Barnstaple, Southampton, Ipswich, Exeter, and Poole, these threatening words were enough to bring the stubborn to compliance.[4] Only in Newcastle did defiance go further. Fifteen men refused to pay even after their names had been sent to the Council.[5] Warrants were issued to bring the fifteen to Westminster.[6] It appears that this action was enough, for a brief entry in the Council's register three weeks later indicates that all had paid.[7]

The levy for the Algiers expedition is a transitional stage in the history of naval finance. It continued the medieval system of putting the burden of supplying naval force mainly on the port towns. The Council, however, did show an awareness of the integrated character of manufacture and overseas trade and did extend the levy to inland towns on occasion. It would, however, be another ten years before the government was prepared to extend the levy system further to include the whole nation. In another sense, the Algiers levy also looks forward to the Ship Money levies of the late 1630s in that it dispensed entirely with the notion that the Crown was asking for ships and not ready money.

The weaknesses and inconsistencies that became evident during

---

[1] *APC*, 1619–1621, p. 291.
[2] PRO, SP 14/107/26; SP 14/108/81 and inclosure.
[3] *APC*, 1618–1619, 23 March 1619, pp. 409–11.
[4] Ibid., pp. 410, 422.
[5] PRO, SP 14/108/48; on the list of refusers, one name had been crossed out hastily with the words superscribed 'he hath since paid'. In contrast, Barnstaple sent the names of those paying: SP 14/107/25 and inclosure.
[6] *APC*, 1618–1619, p. 444; two messengers of the king's chamber, Thomas Roberts and Henry Keyme, were empowered to bring in the Newcastle men. Later, two masters of Trinity House were placed in custody until payment was received: *APC*, 1621–1623, p. 222. Also, the French Company was held in contempt.
[7] PRO, SP 14/109/49.

the period of collection help explain the development of a regular, national system of taxation to support a navy. Many of the disputes described above could only be resolved by abandoning the decentralized medieval system. This episode also serves to bring out aspects of the fiscal weaknesses and administrative incapacity of the Jacobean government. Without administrative machinery of its own, the Crown was dependent on local men. As a consequence, the government was compelled to transfer administration to local administration or companies that could be held responsible for the execution of its policies. The experience of the Algiers levy helps explain why the Crown in this period was so attracted to and dependent on monopolies. Finally, the problems of administration and the disputes concerning assessments were a reason for the delay of the expedition and would affect its chances of success.

3
THE ALGIERS EXPEDITION: DIPLOMATIC BACKGROUND

From its inception, the Algiers expedition was seen as an international venture. As early as 28 April 1617, royal servants, merchants, and naval advisers agreed that it was highly desirable, perhaps imperative, to get support from other nations.[1] Contributions from Savoy, Venice, France, Spain, and the United Provinces were considered at first, but only the United Provinces and Spain had the requisite naval power, money, or ports to warrant inclusion. Though England, Spain, and the United Provinces had a common interest in suppressing the Barbary pirates, so many political, strategic, economic, and religious issues separated them that co-operation would be difficult to achieve.

From the beginning, it was also perceived that making the venture a joint one would cause delay.[2] Time would be lost while negotiations took place; even so, the merchants agreed with the representatives of the Crown that proceeding jointly was:

> ... the fittest way, and likeliest to work the Effect intended, was that his Majesty would be pleased, by his Ministers to treat with other Princes, for the uniting of their Forces, or at least for Joining in a contribution toward the charges.[3]

Negotiations were begun with the United Provinces and Spain

---

[1] PRO, SP 14/90/136,91/52 and inclosure. Details of this paragraph on value and desirability of potential allies are found in this correspondence. Savoy and Venice were dismissed quickly for they had little to offer. French ports were thought too distant to be useful against the pirates of Algiers.
[2] PRO, SP 14/90/136.
[3] Ibid.

almost immediately, but almost three years would pass before agreed roles were reached. The story of these negotiations is worth following for two reasons. First, it is of direct, immediate interest because it provides a partial explanation for the Crown's delays in setting out a fleet against the pirates. Second, it offers a different perspective on early 17th-century foreign relations than one finds in traditional histories of this period. These negotiations show that mistrust, duplicity and conflicting interests were present – that is, the traditional picture – but they also reveal common concerns, hopes, and desires for co-operation – features often overlooked in an age remembered primarily for the Thirty Years War.

The possibility of Dutch involvement in the project was examined on 1 April 1617, when Secretary of State, Winwood, wrote to Dudley Carleton, English ambassador in the Hague,[1] asking him to raise the subject of a joint expedition with Maurice of Nassau and Jan van Oldenbarnevelt, Grand Pensionary of Holland. Less than two weeks passed before Carleton replied that Maurice and Oldenbarnevelt thought that the United Provinces would be willing to join an expedition against the pirates. Moreover, their naval advisers thought it would not be too difficult a matter to blockade the harbours of Algiers and Tunis 'by lying at anchor before them in that manner, as during the war with Spain they were wont to do before Dunkirk, and this they esteem the best course'.[2] Only in the four winter months, when the weather was bad, did they think a close blockade would be hard to maintain.[3]

Carleton also maintained a correspondence with Thomas Lake, Secretary of State,[4] who advised the ambassador that James had heard the Dutch had made an agreement with the Turks which included provisions for the Dutch to supply gunpowder. His master thought it strange, so Lake wrote, that 'they would arm the enemies of Christendom and humane society'.[5] Carleton was told to discover the truth of this intelligence and put a stop to it, if true. He was also informed that the king had in hand a plan for a joint

---

[1] PRO, SP 84/77/f.3.
[2] PRO, SP 84/77/f.24–24v.
[3] J.I. Israel, 'A Conflict of Empires: Spain and the Netherlands 1618–1648', *Past and Present*, no. 76 (1977), p. 45, on Dutch difficulties in maintaining a blockade on Dunkirk all year round.
[4] Normally the monarch had two secretaries at this time. The correspondence and relations with diplomats were divided between the two.
[5] PRO, SP 84/77/f.34. 15 April. Lake was sympathetic to Spain and Catholic interests and therefore he was likely to see Anglo-Dutch relations in a different perspective.

expedition which would include Spain as well as the United Provinces.[1]

On 6 May, Lake wrote again to Carleton with more details of the English proposal. Two or three years' sustained warfare against the pirate towns was now thought necessary to break the pirates' power. Consequently, Spanish ports were needed 'for watering, repairing, succour against storms and all other casualties and without that, there is great hazard in the attempt'.[2] The costs of an expedition would be borne 'by a contribution of money or shipping from all Princes and States who are interested in the loss sustained by their subjects'.[3] Being nearest the danger and suffering most from the pirates, Spain was expected to contribute substantially, but France, Venice, and Savoy would also be approached. James wished the Dutch to provide ships which, like England's, were thought more suitable for employment in such an operation than those of Spain.[4]

While Lake made it clear that Dutch participation was expected, he went on to explain that there was no urgency and it would be advisable for Carleton to suspend his efforts to bring in the Dutch until other, more distant powers, that is Spain, had agreed to join forces or contribute to the expedition. Again, he told Carleton that Digby, a man suspected of strong Spanish sympathies,[5] would soon depart for Madrid to treat with the king of Spain. Until Digby returned with an answer, there was little that Carleton might do other than inform the Dutch that 'it will be too late to do much this year'.[6] Lake's dispatch of 6 May did not arrive until 27 June. Thus Carleton's response was not written until 7 July, when he informed Lake that the United Provinces were prepared to give assistance when particulars were finally settled.[7]

In the meantime, Carleton attempted to discover the truth of the allegations reported by Lake. Were they true, the Dutch would be discredited and jeopardize participation in the venture.

---

[1] Ibid. According to Lake, James hoped 'to draw a concurrency between Princes who are interested in the navigation of those seas for the suppression of them and hath a consultation in hand at London with all his sea Captains what is meet to be done in that case . . . and further given instruction to Sir John Digby going into Spain to deal with that king for contribution toward it and for use of his Ports for retreat'.
[2] PRO, SP 84/77/f.98.
[3] Ibid.
[4] Ibid., f.98–98v.
[5] PRO, SP 14/70/21; SP 14/90/122.
[6] PRO, SP 84/77/f.98.
[7] PRO, SP 84/78/f.16.

The proposed expedition would then be transformed into a purely Anglo-Spanish venture, and England, the Dutch republic's strongest ally, would become detached and move closer to Spain, the republic's deadly enemy.

After a brief investigation, Carleton was able to report that he had learned that the Dutch had made contact with the pirates, but there was no evidence that they had agreed to the supply of powder to Algiers.[1] Private merchants may have done so. It was common practice for merchants, Carleton claimed, to supply the pirates with gunpowder because they paid double the going rate. In any event, Carleton added, Dutch officials had made it clear to him that they were eager to join in an operation to suppress the pirates.

The seriousness of this allegation may be seen from the exchange of letters in June between Winwood, a Dutch supporter, and Carleton. On the 4th of the month, Winwood warned Carleton that the government was greatly upset that the United Provinces were said to treat and contract with the pirates of Algiers, especially when their power was growing so much 'that if present order be not taken to suppress them, our trade must cease in the Mediterranean Sea, nay they will shortly grow so insolent and presumptuous that they will adventure to possess our seas, and to asayle in our ports'.[2] Winwood finished his letter by urging Carleton to get the Dutch to stop their men-of-war from furnishing the pirates with powder and munitions. In reply, Carleton wrote that he had talked to Oldenbarnevelt, who had informed him that while it was true that the United Provinces had treated with the pirates, their consul, now imprisoned in Algiers, had sought only to secure the release of Dutch ships and captives who were being held and ransomed at excessive rates.[3] Oldenbarnevelt admitted that an agreement between Algiers and the United Provinces had been drafted and that it contained a clause allowing the pirates to search Dutch ships for Spanish merchandise, but now the clause was thought unacceptable, and the Dutch government would not proceed with such an agreement. According to Carleton, Oldenbarnevelt hoped his country would join England in such a worthy cause. They expected to send a fleet to the Mediterranean to deal

---

[1] PRO, SP 84/77/f.124.
[2] PRO, SP 84/77/f.182.
[3] PRO, SP 84/77/f.197.

with the pirates, unless it were needed, he added pointedly, to defend the Swedes from an attack by the Hapsburg powers.

The interview ended with Oldenbarnevelt exclaiming how upsetting he found the accusations that the Dutch furnished munitions to the pirates. Only the United Provinces, he added, had made efforts to suppress the pirates. In any case, if the pirates had been supplied, it had never been done by their men-of-war, either openly or secretly. These statements apparently gave satisfaction for the matter was not raised again. The efforts of Oldenbarnevelt, Winwood, and Carleton removed the ground from those who sought to exclude the United Provinces from the proposed co-operative venture.[1]

The diplomatic correspondence indicates that little in the way of negotiations took place between July and August 1617. However, a cryptic entry in a letter from Winwood to Carleton, dated 21 July, suggests that the matter was not entirely in suspension. This letter contained an introduction for two unnamed gentlemen who would have charge of a secret business to press Maurice and Oldenbarnevelt.[2] Ten days later, Carleton wrote to Winwood that these two gentlemen, Sir Edward Harwood and Captain Burroughs, were returning with particulars of which he could only say there 'is a good inclination', but that he would leave it to them to relate the substance and results of their mission to the low countries.[3] Despite his admonition, Carleton proceeded to provide details in cipher on 'the business of 10 33 23 29 20 47 65 67'.[4] Deciphered,[5] the nature of Harwood's and Burroughs's business is clear: they had been sent to discuss an attack on Algiers. But what makes this letter especially interesting is the frankness and fullness of the discussion.

According to Carleton, the Dutch foresaw two major obstacles. First, they were worried whether the proposed force could blockade Algiers successfully: 'any misinformation of the store of

---

[1] Between 31 July and 10 January 1618, only two letters are concerned with the pirate expedition and they are amicable in character.
[2] PRO, SP 84/78/f.66.
[3] PRO, SP 84/78/f.107v.
[4] Ibid. A L G I E R S. Except for the occasional interlinear addition of clear text, substantial parts of Carleton's correspondence survive undeciphered.
[5] If enough cipher text survives, the letter frequency analysis technique may be used to construct a cipher key. This method is applicable to most English ciphers of the period since they are of the alphabetic-numeric substitution pattern. Since constructing a key to decipher this letter, its validity has been confirmed by J. den Tex, *Oldenbarnevelt*, II, pp. 704–5, who also constructed a key for Carleton's cipher.

the town, or any small ship which should enter by Sea, would overthrow it'.[1] Carleton could only reply that if a multitude of shipping were used, a close guard could be kept on the port.[2] They also expressed doubt whether the proposed fleet would be able to surprise the enemy. Being a commonwealth, the Dutch government could not undertake such a matter without communicating it to the provinces. The Levant merchants would have to be notified, and since money would have to be raised the provinces were bound to discuss the proposed expenditure.[3] It was very difficult to maintain secrecy, especially when the merchant community needed to be warned or legislative bodies consulted.[4] Carleton was not entirely convinced by the argument; he 'remembered many extraordinary enterprizes, both of great cost and hazard, which unless they had been resolved of and executed with secrecy could never have taken place'.[5] In any case, the risk seemed worth taking. Shipping losses for three or four years, at the current rate, were as expensive as a year's siege which might bring an end to the problem. Half the burden, he went on to point out, would be borne by England in any case.

All this may have been true, but the Dutch were not easily persuaded. Oldenbarnevelt doubted whether the provinces would accept a breaking of the Levant trade. Moreover, the gravity of the task terrified him. Had not Charles V, he recalled, been utterly defeated when he had attempted to take Algiers.[6] Maurice then pitched in with seemingly vague comments which suggest the real reason for their caution. Given the current distractions, he thought it unlikely that the Provinces would assent to so great a foreign business. They would prefer James delay the project (thus stopping the prospect of closer ties between England and Spain). In the meantime, the United Provinces would send 12 ships to the Straits to counter the depredations of the pirates.

Although Maurice's phrases, especially his reference to 'distractions', may appear vague or indefinite, their meaning would not have puzzled experienced diplomats such as Carleton or Win-

---

[1] PRO, SP 84/78/f.168.
[2] Ibid., f.168v.
[3] Ibid., f.169.
[4] See for example the comment by Coke, in HMC 23, *12th Report, App. i, Cowper MSS*, p. 104.
[5] PRO, SP/84/78/f.168v.
[6] M.F. Alvarez, *Charles V: Elected Emperor and Hereditary Ruler*, pp. 120–3; A.C. Hess, *The Forgotten Frontier: A History of the Sixteenth-Century Ibero-African Frontier*, pp. 74–6.

wood. Nor would they have been perplexed over why the Dutch were seeking to postpone the joint expedition. But to understand Dutch policy regarding the pirate expedition, some consideration must first be given to Dutch politics, for domestic politics shaped and directed all foreign policy considerations at this time.

For the United Provinces, the summer of 1617 was a time of turmoil, as serious in its own way as the dark days of 1584 when Parma appeared on the verge of reconquering the Netherlands. This was the denouement of a conflict that had been growing in intensity during the years since the Twelve Years' Truce. In July and August, it threatened to destroy the cohesion of the Republic. The roots of the conflict were theological, but the disagreement soon widened into a broad public debate which, in turn, was transformed into a political struggle that brought into question the constitutional basis, economic interests, and foreign policy of the United Provinces.

One faction, known as the Remonstrants, drew their strength primarily from the large and wealthy province of Holland and especially the oligarchs who dominated municipal government.[1] They were supported by the Dutch East India Company and those whose trade was with southern Europe or along established lines. This faction supported a more conciliatory, less ideological, approach in foreign policy and wished for the truce with Spain to be perpetuated beyond 1621. Both for reasons of trade and foreign policy, the Remonstrants would be inclined to support the English proposal for a joint expedition with Spain against the pirates of Algiers. This coalition was tied together and personified by Oldenbarnevelt.

The focus of power of the Counter-Remonstrants, on the other hand, rested in exiles from the South (prominent in Amsterdam) and the House of Orange. Geographically, Counter-Remonstrant support came from the landward provinces and Zeeland whose mariners and merchants would gain from conflict with Spain. The Dutch West India Company, whose expansionary trading policy in the Caribbean and South America brought it into conflict with Spain, backed the Counter-Remonstrant party. This coalition

---

[1] The following discussion of internal political conflict in the United Provinces is based on the following works: Geoffrey Parker, *The Dutch Revolt*, pp. 247–53; E.H. Kossman, 'The Low Countries', *The New Cambridge Modern History*, IV, *The Decline of Spain and the Thirty Years War*, ed. J.P. Cooper, pp. 371–4; J.I. Israel, *The Dutch Republic and the Hispanic World 1606–1661*, pp. 8–42, 59–65; C.R. Boxer, *The Dutch Seaborne Empire 1600–1800*, pp. 27–8.

sought a more aggressive foreign policy, thought the Truce had been a mistake, and looked forward to a resumption of hostilities with Spain. The economic interests of this faction were not threatened directly by Algerian pirates. More relevantly, the aggressive, anti-Spanish stance of the Counter-Remonstrants made them unlikely to favour a co-operative project involving Spain. Maurice of Nassau championed the Counter-Remonstrant cause.

The domestic conflict of the United Provinces influenced the course of negotiations for a joint expedition in two ways. First, the bitterness and all-embracing nature of the struggle meant that from 1617 until the spring of 1619 policy-making in the Dutch Republic was paralysed by the deadly partisan feud. Little wonder that from August 1617 until early 1619, even as skilled a diplomat as Carleton could not bring negotiations to a speedy or successful conclusion.

Second, the Dutch were distracted, as Carleton wrote on 3 August, by the imminent end of the Twelve Years' Truce.[1] As the expiration drew closer, Spain and the United Provinces manoeuvred for advantage and interpreted each others' actions in the darkest strategic terms. In the summer of 1617 the focus of Dutch attention was almost exclusively on political developments in northern Italy and Bohemia where both the Dutch and Spanish had vital interests.

The Spanish sought to secure their lines of supply (known as the Spanish Road) which stretched from Genoa through the Alpine passes and Germany to Flanders in the Spanish Netherlands.[2] On either side of this route were Savoy and Venice. Both states had territorial ambitions and were antagonistic to Spain. It was the aim of Dutch policy, therefore, to get Savoy and Venice to join the United Provinces in an anti-Spanish coalition which would cut the Spanish Road, isolate the Spanish Army of Flanders, and thereby reduce the threat to the United Provinces. To prevent this, Spanish agents encouraged the duke of Osuna, viceroy of Naples, to create a naval force in the Adriatic and thereby threaten

---

[1] PRO, SP 84/78/f.169v, and later, SP 84/91/f.175.
[2] This supply route was known as the 'Spanish Road'. For more information on the Spanish supply system and the strategic importance of their supply lines to the Netherlands, see: G. Parker, *The Army of Flanders and the Spanish Road, 1567–1659: The logistics of Spanish victory and defeat in the Low Countries' wars*, pp. 50–5, 80–101.

Venetian trade.[1] The Spanish also schemed to secure the Bohemian Crown for a candidate who would favour Spanish interests in Germany and assist in keeping open the Spanish Road.

Thus, both for domestic and foreign reasons the Dutch acted with caution and were inclined to view English proposals for an expedition against Algiers in the context of European power politics. They were interested in the suppression of pirates, but this was not their only or even primary interest in the Mediterranean. In the period 1617 to 1620, matters relating to state security dominated all policy considerations. Dutch participation in the English-sponsored expedition would be determined not by the appeal of the project itself, but by how it related to Dutch security needs.

Suppression of the pirates would relieve Spain of a need to devote naval resources to coastal defence and Mediterranean trade. Defeat of the pirates of Algiers might be detrimental to Dutch strategic aims, though beneficial in economic ways. The Barbary states were potential Dutch allies and could provide Dutch naval forces with bases to harrass Spanish lines of communication in the Mediterranean.[2] On balance, it appeared that Spain had more to gain from the proposed venture, at least in an economic or military sense. However, the United Provinces had much to lose by not participating, or by appearing uninterested in a joint venture. England had supported Dutch independence. Though the relationship had changed in the last two decades, English support remained valuable. A hostile, or neutral, England would provide Spain with a safe seaward supply route to the Netherlands.[3] Therefore, Dutch statesmen did not wish to alienate the English government.

The realities of power limited the choices available to Dutch statesmen in general, but with the ascendancy of the Counter-Remonstrants, Dutch policy became more narrowly anti-Spanish in focus. The sending of an English fleet to the Mediterranean was viewed with ambivalence. If the English fleet were to destroy the

---

[1] R.A. Stradling, *Europe and the Decline of Spain: A Study of the Spanish System, 1580–1720*, pp. 69–70.
[2] PRO, SP/84/88/ff.122,201v.
[3] In the 1630s and early 1640s a large part of Spanish money and resources came through England rather than going to Genoa and up the Spanish Road: J.S. Kepler, *The Exchange of Christendom: The International Entrepôt at Dover, 1622–51*, pp. 36–9; G. Parker, 'New Light on an Old Theme: Spain and the Netherlands 1550–1650', *European History Quarterly*, XV (1985), p. 227.

pirates of Algiers, a potential ally in a war against Spain would be lost; however, if the English and Dutch fleets were to operate jointly in the Mediterranean against pirates, Spain would feel threatened.[1] Even if the fleet were to operate strictly against the pirates, the mere presence of an Anglo-Dutch fleet would be enough to make the Spanish anxious and perhaps alter the disposition of their forces. But this state of affairs would come about only if the Spanish were excluded from the anti-pirate venture. Dutch statesmen, therefore, wished to avoid the tripartite sort of expedition proposed by James, but at the same time they could not be so negative or obstructive that they would be excluded.

The basic aims of Dutch policy were pursued openly. On 10 January 1618, Noel Caron, the Dutch representative in London, urged James to forget about possible Spanish contributions; the English and Dutch fleets, operating together, could accomplish more and do it more quickly.[2] Little action followed Caron's initiative; indeed on 8 September, Caron informed his masters that the whole project seemed at a standstill.[3] The reasons for the apparent stoppage were financial and diplomatic. The English government, as related above, was having difficulty getting the merchants and port towns to pay up,[4] and the Spanish, for reasons of their own, were procrastinating.

Because Spanish interest in the project seemed to be flagging, James suggested at this point that it might be advisable for England and the United Provinces to go ahead, launch the expedition on their own, and wait and see what Spain would do. James's proposal for an Anglo-Dutch expedition should not be taken at face value; it was made for effect. It would encourage Dutch interest and let the Spanish see that England might be forced to join the Dutch by default if the Spanish did not respond more positively.

In any case, the Dutch responded eagerly, though for reasons of their own. Just as James made his offer for an Anglo-Dutch expedition, reports of a substantial Spanish naval build-up began to arrive in the Hague. Madrid claimed that the fleet was being

---

[1] For example, PRO, SP 84/96/f.96.
[2] BL, Add. MS. 17,677, I, ff.266–7; PRO, SP 84/82/f.75.
[3] BL, Add. MS. 17,677, I, f.329–329v.
[4] See Chapter 2.

prepared for action against Algiers, but Dutch suspicions[1] were not allayed.[2] Ominous developments in Bohemia encouraged Dutch officials to suspect that the fleet was part of some grand Spanish/Catholic scheme to attack Venice, the United Provinces, and destroy the whole Protestant world. English friendship and support now appeared valuable. On January 1619, the Dutch commissioners in London went to James, as instructed by the States-General, and indicated that the Dutch would like very much to join England in suppressing the pirates.[3] James seemed pleased and told the Dutch commissioners that he would almost immediately restart preparations and see that they were prosecuted with vigour and speed.[4]

Fear of the Spanish naval build-up cut wide and deep. Even apparently pro-Spanish officials in England seemed worried. For example, in February the Dutch commissioners wrote that Lord Digby, an experienced diplomat and not easily given to anti-Spanish sentiment, was voicing concern.[5] He made a great impression on the Dutch, as Carleton reported a week later. His words are worth quoting because the nature of Digby's proposal[6] (and hence English policy) is open to misinterpretation unless the precise form of the proposal is considered. Carleton wrote to Naunton the following:

> I find that the States have been written unto by their Commissioners in the name of his Majesty, as moved by my Lord Digby, to join their ships with his Majesty's to assist the Spaniard in case he doth really intend to besiege Algiers; or if his design should be against the Venetians, then to follow the fleet, and assist that Commonwealth, in both of which they find much difficulty. First in the siege of Algiers which would expose their merchants to a danger of confiscation of all their goods in

---

[1] PRO, SP 84/88/f.201. An attack on Scotland was mentioned as a possibility, but the Dalmatian coast was thought more likely in most reports. Ibid., f.215: On 26 February 1619, the Dutch suspected the Spanish fleet was meant for Ireland.
[2] It now seems certain that Spanish preparations were actually intended for a campaign against the pirates of Algiers: C. Fernández Duro, *Armada Española*, III, pp. 353–67.
[3] PRO, SP 84/88/ff.3v–4.
[4] Ibid., f.115.
[5] BL, Add. MS. 17,667, I, ff.389–90.
[6] PRO, SP 14/108/15. It may be assumed that Digby was acting on instructions from James, as he had done before and would do again when negotiating the Spanish match as Sir Edward Harwood observed.

Turkey & the taking of that town by the Spaniard would make him to absolute a master in the Mediterranean. Secondly in assisting the Venetians which would draw them the same inconvenience of loss both of ships & merchandise which they have now in Spain.[1]

At first glance Digby's proposal appears to imply that the pirate expedition was really intended to act as a counter-balance to any Spanish moves in the Mediterranean. This is the conclusion reached by Sir Julian Corbett in his study of English naval involvement in the Mediterranean.[2] However, it should be noted that Digby's proposal was cast in the conditional mood: the fleet would be employed against Spain (instead of Algiers as advertised) only if Venice were actually threatened. The motives behind the proposal must remain speculative, but its anticipated effect is easy to deduce. The proposal would appeal to the Dutch by allaying their fears about Spanish intentions and Anglo-Spanish collusion. It would also prevent the Dutch from withdrawing from the project and entering into an overtly anti-Spanish alliance with Algiers.[3]

On 19 March, as instructed, the Dutch position was related to the Privy Council.[4] The United Provinces were willing to set out a fleet of 20 ships for use against the pirates but did not wish Spain included, nor did they wish to participate in a venture that would offend Constantinople. They would co-operate with the English fleet in any way that would divert Spain from attacking Venice or Bohemia.

These negotiations did not prevent the Dutch from exploring other options. In July, Carleton reported that the United Provinces and Algiers were close to reaching an agreement, though he doubted whether the negotiations would continue smoothly because the issue of the captives had not been dealt with and almost daily there were reports of more Dutch ships taken.[5] James ordered Carleton to convey his anger,[6] but in reply Maurice excused the negotiations with Algiers claiming that they were a contingency 'in regard of the expiration of their truce with

[1] PRO, SP 84/88/f.201v.
[2] See below, Chapter 5 and, especially Chapter 6.
[3] The proposal may represent a contingency plan just in case Spanish preparations were really aimed against Venice, or Ireland.
[4] BL, Add. MS. 17,667, I, ff.402, 404–6.
[5] PRO, SP 84/91/f.64.
[6] Ibid., ff.108–9.

Spain; which if it should not be renewed . . . did import the States much to have a port in the Mediterranean to which their ships might retire'. Carleton put a hopeful gloss on Maurice's words believing that the Dutch would propose unacceptable conditions, as was the case.[1] In fact, a few days later, the Dutch indicated that they were ready to send a fleet to Algiers to arrange an exchange of prisoners. They were even prepared to throw overboard their prisoners within sight of the town if they did not get their way.[2]

In early September, Carleton was told officially that the Dutch government now had no intention of reaching an agreement with Algiers but would send a fleet to the Mediterranean and hoped the English would do likewise so that the pirates might be brought to obedience. They also beseeched James to allow the export of 300 pieces of ordnance needed for the ships intended for use against the pirates.[3] Whether genuine or contrived, this request reflects the preoccupation of Dutch authorities with the coming struggle with Spain and the need for arms.

The English response was both cautious and demanding.[4] The king expressed an interest but was not satisfied with the Dutch explanation regarding negotiations with Algiers. A month later Carleton stated that the Dutch were truly ready to send a fleet of 14 ships against Algiers but success against the pirates would come, they believed, only if the English were also present.[5] On 20 November, James replied evasively informing the Dutch that he was pleased to learn of their preparations and that collections for the English fleet were to be advanced.[6] However, the English response carefully avoided commitment to any proposition that would be solely Anglo-Dutch in character. Though the diplomats continued to talk for another nine months, the basic positions of both countries had been settled by then.[7] While the diplomats talked, English and Dutch naval preparations went ahead, even

[1] PRO, SP 84/91/f.175.
[2] Ibid., f.178v.
[3] PRO, SP 84/92/f.12.
[4] Ibid., f.39.
[5] Ibid., f.167–167v.
[6] PRO, SP 84/93/f.90.
[7] PRO, SP 94/23/f.229. At one point, Cottington, the English agent in Madrid, advised Carleton that Spain would never allow the United Provinces to enter into an anti-pirate league of which they were not part. By no means in the long course of these negotiations were all the delays and difficulties the result of Dutch action or inaction. There was a period when the English government did not pursue the project very actively and Spain was at times just as intransigent as the Dutch.

though no precise agreement defining the nature of their co-operation had been reached.

On 8 August 1620, Carleton passed on the latest proposals from the States-General restating a desire for conjunction of the fleets of England and the Netherlands but avoiding all mention of Spanish participation.[1] The Dutch also thought that a successful siege of Algiers was no longer possible, though in their view it might still be possible to burn the pirate fleet in harbour. If the English still wished to make such an assault, they would assist willingly and suggested a mixed force, including soldiers, commanded by Sir Edward Harwood. In the meantime, a Dutch fleet of 21 ships would undertake patrols with three squadrons: eight ships would sail in the area between the Straits of Gibraltar and Cape Gabba; another eight ships would patrol between Cape Gabba and Cape Pasaro; and the remaining five ships would operate in the Atlantic between the Straits and Cape St Vincent.[2]

Only one day after Carleton transmitted the latest Dutch plans, he sent the following report to Naunton:

> a chief person of the States hath whispered unto me [that the] ... joining the two fleets now preparing in England & the Provinces ... shall be judged the most necessary service of the two either against the pirates at sea or the fleet [may threaten] ... these great armies by land ... which as they here judge would fetch Spinola back though he crossed the Rhine. How this may stand with his Majesty's liking or service, I am not to examine, nor in a conjuncture of so great & so imminent peril to his nearest friends abroad to conceal what is projected for their safety. If hereupon or anything else his Majesty hath any service to command me with this state your honour may please give me direction how to govern myself either by going to the camp (as my predecessors did according to occasions) or remaining here at the Hague.[3]

This letter shows again how much Dutch foreign policy was geared

---

[1] PRO, SP 84/96/ff.92, 94. The pirates were said to have 100 sail.
[2] Algemeen Rijksarchief, The Hague, Almiraliteitsarchieven 954, the journal of William de Zoete (Haultain). I wish to thank Dr Sari Hornstein for procuring for me a microfilm copy of this journal.
[3] PRO, SP 84/96/f.96. Although the language of this quotation may appear obscure to modern eyes, what Carleton is saying is that an important dutch official has intimated that the proposed joint fleet might be used either against pirates or as a means of threatening the supply lines of the Spanish forces in the Low Countries.

primarily to security concerns in the Low Countries and Germany. It also shows how the Dutch sought to draw England into an anti-Spanish coalition.

Pressure of this sort irritated James, and as a consequence the old and friendly relationship between the two states became strained. On 28 August, Naunton replied letting the Dutch know that his Majesty was indignant and that he (Naunton) 'was directed . . . to make no other answer than this, that his Majesty presuming they hath the same ends with him, to extirpate that wicked generation of the pirates, & to secure the common trade, was in that respect very willing to take them into the association, there being hope that by such an increase of strength, the enterprise shall succeed the better'.[1] A week later, Carleton told the Dutch that his master had good reason to join his fleet with any nation but the United Provinces, especially after the massacre of English subjects by the Dutch at Amboyna.[2]

The response of the Dutch was one of injured innocence; they claimed their recent proposal had been prompted solely by English suggestions, specifically that:

> There was some speech held with them by some of his Majesty's Commissioners touching a joint attempt upon the town of Algiers betwixt his Majesty's forces, the king of Spain's, & theirs: which purpose, the town being taken, to put the same into the king of Spain's possession; against which they had many important considerations for their particular not to engage themselves, nor to wish that town in the hands of the Spaniards.

Carleton reassured the Dutch that the English government had never proposed to hand over Algiers to Spain.

Two weeks later and just about the time the English fleet was ready to depart for the Mediterranean, Naunton reviewed at length the course of the Anglo-Dutch negotiations over the expedition.[3] It was the United Provinces, Naunton declared, who had solicited James for aid against the pirates; James had agreed graciously, he said, only to find that they then started to raise objections over the Spanish contribution of money and ports.

---

[1] PRO, SP 84/96/f.160.
[2] PRO, SP 84/97/f.12.
[3] PRO, SP 84/97/f.72.

Warming to his subject, Naunton went on to relate that whatever any might now say about the delivering up of Algiers, he remembered it was not spoken of by Lords of the Council Table; nor was his Majesty made aware of any overture of this nature. He did recall, however, that in March 1619, the Dutch commissioners put in writing to the Council some sort of proposition or answer to what some commissioners had privately intimated but when the king was acquainted, he

> was thoroughly detested at it and remarked it of himself that they had made first suit & motion to have joined with them in that service and gave me [Naunton] order to refer them no answer but this, & that in case only if they should call for it, that he had no other answer to make to this their flourishing relation, but that he understood it well enough. Whereupon all further proceedings with them in that point & of the Pirates ceased.

As a result of delays by the Dutch and their deviousness in negotiation, so Naunton went on to advise the Dutch, James had been forced to make 'equal & indifferent articles of association' between himself and the king of Spain.

On 28 September, the Dutch sent their reply through Carleton, who employed a Latin quotation, perhaps to reduce the sting, for the Dutch had expressed anger and disappointment over what they perceived as a developing Anglo-Spanish understanding now manifest in the joint expedition.[1] In view of Spinola's invasion of the Palatinate,[2] the Dutch had informed Carleton, they found it difficult to comprehend – let alone accept – an Anglo-Spanish rapprochement.

How and why this Anglo-Spanish understanding developed is the subject of the next chapter, but in part it can be credited to a failure of Dutch diplomacy. By refusing to condone any Spanish involvement, the Dutch brought about their own virtual exclusion and encouraged Spanish involvement and a closer relationship between Spain and England. A narrowly partisan perspective,

---

[1] PRO, SP 84/97/f.92.
[2] A state of the Holy Roman Empire consisting of two territories: (1) the Lower Palatinate (now in the state of Rhineland-Palatinate) and (2) the Upper Palatinate (now in Bavaria). At the time, the Palatinate was officially Protestant, ruled by an Elector (Frederick, the son-in-law of James I), and friendly to the United Provinces.

increased by the exclusion of the Remonstrants, blinded the Dutch to the merits of James's vision of a joint venture by the Christian powers against the pirates.

English diplomacy in these negotiations was only partially successful. It proved impossible to bring together the fleets of the three greatest European naval powers in a joint expedition against the pirates. Nonetheless, James and his ministers can take credit for getting the Dutch to co-operate with what was essentially an Anglo-Spanish expedition against the pirates. That this much was achieved came about through the unswerving insistence of the king and his diplomats that the multi-national fleet would be used only for the stated objective: the reduction of piracy in the Mediterranean and North Atlantic.

4
ANGLO-SPANISH NEGOTIATIONS

In many ways English negotiations with Spain were similar to those with the United Provinces. Neither progressed smoothly nor continuously. Spanish diplomacy was also greatly influenced by the approaching end of the Twelve Years' Truce and by an internal political conflict which ended in the destruction of the leader of the peace party. Despite many similarities, however, Anglo-Spanish negotiations were different in character. For a start, the proposed joint expedition was part of a larger, more general English diplomatic initiative bound up with and influenced by parallel negotiations for the restoration of the Palatinate and an Anglo-Spanish marriage treaty.[1] Secondly, Anglo-Spanish negotiations were greatly handicapped by mutual misunderstanding and deep-seated mistrust that went back to the Armada or earlier, though these feelings were increasingly offset by converging economic and political interests which made it desirable for both states to try to co-operate.

Following the Privy Council meetings of March and April 1617, Digby's instructions for his forthcoming embassy were amended to authorize him to negotiate an anti-pirate league with Spain.[2] On arrival in Madrid in early summer, Digby presented a letter from James I to Philip III proposing the naval forces of the two crowns be joined for operations against the Barbary pirates.[3] The Spanish reply, though polite, was neither immediate nor positive.

In part, this response was the consequence of a report sent by

---
[1] The Hapsburg forces had dispossessed Frederick, the son-in-law of James I, of lands in the Palatinate in the Holy Roman Empire.
[2] PRO, SP 14/90/136, 14/91/52 and inclosure, 14/92/11.
[3] AGS, Estado, legajo 2850, letter of James I to Philip III, 24 March/3 April 1617.

the Spanish ambassador in London, Don Diego Sarmiento de Acuña, conde de Gondomar. On 12 July, he warned his government that he had learned from an (unnamed) informant that the proposed league against the pirates was really an anti-Spanish plot, a scheme hatched by the earl of Southampton who hoped to use it to secure the office of Lord High Admiral.[1] From this position of power, according to Gondomar, Southampton then planned to use naval forces sent out against the pirates to attack Genoa or the Papal States and thereby bring about war with Spain. Since Gondomar's report has been taken as proof that the expedition was Southampton's idea and primarily an anti-Spanish operation, it is worth examining carefully before relating the part it played in the negotiations.[2]

Though it is *possible* that Gondomar reported nothing but the truth, it is curious, to say the least, that no evidence has survived to corroborate his story. Neither the discussions of the Privy Council nor letters to or from James ever treat the proposal as a cover for action against Spain. The only document giving colour to Gondomar's contention is a letter from James to the commissioners for the Spanish Business expressing his support for the proposed expedition against the pirates (no other aim is stated), and putting forward Southampton as a possible commander, instead of the aged and infirm Nottingham.[3] Southampton may have had connections with some of the City merchants, though this does not mean they were his agents, nor even had the same motivation or objective, even if they did propose an expedition.[4] At best, Gondomar's story is only hearsay.

It is *equally possible* that there is no truth whatsoever in the report. Gondomar may have been deceived, manipulated or even fabricated the story himself. Evidence undermining Gondomar's credibility is plentiful, though largely circumstantial. Recent research has gone some way (though not far enough) to amend the impression that Gondomar was a machiavellian super-diplomat extraordinary with spies in every council chamber and King James wrapped around his little finger. In fact, as he was forced to

---
[1] Ibid., 2850, Gondomar to Philip III.
[2] For example, C.D. Penn, *The Navy under the Early Stuarts and its Influence on English History*, pp. 48, 87.
[3] PRO, SP 14/90/136. Three years later the Venetian ambassador suggested that Southampton and his relations were prepared to put up £100 000 for the expedition: *CSPV*, 1619–1621, pp. 298–300.
[4] *DNB*, vol. 21, pp. 1055–61.

acknowledge on more than one occasion, his spies were next to useless, and his influence at court has been much exaggerated.[1] Gondomar was adept at taking credit for all actions favourable to Spain (after they had occurred), but never took responsibility for the failures of Spanish policy.[2] Short in stature, he liked to play the grandee at court, and gloried in his intimacy with the English monarch. James was no fool and flattered the Spanish ambassador, speaking of him, when he was present, as though he were an equal. They were 'two Diegos', leading Gondomar to believe that he was responsible for much of English policy.[3] The Spanish ambassador's vanity had few limits, though once in a rare moment of truth, he acknowledged that 'as often as not it seemed James was deluding *him*' – though even then he could not conceive that he might be duped *more often than not*.[4] He was a great self-publicist, as is evident in his voluminous correspondence, the survival of which may help explain his reputation.[5] His reputation as an outstanding diplomat is surprising since he lacked the essential characteristic of a good ambassador.[6] He was deeply prejudiced and this distorted and diminished his understanding of England and the policies of James's government.

That Gondomar apparently believed what he reported about the English proposal for an expedition is a measure of his misunderstanding: it runs against the main thrust of English foreign policy at that time. In simple terms, English foreign policy reflected the

---

[1] In particular, C.H. Carter, 'Gondomar: Ambassador to James I', *The Historical Journal*, VII (1964), pp. 189–208. Carter corrects the spy-master image and also shows how even as reputable a scholar as S.R. Gardiner exaggerated Gondomar's presence and importance at Court. It is ironical that Gondomar's inflated reputation is as much a product of his Puritan enemies as of his own boasting.
[2] For an example of Gondomar's spurious claims, see PRO, SP 94/23/f.120, in which he takes credit for weakening the navy.
[3] Carter, 'Gondomar', pp. 205–6.
[4] Ibid., p. 206.
[5] Ibid.
[6] Many of Gondomar's letters have been published in *Documentos Inéditos para la Historia de España*, I–IV, but many others remain unpublished. These are mainly in AGS, Estado, and cover the periods of his embassies. For a recent example of a work which rates Gondomar highly, see G. Mattingly, *Renaissance Diplomacy*, Chap. XXVI. Gondomar's reputation is closely tied to interpretations of English foreign policy and its mainspring. Some contemporaries saw the rapprochement with Spain as the result of intrigues by Catholics or crypto-Catholics. Others, and historians such as Mattingly and to a lesser extent C.H. Carter, in *The Secret Diplomacy of the Hapsburgs*, attribute this policy to Gondomar's skill. One of the chief arguments of this book is that the shift in English foreign policy in the early 17th century was not a consequence of manipulation by native or foreign individuals but a reflection of the changing distribution of power in Europe.

changing balance of power in Europe. James was attempting to achieve a rapprochement with Spain to counter the rising power of France and the United Provinces.[1] This policy was symbolized by the Crown's pursuit of the Spanish marriage. Gondomar's report also shows little appreciation of English politics. Southampton was not a member of the Council nor a close confidant of the king. He never became Lord High Admiral, and few any longer looked upon Southampton as a serious leader; those in the know thought him but a tool of Sir Edwin Sandys.[2]

The improbable nature of Gondomar's report becomes more apparent when one considers its implications. Is it really likely that James or his close adviser on foreign affairs, Lord Digby, would have promoted, even covertly, a course of action that aimed at hostilities with Spain at the very time they were expending so much effort in trying to achieve a successful conclusion to the Spanish match? Would these same men – long experienced in statecraft and politics – then embarking on a delicate but fundamental foreign policy initiative, allow themselves to be manipulated by Southampton? Were they so insensitive that they would choose a man of known anti-Spanish sympathies and impetuous character to lead an expedition needing Spanish support?[3] However absurd Gondomar's report may seem to us, it could not be dismissed by the Spanish government.

Martín de Aroztegui, Secretary of War, was appointed to treat with Digby and learn what the English had in mind.[4] About a month later, the Council of State met to discuss the English proposal.[5] They were conspicuously less suspicious and hostile to the proposal than Gondomar. Opinions differed within the Council mainly on regional lines: those with northern connections were against the proposal; those from Valencia or Andalusia (the provinces suffering most from the pirates) were generally in favour

---

[1] For contemporary appreciation of this, see for example, Sir George Carew, 'A relation of the State of France with the Character of Henry IV and the principal persons of that Court', in *An Historical View of the Negotiations between the Courts of England, France and Brussels, 1592–1617*, ed. Thomas Birch; BL, Add. MS. 36,444 ff.14–61 (Sir Charles Cornwallis, Discourse of the Estate of Spain Anno 1607). This realism is also evident in Anthony Sherley's treatise, *Political Power in the Whole World*, completed in 1622 initially in Spanish as *Peso politico de todo Mundo*; Sherley's ideas are discussed in R.A. Stradling, *Europe and the Decline of Spain: A Study of the Spanish System*, pp. 60–1, 64, 84.
[2] BL, Add. MS. 36,445, f.187v.
[3] *DNB*, vol. 21, p. 1059. He was not on the Privy Council until 1619.
[4] AGS, Estado, legajo 2850, 30 October/9 November 1617.
[5] Ibid., 25 November/5 December 1617.

of the English plan.[1] Aroztegui began with a summary description of his negotiations with Digby and laid before the Council English plans for a blockade of the pirate bases for two or three years.[2] The Spanish considered the English plans generally good but thought it doubtful that the pirate fleet could be set afire within the harbour of Algiers.

These deliberations show that the Spanish government was both divided and uncertain. Don Juan Hurtado de Mendoza, the Duke de Infantado, thought that the case for action against the pirates was clear enough and the plan of campaign sound, but stated that he would rather it were carried out by Spanish forces alone. For the time being, he suggested Digby be put off while they investigated the possibility of doing it themselves. Next, Don Agustin Messia, a veteran soldier, advised the Council that the idea of burning the pirate fleet in harbour was militarily impractical. He did not think they should accept Digby's offer, but in any case the matter should first be referred to the Council of War for their views before any final decision was taken. Father Aliaga, confessor of Philip III, was not opposed to the idea, but suggested that Digby should be asked to provide details of the cost of the venture before they determined the form of their response. Finally, Don Baltasar de Zúñiga recommended Digby be thanked for his efforts in explaining the plan and its purpose. Zúñiga thought such a league advisable, and his only concern was over the strength of the English fleet. He would prefer merchant captains in command of the English ships. He would also prefer it if the size of the English fleet were limited. In any case, the matter should be referred to the Council of War. It was thus agreed to give Digby a cautious, non-committal answer while the matter was looked into more thoroughly by the Council of War.

The response of the Council of War to the English proposal was very much concerned with their appreciation of relative naval strengths and threats. Some understanding of these is necessary before the policy of the government can be grasped.

---

[1] For example, Aliaga was a southerner and more concerned with the promotion of Spanish interests in the Mediterranean, while Zúñiga, a northerner, wished to direct resources towards the Netherlands. This division was general and not just evident in the discussions over the anti-pirate league. This is brought out in J.I. Israel, *The Dutch Republic and the Hispanic World, 1606–1661*, pp. 12–14, 64, 66–76. For biographical information on the council, P.L. Williams, 'The Court and Councils of Philip III of Spain' (unpublished PhD thesis, University of London, 1973), vol. II, pp. 417–20.
[2] AGS, Estado, legajo 2850, 25 November/5 December 1617.

Throughout the reign of Philip III the navy had been reduced in tonnage, numbers, and operational readiness. This trend was especially marked in the years following the truce with the Dutch in 1609. Expenditure declined sharply reducing the number of serviceable ships and preventing any replacement programme from being put into practice. By 1616 the nadir was reached; in that year the entire *Armada del Mar Océano* consisted of only eight galleons, five naves, two caravels, and tiny advice boats.[1] By the beginning of 1617 the possibility of a Dutch-Venetian-Savoyard alliance made the Spanish government anxious. Such a combination would possess overwhelming naval superiority in the Mediterranean and Atlantic.[2]

Potentially this threat was very dangerous, but the Barbary pirates posed a more immediate danger in these years. The weakness of the Spanish navy in the years of the truce was matched by the growing power of the pirates of North Africa, who raided Spanish shores and threatened the trade and communications links of the empire. The Barbary pirates became, in the words of I.A.A. Thompson, 'the major preoccupation of Madrid' as far as naval matters were concerned.[3] Thus, the Spanish government, faced with this combination of threats, began the long and costly process of revitalizing the navy. In August 1616 the Council of War informed Philip that the number of ships was so few and worn-out that unless new vessels were laid down in the coming months, there would be no men-of-war fit for service in 1617.[4] Even with this warning, the royal government moved slowly for it was early 1617 before any positive action was taken.

To meet the threat of the Barbary pirates, a proposal was submitted on 23 April 1617 requesting that new squadron of six fast sailing ships be created and employed in operations against the marauding pirates in the Straits and along the coasts of southern Spain.[5] This proposal was approved, but months passed before the navy budget was increased enough to begin building six new galleons and five other men-of-war. When finally put into service in 1617 to 1618, these ships were effectively replacements for

---

[1] AGS, Guerra Antigua, legajo 808, 4 August 1616. Thus, the fleet was a quarter of its former size.
[2] AGS, Estado, legajo 1881, warns of a Venetian-Dutch-Savoyard-English alliance.
[3] I.A.A. Thompson, *War and Government in Hapsburg Spain 1560–1620*, p. 198.
[4] AGS, Guerra Antigua, legajo 808, consulta 4 August 1616.
[5] Thompson, *War and Government*, pp. 198–9.

scrapped or unserviceable ships, rather than fresh additions to Spanish naval strength.[1]

The evidence of Spanish naval weakness prior to 1617 and the rebuilding programme of 1617 to 1623 must be taken into account when considering Anglo-Spanish relations in these years.[2] The naval balance of power was more than just a backdrop against which discussions took place. First, the utter decay of the Spanish navy made immediate acceptance of the English proposals virtually impossible. Philip III simply lacked sufficient naval forces to contribute to a joint venture. A simple financial contribution, as first mooted by the English, held no attraction. If the money were available, it was better spent on revitalizing the Spanish navy than financing a potential enemy.

Second, Spanish naval weakness meant that no Spanish statesman could in good conscience encourage the presence of a powerful and potentially dangerous fleet on the coasts of Spain.[3] Even if friendly when it set out, an English fleet might become hostile, and, in that case, Spanish trade and troop movements would be at the mercy of the enemy. The mentality and bureaucratic nature of the Spanish state discouraged risk-taking; prudence encouraged policies based on assessments of the capacity of a state rather than intention.[4] Until Spanish naval forces were sufficiently strong, the presence of a foreign naval force on the coast of Spain was to be discouraged.

The Council of War judged the English proposal primarily from a military perspective.[5] The objective of the project met with favour: they had long recognized the need for action against the pirates. They also agreed with the English assessment that considerable naval forces would be needed. The *consulta* produced by

---

[1] Ibid. In all, the rebuilding programme of the Spanish fleet seems more successful than perhaps is implied here. A list prepared by Aroztegui in March 1629 shows a fleet of 22 ships, including 15 galleons: AGS, Estado, legajo 2850.

[2] PRO, SP 94/23/f.60v. In August 1618 the king of Spain could set out 34 ships: 13 ships of the *armada real*, 9 Portuguese, 12 of the Biscay squadron. By January 1621 the *armada del mar océano* had 26 ships including the Basque and Santander flotillas and there were another 18 in the *armada del Estrecho*: AGS, Guerra Antigua, legajo 873.

[3] This was the period when the war party was advancing and Lerma and the peace party were on the defensive: Israel, *Dutch Republic*, pp. 66–85.

[4] Williams, Thesis, vol. I, pp. 327–35; P. Brightwell, 'The Spanish System and the Twelve Years' Truce', *EHR*, LXXXIX (1974), pp. 276–89; P. Brightwell, 'The Spanish Origins of the Thirty Years' War', *European Studies Review*, IX (1979), pp. 413–22, provide a portrait of this administrative system in action.

[5] AGS, Estado, legajo 2850, consulta dated 14/24 April 1618.

the *consejo de guerra* stated that a minimum of 25 to 30 substantial vessels would be required for such an operation. They were uncertain about the financial arrangements but clearly preferred separate Spanish and English fleets acting in a co-ordinated way. They wished to maintain absolute control over the Spanish fleet, and a joint fleet would pose problems of command, control, and administration.

After accepting the advice of the Council of War, the Council of State informed Digby that the king of Spain was inclined to accept the English offer.[1] An English fleet would be permitted to come and operate in Spanish waters. In the meantime, detailed arrangements covering the operations of the fleets of both nations would need to be discussed and terms settled. However, before these discussions took place, the news that Raleigh had taken and burned San Thomé caused the government to reconsider the project.[2] Raleigh's raid put the expedition in a new light and fuelled the fears that the English fleet might really be intended, as Gondomar had warned, for an attack on Spain or its dependencies.[3] Thus, in the spring of 1618, the Spanish decided to go their own way.

Between May 1618, when reports of Raleigh's raid arrived, and March 1619, Spanish policy was also influenced by more general developments. The reform movement made a go-it-alone policy regarding the pirates appear more attractive and worthy of Spain. These are the years of the *arbitristas*, the *Junta de Reformacion*, the fall of Lerma, and government by strong and able councils.[4] It is the time when Spanish naval power was being revitalized, and the efforts of renewal were beginning to bear fruit. It was possible for Spanish ministers to hope for a return to the supremacy of former years, and these dreams had not yet been dimmed by the realities of Dutch power or straitened circumstances of the Crown. At the end of April, Francis Cottington, the English agent in Madrid, signalled the change in policy. He wrote that a great fleet was then being prepared and that the Spanish

> are very unwilling his Majesty should intermeddle in the clearing the seas of them, partly for that they would be loth

---

[1] AGS, Estado, legajo 2850, 18/28 April 1618.
[2] AGS, Estado, legajo 2850, 7/17 January 1619.
[3] This consequence of Raleigh's expedition has been largely overlooked by historians, and may help explain why James showed no mercy to Raleigh.
[4] Stradling, *Europe and the Decline of Spain*, pp. 50–1, 62–3.

there should be any arming of that kind in England, and partly for it is conceived it would be a precedent of much dishonour for this Crown and monarchy in the future, but chiefly for that in admitting into their ports a few Holland men-of-war (employed in that kind), they have already found many inconveniencies and suffered much by the insolences of seamen who though they were not past 6 or 7 sails of ships, yet were always masters of the harbours into which they were admitted, and in many places committed great outrages.[1]

In the summer of 1618, squadrons of warships went to sea against the pirates, and on one occasion intercepted a fleet of 26 pirate vessels in the Straits, destroying five ships and making prize of several others.[2] Throughout these months considerable effort was invested in preparing a large force for use against Algiers. Though the expedition never sailed, the magnitude of the preparations (which were widely reported) gave the impression that Spanish naval power was revived.[3]

This revival and the preparations against the pirates frightened most of the rest of Europe.[4] As intelligence on Spanish preparations grew in 1618, and reports of the supposed destination of the armada became more ominous, the government of James I responded with increased interest in preparing a fleet for the Mediterranean; activity in the dockyards, for example, proceeded with new vigour.[5] Ironically, this time Gondomar would have been correct had he written that these preparations had an ulterior purpose. Writing from Venice, the English ambassador, Sir Henry Wotton, spelled out James's aim at this time:

that your Majesty had at his [the Venetian ambassador's] instance, (as I conceive them to take it) resolved to send out some sufficient number of his own ships, or likewise other vessels belonging to the merchants of your kingdom towards the coast of Spain, to invigilate for the common safety over the preparation and designs of that king who will thereby, as they

[1] PRO, SP 94/23/ff.27v–28, 13 April 1618.
[2] PRO, SP 94/23/f.55v., 16 July 1618.
[3] AGS, Estado, legajo 711.
[4] For the Venetian fears, see S.R. Gardiner, *History of England: From the Accession of James I to the Outbreak of the Civil War, 1603–1642*, III, p. 287, n. 2.
[5] PRO, SP 14/111/13; KAO, U 269 – Sackville Knole MSS (Cranfield Papers), ON 8690, 24 November 1619.

will imagine, be so injealoused, as may preadventure keep him from molesting these nearer seas, which consequently will redound (say they) not only on the quiet of Italy, but likewise to much advantage of the German affairs, as meaning that without some such distraction of Spanish power an attempt perchance might be made to transport soldiers by this gulf to Trieste in succor of the house of Austria against the Bohemians whom the United Provinces do favour.[1]

Soon thereafter, an even more authoritative figure laid bare the king's true purpose in reviving the fleet preparations. Digby's letter to Buckingham about his briefing of the Privy Council gives the game away:

I intimated unto them, how much the state of business was now changed from what it was, when both the suppressing of the pirates, and the preventing any unfitting attempt which might be made by the Spanish fleet were jointly in consultation.[2]

In the history of these negotiations – with all the starts and stops and twists and turns – this letter of Digby's stands out as a rare example of a policy-maker setting down in plain language the aims of the government. But paradoxically, the unexpected frankness of Digby's words has led to as much misunderstanding as the more cryptic expressions characterizing most diplomatic correspondence. The wording and context of this letter must be considered very carefully if misunderstanding is to be avoided.

First, it is important to note that the letter was written on 5 April 1619, that is *after* the great scare over Spanish naval preparations had subsided. He wrote:

For your Lordship may consider, how much we have been troubled with the noise of the great preparation making this year in Spain, the which are not absolutely relinquished or laid down, but only deferred.[3]

Digby's letter is concerned with what course the government should take, *post-scare*, regarding the pirate fleet. When Digby

---

[1] PRO, SP 99/22/f.280–280v.
[2] BL, Harl. MS. 1580, f.106.
[3] Ibid., f.107v.

describes the expedition having a second, covert anti-Spanish purpose, this is predicated on the assumption that the reported Spanish preparations were hostile.

Second, even during the emergency in 1618, the counter-Spanish role of the fleet was only one of two functions, a new task added to the earlier mission of suppressing pirates. Neither objective was given primacy; it was hoped that both would be pursued jointly, but when the Spanish threat did not materialize, the initial and primary aim of the English fleet reasserted itself.

This letter again shows how unfounded was Digby's pro-Spanish reputation.[1] Not only was he suspicious of Spanish aims but quite willing to use force against Spain to achieve political objectives considered worthwhile.[2] It also shows that English foreign policy, as enunciated by Digby, was motivated very much by considerations of power and not ideology. His advice was far-sighted and practical, based on realistic assessments not ideological preferences, as is evident in the following passage:

> for an addition and increase of greater strength against the next year, for that they now held not their power suitable to their design; And if it were held fit that this year his Majesty should put himself in order, in regard of these preparations; I conceive that same reason will hold for the next, when the Spaniard is likely to be stronger; And therefor it may be not unworthy consideration, whether it will not be fitter to reserve this to augment our preparations the next year, then to it now upon an uncertain enterprise.[3]

He was not in favour of sending out a fleet, reduced in number, as advocated by some, because, as he put it:

> For myself, I concurred with my Lords for the continuance of the action; but to be undertaken at such time, as all things belonging unto such an action, shall be deliberately consulted of & settled, and not to set a fleet to sea like adventurers to seek an enterprise; and I conceive it would be ten times more dishonour to his Majesty & the state to set out a fleet which should do nothing remarkable or that should want means to

---

[1] PRO, SP 14/70/21,14/90/122.
[2] PRO, SP 80/4/f.138v. Digby would show a willingness to use force against Spain in 1621 as well.
[3] BL, Harl. MS. 1580, ff.107v–108.

effect the attempt they went about, then to suspend a resolution, until all things might be fully & fittingly provided and settled.[1]

In his opinion, it was premature to send out a fleet in the spring; it would be better to wait until August when the pirates might be caught returning to their bases.[2] In the meantime, Digby thought the plan of operation should be settled for it had not been determined 'whether we were to attempt the pirates in their ports, or seek them at sea'. Then they should decide what forces would be needed, how they were to be supplied beyond the initial supply of the six months' victuals, and how the resupply was to be financed since the initial funds (£20 000) would all be expended on setting out the fleet, and 'no part of the twenty thousand pounds for the next year can be raised till this time twelve months'.[3]

In ending his letter to Buckingham, Digby raised the question of whether the expedition might not prove too advantageous to Spain. He wrote:

> Secondly, it is certain, that there is no nation so much annoyed & infested with the pirates as the dominions of the king of Spain, very many of them being Moriscos which were expelled thence, & every year are guides to the Turks and Moors to do mischiefs upon the coast towns of Spain; so that it may be considerable, whether we should make too much haste to pull this thorn out of the king of Spain's foot or not.[4]

Regrettably, the Lord High Admiral's reply is not extant, but judging by the events that followed, Buckingham agreed with Digby's recommendations, even if he and his officials at the Admiralty were remiss in executing them as diligently as Digby would have wished.

Ironically, at the very time the English were most fearful of Spanish naval preparations and were preparing a fleet to counter the rumoured attack on Venice, the Spaniards, who never intended to attack Venice but instead had planned to assault Algiers, were coming to the conclusion that such an attack was

[1] Ibid., f.107.
[2] Ibid., f.107–107v.
[3] Ibid., f.107v.
[4] Ibid., f.108. This is yet another example which shows how unfounded was Digby's pro-Spanish reputation.

beyond their means. At the end of September 1618, Cottington wrote that he had learned that the Spanish now reckoned that Algiers was too strong and could boast at least 30 000 fighting men for use in defence.[1] They estimated that an assault on the city would require at least 50 000 men for the siege operation, besides those needed for the navy and transports.[2] As a result, the Spanish cancelled preparations for the armada, as Cottington informed Carleton some time later.[3] He also reported that he could now confirm that it had been intended for use against Algiers.[4]

Cancellation brought a shift in Spanish policy. In May 1619, officials were expressing renewed interest in a joint expedition against the pirates.[5] It appears that the Spanish interest had begun some time before they brought up the matter with Cottington because draft articles for an agreement are dated 26 April 1619.[6] By early June, Cottington had come to believe that the agreement would be achieved.[7] In general, Cottington's forecast was correct, though it took many more months before an agreement was finally concluded.

On 5 January 1620, Sir Walter Aston received instructions for his forthcoming embassy to Spain ordering him to negotiate agreements on: (1) the marriage; (2) the Palatinate; (3) the settling of a 'joint force for the extirpation of the pirates (Turkish & others)'.[8] As matters then stood, Aston and his Spanish counterparts needed to resolve particular details only; and these discussions were then 'well advanced'. The ambassador was informed that he should explain the 'joint benefit to both Crowns & subjects in joint action' and the forwardness of English preparations. The fleet would set out in the summer so a speedy conclusion of the proceedings was desired.

From Aston's correspondence it appears that the settlement did

[1] PRO, SP 94/23/f.71–71v. Cottington writes that 'the strength of Algiers is well known to all men and how impregnable it is, without a long and strongest [?] siege by both sea and land'.
[2] This force is almost double the size of that sent against England in 1588.
[3] PRO, SP 94/23/f.169–169v.
[4] Ibid. Spanish shipping movements and embarkation points support this conclusion, as does the stated intention of the government: AGS, Estado, legajo 711.
[5] PRO, SP 94/23/f.192.
[6] BL, Add. MS. 36,445, ff.11–14v; AGS, Estado, legajo 2850, legajo 845, f.145.
[7] PRO, SP 94/23/f.198–198v. Also AGS, Estado, legajo 2038; the officials were Agustin Mexia and Don Diego Brocharo de Anaya.
[8] PRO, SP 94/23/f.279v. Aston's instructions include a brief review of English policy and the course of negotiations through 1619.

not progress as smoothly as he was led to expect.[1] On 6 August 1620, he wrote the following from Madrid:

> I doubt not but your lordships hath formerly understood a certain treaty (if so I may call it) between his Majesty and this king for the joining of their sea forces in some action against the pirates which union should have continued for some years but I must acquaint you that whether it be they do here repent them (for many reasons both of state and reputation or that their natural and habitual slowness be the cause) the articles that were conceived to be the rules of this conjunction are yet so imperfect as in mine opinion Sir Robert Mansell must be fain to undertake the work alone without any joint assistance from the Spaniards howbeit this king's armada is now at sea in search of the pirates.[2]

The uncertainties of Madrid were not matched in London for Buckingham writing in a positive mood told Gondomar that:

> It is agreed (as your Excellency knoweth) betwixt both the kings our masters to join their fleets together against the pirates: and so in performance thereof the king my Master sendeth now the twenty ships agreed on, and for general Sir Robert Mansell.[3]

After explaining Mansell's intended course (departure estimated to be about 5–10[?] August), the Lord High Admiral gave the Spanish ambassador assurance of English good will, telling Gondomar that:

> Our general . . . and all that accompany him have special order from the king my master to serve his Majesty of Spain, and in all things to observe his will and service, as if it were for the king my Master . . . and he had likewise order not to stand upon ceremonies and punctilios, which do oftentimes overthrow business of great importance.[4]

---

[1] BL, Add. MS. 26,444, f.159–159v. In June, Aston felt the Spanish would prefer to put off the expedition until the next year, though they would keep their fleet at Cadiz in readiness.
[2] PRO, SP 94/24/11v.
[3] BL, Add. MS. 36,444, f.165.
[4] Ibid., f.165–165v.

The Lord High Admiral hoped the king of Spain would give a like order to his people and furnish the English 'with all things that [they] shall have need of . . . according to what hath been agreed'.[1] Gondomar was asked to write letters, sent open, for Mansell to carry with him on his voyage to the Mediterranean.[2] Buckingham ended in fine style:

> The mind and resolution here is to confer the good correspondency we have with Spain, and more and more to increase it every day in all things . . . and as this is but a beginning of the conjunction in arms of the two nations, so I hope there shall be thereafter many occasions to increase all good correspondency and friendship betwixt them by the experience which they have of one another.[3]

Formal sentiments, no doubt, but they also reflect a genuine desire that underlay English foreign policy.

The negotiations had begun in a time of hope when peace in Europe seemed possible. This was the time when the influence of men of moderation, Lerma, Oldenbarnevelt, Digby, and James, was at its greatest.[4] They wished the peace to continue and shared a sense of the unity of Christendom and the benefit that would accrue if the costly and destructive energies then present could be directed toward the common enemy.

Yet this vision could not be sustained as the end of the Truce approached. By 1618, both in Spain and the United Provinces, a war party had gained ascendency, and fear began to distort perceptions and foreign relations. Only in England was the war party excluded from power. As a consequence, a policy of co-operation could be continued, and this made it possible in 1620 for negotiations with Spain to be concluded.[5]

---

[1] Ibid., f.165v.
[2] Gondomar did write letters to assist Mansell when he entered Spanish ports: PRO, SP 31/12/23, f.74–74v, 3 August 1620.
[3] BL, Add. MS. 36,444, f.165v.
[4] One can also see this in the work of Grotius: C. Wilson, *The Dutch Republic: And the Civilisation of the Seventeenth Century*, pp. 60–1. French foreign policy under the Duc de Luynes also shows a similar spirit of restraint.
[5] The agreement between England and Spain is more significant than it may appear for as well as embodying the good will and skill of a few, it also reflects a convergence of interests that corresponds to shifts in the distribution of power in Europe.

Part 2
THE ALGIERS EXPEDITION AND THE COST OF PIRACY

5
THE ALGIERS EXPEDITION

Although the Earl of Southampton had been mentioned early on as a possible commander of the expedition, Sir Robert Mansell was appointed to lead the fleet against Algiers.[1] Born in 1573, Mansell was the fourth son of a Glamorganshire gentleman of no great fame or wealth.[2] He was related to Charles Howard, Earl of Nottingham, the Lord High Admiral, and it was probably through his kinsman that Mansell secured entry into the navy.

He may have served under Howard against the armada; certainly he was in the expedition against Cadiz in 1596 as captain of the *Mer-Honour*, flagship of the fleet of the Earl of Essex. Mansell was knighted during the expedition, and it may be indicative of the quality of his service that he retained his knighthood while many of those knighted by Essex were repudiated by Elizabeth I.[3] During the last years of the war against Spain he commanded several small squadrons operating near Ireland or in the Channel. In recognition of his service, he was appointed 'vice-admiral of the Narrow Seas' in 1603.

Following the war, Mansell went as part of Nottingham's embassy to Spain where he gained a modicum of fame, chiefly for apprehending thieves. Once at a dinner party, Mansell observed a

[1] PRO, SP 14/90/136, for Southampton; Lords Danvers and Sheffield also desired the command. *Calendar of the Clarendon State Papers in the Bodleian Library* hereafter *Cal. Clarendon Papers*, vol. I 1623–1649, ed. O. Ogle and W.H. Bliss (1872), p. 13, no. 122; and for Lord Sheffield, SP14/105/104.
[2] This account of Mansell's career is drawn from J.K. Laughton's entry in *DNB*, vol. 12, pp. 973–4, and G.T. Clark, *Some Account of Sir Robert Mansell, Kt., Vice Admiral of England . . . and of Admiral Sir Thomas Button, Kt.*
[3] Mansell was no creature of Essex, arresting several of those involved in Earl's rebellion.

Spaniard concealing a plate in his clothing. Immediately he went over and grabbed the culprit, shaking him so vigorously that the silverware fell to the floor. On another occasion, a thief snatched Mansell's hat and fled through the streets. Mansell gave chase catching up with him at a magistrate's house where the thief had taken refuge. Without a moment's hesitation Mansell forced entry with sword in hand, grabbed the thief, and recovered his hat. These incidents illustrate a directness and fearlessness widely attributed to him.[1] Many years later, in 1641, when MPs thought they smelled gunpowder and rushed out of the House 'scared out of their wits', Mansell did not even shudder but drew his sword and bid them to 'stand for shame', but no man stood 'with the good old knight'.[2]

In 1604, Mansell became Treasurer of the navy, an office he retained until 1618 even though he had gained a deserved reputation for corruption. For example, in partnership with two other Admiralty officials, Mansell built, fitted out and rigged (all with materials belonging to the navy), a ship called the *Resistance* which he then freighted with stores from the Admiralty's warehouses. The ship was then sent to Spain where its cargo was sold, as was the cargo of Spanish goods brought home. The profits were staggering for even the wages of the master and crew were charged to the Crown. Such abuse of office was too extensive to be concealed for very long. In 1608, a royal commission was appointed to investigate frauds and mismanagement in the navy. The commission collected a mass of evidence showing needless expenditure, the deplorable state of the fleet, and malfeasance by Mansell and other officials, but when James came to pass judgment, Mansell was let off with no more than a verbal admonishment.[3]

Although Mansell's reputation was tarnished as a consequence of this investigation,[4] his appointment to the command of the

---

[1] Mansell was known as a man of action; he fought at least one duel, a notoriously savage combat in which he killed Sir John Heydon.
[2] Quoted by A. Fletcher, *The Outbreak of the English Civil War*, p. 27.
[3] BL, Cotton MS. Julius F.III, ff.1–2v, 5, 9, 15, 24–24v, 26, 98, 184, 219–219v, 229. The fullest discussions are in A.P. McGowan, *The Jacobean Commissions of Inquiry, 1608 and 1618* and M. Oppenheim, *A History of the Administration of the Royal Navy and of Merchant Shipping in Relation to the Navy*, pp. 184–95. Also useful are L.L. Peck, 'Problems in Jacobean Administration: Was Henry Howard, Earl of Northampton, A Reformer?', *The Historical Journal*, XIX (1976), pp. 835–40.
[4] In 1618, another commission investigating the navy also discovered malfeasance and inefficiency.

Algiers expedition is not as startling as it may seem. No one among the nobility had sufficient naval experience, except Nottingham, who was too old and infirm. Mansell was experienced and the second highest ranking naval officer. His appointment suggested that the Crown was really determined to reduce the pirates, whereas the appointment of a courtier would not have inspired confidence.

Political attributes also made Mansell a good choice to lead the expedition. He was not associated with either the Spanish or anti-Spanish factions at court. A man of anti-Spanish reputation would have been unacceptable to the Spanish whose co-operation was essential. However, a commander with strong Spanish sympathies would have offended the Dutch and also fuelled fears in England that the expedition had been conceived in Spain for the benefit of Spain.[1] In Sir Robert Mansell the Crown had found a man of just the right political complexion.

He was equally acceptable to the City. His involvement in business, both as Treasurer of the navy and as projector and manager of the glass monopoly, added to his suitability for the post. He was well known to the merchants and shipowners of London who were being called upon to provide a majority of the ships and money. Their co-operation was essential and could not have been obtained by the appointment of a politician or courtier.

In another way, Mansell's political reputation made him attractive to the Crown. His political past contained nothing that would make him a political liability. He was unusual, if not unique, among high-placed Stuart officials in this respect. He was a man of high ambition, but his ambitions did not lie in the political sphere. He was not identified with a particular policy or faction. He was loyal to the Crown but not sycophantic.[2] To the end he remained a man of no deep or obvious political commitments. In 1642 when a lack of political enemies was the chief qualification for command of the navy, Mansell was acceptable to all parties, though by then he was rather old for such an active command.[3]

---

[1] One can see an example of this fear in Act III, Scene I, of Thomas Middleton's *A Game At Chess*, p. 44, when the Black Knight (Gondomar) announces, 'Was it not I proclaimed a precious safeguard/ From the White Kingdom [England] to secure our coasts/ 'Gainst the infidel pirate, under pretext/ Of more necessitous expedition?'

[2] Throughout the 1620s he expressed an open dislike of the king's favourite, but his opposition to Buckingham was more personal than political.

[3] *DNB*, vol. 12, p. 974. Mansell was 69 at the time.

Mansell's ambitions centred on wealth not political power. His inheritance was much too meagre to match his needs. Only marriage, office, and business offered security. Contemporaries claimed he made tens of thousands of pounds from his treasurership; perhaps he did, though it is impossible to substantiate such charges.[1] James was not blind to Mansell's weaknesses but rather had a good measure of this Vice Admiral. The king recognized Mansell's acquisitiveness, and sought to use it to his advantage. James pardoned Mansell but allowed him to continue in office. Until then, Mansell had been a client of Nottingham. His advancement and fortune were owed to his distinguished relation. But as a consequence of the royal pardon, Mansell became dependent on the king, a client tied directly to the Crown.[2] By co-opting Mansell, James thereby gained a measure of control over a royal servant and the execution of royal policy. Power was the king's in name, but in fact all too often it was exercised by subjects who might frustrate or distort the king's will. Control of the Algiers expedition was especially important for the king. The fleet would be far away and effectively beyond direct royal control for months. James needed a commander directly tied to him, not someone who might wish to make policy or be manipulated by those who wished to overturn the Crown's foreign policy.

Mansell's appointment was fitting and just in an ironic way that would have appealed to James who delighted in posing and playacting. In 1613 to celebrate the marriage of his daughter the Princess Elizabeth to the German prince, Frederick, a mock seafight was staged in the Thames. As Vice Admiral of the 'English fleet', Mansell had gloried in his role of victor over the 'pirates of Algiers'.[3]

Mansell selected as flagship the *Lion*; like other royal warships, the *Lion* was strongly built and armed, able to hold her own against any potential enemy warship.[4] These vessels were deep-draft warships best suited to battering opponents or bombarding fortresses but lacking speed and manoeuvrability. With her sister ships, the *Lion* formed a powerful battle group which no pirate

---

[1] With a boldness typical of the man, Mansell destroyed or denied having accounts when questioned by the commissioners looking into abuses in the navy.
[2] Historians have seldom considered the weakness of James's position. He was foreign born and came to the crown of England without an established political base or client network. He was faced with several strong patrons and patronage networks which could effectively control the execution of government policy.
[3] Clark, *Sir Robert Mansell*, p. 15.
[4] Mansell carried the title Admiral or Captain-General for the expedition.

fleet could match; it was expected that these ships would serve as an anvil against which weaker enemy vessels might be hammered.

Second-in-command was Sir Richard Hawkins who held the rank of Vice Admiral and sailed in the *Vanguard*. Hawkins was a member of an illustrious naval family and a man with considerable naval experience, but he had not had a sea command since 1594 when he had been captured by the Spanish.[1] Following capture, Hawkins spent a number of years in harsh confinement in Spain.[2] He was an unexpected choice as the second-in-command since he was then nearly 60 years of age and his last active duty had been almost 25 years ago. He had in his favour, however, a good name and was a familiar figure to leading members of merchant companies and the maritime community. Since they were contributing a large part of the money and ships, Hawkins would have been a satisfactory choice.[3] Early on in the planning stage, the merchants had expressed a desire for influencing the choice of command rather than leaving it entirely in the hands of the appointees of James or his Lord High Admiral.[4]

Hawkins was also an attractive choice for the Crown for political reasons. His name, reputation, and wartime experience would quiet those who suspected or feared that the expedition was some Spanish design or would be used by the Spanish.[5] James needed to guard carefully against an untrustworthy zealot coming into command in case of Mansell's death. Also, the king would wish to prevent anyone high in the command structure of the fleet influencing Mansell unwisely.[6] Although no friend of the Spanish, Hawkins was not an anti-Spanish zealot and had shown over a long career that he was a loyal servant of the Crown and one who could be trusted.[7] His age may also have served the Crown. He

---

[1] Hawkins was captured in an action which lasted three days; he had acquitted himself with courage against a greatly superior enemy before being taken prisoner.
[2] *DNB*, vol. 9, pp. 223–5.
[3] In fact, they may have put forward his name as a leader to look after their interests.
[4] From the first meetings in 1617, merchants and mariners advised the Crown: see above, Chapter 2.
[5] BL, Harl. MS. 1581, f.76, Hawkins is described as 'a very grave, religious and experienced gentleman'.
[6] This was especially so when the fleet set out, for international tensions were rising. The end of the Twelve Years' Truce between the Dutch and the Spanish was fast approaching, and the recrudescence of warfare between these two states brought with it the possibility that the conflict might expand into a devastating European war into which England might be dragged.
[7] In fact after the expedition he dedicated a work on his voyage to the South Seas to Prince Charles.

Table 2
The chief characteristics of the royal warships

Ship	Commander	Tonnage	Guns	Men
Lion	Rainsborough	600	40	250
Vanguard	Hawkins	660	40	250
Rainbow	Button	600	40	250
Constant Reformation	Mainwaring	660	40	250
Antelope	Palmer	400	34	160
Convertine	Love	500	36	220

had none of the impetuosity of youth that could endanger an expedition so distant and difficult to control.

Sailing in the *Rainbow*, as Rear Admiral, was Sir Thomas Button. Of the flag officers, Button could claim the most recent naval experience. He gained fame in 1600 when he held the harbour of Kinsale against the Spanish invading force with only a small pinnace. Since then he had been in almost constant service protecting the Channel and coasts of Ireland against pirates.[1] Based on active sea duty and experience in dealing with pirates, Button was well qualified to lead the expedition and he was offended that he was not made Admiral or Vice Admiral. It appears that Button was passed over through inadvertence rather than inadequacy or personal offence.[2]

The other three king's ships were also commanded by experienced men, though of lesser fame. Sir Arthur Mainwaring was given command of the *Constant Reformation*,[3] Sir Henry Palmer was placed in charge of the *Antelope*, and Sir Thomas Love captained the *Convertine*.[4] See Table 2 for details on the chief characteristics of these main royal warships.

Twelve merchant ships were sent on the expedition. All were

---

[1] *DNB*, vol. 3, pp. 551–2. Button was a kinsman of Mansell and one of several naval officials of Welsh background.
[2] BL, Harl. MS. 1581, f.76–76v. In a letter dated 10 July 1621, Mansell writes that he had recently given Sir Thomas Button some [unspecified] cause for offence, and that this was the second injury done to him: the first was engaging Hawkins as Vice Admiral, but this had been done before he knew that Button would be free from his Irish employment. Mansell was later to recommend him for further naval service when the fleet returned to England.
[3] Arthur Mainwaring was the brother of the pirate 'admiral': C.M. Senior, *A Nation of Pirates: English Piracy in its Heyday*, p. 72.
[4] This ship, originally called the *Destiny*, had been built by Sir Walter Raleigh and later confiscated from him: BL, Add. MS. 36,444, f.167.

Table 3
Merchant ships in Mansell's fleet[1]

Ship	Captain	Tonnage	Guns	Men
Golden Phoenix	Samuel Argall	300	24	220
Samuel	Christopher Harris	300	21	120
Marygold	Sir John Fearne	260	22	100
Zouch Phoenix	John Pennington	280	26	80
Barbary	Thomas Porter	200	18	80
Centurion	Sir Francis Tanfield	200	22	100
Primrose	Sir John Hampton	180	18	80
Hercules	Eusabey Cave	300	24	120
Neptune	Robert Haughton	280	21	?
Merchant *Bonaventura*	John Chidley	260	23	120
Restore	George Raymond	130	12	50
Marmaduke	Thomas Hughes	130	12	50

smaller, and more lightly built and armed than the royal warships. Most were London vessels built and used for trade in areas like the Mediterranean where a fairly large armament was required. All were commanded by experienced seamen; some, such as Sir John Fearne, had gone to sea as privateers during the Spanish War.[2]

Work on fitting out the fleet began in late 1619 with the navy commissioners instructing the dockyards at Chatham and Deptford to go ahead as quickly as possible.[3] However, by the 19th of July the king's ships were not ready, though Buckingham wrote to Gondomar that he expected the fleet to be at sea before mid-August[4] when the returning vintage fleets would need protection. This was also the time when the Algerines sailed out of the Mediterranean to infest the Atlantic.[5] If the English fleet were in the Straits or before Algiers by September, the returning pirates would be cut off from their bases and market for prizes and captives. In the event, it took another month before the dockyards

---

[1] There are several lists of the ships on the expedition: see, for example, BL, Add. MS. 36,444, f.167.
[2] Fearne served under Raleigh as captain of the *Star* on the Guiana expedition. Also on the expedition was Robert Walsingham, a former pirate who had captained an Algerine man-of-war: Senior, *Nation of Pirates*, p. 146.
[3] PRO, SP 14/111/13, indicated a spring departure for the fleet.
[4] BL, Add. MS. 36,444, f.165.
[5] See below, Chapter 7.

could get the ships ready and victualled.[1] On 6 August, Mansell reported to Cranfield that the ships were at last ready (see Table 3), but they could not sail because they lacked sailors and gunners.[2] In the end, a large number of sailors had to be pressed to provide sufficient crew.[3]

On 7 September, Mansell sailed from the Thames but went no farther than the Downs where he encountered part of a Dutch fleet, also heading for the Mediterranean.[4] Because of contrary winds, both fleets remained anchored for some time. In this interval, Mansell and his captains took the opportunity to return to London. Their reason is unknown, though their action may have been related to the presence of the Dutch fleet.

As related previously, the negotiations with the United Provinces never resulted in a formal agreement. When the Dutch finally realized that the English really did intend to set out a fleet, they approached James through his ambassador and again suggested that the fleets of the two nations be united.[5] James had responded with studied equipoise. He rehearsed English complaints about the Dutch, noting that they showed no sign of wishing to co-operate in the Indies or on matters of trade. His past offers for a joint expedition had been spurned. As a consequence, his government had come to an agreement with the Spanish, though sincere contributions by the Dutch would still be appreciated.[6] The studied ambiguity of the English reply while admirable from a diplomatic viewpoint was of little use to Mansell. He needed to know whether to co-operate with the Dutch fleet, and, if so, what form this co-operation should take. English plans

---

[1] PRO, SP 14/116/4. On 4 July, three ships were still wanting and there were problems over the financing of supplies. Trinity House indicated it intended to levy £1000 per annum to pay for the supplies that the ships of the fleet would need.
[2] KAO, U 269 ON 311.
[3] *APC*, 1619–1621, p. 248, includes an order for the impressment of 680 men, a quarter of the expeditionary force. See also PRO, SP 14/116/17,53–4 and inclosure, 65, 70, for particulars of how impressment was carried out. These delays and difficulties were not unique to the Algiers expedition; almost every other major naval operation of the 16th and 17th centuries experienced similar delays and needed to press crew.
[4] This was the fleet of 22 ships under William de Zoete, Admiral Haultain.
[5] PRO, SP 84/96/f.92. Also, *Letters from and to Sir Dudley Carleton, Knt., during his Embassy in Holland, from January 1615/16, to December 1620*, p. 491.
[6] PRO, SP 84/96/f.160; SP 84/97/ff.12–12v, 72. As a diplomatic statement, the king's reply was admirable: at one and the same time he warned the Dutch not to take English support for granted and offered them hope that support might be forthcoming if they were to be more helpful on a range of matters concerning the two countries.

depended on Spanish support and ports, but this might be put in jeopardy if the English ships were seen in company with the Dutch. Since both fleets could be in the Mediterranean at the same time, they were bound to encounter each other and co-operation would be useful.[1] Mansell needed to know how he should treat the Dutch.

The surviving copy of Mansell's instructions supports this interpretation. They are dated, 10 September, i.e., three days after he anchored in the Downs.[2] Article 4 of these instructions provided the following guidance:

> And forasmuch as we are also informed that the States General of the United Provinces out of the like laudable respects have this summer armed to sea, or do intend to arm certain ships against the said pirates, Our pleasure is, if you shall in like manner, with their fleets hold friendly correspondency, to the public ends, and carry yourselves towards them with such offices of courtesy, as shall best betoken our honour, and the good amity which is betwixt us and that state.

And Article 5 went on to clarify the position Mansell should take *vis-à-vis* the Spanish and the Dutch:

> Provided always, and therefore we have thought fit to give you warning that if it so fall out (which we hope it will not) that the King of Spain shall by virtue of any former treaty or capitulation or for any other reason of state (whereof it appertaineth not unto us to judge) deny port unto any of the States' ships, or being entered shall embarque or detain them, our meaning is not that you shall engage yourself or us by any article of yours to assist the Dutch in that case, or otherwise than by mediation.

Mansell was thus informed of the dangers of too close an association with the Dutch fleet and also of potential trouble between the Dutch and the Spanish. The English government was clearly trying to avoid being drawn into a dispute between the Dutch and the Spanish.

Customarily, commanders of naval expeditions kept journals,

---

[1] In January 1621, Mansell met a Dutch squadron of seven ships off Malaga, part of Admiral Haultain's fleet: BL, Add. MS. 36,445, f.153v.
[2] BL, Add. MS. 36,445, ff.15–19.

but unfortunately only part of Mansell's has survived.[1] However, two journals by members of the expedition are extant. One journal was by a captain of one of the ships or someone in a similar position. It is a rudimentary logbook, though it does not contain entries for every day, but includes information about wind, weather, course, and position, as well as a brief description of any noteworthy incidents.[2] The other journal was made by John Button, kinsman of Sir Thomas Button, the Rear Admiral.[3] By supplementing these journals with letters and other records, it is possible to reconstruct a virtually full, day-by-day relation of the expedition.

The activities of Mansell's fleet during its year-long voyage fell into seven distinct chronological phases with each phase associated with a particular type of operation or activity:

(1) The voyage to the Spanish coast.
(2) Patrolling Spanish waters.
(3) The actions at Algiers.
(4) The return from Algiers and actions on the Spanish coast.
(5) The second voyage to Algiers and attack on the port.
(6) Post-Algiers operations and resupply activities.
(7) The planning and preparations for a second attack, and finally, the return of the fleet.

The first phase of the voyage began on 20 September, the day the fleet left the Downs, and lasted until 6 November when the actions against the pirates commenced.[4] This phase was largely uneventful, and therefore there is no need to describe events in detail.[5] On the 31st of October, the fleet finally reached Gibraltar

---

[1] PRO, SP 71/1/ff.21–25, covering 27 November to 8 December.
[2] Bodleian Library, Ashmole MS. 824/XV, ff.149–66.
[3] John Button, *Algiers Voyage [in a Journall or Briefe Repatary of all occurents hapning in the fleet of ships sent out by the King his most excellent Maiestie, as well against the Pirates of Algiers, as others; the whole body consisting of 18 ships]* (1621). A copy of this journal with Coke's annotations is in PRO, SP 14/122/106.
[4] The following account of the expedition is drawn from the journals cited above and Mansell's letters. All quotations are from these three sources. Mansell's letters to and from the Bashaw are in PRO, SP 71/1/ff.27–8, and he sent Aston a relation of his proceedings: BL, Add. MS. 36,445, ff.22–9.
[5] Ten days were lost at Plymouth where additional men and provisions were taken on board because the weather was 'foggy and dirty'.

where they met with five Spanish ships. After saluting each other, the Spanish Admiral came aboard and reported that the remainder of his fleet was at Cadiz, and 'that a great store of pirates were abroad' and that recently they had raided the coast and 'carried away divers prisoners'. After putting ashore some sick men, Mansell left for Malaga where he arrived on 3 November. Upon saluting the town 'with a great store of ordnance' he went ashore and was entertained by 'the best sort of townsmen'.

Three days later the fleet weighed anchor and sailed for Alicante. Mansell divided his forces into three squadrons and ordered them to assume 'a halfmoon formation'.[1] Button's squadron was positioned closest to shore at a distance of three leagues. Mansell was in command of the centre squadron which formed a line three leagues across. The third squadron, under Vice Admiral Hawkins, sailed another three leagues seaward.[2] For over two weeks, the fleet made its way along the Spanish coast in formation reaching Alicante on 19 November where the ships anchored 'the whole fleet saluting the town with our ordnance and the town us (though not in so royal a fashion as other towns)'. Mansell put ashore more sick men at Alicante in houses provided for that purpose by the Spaniards and left the *Goodwill* in the harbour to serve as a hospital ship. Provisioned with wine, water, etc. from the town, the fleet set out on the 25th for Algiers.

Two days later, the fleet dropped anchor before Algiers, though far enough from the fortifications to be out of range.[3] Not until the following day, 'the violence of the storm being somewhat appeased' did anyone go ashore. Then Captain Squibb went to the Bashaw[4] to present letters from King James and to demand hostages.[5] After receiving Squibb, the Bashaw dispatched two Turks and an interpreter to Mansell's ship with a letter and the promise of safe conduct for the men of the English fleet. Time now

---

[1] This was a traditional formation of the period; the Spanish formed up this way in the famous armada of 1588. It allowed a fleet like Mansell's to sweep a path along the coast 36 nautical miles wide.
[2] After sailing along for a day in this way, a boat was sent ashore to enquire 'if any pirates were at anchor, either in bays or coves'.
[3] The fleet anchored in 27 fathoms of water, i.e., some distance from the harbour. Mansell saluted the town on arrival but received none in return. Some of the ships were forced out of the road because their anchors would not hold.
[4] A title of honour in the Ottoman empire used to describe important Turkish military or civil officials.
[5] The need for the expedition was brought home that evening when two English ships were brought in: one was from Plymouth and the other from North Yarmouth.

became critical for the English fleet because of 'the openness of the road, the ill anchor hold, and the many dangers the whole fleet was subjected unto'. Squibb, therefore, was sent ashore the very next day to demand a speedy answer, but the Bashaw replied that nothing could be done until the following Saturday – at the very earliest – when he would bring the Doana, an assembly, into session. Mansell decided to hold a council of war to decide whether to risk waiting so long for an answer. He was of the opinion that 'in respect of the expectation he had of the good success of His Majesty's letters' and because the Bashaw's 'verbal promise gave me great hope' the fleet should wait.

However, a short while later, Mansell learned that ships within the Mole were taking on board English captives. Squibb was ashore almost immediately with instructions to get the Bashaw to agree to stay all ships in harbour so that English captives could not be sent abroad. Mansell could not prevent this occurrence because 'the [English] ships being moored topmasts down and yards upon the deck, I could not hinder any ships to enter or go out'.[1] The Bashaw was unwilling to agree and instead asked for Mr Frizell to be sent ashore since 'he well understood the course of their proceedings'.[2]

Two days later, Mansell sent Captain Roper ashore to demand:

> of such satisfaction as was required . . . [and] restitution . . . of 150 sail of ships taken in the five years past from His Majesty's subjects besides those taken since April last. That the pirates and their armadors who are there harboured might [be] cut off by the sword of justice or otherwise delivered up unto me to receive . . . punishment . . . That all English bottoms . . . [and] goods remaining in them or landed on the shore might be presently sent unto me. That all His Majesty's subjects: either slaves, renegades, boys or freemen might be presently sent aboard me.[3]

This demand had greater effect; the Bashaw agreed to advance the

---

[1] Mansell provides no explanation why he unrigged the ships, though his anchorage on a dead lee shore and a poor holding ground may help explain his action.
[2] Frizell was a Barbary merchant who continued to trade with Algiers and look after English interests there through the 1630s.
[3] PRO, SP 71/1/f.21v. The number of English losses appears high; for a more detailed discussion see below, Chapter 7.

meeting of the Doana to the following afternoon and to make an attempt to stop ships departing with English captives aboard.

On Sunday morning, 3 December, the Doana met with Captain Roper and Mr Frizell in attendance. Proceedings began seriously, but the meeting ended in something resembling a farce. Roper began by delivering James's letter to the Bashaw who proclaimed he could not read it. Roper then gave him three copies: one in Turkish, a second in Italian, and a third in Latin. The Bashaw read the Turkish copy to himself but refused to read its contents to the Doana. Roper was then asked whether he had any letter from the Grand Signor, the Ottoman ruler, nominally in authority. Roper replied that he had no such letter. On hearing this, the Bashaw called on the representative of the Grand Signor to inform the Doana that it could not take notice of the English communications since the authority of the Grand Signor was required before they could be officially read. On hearing this, 'divers of the Doana, whom Mr Frizell had formerly prepared for that purpose, earnestly pressed to know the contents of the letters . . . which the Bashaw denied, affirming that he could not read it and demanded of Capt. Roper what was desired in His Majesty's letters'. Roper answered that he had delivered a letter in their own language which even he [Roper] could read. Perceiving then 'the importunity of the Doana to know the same and the unwillingness of the Bashaw to have it published', Roper announced that the letter called for the restoration of 150 ships (and their crew and contents) taken in the last five years, and the punishment of the offenders. On hearing this the Bashaw replied that many of these ships had been taken a long time ago: many ships had been lost or sold; many of the men were dead; and the goods had long been sold or eaten. As a sop, he added that those remaining would be delivered up shortly.

Roper was not satisfied, whereupon the Bashaw proclaimed that Algiers had suffered greater losses from the English.[1] Roper replied that even if this were the case, which he doubted, their complaints should be addressed to the King of England from whom, doubtless, they would receive satisfaction. The Bashaw retorted that by their law they could not take away the life of a thief, but he promised to make restitution of English ships, men,

---

[1] The Bashaw named William Mellin, Captain Gifford, Richard Alline, and William Garrat as culprits. Alline and Garrat were said to have taken three ships bound for Tetuan worth 300 000 pieces of eight. None of these cases was recent, dating back to 1604–8.

and goods then in the town, if a consul were appointed to reside in Algiers. In that case, any ships, men, or goods taken in the future could be delivered unto him and the offenders punished.

Members of the Doana then began to debate the matter. Some favoured the English demands while others supported the armadors.[1] At last, the Bashaw announced that the matter should be settled with the losses sustained by each side set against the other, cancelling out each other. Additionally, he went on, the ships and goods currently within the Mole would be delivered up to Mansell and a proclamation proclaimed throughout the town saying that 'whosoever had any English captives or boys should presently bring them in on pain of losing their heads, the captives . . . to receive trial and such as were found to be Christians and likewise such as never had turned Turk and would revolt should be presently sent aboard'. The Bashaw's proposal was soon accepted by the Doana and the proclamation announcing the settlement was duly read.

The proclamation brought meagre results: only 18 captives were delivered to Roper. In consequence, Roper and Frizell returned on 5 December to speak again to the Bashaw and Doana. Mansell had no authority to appoint a consul, they said, but he would leave Frizell's man to keep a register of ships taken. On hearing this 'a tumult was raised through the whole body of the Doana' and so dissatisfied were they that 'the poor captives that were formerly delivered up to Captain Roper [were] clapped in prison, the gates of the town to be shut up and a guard set upon Mr Frizell's house where Captain Roper and himself were'.[2]

After some shouting and debate within the Doana, calm returned, and eventually Roper and Frizell were released when Mansell agreed 'that rather than I would leave him [Roper] and Mr Frizell behind me and the English captives delivered unto him, I would appoint one Ford, an ordinary sailor whom I had accommodated for that purpose . . . to remain there for the purpose of keeping a register'.[3]

Mansell went on to admonish Roper and Frizell to return to the ships as soon as possible for he had learned that the Turks were

---

[1] That is those who owned and fitted out the pirate ships.
[2] Frizell was told that they would not be released until the hostages on board Mansell's ship were returned.
[3] Ford was dressed up for the part and remained there after Mansell had departed: PRO, SP 71/1/f.31. The Levant Company refused to accept the debts he incurred in trying to assist captives: SP 105/148/f.96v.

just delaying and had no intention 'but to abuse me & that I would depart without any longer stay upon the viceroy's promises'. On 6 December, Ford was sent ashore and Roper and Frizell 'perceiving their perfidious dealing' and fearing a longer stay 'might occasion further trouble . . . did repair presently with those few captives leaving Ford to solicit the delivery of the rest as they have formerly promised'.

On 7 December, Ford wrote to Mansell that he had discovered that 'they intended nothing but delays and had put him off till Saturday'. That evening Mansell concluded that 'there was no hope that any more captives would be delivered nor ships nor goods restored for that they were unrigging their ships and unloading the goods'.[1] As a result and according to a resolution taken by a council of war, Mansell prepared to set sail the next morning.

On 13 December the fleet arrived in Majorca having achieved little. Over five months were to elapse before the fleet would again set out for the pirate stronghold. The first two weeks in Majorca were spent refreshing the men, taking on wood, water and ballast which were much needed. The English fleet was pleased to find 'the people very kind and courteous bringing us great store of all manner of provisions which we bought at easy rates'.[2] On Christmas Eve, Mansell ordered the fleet to sea, and on the following night they came across eight or nine pirate ships which they chased but could not catch because, '. . . it is almost incredible to relate in how short a time those ships out-sailed the whole fleet out of sight'.[3]

From 26 December until 6 February the fleet was based at Alicante, where more sick were put ashore. During this time, individual ships or squadrons made forays to search for pirates, all to no avail.[4] In early February, Mansell's fleet left for Malaga arriving on the 13th where the *Mercury*, *Spy*, and two resupply ships were found. After a few days stay, the English fleet set out for Gibraltar. Whilst approaching the Straits, Mansell divided the fleet into squadrons. Five ships were sent to the Straits, where the *Antelope* captured a 'small Frenchman which had 50 butts of oil in here and divers Moors and Jews, men, women, and children –

---

[1] The actions by the Algerines indicate that they were expecting an attack.
[2] 240 sick men were put ashore to recover.
[3] BL, Harl. MS. 1581, ff.70–2, a report sent to Buckingham in January from Alicante.
[4] Such forays were made on 27 December, 1–4, 4–5, 13–18, 21–24, 25 January.

passengers bound from Tetuan to Algiers'.[1] Another group went to the coast of Barbary where they met Captain Gyles Penn in a ship of Bristol. With Penn were two Moors who wished to treat for the redemption of their people in exchange for some English captives they had bought from the pirates. Negotiations continued for the next two weeks but proved fruitless and ended on the morning of 10 March, when 'Capt. Penn being overconfident of the Moors' good faith and promises with whom he had long traded went ashore without cautions;' the Moors made stay of him, 'hoping thereby the better to recover their own people whom we held'.[2]

The fleet returned to Malaga on 13 March where it remained until the 28th, leaving behind Rear Admiral Button and five ships to await the supply ships from England. After waiting 12 days without sight of the ships or any word of their whereabouts, Button sailed for Alicante. On 14 April, the fleet was reunited in the roadstead of Alicante. Here Mansell purchased a 120-ton Spanish ship, reported to be 'an excellent sailor, and likewise bought three brigantines which rowed with nine oars on a side'.[3] A week later, news reached Mansell that the supply ships had arrived, but by then he had resolved not to press on for Algiers. Four days later, the fleet sailed to Majorca where they spent a little over two weeks taking on provisions, training the men to use fire ships, and practising how to execute an attack on the harbour of Algiers. On 16 May, they weighed anchor, and five days later an English battle fleet was again riding before Algiers.

The fleet anchored a half league from the town, but this time the ships were not unrigged nor was there any attempt to parley. The fleet divided into three columns with the king's ships and the *Golden Phoenix* placed nearest the Mole, the Vice Admiral's squadron was to the south and the Rear Admiral stationed to the north. Six of the merchant ships were then ordered to ply off the town keeping as close to shore 'to prevent the coming in of any pirates between the fleet and the shore'. On the first evening, two boats and three brigantines were prepared for action. In the boats were laid 'plenty of dry wood, wood of oakum, pitch, resin, tar, brimstone', while the brigantines were fitted with 'chains and

---

[1] None of the accounts of the capture of this ship actually describe her as a pirate vessel. All the Turks saved themselves by fleeing in a boat.
[2] Penn remained a Barbary trader for the next 20 years: see below, Chapter 11.
[3] Mansell sold the prize goods and ransomed the captives: HMC 23, *12th Report, App.i, Cowper MSS* (Cal. of Coke MSS), p. 115.

grapples of iron . . . fire-balls, buckets of wildfire, and firepikes'. Seven boats were put in the water and filled with armed men. When all was in hand, the wind moved around to the west and then dropped; Mansell called the captains and masters aboard to advise him whether to make the attempt that evening.[1] The council of war concluded that it was better to defer until another 'fitter opportunity was offered'. On 22 May, like preparations were made but put off for like reasons. The next night, after waiting two hours for a gale to blow out, the brigantines and boats at last set out for the Mole, only to have the wind shift before they could get near.

The night of the 24th also started badly, for a rain squall swept over the fleet, and the wind was out of the bay. But as the night went on, the weather became more favourable, and the small English flotilla was able to move forward once more:

> The boats performed their directions in towing on the ships; but considering, that by the continuance of the course, they should expose their principallest men to hazard, by reason of the great store of ordnance and small shot, which played upon them, they debated among themselves what to do; Captain Hughes (who commanded one of the brigantines) replied, Go on, and give the attempt with the boats; which they cheerfully pursued, crying out without cessation, *King James, King James, God Bless King James*; and fearless of the danger even in the mouths of the cannon and small shot, which showered like hail upon them they fired the ships in many places, and maintained the flame, to the great comfort of us that were spectators, so long as they had powder left in their bandoleers, and striving in the end who should have the honour to come off last; the which at length, as a due to the former resolution and courage, they left to Captain Hughes, and so retired, all the ships continuing still their cheerful cry, *King James*, . . . and leaving the fire to flame up in several places, which continued in some of them long after their retreat, and being aboard his majesty's ships.

The cowardly Turks, who before durst not show themselves to so weak a force but from the walls or tops of their houses, so soon as they perceived all the boats retired, opened their gates and sailed out in the thousands; and, by the help of so great

---

[1] The harbour was protected on the north and west sides; the only entrance was from the east and therefore impossible to enter when the wind was from the west.

multitudes, and a sudden shower of rain seconded with a calm which then happened, the fire was extinguished, without doing any more hurt than making two of their ships unserviceable.[1]

Although the attack came ever so close to succeeding, in the end it failed. No enemy ships were destroyed, though ten or eleven of Mansell's men were killed and thirteen wounded from 'both small shot and ordnance [that] played continually upon them; the hurt being done . . . at their coming off for that they got into the Mole before the town was risen'.[2] As if to celebrate their triumph, four pirate ships slipped into the harbour the next day despite the best efforts by six English vessels. Only the *Bonaventure* got within shot of the pirates.[3] This incident shows that a tight blockade could not be maintained without shallow-draft, oared vessels. Without galleys or similar vessels, Mansell could not prevent pirate vessels from entering or leaving the port.

That evening the English fleet weighed anchor and stood out to sea. Two nights later the *Bonaventure* and *Hercules* drove ashore a Turkish vessel with over 140 on board, including 12 Christians, all of whom were drowned except for 12 Turks who were able to swim to the shore. On last day of May, two Genoese men managed to swim out to one of the English ships, bringing with them the unfortunate news that 'the same night our ships stood off to sea, there came into the Mole seven of the best ships of Algiers and that if we had stayed, they had fallen into our laps'. The Genoese also informed Mansell that the Turks had now put a boom across the harbour so that it was now impossible for boats to get close enough to fire the ships within the Mole.[4] And from the Italians, Mansell also learned the enemy now kept three galleys and 15 boats at the ready to guard the boom.

On the 2nd of June in the evening, two or three galleys ventured out from the Mole, but only a few shots were exchanged before they went back; neither side suffered from this encounter.[5]

[1] BL, Harl. MS. 1581, f.72–72v.
[2] Casualties were fairly high; altogether 14 vessels and 232 men took part in the attack.
[3] Mansell's comment on this subject can be found in BL, Add. MS. 36,445, f.133.
[4] That the harbour had not been boomed earlier suggests that the Algerines did not take Mansell to be a serious threat.
[5] On this day, ships of Mansell's fleet at last took a prize, a merchantman from Leghorn bound for Algiers 'with divers Jews in her and . . . laden with . . . two or three thousand pounds in ready money'. There is nothing in the evidence to suggest that this ship was anything other than a merchantman intent on trading with Algiers: Bodleian Library, Ashmole MS. 824/XV, f.161v.

During this period, when the fleet was riding before Algiers, Mansell kept several boats between the fleet and town to give warning and take up 'such poor Christian captives as would adventure to save themselves by swimming from the slavery of the Turks'.[1] A few captives were able to make it to the English ships, and from them Mansell learned that all chance of surprising the Turks had been lost. Since many of the ships now wanted for victuals, he ordered the fleet to abandon Algiers once more, and on 4 June they departed for Alicante.

The fleet returned to the coast of Spain on 8 June where they were greeted by Captain Roper, who had come from England carrying letters from the Lord High Admiral. Mansell was ordered to relinquish the royal warships, *Vanguard*, *Constant Reformation*, *Rainbow*, and *Antelope*. A week later, after refreshing the crew, victualling, and paying off debts with prize money, Mansell set sail for Cadiz, stopping at Malaga and Torremolinos on the way.

By 12 July, while four miles off Cadiz, Mansell gave order for the homeward-bound ships to leave. Because the *Lion* was 'so defective that she could not any longer be continued without eminent peril of perishing' she was sent instead of the *Vanguard*.[2] For similar reasons, the merchant ships, *Zouch Phoenix*, *Marigold*, *Primrose*, and *Restore* were dispatched home. As they left, the ships heading for England took their leave with 'four or five hundred pieces of ordnance being discharged by both sides for a farewell'.[3]

The two journals which have formed the basis for much of this account of the expedition were written by individuals who returned to England in July/August 1621, and, therefore, it is difficult to render a precise day-to-day relation of Mansell's fleet during the last two months of the expedition. Mansell himself, however, wrote several letters during this time which contain enough information about his actions and intentions to complete this account of the expedition.

Even before going to Algiers, he had written to Sir Walter Aston[4] of his plans, enclosing instructions for Mr Rice to take to

---

[1] Several French, Dutch, and Spanish captives were able to escape in this way.
[2] For the defects of the *Lion*, see Chapter 6. These ships went under the command of Admirals Hawkins and Button.
[3] By 3 August they were safely back in England. (In the source used here, the ship *Marygold* is called the *Marigold*. It was not uncommon for the spelling of ships' names to vary in this period.)
[4] The English envoy to Spain.

England to acquaint Buckingham of the needs of the fleet.[1] Because of the worn state of his ships, Mansell thought it would be necessary to spend July and August refitting and that he could not operate against the pirates before September at the earliest. The ships had deteriorated markedly because of the weather and length of time at sea. Mansell believed the king's ships might be kept at sea for another six months but only with great difficulty. Careening[2] would not be sufficient, these ships were too foul and could be put right only if they were dry-docked. All the royal ships were in need of a completely new set of sails, tackle, and rigging. It would be difficult to undertake such a complete refit in Spanish ports.[3] The fleet's prize money would not cover the costs. Therefore, Mansell recommended that a fresh fleet be sent out. Twelve months was too long a time to keep a fleet at sea, especially when the ships were unsheathed.[4] It was better and cheaper, Mansell claimed, to employ two fleets, keeping one on station nine months at a time while the other refitted at home.

Notwithstanding earlier admonitions, Mansell was now of the opinion that he could keep his fleet at sea for another six months if necessary as long as the *Lion* was replaced and fresh supplies received. A few days later, Mansell had second thoughts about the viability of keeping his ships at sea for so long. He informed Aston that if he had not received news of a replacement fleet on return from Algiers, he intended to sail promptly for England, unless commanded to stay out longer.[5]

When Mansell did come back from Algiers in June, he found orders awaiting him at Alicante. A new fleet was not being sent out, as he had recommended; instead, he was ordered to send home four warships but remain with the rest of the fleet to continue operations against the pirates. On the 28th, he wrote that he was sailing to Cadiz to refit and supply the fleet.[6] About three weeks later, Mansell wrote to Aston from Cadiz reporting on the readiness of his fleet.[7] In this letter he states that he expected to

[1] BL, Add. MS. 36,445, ff.64–5.
[2] Careening was the process (done periodically) of turning a ship on its side for cleaning, caulking, or repairing.
[3] Mansell expected a refit in Spanish ports to be expensive, more so than if undertaken in England.
[4] This was before cooper sheathing was used to prevent marine growth on the underwater portion of a ship's hull.
[5] BL, Add. MS. 36,445, ff.66–8, 102v.
[6] Ibid., ff.153–4. No port within the Straits could meet the fleet's needs.
[7] Ibid., f.183.

put to sea by 1 August. The refit had been completed almost a month early, as Mansell noted, 'by reason of the great forwardness' of the Spanish. Four days later, Mansell paid his Spanish hosts another compliment advising Aston that the Veedor General had been exceedingly helpful, going so far as to supply 'all wants many of which he does secretly and cannot be had anywhere else'.[1]

Support from England, on the other hand, was either inadequate or late. Throughout July, Mansell wrote anxiously about the whereabouts of supplies from England.[2] When he returned from Algiers, he had been informed that the supply ships were expected to arrive on 24 June. But as he learned in a letter from his wife, dated 28 June, the supply ships were still anchored in the Thames.[3] By 25 July these supplies had still not arrived. In fact, Mansell had no definite information when they might arrive. By that date, matters were getting desperate for the fleet possessed only four days victuals and had no money or credit left.

From late July onwards, Mansell's actions were dictated by want of supplies rather than strategic or tactical considerations. By 21 July he had resolved to take the fleet to Gibraltar so it might be better placed to intercept the supply ships.[4] A few days later, Mansell was forced to put to sea in search of the missing supply ships. By 29 July, the victuals of the fleet had been exhausted; yet still there was no sign of the supply ships.[5]

Until this moment, Mansell had remained confident in the eventual success of the expedition. It appeared inconceivable to him that the Lord High Admiral and the navy commissioners would let the fleet go hungry or fail to provide necessary supplies. For months, he had worried about the deplorable condition of men and ships. Lack of support had adversely affected morale of his officers and men, but his faith had not been shaken.[6] But by the end of July, even Mansell had begun to despair. It seemed that the fleet had been abandoned. The supply ships had not come; there was not even news of them. Indeed there was no news of any

[1] Ibid., f.187–187v.
[2] 6 July: BL, Add. MS. 36,445, f.164v; 21 July: ibid., f.183; 25 July: ibid., f.187; 29 July: ibid., ff.168–9; 31 July: ibid., ff.207v–208.
[3] Ibid., f.87.
[4] He dared not risk having the supply ships pass on their way to the Mediterranean while his ships were anchored in the Bay of Cadiz.
[5] BL, Add. MS. 36,445, ff.207v–208.
[6] Ibid., f.168v. At one point, over 600 men of the fleet were sick and what food they had was bad.

sort out of England, and what made matters worse, as Mansell observed, for weeks the weather had been favourable for ships to sail southwards.[1]

After 31 July, Mansell wrote no more, nor does the correspondence of Aston contain more than rumours of the fleet's activities. Thus, from 1 August until the second week in September, the exact whereabouts and actions of the fleet remain a mystery. However, from Mansell's earlier letters and from parole evidence, it is possible to deduce what probably occurred.

Subsequent to his second voyage to Algiers, Mansell made plans for another assault on the pirate stronghold, but to succeed he now realized that galleys would be needed to press home a new attack on Algiers. Mansell had informed Aston that his last effort would have been much more successful if he had had but two galleys with his fleet.[2] On 6 July, Mansell requested Aston obtain eight galleys from the Spanish.[3] On 21 July, Mansell revised his request: eleven galleys were now the minimum, though thirteen would be better.[4] Mansell intended to use the galleys to choke off the harbour. With oared galleys from Spain, Mansell would no longer be dependent on the wind, and a tight blockade could be maintained. In the past, contrary winds and currents had prevented him from pressing home the attack. This time the galleys would tow the English warships into position close to the enemy where their heavy cannon could cover the small boats and fireships that Mansell intended to use to cut the boom and fire the pirate ships within the harbour.[5]

Aston presented Mansell's requests to the Spanish Council of War, and on 26 July he advised London that Martin Arostegui, Secretary to the Council of War, believed almost all of the English requests would be met.[6] Orders had been given for the galleys to sail to Majorca to await Mansell's fleet. The viceroy at Majorca had already been given orders to furnish the English fleet with any victuals, munitions, or fireships they might need or think necessary. Don Juan de Aya la Mannique, commander of the Spanish forces, had been given specific orders to co-operate with Mansell and to conform to the wishes of the English Admiral.

---

[1] Ibid., ff.207v–208.
[2] Ibid., f.132v.
[3] Ibid., f.164. He added that six galleys would suffice.
[4] Ibid., f.183–183v.
[5] Ibid., f.133.
[6] Ibid., f.189–189v.

On hearing this news, Mansell informed Aston that he would have liked to discuss in detail with the Council of War plans for a joint operation, but a lack of time (brought on by the lateness of the resupplies) precluded such a meeting.[1] Instead, Mansell intended to press on, trusting in the judgement and affection of the Spanish commander of the galleys.

Mansell understood that surprise and secrecy were needed for this new assault to succeed. Four days prior to his last attempt, launched from Majorca, a French merchantman had carried with her to Algiers news of the English fleet.[2] This intelligence gave the enemy time to prepare their defences. Mansell now planned to launch the operation directly from Alicante or Cartagena so that the pirates would not be forewarned.[3] He was, therefore, perturbed to learn in July that the Spanish galleys had been ordered to go to Majorca. Immediately he sent a letter to Aston requesting him to get the Spanish to stay the galleys at some Spanish port until the English fleet arrived.[4] On 31 July, Mansell reiterated his request and also suggested that the governor of Majorca should be given orders to stay all vessels if the galleys had arrived and that some pretext for their presence must be given out. This letter shows that as of the end of July, Mansell was still planning to mount another attack on Algiers. But to do so, he needed a well-provisioned fleet. The Spanish galleys would count for little, if he did not have a squadron of powerful men-of-war to defeat any pirate ships that put to sea. They would have to be in reasonably good condition and well provisioned for they would be expected to keep station in all weather and for weeks, certainly, and probably months.[5]

The king's ships were probably the most powerful warships in the Mediterranean, and without them the fleet would be at risk. In July, the strength of the English fleet was substantially reduced when four royal men-of-war and five of the armed merchantmen were sent home. Replacements were expected. As far back as March, an order had been given to equip *Victory* and *Dreadnought*

---

[1] Ibid., f.183–183v.
[2] Ibid., f.165–165v.
[3] Ibid., ff.165, 207v–208.
[4] Ibid., f.207v.
[5] Ibid., f.164v. as far back as 6 July, Mansell had concluded that the fleet would have to keep station before Algiers for months, perhaps even up to a year, to succeed. Eventually, he anticipated that the honest townsmen would rise up and overthrow the armadors.

for six months at sea.[1] When these powerful replacements arrived, Mansell's fleet would again be just strong enough to go forward with the attack on Algiers.

Thus by the end of July Mansell had evolved a precise plan of attack. It assumed the galleys would be available, as promised. It also assumed that secrecy could be maintained. The English men-of-war were Mansell's greatest concern.[2] The non-arrival of the replacement warships and supplies made his position even more precarious by the beginning of August.[3] Some of the much needed provisions could be acquired from the Spanish. Some supplies were acquired in August, for the fleet was able to remain at sea over six weeks after Mansell reported at the end of July that his original supply of victuals was exhausted.[4]

If Mansell needed an excuse to abandon the operation, the weakness of his fleet and the lack of adequate provisions would be sufficient. However, he expressed no wish to abort the operation; to the contrary, several documents suggest that Mansell wished to carry on, despite the odds, but that the fate of the expedition was determined by the king and Council, though they, in turn, were influenced by reports from Mansell.

Opinion in London was not impressed by the early actions of the expedition. As usual, rumours of great victories and catastrophic defeats circulated in London, but the first real impression of Mansell's doings came from reports and rumours about his actions at Algiers derived from Spanish ministers or agents. Before Mansell had even come back from Algiers the first time, Gondomar was complaining that Mansell had 'made truce with the town and become good friends with the pirates, and that the English and those robbers are now all one'.[5]

[1] PRO, SP 14/120/37,64. Victualling and wages for six ships for six months was estimated to cost £14 094 13s 4d.
[2] BL, Add. MS. 36,445, f.169–169v. Mansell thought the odds were 12 to 1 against him unless he were re-equipped.
[3] At the end of May, the Admiralty still intended replacement ships and resupplies to be sent: PRO, SP 14/121/57. *Victory* and *Dreadnought* were to join Mansell at Gibraltar. In fact, though manned and equipped, the two ships were eventually diverted to duty in the Narrow Seas. And to make matters worse, the resupply ships had still not appeared by the beginning of August.
[4] He may have received victuals from the Spanish. Aston wrote in August that Mansell was still at Cadiz awaiting supplies and intent on making another attempt on Algiers: PRO, SP 94/24/f.284.
[5] For an example of a false rumour of the destruction of the fleet: BL, Add. MS. 36,445, ff.82, 103. Mansell believed that Cottington was a source of the malicious reports.

Efforts were made to correct these false reports. Digby and Buckingham, for example, wrote to Mansell ordering him to send Aston copies of his journal and orders so that the Spanish might see he was acting honourably.[1] He was also advised 'that he be careful not to give any cause of jealousy unto them by his carriage but in all things exactly to perform the Articles of the Treaty, as likewise to use all courses of courtesy, as he knows was his Majesty's pleasure'. Mansell complied and took care on his second voyage to Algiers to bring Spaniards to witness the true nature of his actions. As requested, Aston also supplied the Spanish government with an accurate record of the fleet's actions and intentions and tried to counter the malicious rumours.[2]

However, the attempts to discredit the expedition continued. After his second attempt on Algiers, Mansell returned to find more complaints. He wrote to Aston on 28 June that he was surprised his zeal and services were rewarded with discouragements, censures, aspersions of concluding a peace with the pirates, acts of piracy, and breaches of the Articles of Capitulations.[3] He went on to add that he also found it surprising that the Spanish king would accuse him before being fully informed. Mansell and Aston attempted to put the record straight both in Madrid and London, but as Mansell noted, he feared that Gondomar's complaints would be hard to erase.[4]

The unfavourable image of the enterprise was not entirely due to the machinations of Gondomar or his agents. After almost a full year at sea, little real success could be reported. There had been nothing to enthuse or encourage additional support. Most of Mansell's letters to Buckingham, Aston, Calvert and Cranfield, make for dismal reading. They are filled with descriptions of the poor condition of the fleet, the defects of the ships, the lack of supplies, the sickness of the crews.[5] The discouraging tone of these letters may have been unintended, but his letters were unlikely to engender support. The reports disclosed substantial weaknesses and defects; the remedies would be costly and funds were desperately short. The Crown was still having difficulty collecting money promised before the fleet set sail.[6] To continue

[1] BL, Add. MS. 36,445, ff.82, 105v.
[2] Ibid., f.136v.
[3] Ibid., f.153–153v.
[4] Ibid., f.162.
[5] For example, PRO, SP 94/24/f.124; BL, Add. MS. 36,445, ff.64–65v, 168–9.
[6] PRO, SP 14/122/123; SP 14/123/33.

the fleet in the Mediterranean or replace it with fresh units, as Mansell advised, might be desirable, but would be costly, and other policy considerations had emerged since the expedition set sail. The end of the Twelve Years' Truce and the occupation of the Palatinate posed new threats to English interests. At the very least, England's role as a neutral shipper would need to be supported and perhaps defended from one or both of the warring parties. The occupation of the Palatinate might be countered by use of the navy. Either development would put new pressure on the scarce naval resources. By early 1621, these new threats were apparent enough for the Council to discuss possible measures needed to make England ready for war.

The resumption of hostilities between the United Provinces and Spain strained Anglo-Dutch relations. In the years of the Truce, commercial and maritime competition with the Dutch became so fierce that armed conflict occurred in the Indies. With the advent of war, English shipping took advantage of neutrality to carry goods from Spain to Flanders, and the Dutch attempted to cut the flow of supplies to the Spanish Netherlands by stopping, searching, and seizing English ships. These infringements of English neutrality and sovereignty brought protests from the government. They also led to a consideration of ways to protect English shipping and national rights in the Narrow Seas. The Council, according to Heath, considered recalling Mansell's fleet from the Mediterranean to guard the Narrow Seas.[1] On 28 August, Sir Edward Conway was informed that an English fleet was being prepared as a counter-measure to seize Dutch East India ships when they returned to the Narrow Seas.[2] This letter does not indicate whether this fleet was to be based on warships recalled from the Mediterranean, but it shows that international relations were becoming more tense and that the government believed that neutrality could be maintained only by the application of naval force.

Events on the Continent also encouraged consideration of the use of naval power to support royal foreign policy. The expulsion of Frederick from the Palatinate brought in its train recommendations that Mansell's fleet be diverted from its original objective and used, if need be, to bring pressure on Spain to restore the Palatinate for James's son-in-law. Only Spain had influence with

[1] PRO, SP 14/120/121.
[2] PRO, SP 14/122/94.

the Emperor, and it was hoped that the Spanish would support Frederick's claims so as not to alienate England. From Vienna on 26 July, Digby advised that it was then vital to make the Spanish realize what was at risk:

> I shall conclude with telling your lordships only this. That, although I despair not of good success in this knotty business, yet I hope his Majesty and your lordships lay not aside the care of all fitting preparations for a war, in case a peace cannot honourably be had; and, amongst other things, I must earnestly recommend unto your lordships, and by your lordships unto his Majesty, the continuing abroad of Sir Robert Mansell's fleet upon the coast of Spain; which, in case his Majesty should be ill used, will prove the best argument he can use for the restoration of the Palatinate. And so, with the remembrance of my humble service, I recommend you to the protection of God, and rest.[1]

Digby's letter did not arrive until August, but by that time the Council was already discussing what to do with Mansell's fleet. As late as 20 July, however, a draft was circulating which recommended that Mansell's commission should be enlarged to permit a direct attack on Algiers and to chase the pirates as far as Zante.[2] This recommendation was never implemented; instead, the government had decided to recall the fleet. As early as 28 July, Chamberlain had learned that Mansell's fleet was being recalled to guard the Narrow Seas.[3] Almost two weeks later, the committee of merchants was formally told that the fleet was being recalled since it was 'unable to brook the sea longer'.[4]

Yet by September the government had second thoughts. On 12 September, Calvert let Cranfield know that the government that morning had decided to keep the fleet out longer. Additional contributions from the merchants would be required but, as Calvert observed, it was likely to prove difficult to convince them,

---
[1] PRO, SP 80/4/ff.136–8v.
[2] PRO, SP 14/119/144. It was entitled 'Certain Particulars concerning Sir Robert Mansell's Employment worthy of your Lordships Consideration' and contained eleven recommendations, most of which related to supply matters.
[3] PRO, SP 14/122/46. Aston writes that he received two letters from Mansell dated 20 and 26 July but does not specify their contents. SP 94/24/f.284, Aston wrote to Buckingham that he had sent the Lord High Admiral's letters on to Gibraltar and Alicante.
[4] PRO, SP 14/122/65.

especially after they had just been informed to the contrary. Calvert told Cranfield that:

> the best reasons that we could think upon this day at court to resume the business was to tell them that the principal reason why the king did recall Sir Robert Mansell was because the king of Spain was jealous of his proceedings, which is now so well satisfied and cleared as he desires that he may go on with the former enterprise, whereof . . . the king of Spain hath sent Sir Robert Mansell a great supply of fireworks, galleys, and other vessels with which . . . he was resolved to give a new account, and will if his Majesty's letters in the meantime do not invoke.[1]

He went on to ask cynically, though uncertainly, 'If you think this will hold water and bring on the merchants, I will call a council tomorrow morning for it requires haste'.

Although the true reason for the sudden change of policy cannot be documented, recent developments on the Continent was the most likely cause. Digby had learned that the Spanish were reluctant to take any action to assist in the restoration of the Palatinate. Unless force were brought to bear, James would become merely a suitor for grace.[2] Mansell's fleet was the only force which England had which might be used to put pressure on the Spanish. When the government changed its mind in September about keeping the fleet abroad, Mansell responding to earlier orders was, however, already sailing for home. In a few days, his tired and worn vessels would drop anchor in English waters. Mansell's ships had been at sea almost a year to the day, much longer than any English fleet up until that time and for many years to come. The fleet could also claim the distinction of serving in more distant waters than any that had gone before, and of marking the beginning of an English naval presence in the Mediterranean, a development that would continue with few breaks down to the present day.

---

[1] KAO, U 269 ON 6860.
[2] PRO, SP 80/4/ff.132, 212.

6
THE ALGIERS EXPEDITION: ASSESSMENTS, AIMS AND ACCOMPLISHMENTS

Though the fleet could rightly claim several distinctions, no fanfare greeted the return of Mansell's ships. Indeed, the event passed almost without notice. The only official indication at all comes in the form of bills presented after the expedition was over. Even as well-informed and assiduous an intelligencer as Chamberlain only noted the event in passing and gives no date for the return of the fleet.[1] That contemporaries took so little notice may simply reflect a preoccupation with other matters, but it may also indicate their estimation of the fleet's accomplishments. There were no triumphal celebrations, no rich prizes, no heroic actions worthy of praise. The fleet slipped into harbour silently and the expedition passed almost as quietly into history.

An account of the expedition was written by John Button (who returned with Hawkins's squadron in July 1621)[2], and though the journal is positive in tone, it is hard to discover in it any action of major importance or lasting gain. The marginal notes that Sir John Coke added to a copy of Button's journal encapsulate the official view of the expedition. For example, Coke wrote:

3 November:	'hitherto nothing but shooting and ostentation'.
25 January:	'ostentation'.
12 February:	'still inviting them to harbour from harbour'.
21 May:	'why was not this done the first time they came to Algiers'.
2 June:	'here was a merchant ship but not pirate taken'.

---

[1] PRO, SP 14/123/46.
[2] John Button, *Algiers Voyage*. A copy, annotated by Coke, is in PRO, SP 14/122/106.

	'this time had been better begottened[?] at sea, for there was no hope of good by lying still'.
12 July:	'more ostentation after so prospering a far way. quero why they went to Cadiz'.

Coke went on to summarize his doubts about the action at Algiers writing:

> I do conceive by the pirates lax defending themselves, until the attempt upon them in the mole of Algiers, as also for that they used no stratagems upon our fleet at an anchor, that they did not account us enemies, but thought by the treaty no hostility was meant them. Otherwise they would have boomed their harbour as well before as now.
>
> And for the second if they had esteemed us as enemies, having galleys and numbers of unserviceable vessels with a northerly wind, they might have towed fire ships amongst ours, and either have burnt us, or par force with that wind put us on shore where we could not avoid shipwreck.
>
> The danger of the sea was not much less, that road being fatal to Christians, as appeared by the loss of Hugo Moncado, and after Charles the Fifth wrecked in that very place with storms of northly winds.
>
> The mischief that fell to our English merchants and mariners upon this voyage is too truly, and commonly known.

And Coke was not alone in criticizing Mansell's expedition. On 20 October 1621, Chamberlain wrote to Carleton that the late expedition had done nothing but irritate the pirates; recently 57 ships had been taken.[1] A month later, Sir Thomas Roe wrote from the Mediterranean that piracy was on the increase.[2]

The most damning criticism came from Sir William Monson a tract entitled *The ill-managed Enterprise upon Algiers in the Reign of King James, and the Errors committed in it*.[3] Monson thought the 'voyage proved little better than a public scorn for all nations to laugh at considering the reputation this realm had gained in

---

[1] PRO, SP 14/123/46.
[2] BL, Add. MS. 36,445, f.283. Roe reported an increase in piracy and that merchants of the Levant trade had written to Calvert for help.
[3] *Sir William Monson's Naval Tracts*, ed. M. Oppenheim, III (Navy Records Society 1913), pp. 94–8.

their former expeditions by sea'.[1] Monson put the blame for the failure of the expedition almost entirely on Mansell. Reflecting the criticisms made by Coke he wrote:

> But such was the mis-government of those ships, and the negligence and vain-glorious humours of some to feast and banquet in harbour when their duty was to clear and scour the seas, that they rather carried themselves like amorous courtiers than resolute soldiers, by which means they lost the opportunity which offered itself to do hurt upon those hellish pirates; as may be collected out of a pamphlet published at their return to which I refer you. But with this observation, that besides their going and coming, they spent not twenty days at sea whilst they continued in the Straits, but retired into harbour, where the pirates might find them, but not they the pirates.[2]

Others agreed that the expedition was a failure but were not so ready to blame Mansell. Sir Robert Phelips, for example, blamed the Spanish for the expedition's lack of success and considered Mansell unfortunate to have been in command.[3]

Until the beginning of the 20th century, the judgements of Coke, Monson, Phelips, *et al.*, held sway, but with the publication of *England in the Mediterranean* (in 1904), Sir Julian Corbett reached very different conclusions regarding the aims and accomplishments of the expedition.

Corbett believed that Mansell operated under several restrictions which influenced the outcome of the expedition.[4] First, Mansell was restricted geographically: he was prohibited from sailing beyond Cape Spartivento on the southern tip of Sardinia. Second, there were tactical constraints: Mansell was prohibited from undertaking a frontal attack on the city of Algiers. Third, Mansell had been instructed not to risk the king's ships. To Corbett these restrictions seemed unwarranted. To Corbett, the stated mission of the fleet, i.e., the suppression of the pirates of Algiers, could not have been accomplished by any commander

---

[1] Ibid., p. 95. Monson was by no means an impartial observer having earlier sought and been denied the command of the expedition.
[2] Ibid., pp. 94–5.
[3] BL, Harl. MS. 6383, f.89v.
[4] J.S. Corbett, *England in the Mediterranean: A study of the Rise and Influence of British Power within the Straits, 1603–1713*, I, 2nd ed., pp. 100–1.

under those conditions. Therefore, Corbett concluded that Mansell's fleet must have been sent with another purpose in mind.

Corbett believed that 'at the time the true significance of Mansell's fleet was recognised in all the cabinets concerned'.[1] This significance was not to be found in the actions of Mansell before Algiers. Coke and Monson were wrong. The 'merciless contempt' which they had for Mansell and the expedition needed to be cast aside because their judgements were the result of 'haste and lack of information'. They could not appreciate the significance of Mansell's expedition because of their 'ignorance of the dual object of the expedition'. Mansell's strategy was condemned without a full knowledge 'of the political considerations that deflected it'.[2]

At the centre of Corbett's account of the expedition was a belief that the fleet had been sent out with a second secret role: Mansell's fleet was sent out to threaten Spain. The strength of Corbett's naval history, in general, and not just in *England in the Mediterranean*, was his insistence that the navy existed to contribute to the government's wider political and strategic purposes, and not just to fight battles. For an historian of such a cast of mind, the 17th century and especially the period of the Thirty Years War offered ample scope to discover high political purpose behind naval orders and actions. Thus it is not surprising that Corbett sought to relate Mansell's expedition to the international political manoeuvres that marked the opening of a protracted conflict over the preponderance and place in Europe of Hapsburg power.

But as well as having a philosophical predisposition to discover high political purpose, Corbett saw in documentary evidence a connection between the expedition against pirates and other objectives of English diplomacy. In particular, letters from Coke, Lord Danvers, and Digby led Corbett to re-evaluate the purpose and accomplishments of the expedition.

First, Corbett found evidence of a secret purpose in a minute by Coke, written in 1619. Coke believed:

> In this preparation against pirates it may be conceived the State hath some further design, and if it be governed by such general warrants it will go slowly on, the Gazettes of Venice will take

---

[1] Ibid., p. 115. A search through Corbett's papers and manuscript notes has failed to provide any evidence to support this statement.
[2] Ibid., p. 100.

ASSESSMENTS, AIMS, ACCOMPLISHMENTS 109

notice of it . . . But if it be thought fit to carry it by the trust of a few . . . foreign princes will with more respect proceed in their attempts, and if they find any interruptions in their principal designs they shall not have the advantage of our security and nakedness to redeem their honours by falling on us.[1]

A more direct expression is found in a proposal by Sir Henry Mainwaring,[2] who recommended that a fleet be sent which:

may have orders to go forth – with this commission, that if the Spanish fleet bear in with the Straits they may follow them, and so stand for the Gulf, whither they will arrive first, because the Spanish fleet must stop at Messina. If the Spanish fleet go not to the southward, then the Venetians have no need of supply, and the ships are ready to proceed on his Majesty's own designs. But if the Spanish fleet should dissolve, the ships being forth might be employed against the Turkish pirates.[3]

Although Mainwaring's proposal was submitted before Mansell's fleet had been organized, and therefore might be dismissed, similar advice, as we have seen, was offered by Digby to James I on 26 July 1621, when Mansell was operating in Spanish waters. Corbett used this letter, though he does not appear to have seen an earlier one in which Digby suggested that the fleet might be used against Spain:

According to your lordship's pleasure I have moved my lords in the business of the pirates letting them know, that it was your lordship's desire, that they would be pleased to take into consideration, how the enterprise against the said pirates was to be prosecuted, as looking upon it singly, without any relation to the preparations of Spain. I intimated unto them, how much the state of business was now changed from what it was, when both the suppressing of pirates, and the preventing any unfitting attempt which might be made by the Spanish fleet were jointly in consultation.[4]

[1] HMC 23, *12th Report, App. i, Cowper MSS*, p. 104.
[2] Corbett, *England in the Mediterranean*, p. 80.
[3] PRO, SP 14/105/148. James's ambassador to Venice, Henry Wotton, offered similar advice on 5 March 1619: SP 99/22/f.280.
[4] BL, Harl. MS. 1580, ff.106–8. 5 April 1619.

A month earlier, Lord Danvers had written to Buckingham (newly appointed Lord High Admiral), setting forth (what he conceived to be) the true political reasons of the expedition. Danvers believed that the expedition had been prepared, ostensibly for action against the Algerian pirates but really it was being sent 'to watch the Spaniards' motions and check their growing power by sea'.[1] Finally, in the instructions issued to Mansell, a copy of which only came to light shortly before *England in the Mediterranean* was written, Corbett believed he could see evidence of a secret purpose for the expedition.

Corbett's book grew out of a series of lectures he gave in 1902 as part of a revitalized course for Senior and Flag Officers at the Royal Naval College, Greenwich. Thus from the start this work had a special didactic purpose. He was sponsored and advised by Sir George S. Clarke, First Secretary of the Committee of Imperial Defence, and by Captain W.J. May, Director of the Naval War Course. The work's strategic framework, as Corbett later acknowledged, was suggested to him by Clarke, and, as he also noted later, he was much influenced at this time by May, who advised him to build his lectures around the theme of the deflection of strategy by politics.[2]

The provenance of this work and in general Corbett's role as naval controversialist are vital in assessing his interpretation of Mansell's expedition. His conclusions about the purpose of the expedition and its accomplishments can only be evaluated fairly when one has grasped the intellectual process behind them and the peculiar political context of *England in the Mediterranean*. In no way is this comment meant to infer that Corbett approached his study of history in an unscholarly way. However, it would be doing an injustice to the range of his intellect and interests not to recognize that in writing this book, and the histories that followed, he was engaged in an attempt to educate British naval thinking and influence public opinion. This purpose is made explicit in the preface:

> For I am bold to hope that by this means he [the reader] will find in Stuart times a lamp that will light up much that is dark in later ages, that will even touch Nelson with a new radiance, and perhaps reveal more clearly why it is that our Mediterranean

---

[1] *Calendar of the Clarendon State Papers in the Bodleian Library*, vol. I, 1623–1649, ed. O. Ogle and W.H. Bliss, p. 13 (no. 122).
[2] Corbett, *England in the Mediterranean*, I, pp. v–viii.

Fleet stands to-day in the eyes of Europe as the symbol and measure of British power.[1]

For British naval strategists, the early decades of the 20th century were a time of great anxiety. For the first time in a hundred years the defence of the realm was threatened by a potential enemy whose strength appeared a match for the Empire. But what made this threat – Germany – so menacing was not simply the magnitude of German power but the particular form that it took. By 1902 it had become clear, at least to some, that Germany was determined to challenge the supremacy of the Royal Navy and the world system which the navy underpinned. The threat posed by the German High Seas Fleet was great, but the essence of German strength was not naval. Germany was a continental land power and thus virtually invulnerable to British power which resided in the Royal Navy. It appeared that Britain would not disregard or prevent the establishment of a German hegemony in Europe. Additionally, Germany, unlike Britain's historic enemies, had no colonies of value which might be taken hostage and later traded at a peace conference.

The strategic problem of Germany was real, immediate, and deeply disturbing. It dominated Corbett's thought and infused all his writing for a decade or more. Like many, when faced with an immediate and vexing problem, a dark future, he turned to the past for guidance. There he found comfort in Britain's triumphs over Spain and France, the preponderant and threatening continental powers of an earlier age.

Corbett's study of history led him to identify several distinct features of British strategy which had brought success and seemed relevant for use against the new continental foe. First, he came to believe that a maritime strategy could succeed against a stronger European enemy.[2] At the time the basic philosophy of the Royal Navy, reflecting the experience of the Napoleonic era and the doctrines of A.T. Mahan, saw the navy's objective simply as gaining 'command of the sea' by a decisive fleet action. Corbett thought this approach unrealistic and impracticable. He sought to educate the officer cadre not to see naval action as autonomous military activity, unrelated to the actions of land forces; both land

---

[1] Ibid., p. vii.
[2] M. Howard, *The British Way in Warfare: A Reappraisal*, pp. 10–11. See also, D.M. Schurman's thoughtful study *Julian S. Corbett, 1854–1922*, pp. 19–33, 63 for additional illumination of these points.

and naval forces needed to be harmonized and directed towards a single objective defined within the political strategy of the government.

Second, Corbett believed that sea power was most effective when used to strike at an enemy's lines of communication, shipping interests, or when used to blockade, bombard, and launch diversionary raids which could pin down enemy forces of far greater strength.[1] This, he believed, was the strategy employed by the Elizabethans successfully against Spain. This was also the approach perfected against France by Pitt, and was also the strategy of the Navy war plan of 1907 which Corbett helped to draft at the very same time he was writing his history of the Seven Years War.

Lastly, Corbett came to the fortuitous conclusion that by the application of limited power in certain circumstances, sufficient leverage could be obtained to secure unlimited objectives. Specifically, he saw the use of naval power by Britain in the Mediterranean as a fulcrum that had been and could be used to shift a stronger continental foe. *England in the Mediterranean* is subtitled *A study of the rise and influence of British power within the Straits, 1603–1713*, and in it Corbett sought to convey by historical example how 'the presence of British warships in the Mediterranean exercised an indirect influence which far outweighed their actual achievements'.[2] In Mansell's expedition, Corbett saw the beginning of a role which he portrayed as follows:

> The dawn of England's career as a Mediterranean power was as unpromising as her first attempts at colonisation. There was no trace discernible of how it was destined to press upon the world and force history into the channels in which it flows to-day. Yet Mansell's fleet was the beginning, and we must see in it the pale dawn of all that it heralded. England was about to step into the primeval arena upon which the greatest dramas of dominion had found their catastrophe. It was here upon the sea which the three continents embraced that empire had broken empire since the ages began in unending strife, and for the first time the British navy was entering its bloodstained waters. For Englishmen at least it proved to be one of the most momentous departures in history, redeeming a contemptible reign from

---

[1] Howard, *The British Way in Warfare*, p. 12.
[2] The phrase comes from an anonymous review of the work in *The Quarterly Review*, July 1906, p. 6.

much of its insignificance; and as we see the little squadron thus trailing, as it were, a fiery wake behind it across the Bay, it glows with an attraction too real and too romantic for us not to linger a while over its fortunes.[1]

Both Michael Howard and Donald Schurman have detected and described the influence of history on Corbett's strategic proposals: Corbett openly sought to learn from his study of history lessons that would be applicable to the problems of his own day. But what has not been observed – and it appears that Corbett himself was not fully conscious of it – is the extent to which his concern with the pressing strategic problem of Germany shaped his interpretation of historical experience and coloured the evidence selected in interpreting events. To make the past serve the present, he had first to remake the past. This process lies behind his interpretation of Mansell's expedition.

Corbett's view of Mansell's expedition, and in particular the covert anti-Spanish character he perceived, was largely derived from the instructions given to Mansell and the letters that Mansell sent while abroad. His treatment of Mansell's instructions is especially interesting in that it shows how far he was prepared to move away from the explicit meaning of the document to support his inclination that the expedition had a secret political purpose. For example, Corbett chides Monson for 'his ignorance of the dual object of the expedition', then writes:

> Fortunately, after nearly three centuries of oblivion, a copy of Mansell's instructions has come to light to secure him a fair hearing, and to emphasise the injustice of condemning an admiral's strategy without a full knowledge of the political considerations that deflected it.[2]

However, this deflection of the Admiral's strategy by political considerations is by no means apparent and needs to be demonstrated.

The next sentence reveals with astonishing transparence the line of the argument that Corbett followed and also its weakest point. He explains:

---

[1] Corbett, *England in the Mediterranean*, I, pp. 97–8.
[2] Ibid., p. 100.

Though in form they [Mansell's instructions] of course disclose nothing but an intended campaign against the Barbary corsairs, they are framed in such a way as to secure a diversion of the expedition on the shortest possible notice.

Corbett is right: the instructions disclose nothing but a campaign against pirates. He is also correct in that the instructions express the motives that induced James to set out the fleet, but they do so explicitly in the opening paragraph:

First you are to understand, that the principal motive inducing us in the beginning to undertake this enterprise, was the welfare of our subjects, and the securing of their trade, which hath been so long infested by the continual spoils of that wicked crew of pirates, haunting for the most part the Mediterranean Seas, though sometimes roaming[?] without the Straits upon other coasts, and namely of <u>England Ireland</u> and <u>Spain</u>, our pleasure and commandment is, that for the clearing of those seas, and the utter extirpating of the said common enemies of mankind (so far as God's assistance we may hope to prevail) you shall in your way towards the Straits, to which you are principally to direct your course, prosecute and give chase to any pirates of what nation soever they be, doing your uttermost endeavours to take and apprehend them, and afterwards to dispose of their ships, persons, and goods, as hereafter by these Instructions you are directed, for which purpose you may not unnecessarily upon uncertainties, spend so much time in search of them on this side of the Straits, whither you are to make all speed you may, our High Admiral of England hath by our direction dispatched away one of our ships unto Ireland, there to take information of such pirates as shall be discovered to be upon that coast, and hath given the same order unto the vice admiral of the West part of England to make like enquiry there, and accordingly give notice unto you, and to the end you may be assured not to leave any of them behind you, to spoil and rob in those seas for the want of due information whilst you are in prosecution of them within the Straits, we have in like manner taken order by letters sent which shall speed to our Ambassador in Spain, that advice may meet you upon the coast of Spain or Portugal of the pirates abroad in those seas, the diligence being used by the <u>Conde de Gondomar</u>, Ambassador extraordinary with us from our good brother the King of Spain, by his effectual letters written also to the same purpose, and that you may the more certainly receive the said advice, we think fit when you come to the North Cape, that if the wind be trade you come close aboard the shore with the fleet, if the wind be out at sea and Westerly, then to sail about 12 leagues of the North Cape, and between 20 and 25 leagues of the shore in the height of Lisbon, and howsoever the wind be to come close aboard the South Cape because at some or all those places we doubt not but you shall receive advice.[1]

The purpose of the expedition is unambiguous: Mansell's fleet was dispatched to suppress the pirates of Barbary.

Because the instructions indicate that the expedition was sent to suppress pirates, Corbett had to infer the existence of a second, secret set of instructions. Mansell, however, never even alluded to a second set of instructions even later on following his return to England when his leadership of the expedition was criticized. Moreover, Mansell's conduct weighs against this assertion. In defending himself, Mansell never said nor implied that he had been sent out to do anything other than campaign against the Barbary pirates. His only comments regarding his instructions were that they did not allow him to take as aggressive an action *against the pirates* as he wished.[2] Mansell was quick to attribute the blame elsewhere: the Spanish, the Admiralty, the weather, the state of his ships, or a lack of supplies, all were held responsible. He was never at a loss for reasons to explain why the fleet had accomplished so little. Yet never once did he defend himself by saying that the expedition had a dual purpose, that secretly he was as much concerned with countering Spanish threats, and that this was why his expedition appeared to lack purpose and direction. Such a defence would have been credible and, in the mid-1620s when anti-Spanish feeling was strong, would have been a popular way of redeeming a blemished reputation.

As we have seen, Mansell's instructions explicitly ordered him to suppress pirates. Yet Corbett contrived to see in them signs of another, more fundamental design. For example, Mansell was restricted in several ways; section 9 of the instructions specifically warned him 'not to engage any of our own royal ships or the rest of

---

[1] BL, Add. MS. 36,445, ff.15–19; instructions for Sir Robert Mansell in the Aston papers. The 'North' and 'South Capes': Cape Ortegal and Cape St Vincent.
[2] PRO, SP 71/1/ff.27–28, 17 January 1620/1.

the fleet in manifest peril'.[1] Corbett believed this admonishment was included to prevent the fleet from becoming so heavily engaged against the pirates that they could not divert to undertake actions against Spanish naval forces. However, though it is possible to infer such a design, another and more direct explanation seems likely.

In the first place, a warning of this sort was commonly included in naval instructions. Care was always to be taken with royal property, and ships were valuable, costing about £5000 each. Second, the risk of loss was considerable. As noted above, contemporaries were only too well aware of the dangers. The memory of the disaster that befell the fleet of Charles V while riding in the Bay of Algiers was still vivid.[2] The fortifications of the pirate stronghold were believed to be great. Warships were at a disadvantage when engaging stone forts and likely to be heavily damaged or sunk if taken too close or used rashly.[3]

The instructions also prohibited Mansell from making a direct assault on Algiers. At first glance this seems unduly restrictive, even strange, and perhaps indicative of a desire to keep the fleet free to secure a diversion at the shortest possible notice. But the instructions go on to state exactly why Mansell was not permitted to assault Algiers:

> But because the town itself is of that strength as it is not to be imagined, this (the destruction of it as a base for pirates) cannot be done by any such open assault upon it, & besides for we are at this present in such terms of amity with the Grand Signor, under whose dominion the said town is acknowledged to be, as we would not willingly give him cause to be jealous of any enterprize upon that place: our pleasure is that you shall not attempt any hostile act against the town or castles.[4]

Later, Buckingham explained to Aston the reasons why such precautions needed to be taken:

---

[1] BL, Add. MS. 36,445, f.17.
[2] A large part of the fleet had been lost in 1541: M.F. Alvarez, *Charles V: Elected Emperor and Hereditary Ruler*, pp. 121–3.
[3] A later part of the instruction itself gives an indication of the concern behind the stricture. Mansell was instructed 'we are well contented and for the same do give you full authority to set fire of any two or three of the smallest ships of the fleet, such as you think fittest (our own royal ships excepted) . . . to fire the pirate ships within the Mole, if in likelihood it may be done'.
[4] BL, Add. MS. 36, 445, f.16v.

His Majesty's Instructions to Sir Robert Mansell were, to prosecute all pirates to the death, but not to commit any hostile act upon the town of Algiers (knowing the cruelty that would have been used thereupon to the ambassador and merchants at Constantinople).[1]

The reasons for this prohibition were certainly not contrived. Algiers was thought to be virtually impregnable. Almost all of the city was surrounded by high walls and there were several fortresses incorporated in the city's defence system.[2] Algiers was a large city; estimates put its population between 40 000 and 100 000, that is, about the size of London. Substantial reserves of manpower were available to supplement a garrison that greatly exceeded the 2600 or so men that Mansell could muster. When Charles V attacked Algiers in 1541 he had an army of over 20 000 soldiers, 65 galleys, and 30 other ships, and even this force proved inadequate to take the city. The strength of the city leaves one in no doubt that the prohibition was a wise and necessary inclusion in the instructions. And experience suggested that retaliation against the English community in Constantinople was more than a mere spectre.

Corbett also noted that Mansell's instructions prohibited him from taking the fleet east of Cape Spartivento in Sardinia. Regarding this restriction, he wrote:

> It will be seen that this prohibition insured as far as possible that his operations should not draw him out of that part of the Mediterranean which lay between Spain and her North Italian possessions, so that his fleet might remain a constant menace if any attempt were contemplated to send assistance to the Emperor by sea.[3]

As with Corbett's other inferences, no positive evidence is advanced to support this interpretation. Although this inference is possible, hypothetically at least, there are several pieces of evidence that make Corbett's suppositions improbable.

First, convoys from Spain to Genoa[4] did not sail out into the

---
[1] Ibid., f.82, dated 8 April 1621, received 22 May 1621.
[2] AGS, Estado legajo, 2596, f.94, reports that two English captives had just returned to London having reconnoitred the defences of Algiers and found them strong and in good order.
[3] Corbett, *England in the Mediterranean*, I, p.101.
[4] The port at the beginning of the 'Spanish Road'.

central Mediterranean. They followed the coast northeastwards from Cartagena or Barcelona directly along the Riviera to Genoa.[1] These ships were never within 400 miles of Cape Spartivento. Even if Mansell stayed in the area east of Cape Spartivento, his fleet would never have been in a position to intercept a convoy from Barcelona, because the Spanish would always be closer to their destination of Genoa than Mansell. As a matter of fact, the letters and journals of the fleet show that it operated too far to the south or west to be able to intercept any Spanish Mediterranean fleet, even one from Cartagena or Alicante.

Furthermore, if the Spartivento restriction had been framed to ensure that Mansell kept his fleet in a position between Spain and northern Italy, then Mansell does not seem to have appreciated the aim. His operations along the North African coast near Tetuan put him about as far as possible (within the Mediterranean) from any conceivable point of interception.

A more likely explanation for this geographical restriction may be found in the instructions themselves. The appropriate section reads as follows:

> we think fit and have resolved that for no respect you are to suffer our fleet, or any part of it to go to go [sic] farther Eastward then Cape Sparta Venta, whence the pirates of Tunis usually haunt, without other direction from us or our Council of State unless it be in a chase, and that in fight or forced by foul weather, which chase being lost, or the weather serving you, then to return presently again because the sea beginning from thence to dilate itself into a spacious largeness, and there being so many retreats for that kind people in the islands of Archipelago, it were a wild chase and to little purpose.[2]

Finally, on the subject of this restriction, there is one more piece of evidence that tells against Corbett's view. On 21 July 1621 the Council considered 11 measures to continue operations in the Mediterranean. First among these was the enlargement of Mansell's commission so that 'whereas he is confined to go no farther then Cape Spartivento, he may have power to follow the

---

[1] G. Parker, *The Army of Flanders and the Spanish Road 1567–1659: The Logistics of Spanish Victory and Defeat in the Low Countries' Wars*, p. 51.
[2] BL, Add. MS. 36,445, f.17v.

pirates as far as Cephalonia, Zante, and the Islands adjacent'.[1] This measure, which would have allowed Mansell to sail another 700 miles east of Cape Spartivento must signify that the Council did not intend to position the fleet for diversion against Spain and the interception of supply convoys bound for Genoa. Mansell's fleet would have posed as much of a threat to Spanish coastal shipping had it remained in the Downs.

Corbett also saw in many of Mansell's letters signs of a secret design, particularly in the many attempts made by Mansell to get news whenever he came into port. When the fleet first came to Malaga early in November 1620, Mansell went ashore. 'Here', in Corbett's words, 'the Admiral hoped for his final orders'. In the next paragraph, Corbett developed this theme:

> At Alicante there was still not a line to guide him, and he despatched yet another officer to Cartagena. Nothing is more eloquent of the uncertain object of the expedition than this incessant anxiety for orders.[2]

In neither case, though, do any of the documents refer to 'orders' or 'final order'. When Mansell arrived in Malaga, he went ashore because, as one account puts it, he 'expected letters of Advice'.[3] When at Malaga, he sent a messenger, Master John Duppa, to Madrid 'to let him [the English ambassador] know of our arrival and proceedings'.[4] Again, when Mansell wrote from Alicante, he did not enquire about orders, rather he wrote that 'if any directions for me shall be come to your hands, he [Duppa] might convey them unto me with all speed'.[5] On no occasion do Mansell's letters or related documents reveal a hope or anxiety for final orders. All that these pieces of evidence show is that Mansell made efforts to establish lines of communication with his government when he arrived on the coast of Spain and that in doing so he naturally enquired about any letters of advice or direction that might have been sent to him.

Communications between the fleet and the Admiralty were slow

---

[1] PRO, SP 14/119/144.
[2] Corbett, *England in the Mediterranean*, I, p. 102.
[3] Bodleian Library, Ashmole MS. 824/XV, f.153. Furthermore, when Mansell wrote to Buckingham from Malaga, his letter displayed no anxiety for orders: KAO, U 269 ON 6755.
[4] Button, *Algiers Voyage*, (unpag.), entry for 6 November 1620.
[5] BL, Add. MS. 36,444, f.229.

and difficult. Mansell displayed a considerable interest in communications from England, as Corbett perceived, but his interest cannot fairly be characterized as 'incessant anxiety', nor does this interest indicate a covert aim for the expedition.

To begin with, Mansell's instructions order him to make frequent visits to the Spanish ports to get advice. Section 7 states that:

> we think it very requisite that you do use all industry you may to procure continual advertisement of their [the pirates] being from all parts, for which we doubt not but you may obtain 2 or 3 small boats in some of the king of Spain's ports, to send forth Avisoes upon all occasions.[1]

Secondly, the logistics of the expedition alone compelled Mansell to send urgent dispatches and enquire repeatedly about messages from England. He needed to know if his requests had been received, what responses had been sent. At the same time he needed to inform the Admiralty of the state of his ships, his proceedings, and his intended actions and whereabouts.

It is also only natural that the commander of a distant naval force should try to keep in close touch with his government. But in all the correspondence between Mansell and Aston, Digby, Cranfield, Calvert and Buckingham, there is virtually no detailed discussion of the course of international politics. If Mansell had been sent to counter possible Spanish moves in the Mediterranean or menace Spanish supply routes, then one might expect in the correspondence evidence on recent developments in the international situation for these would influence the way a commander deployed his forces.

Mansell's concerns were of a different character as those in a letter to Aston, dated 13 January 1621, indicate. He writes that he has heard nothing from his wife from whom he hopes for a letter; instead, all he received was

> The letters that came from my Lord Admiral, and my Lord Digby [which] contain only business, and I neither received this time, nor since my coming out of England any one letter from any private friend that I have, and therefore am a stranger as well to their welfare as to the condition of my own fortunes.[2]

---

[1] BL, Add. MS. 36,445, f.16.
[2] Ibid., f.7–7v.

As well as family concerns, Mansell had a particular interest in events in England at this time. Members of parliament were then in the midst of making a vigorous attack on monopolies, and Mansell held a valuable monopoly covering the manufacture of glass. On 25 July 1621, he wrote to Aston that he had recently received a letter from his wife and had been advised of:

> courses taken by Sir Edward Coke to ruin my poor wife, & to turn her out of the glass business now in my absence without any reparation for £25,000 disbursed by me, the most part whereof hath been paid to his Majesty & his servants, had not his Majesty & the Prince, his Highness, by his mediation, been gratuitously pleased to prevent his malice.[1]

Throughout his stay in the Mediterranean, Mansell showed a greater interest in English politics than he did in international relations. His letters contain occasional comments and some of these give a valuable insight on personalities or events, such as his observation that:

> Touching my Lord of Southampton, I conceive that his overmuch crediting the advice & counsel of Sir Edwin Sandys, hath drawn him into some error – & I did ever assure myself that that man's busy head would never be the author of any good to that Lord.[2]

But his interest in English political developments was not simply curiosity. He was aware that his command of the expedition was being carefully scrutinized. There were many who wished to discredit the expedition and in so doing damage Mansell's reputation. In April 1621 he was informed, perhaps by his wife, that Lord Cottington had done him ill at Court by letters which friends had read.[3] There appears to be some truth in this accusation, for at the same time Digby wrote to Aston that 'My Lord the Spanish Ambassador here is very much troubled with the reports which daily come from thence of Sir Robert Mansell's carriage at Algiers, diverse writing that he should have made peace with the pirates'.[4] In June of that year, Mansell wrote two letters to Aston

---

[1] Ibid., f.187.
[2] Ibid., f.187v.
[3] Ibid., f.103.
[4] Ibid., f.105v. Also Buckingham to Aston, ibid., f.82; and for Aston's explanation, ibid., ff.136, 157.

telling the ambassador that he was much troubled by those aspersions. He thanked Aston 'for pains taken to preserve my reputation against malice'.[1] Any concern Mansell may have displayed over the receipt of correspondence from England was more likely grounded in matters as real as these rather than 'orders' as Corbett inferred.

Although the overwhelming weight of evidence indicates that the expedition was sent out to suppress pirates, and not for some dark political purpose, this does not mean that other uses for Mansell's fleet were not from time to time considered, nor that the fleet was sent out without contingency orders. In one letter Mansell refers to a box that should be opened in case of his death.[2] It is certainly possible that it contained special orders to advise the commander if certain contingencies came to pass. To send a fleet thousands of miles from home, where communications might take months, without providing orders to deal with the eventuality of war between England and her former and perhaps potential enemy would have been gross negligence. It seems likely that Mansell had carried orders of this sort.

Since it now appears that there is insufficient evidence to believe Mansell's expedition was sent to the Mediterranean to influence or impede Spanish policy, then it is also no longer possible to follow Corbett and judge the expedition in terms of possible diplomatic or international political accomplishments. Consequently, any evaluation must be made on the basis of the aims set forth in the instructions given to Mansell.

From the very first meeting in 1617 regarding the expedition and lasting until Mansell returned to England in 1621, there was present an ambivalence in the tactical approach that the fleet was to follow. On the one hand, the fleet was instructed to scour the seas of the western Mediterranean and by this approach capture and sink pirate vessels until their power was destroyed. Yet, on the other hand, a lengthy blockade of Algiers was envisaged by which pirate ships would be destroyed within the Mole or penned up until such time as the ships rotted or ceased to be fit for service. Each approach was feasible, had either of them been pursued with single-minded determination, but each required particular types of ships, manpower, and logistical support. Both could not be pursued by the same force: a choice existed but was never made.

[1] Ibid., ff.132, 153, 162.
[2] PRO, SP 94/24/f.124.

Instead, Mansell tried both alternately; though by the latter part of the voyage he appears to have concluded that success was more likely to be achieved by a tight blockade of Algiers and attack on the shipping within the harbour.[1] In the first six months of the expedition he cruised along the coasts, and though the presence of his fleet may have frightened pirates and forced them to abandon operations in those areas, success was only temporary and local. His ships were too slow and ponderous ever to catch up with the pirate vessels.

Since there is no evidence that Mansell participated in the drawing up of the instructions issued to him, it would be unfair to blame him for the inherent ambiguity of his instructions. Normally, the responsibility for naval and tactical matters rested with the Admiralty. Thus, deficiencies in the instructions must be laid with the naval administration, and ultimate responsibility rest with the Lord High Admiral, Buckingham.

As well as suffering from deficiencies in its conception, Mansell's expedition was hindered by other, more mundane factors, such as bad weather which played a large part in the fate of the expedition. The letters of Mansell and Hawkins and, in particular, the journals of the expedition make frequent reference to the influence of weather on the course of the expedition. These accounts are littered with phrases such as: 'so great a sea, we could do little'; 'but little wind, we gained not much'; 'blew so hard we were forced to bear up'; 'storm increasing, all the kings long boats lost'.[2] Such statements are not unusual or peculiar to this expedition. Almost any sea journal or captain's letter of the period will display similar complaints. Heavy seas or strong currents were a great hindrance to ships of the period. Bad weather or unfavourable winds might have been expected especially in the winter months when even the pirates seldom put to sea. Though weather delayed and hampered the fleet at times, it did not affect the outcome of the expedition in a significant way.

In fact, only during one phase did weather greatly influence operations. When Mansell returned to Algiers, it was his intention to launch an attack immediately, but the first four nights after his

---

[1] BL, Add. MS. 36,445, f.164–164v. Mansell believed that if the pirate ships were burned and a blockade maintained, within a year 'honest townsmen' would overthrow the pirate faction. He also claimed that the fleet 'wanted neither will nor power to have battered down the town upon their heads': ibid., ff.7, 9v.
[2] Bodleian Library, Ashmole MS. 824/XV, ff.152, 157v; Button, *Algiers Voyage*, 10 November 1620, 10 February 1621, 9 March 1621.

arrival the winds were contrary, preventing him from using fireships that were the basis of his plan of attack. Each day's delay strengthened the enemy and made surprise less likely. When finally launched, the assault was in less than ideal conditions, yet it almost succeeded; but for a change of wind and rain at the last moment, the fireships would have destroyed the pirate fleet. For 20 days thereafter, as Mansell noted sadly, the contrary winds prevented a second attempt.[1]

In addition to weather, operations of the fleet were inhibited by problems of communication. Although Mansell was able to use Spanish ports to rest men and obtain water and some food, he was still very much dependent on England for major items of supply and money. Being at the end of a very long supply line made matters worse. Some communications were sent by sea and therefore dependent on variable factors such as wind, weather, speed of the ship, and directness of the course. Other correspondence went overland for much of the way and was routed through the English embassy in Spain.[2] Journey times varied considerably, but on average it took about a month for a letter to or from Mansell to arrive. Therefore almost two months lapsed between request and reply. Letters were intercepted, lost, or simply delayed. In writing to Aston on 24 April 1621, Mansell thanked the ambassador for sending on a letter from his wife, but added that many packets which had been sent overland had not been received.[3]

The problems of the fleet were exacerbated by the lack of facilities available in Spanish ports. Only after several months at sea did Mansell discover that Cadiz was the only port that could supply the fleet.[4] Also, a basic ignorance of the geography of the Mediterranean hindered the fleet. In writing to Buckingham on 13 January 1621, Mansell admitted that he had been misinformed: the distances were greater than he had been led to believe, the seas more open, and the harbours not as good as he expected.[5]

Communications were made worse by the constant movement

---

[1] BL, Harl. MS. 1581, f.72.
[2] The volume of letters in the Aston papers attests to the embassy being used as a conduit. See, for example, BL, Add. MS. 36,445, f.82, postscript by Buckingham directing Aston to send on letter.
[3] BL, Add. MS. 36,445, ff.102v–103. For an example of the time it took for correspondence, see ibid., f.82. Buckingham's letter took seven weeks to reach Mansell.
[4] Ibid., f.154.
[5] BL, Harl. MS. 1581, f.70.

of the fleet. Letters were sent to Cartagena only to find that the fleet had sailed to Malaga. No suitable base of operations had been arranged nor a line of communications fixed before the fleet set out. The difficulties arising from poor communications are graphically displayed in a letter from Mansell to Cranfield, dated 22 January 1621:

> I find my instructions & the Articles of Treaty delivered me for direction by His Majestys commandments; that His Majesty intends to continue the employment of forces in these parts, for the space of 3 years; my late direction from my Lord Admiral is that I shall continue these ships under my charge for six months longer; In which direction, I neither receive order to return home with the ships under my charge when the next supply shall within two months of expiration, nor order to repair to any place to expect further direction. I beseech you to be pleased to take into your consideration the many dangers I may happen by the delay of a direction to a late hour in my employment thus remote, but especially of this nature which must ever alter my intentions & purposes, as the enemies I am to pursue I shall alter their courses.
>
> It is not contrary winds that I fear, though they may keep back a direction sent by sea three months, nor intercepting of letters overland, but my certain knowledge that no directions can be safely sent unto me after I have filled my ships and received in my victuals, and once put to sea from the Christian shore for being resolved in my intention to spend most of this summer on the Turkish shore, I know not whither the pirates may lead me & therefore I must entreat your favours, out of the interest you have in all his Majestys employments by reason of the affection you bear to this above all others tending to the public good, if you will be pleased to move my Lord Admiral, for this bearers sudden dispatch, who I have directed to return to this place, where I will leave order for his safe passage to Majorca where God willing I purpose to settle to sea: and that by him I may perceive direction for my repair home with His Majestys fleet, or direction in what place I shall attend His Majestys further pleasure – the 15th of July – for by that time I must of necessity . . . be forced either to bear up for England or repair to some certain place where I may careen the ships, & cherish and relieve the sick men if it be His Majestys pleasure to have these ships to continue for any longer time.

... And seeing I have ffalme[?fain] casually to name the place I cannot but let you understand what wounds it hath given this service that misinformation from some seaman which hath procured the direction of going to Malaga to receive our supplies.[1]

The incident mentioned in the last paragraph clearly angered Mansell for he wrote of it several times. On setting out, the captains of the resupply ships received orders to go to Malaga. They would go no further, refusing to obey Mansell's order. In the end he was forced to bring the fleet to Malaga to get the much-needed supplies.[2]

Poor communications between the Mediterranean fleet and London were not the only source of trouble. A lack of effective communications between English and Spanish officials made matters worse. A little over a month before the fleet set sail, Aston observed that 'the rules of this conjunction are yet so imperfect as in mine opinion Sir Robert Mansell must be fain to undertake the work alone without any joint assistance from the Spaniards . . . .'.[3] There is nothing in the evidence to suggest that a detailed plan was ever worked out. Only the vague pronouncements of the early September 1620 articles 'touching the joining of His Majesty's fleet with this King's' had been agreed. The first version of the draft articles called for two fleets of 20 ships (14 English and 6 Spanish within the Straits; 14 Spanish and 6 English in the Atlantic), but in the final version this was modified to read, 'It is likewise now thought better that the fleets keep their courses each one by itself, unless it shall fall out that necessity compel one commander to require ships of the other'.[4] When Mansell arrived at Gibraltar at the end of October, he met with a Spanish admiral but little was decided other than that Mansell would operate within the Straits while the Spanish would concentrate their forces in the Straits and Atlantic.[5]

Until December there was virtually no communication between the fleets; until that time there appeared to be little need for a close co-ordination. Mansell's voyage to Algiers demonstrated the weakness of this approach. First, the suspicions of the Spanish

[1] KAO, U 269 ON 6874.
[2] BL, Add. MS. 36,445, f.102. Supplies were three months late well as at the wrong place. Mansell had sent orders over a month earlier to resupply ships: ibid., f.67.
[3] PRO, SP 94/24/11v.
[4] BL, Add. MS. 36,445, ff.11–14.
[5] PRO, SP 94/24/f.124.

were aroused when they saw the English fleet peacefully anchored in the road of Algiers and learned that the commander was ashore holding discussions with the pirate leaders. For several months this incident poisoned relations and fuelled the fears present in each court. Only after letters from Madrid to London, London to Mansell, Mansell to London, and London back to Madrid, were suspicions allayed. As Aston reported on 22 May 1621, the Spanish had expected Mansell to attack Algiers and thus began to doubt the fleet's intentions; only when they learned that Mansell was prohibited from assaulting the town and that the English intentions 'were only the rooting out and destroying of that base and wicked kind of people' were they satisfied.[1]

But during this period Mansell realized that he would need small fast ships and galleys if he was to deal with the pirates successfully. However, when he requested ships and galleys on his return from Algiers in January 1621, the Spanish response was vague.[2] This cautious response of the Spanish may not have been a reflection of uncertainty about Anglo-Spanish relations or even about the intentions of Mansell's fleet. It may simply have been a reflection of their naval strength and fleet policy. On 21 January 1621, Aston wrote to Carleton that the Spanish were reducing the number of galleys they had in commission from 18 to 10; this retrenchment was 'due to the great charge and little usefulness' of the galleys.[3]

By the middle of March 1621, Mansell learned from Aston that the Spanish Minister of War had agreed to supply a number of galleys, but neither the date nor place of collection was communicated.[4] By this time Mansell had obtained three ships from the local Spanish commander and resolved to sail for Algiers with or without the galleys.[5] In any case, Mansell wrote that he would not postpone his forthcoming operation against the pirates any longer.

In the summer of 1621, Spanish officials again attempted to assist Mansell. On 6 July, while Mansell was refitting the fleet at Cadiz, it was suggested that he should meet with Spanish naval officials at some convenient point between Seville and Madrid to co-ordinate efforts. Mansell's reply, dated 21 July, displays a note of indifference which seems curious considering the importance

[1] BL, Add. MS. 36,445, f.136v.
[2] Ibid., f.9; PRO, SP 94/24/f.100.
[3] PRO, SP 94/24/f.91.
[4] BL, Add. MS. 36,445, f.66
[5] Ibid., f.102v.

placed earlier on the need for galleys and other forms of Spanish aid. He wrote that though he had hoped to meet representatives of the Council of War, he no longer had the time for discussions of matters of joint operational interest. Instead, he intended to set sail with the ships at hand and put his trust in the judgement and affection of the Spanish General appointed by the Council.[1]

As well as serving as an example of inadequate communications, the correspondence concerning the galleys highlights another fundamental weakness of the expedition: the lack of the right types of ship. For close blockades, galleys or similar oar-powered, shallow-draft ships were mandatory. By the early 17th century, England no longer possessed galleys, and the correspondence that preceded the expedition contains no indication that the Admiralty or Trinity House advisers had a proper appreciation of the value of such ships in warfare in the Mediterranean.

Mansell had to be content with the royal men-of-war and armed merchantmen. Two small and fairly nimble pinnaces were authorized and built for the expedition, but they were not completed in time to sail with the fleet and only arrived in the Mediterranean six months later.[2] Taken as a whole, the fleet was only partially suited for the tasks it was called on to perform. The royal men-of-war gave the fleet a marked superiority in a defensive sense: the fleet would not suffer defeat at the hands of the pirates. These ships were also useful in operations against fortifications where they could provide covering fire and block a harbour entrance with their guns. The tactical situation called for an anvil and hammer approach. The royal men-of-war could act as an anvil and therefore were useful, but the fleet never possessed a hammer: quick, nimble, shallow-draft ships or galleys to drive the pirate vessels up against the guns of the men-of-war or seal tight a blockade.[3] Mansell claimed that if he had had galleys, he could have taken 70 pirate vessels.

As well as being partly of the wrong type, the expedition's ships were poorly prepared or defective. As soon as the fleet set sail, weaknesses became apparent, and more were revealed after a few months at sea. On 8 February 1621, Sir Richard Hawkins informed the Lord High Admiral of the sorry state of the fleet:

---

[1] Ibid., f.183v.
[2] PRO, SP 71/1/ff.27–28, letter of Mansell, 17 January 1620/1, shows how important pinnaces were. See also BL, Harl. MS. 1581, ff.70–1. Their arrival was several months late: Harl. MS. 1581, f.238v.
[3] BL, Add. MS. 36,445, f.133–133v.

if it pleases His Majesty to resolve upon a second supply under correction that will be fit to send other ships in places of the *Lyon* and *Vanguard & Rainbow* for they are very unfit for these seas being very laboursome and unable to carry out their lower tier of ordnance in any gale of winds and the latter two hardly be careened without which they cannot be cleansed or made fit to do service and that these ships should be called home in the winter time I assure Your Lordship they would be in great danger. The *Reformation*, the *Convertine*, and the *Antelope* are good ships and therefore more fit to be continued. The *Lyon* is weak about the bows and in any foul weather labours much.[1]

Hawkins was not given to exaggeration and when he declared several of the ships to be 'very unfit' or, as in the case of the *Lion*, 'weak about the bows', his description understates the deplorable condition of the ships, as the following description will make clear. A month after Hawkins's letter, Mansell included in one of his letters the sworn testimony of the master carpenter and survey commission. Among the faults of the *Lion* they noted were the following:

> beams of the main orlop too labour[some?], the main pillars ratch [wrench?] their bolts in pieces & some of their standers too labour; the bows very weak, the inward building insufficient for strengthening the same, & the hooks to slender, & the false stem decayed, & the hauce pieces imperfect by reason whereof all the foreparts so laboureth especially in a head sea, as enforceath continual pumping; the second orlop is very laboursome both of insufficient building fore and aft, & also for the want of knees, which are but singly placed & and very thin in distance; the upper works generally very weak, the timbers thin & of small scantling & weakly kneed, by reason whereof all places are so weak, that notwithstanding the continual caulking, yet in the least foul weather, it laboureth all that oakum out of the seams again.[2]

The survey commission went on to warn that the ship was unsafe and that it would be hazarding both ship and the men if she were

[1] BL, Harl. MS. 1581, f.238v.
[2] BL, Add. MS. 36,445, f.68. 'Standers' are standards; 'hooks' are breasthooks; and 'hauce pieces' are hawse pieces: all provide strength to the hull.

kept abroad in winter. Many letters contain comments on the unfit nature of the ships. For example, on 6 July 1621 Mansell complained about the poor state of the fleet in a terse note, adding that, besides the four already sent home, he had dispatched five more merchantmen because they were so unserviceable.[1]

Inadequate support and at times negligent treatment of the men also hurt the expedition. Warships of the period were notoriously foul and unhealthy places, but even experienced seamen such as Mansell and Hawkins remarked on the exceptionally sickening stench found in the holds of the ships of the fleet and of the pitiful condition of the seamen who lived, worked, and fought aboard them. In March 1621, for example, Mansell wrote:

> It may please your Honour to understand, that the great sickness and mortality wherewith it hath pleased Almighty God to visit this fleet hath proceeded from no other cause then the Nastiness of the poor men for the want of clothes to shift them, and now that there is 6 months and more already expired, and order come for supplies for six months more, I find no mention of any means sent unto them, either out of their wages already due, or by any of imprest for that to come now any refreshment at all to relieve them.[2]

Although this quotation is cited to illustrate the pitiful condition of the men, it is worth noting that Mansell was in no doubt that the fault lay with the naval administration which failed to supply the fleet adequately. It is also worth noting that Mansell did not address his complaints to the Lord High Admiral, his normal channel for communication. Mansell states specifically that he hopes Calvert will remedy the errors of those 'at home' that have caused the men and service to suffer. This was not the only occasion Mansell felt compelled to seek redress from those outside the naval administration. On 22 January 1621, Mansell wrote a letter in a similar vein to Cranfield in which he explained the inadequacies of supply, adding '& therefore I must entreat your favours, out of the interest you have in all His Majestys employments by sea, & out of the affection you bear for this, above all others tending to the public good, that you will move my Lord Admiral for this bearer's sudden dispatch'.[3]

---

[1] Ibid., f.164v.
[2] PRO, SP 94/24/f.124.
[3] KAO, U 269 ON 6874.

Inadequate supplies were a problem. At one point Mansell wrote that he was in desperate need of everything but anchors.[1] Inadequate supply affected the health of the men. At times, sickness reached truly epidemic proportions. In January 1621, Mansell wrote that over 400 were seriously ill.[2] Six months later over 600 were listed as being too sick for action.[3] There is no evidence as to the total number of men lost in the course of the expedition but at least two captains died during the voyage. A measure of illness may be found in Mansell's request early in 1621 for a physician and two surgeons, the cost of which the officers and men were willing to cover out of their pay.[4]

When the ships reached Spanish ports, sick men were put ashore in large numbers with the local officials providing houses where the men could be treated and recover if possible. At times the fleet was so weakened by sickness that it was unable to set sail. For example, on 21 March 1621 Mansell wrote that he was unable to leave for Malaga because not enough men were fit to crew the ships.[5]

Illness and inadequate supply affected morale. On more than one occasion Mansell observed how dispirited the men had become.[6] His comments contained no criticism of the men; he vented his anger only against those in England who had let them down. Hawkins also commented on the sickness and lamentable condition of the men, adding that 'I think your Lordship [Buckingham] would do His Majesty an acceptable service and yourself much honour to move Him that some supply might be sent of four or five months pay which will be a great encouragement for them to be forward in any difficult attempt and relieve their necessities to keep them clean and in health'.[7]

The lack of pay troubled the men as well and serves as an example of the type of administrative incompetence or blindness which undermined operations of the fleet. For months, nobody was paid because the paymasters in the office of the Treasurer of

---

[1] Ibid.; BL, Add. MS. 36,445, ff.64–5.
[2] KAO, U 269 ON 6874.
[3] BL, Add. MS. 36,445, f.168v.
[4] KAO, U 269 ON 6874.
[5] Ibid., ON 6755. BL, Add. MS. 36,445, f.65, speaks of a need for more men indicating that they did not last long in the foul air of the ships.
[6] For example, see Mansell's comments in BL, Add. MS. 36,445, f.168v.
[7] BL, Harl. MS. 1581, f.238v.

the navy were unable to issue payments until they had received and examined the muster books, which were on board the ships in the Mediterranean.[1]

Mansell's own health suffered little and his spirits held up remarkably well judging by expressions of confidence contained in his letter, but by the end of the expedition frustration with problems of supply and pay seems to have tempered his optimism. When he received a picture of James and the princes, he wrote that this gift had 'infused a new life into me'.[2]

Much of the anguish was brought on, in Mansell's words, by 'the unseasonable sending of the supplies by piecemeal'.[3] The original provisioning of the fleet was inadequate. Much of the victuals loaded on board were 'stinking, mouldy, and undersize',[4] and the leaky condition of the hulls caused even further losses. Hawkins informed Buckingham that one ship, the *Vanguard*, had lost 30 barrels of gunpowder and match (of which they were short) to dampness 'through the negligence of the carpenters by a leak'.[5]

Though it was intended to keep the fleet in the Mediterranean for a year or more, it left England with less than six months' supplies. Consequently, Mansell was utterly dependent on adequate supplies being sent out. As indicated above, the resupply ships were late setting out and did not arrive until almost three months after they were expected.[6] When at last they arrived in the Mediterranean, they anchored at a port some distance from the fleet and refused to sail further, leaving Mansell to sail to Malaga to collect these supplies.

After six months at sea, the fleet was in need of almost everything. The ships were short of powder and needed fresh sails and rigging. The men were short of food, stockings, shirts and shoes. In January 1621, Mansell wrote to Cranfield that they were desperately short of supplies and that over 400 of his men were weak and becoming more so daily. He wrote that they had begun to eke out their beer; much had putrified and had earlier been cast overboard. To Cranfield he pleaded that order be given for beer to be sent in every ship that sailed for the Straits; as Mansell put it:

---

[1] KAO, U 269 ON 6874. This was a problem that the navy did not completely solve until the 19th century.
[2] PRO, SP 94/24/ff.124–5.
[3] Ibid. Also KAO, U 269 ON 6755, and BL, Add. MS. 36,445, ff.64–5, in which Mansell blames lack of and lateness of supplies for several months' inaction.
[4] BL, Add. MS. 36,445, f.163v.
[5] BL, Harl. MS. 1581, f.238v.
[6] BL, Add. MS. 36,445, ff.64–64v, 168v–169.

Our sick men by the hundreds at a time cries out for English beer which makes me beseech you however that some small proportion of small beer may be brewed purposely to continue long.[1]

In the absence of good English beer and other supplies from home, the fleet had to purchase what it could from Spanish ports.[2] But this expedient posed problems. For example, closest Spanish ports were too small or lacked sufficient supplies or facilities to maintain a fleet of almost 2700 men. Of the Spanish ports, only Cadiz had sufficient facilities for a fleet of the size of Mansell's.

But even attempts to obtain needed supplies from the Spanish were hindered by inadequate arrangements by those in England. Merchant captains had been sent with insufficient funds to pay for provisions.[3] Some letters of credit were refused by the Spanish. A £1500 bill of exchange drawn on Philip Burlamachi was refused. Those that had been accepted went unpaid at home to the further detriment of the fleet. The Privy Council had to write to Leate and Abbot, the leading merchants, to honour these letters.[4] At one point the captains of the fleet had to engage themselves personally in order to obtain supplies for the fleet.[5] Financial support did not improve during the course of the expedition despite Mansell's frequent complaints and pleas. Near the end of the voyage on 25 July, he wrote that he had only four days' victuals left, and neither money nor credit left to purchase supplies, a statement that alone does much to indict those responsible for supporting the expedition.[6]

After the expedition was over, some commentators accused the Spaniards of not supporting the English fleet, but there is no evidence to support this contention. Spanish ministers wrote to local officials indicating that they should supply the English.[7] With one or two early exceptions, possibly the result of misunder-

---

[1] KAO, U 269 ON 6874.
[2] PRO, SP 94/24/f.124v; KAO, U 269 ON 6755.
[3] BL, Add. MS. 36,445, f.168–168v.
[4] PRO, SP 14/123/49; BL, Add. MS. 36,445, f.64. Mansell wasted a month trying to settle Burlamachi's and Smith's bills of exchange.
[5] PRO, SP 94/24/f.124v.
[6] BL, Add. MS. 36,445, f.187. In ibid., ff.207v–208, Mansell relates that supplies had not arrived and the fleet's victuals had been exhausted two days previously.
[7] PRO, 31/12/23, f.74, letter from Gondomar to Spanish official directing him to assist Mansell; BL, Add. MS. 36,444, f.229, Mansell reports that Spanish port officials had received orders to render him aid.

standings, Mansell's letters support the extent of Spanish co-operation. On 21 July 1621, for example, he wrote that all was ready 'by reason of the great forwardness that all the officers of His Catholic Majesty in this place, & especially the General of the Armada, have expressed in furnishing us with all necessaries for our dispatch, at the same prices that are usually paid by his Catholic Majesty's ships'.[1] In the Aston papers is an itemized bill from the Veedor General at Cadiz for almost £2000-worth of supplies and a request that money be sent for payment since the Veedor received no money and furnished the supplies on his own credit.[2]

It is clear that the difficulties encountered by Mansell's fleet are not caused by Spanish ministers nor local officials. The responsibility for the failure of the fleet to achieve its objectives rests with those who formulated the flawed strategy and compounded their negligence by failing to supply the fleet adequately. At the time, Mansell was criticized for his leadership of the expedition, and some of these criticisms seem justified, at least for the early part of the voyage when his operations appear to have lacked a clear purpose or pointed tactical approach. This is the period when he was 'scouring' the seas. Subsequently, however, his attempt to destroy the pirate fleet within the Mole was well conceived and suffered primarily from ill-fortune, not incompetence. For the last half of the expedition, his efforts were hamstrung by inadequate supplies and ships. Time and effort was spent looking for victuals or equipment from Spanish sources instead of engaging the enemy.

In the end it must be said that the fleet accomplished little of lasting value.[3] The western Mediterranean and Atlantic were largely free from pirate attacks – or, to be more accurate, attacks on English ships – during the time the fleet was operating. In one of his letters, Mansell gave a fair summary of his accomplishments:

> I am sure I have chased more pirates in this short time of my employment then the Spanish & Dutch fleets have done in two years, & if I have not fetched them up it hath not been my fault,

---

[1] BL, Add. MS. 36,445, f.183. Mansell's letters are filled with praise for the supplies and support given him by the Spanish: for example, ibid., ff.67, 187.
[2] Ibid., f.209.
[3] Probably one of the most significant long-term benefits of the expedition was the introduction of a new variety of apricot brought back by or for John Tradescant: *The Agricultural History of England and Wales, IV, 1500–1640*, ed. J. Thirsk, p. 196.

yet I have forc'd them out of my limits, where they daily used to commit their rapines, to seek their preys in other men's walks, so that these coasts have not had news of one pirate for divers months past.[1]

Had this achievement been lasting, Mansell would have done a good service, but as it was, the respite provided by his fleet was only temporary. By November 1621 reports were beginning to arrive in London of a recrudescence of pirate activity.[2]

---

[1] BL, Add. MS. 36,445, f.102.
[2] PRO, SP 94/24/f.323, reports 30 English sail taken, 16–20 from Bristol; SP 14/123/46 reports 57 taken. Mansell anticipated this result if extirpation was not effected: BL, Add. MS. 36,445, f.65. In March 1622 it was reported that 'In the Exchange there is lamenting for the loss of more English ships which have been taken by the pirates to the value, as it is reported, of £40,000': Berkshire Record Office, Trumbull MS. Alph. VII, f.50.

7
CAPTIVITY AND REDEMPTION

If Mansell's expedition proved nothing else, at the very least it showed that suppressing the Barbary pirates would not come easily or cheaply.[1] A very large sum of money had been expended,[2] and the government and people of England had few benefits to show. Before reaching any conclusions on the merits of the government's policy of attempting to suppress pirates, one needs first to determine the economic and social costs of piracy.

Surviving records do not provide exact figures of the cost of piracy *per se*, but enough material is extant to develop reasonably accurate estimates.[3] As a first step, one can look at the number of

---

[1] The Chancellor of the Exchequer put the cost at £64 585: Diary of Sir William Spring (Yale Transcript), 11 March 1624. I wish to thank Professor C.S.R. Russell for this reference.

[2] There were other costs, such as political costs, and these will be discussed later in Chapters 9 and 10.

[3] Reports of seizure by pirates are scattered in a wide variety of records, and although there are some general estimates of ships lost and captives held by the pirates, the accuracy of these reports requires careful scrutiny. For example, in his autobiography, the Reverend Devereux Spratt, a former captive, relates that he was informed by the armadors of Sallee that 1700 ships had been brought into that port alone in recent years: *Autobiography of the Rev. D. Spratt, who died at Mitchelstown, Co. Cork, 1688*, ed. T.A.B. Spratt, p. 2. Other estimates appear more reasonable. Henry Robinson, best known for his mercantilist writings, estimated that 4000 English captives were in Barbary in 1642: H. Robinson, *Libertas or Reliefe to the English Captives in Algier*, pp. 4–5. Robinson was a Levant Company merchant and had much firsthand knowledge about trade and shipping in the Mediterranean having resided in Leghorn in the 1620s. Although his figure was not substantiated, it is close to that given in parliament on 1 March 1641. In parliament many loss figures were bandied about, especially in the Commons in the 1620s, but the figures were seldom precise and their basis is unknown. On 26 February 1626, for example, Mr Whitby told the House that there were 2000 English persons held captive in Barbary. Cambridge University Library, MS. Dd.

ships lost to pirates. No single source provides comprehensive information on losses, but one can begin by examining the number of English ships taken by Algiers since this was the main pirate base and since documentation on the port is relatively complete because an English consul or representative of the Levant Company resided there for much of the 17th century. In addition to the usual commercial and political functions, these officials informed the government of the number of ships and captives brought into Algiers. Not all of their reports survive, but enough are extant to establish the level of English losses.

For the years 1627 to 1640, four lists are available. Two are among the State Papers Foreign, Barbary in the Public Record Office: one dated 21 October 1627 lists the ships brought into port; each ship is recorded by name and the master given.[1] A second list covers the period April 1629 to January 1640 in much the same way but also provides the exact date the ship was brought into port as well as the number of captives taken from each vessel.[2] With a few exceptions, this list also includes details on the port of origin or destination of the captured vessel and the nature and value of the goods on board. A few entries contain information on the capture or about the subsequent disposition of the ship, cargo, or crew. The British Library holds a third list which records all ships brought into Algiers between 14 February 1638 and 26 April 1640.[3] In most cases this list includes the name of the ship, home port, the master, and the day the ship arrived in Algiers. Unfortunately, it does not include any information on crew size, cargo and final disposition of the ship. Lastly, the House of Lords Record Office has a list of ships captured between 18 May 1639 and 15 January 1640.[4] This list does not provide information on the exact date of capture, the cargo, the home port or the tonnage of the ships, but does give figures for the number of persons taken captive.

When pieced together, these lists reveal a startling picture:

12–20, diary of Bulstrode Whitelocke, f.83. Yet only two days later, Mr Delbridge informed the Commons that 'above 2,000' English were held captive in Sallee alone. Ibid., f.57.

[1] PRO, SP 71/1/f.77.
[2] PRO, SP 71/1/f.157.
[3] BL, Add. MS. 5500, f.7, 21 April 1640. I wish to thank Dr P.E.C. Croot for this reference.
[4] HLRO, Main Papers, list dated 5 March 1641.

between 1627 and 1640 at least 164 ships and 2828 persons were taken captive by the pirates of Algiers.[1] These figures alone attest to the magnitude of the threat of the Barbary pirates. Yet these lists are by no means comprehensive. In the first place, although they overlap, none covers the period from the end of October 1627 to the beginning of April 1629. If losses for this period were only average, then approximately 20 ships and 400 men should be added, making 184 ships lost and 3228 captives.[2]

Even when losses for the period 1627 to 1629 are included, the total figures underestimate the true extent of damage to English shipping in this period because the lists refer solely to ships and captives brought into Algiers.[3] Because no English agents were resident in Tripoli, Tunis, Safi, or Sallee, there are no lists of ships or captives brought into those ports. This deficiency is especially important because Sallee came to rival Algiers from the late 1620s as the leading pirate base for attacks on English shipping.[4] However, one source gives fairly reliable figures, at least for those taken to Sallee in the mid-1620s. In March 1626, the Privy Council ordered Trinity House officers to provide information on English losses to the pirates of Sallee. The officers concluded that some 1200 to 1400 English subjects had been taken captive.[5] This was

---

[1] The totals come from adding the figures found in the above-cited lists. Where a list simply indicates 'boats' the figure of two has been used, though the actual number might be greater.
[2] We know from Roe's appraisal that the peace was not holding in these months and that it is likely that the average number of ships were taken. See below, Chapter 8.
[3] These lists occasionally indicate that ships of Algiers brought some prizes into other ports, such as Mamora or Tunis. For example, PRO, SP 71/1/f.157, entry of 8 April 1632: the *Falcon* of London, sunk in Tunis Bay and prisoners brought to Algiers. Also, *Hearts Desire* of London, carried to Sallee: SP 71/1/f.77. Frizell wrote 'Many other wrongs there is which are not here mentioned that were [taken] at sea which are unknown to us in Algiers'. One of the most unfortunate of those taken to Tunis was the son of William Wood of London. After three years' captivity he was ransomed by his father who borrowed over £73 from Nicholas Leate. On his voyage back to London, young Wood was taken by a pirate of Algiers and sold again into slavery: PRO, SP 16/14/82.
[4] PRO, SP 16/330/10. 4 August 1636, Giles Penn to Secretary of State Edward Nicholas: 'of the heathen moors of Sallee, of whom there come such grievous complaints of taking men, women, and children, besides ships and goods, to the number of 1,000 within these six months, of England and Ireland'.
[5] Trinity House, Transactions, f.93v. (26 March 1626). Most had been captured within 20 or 30 miles of the west country ports.

not just a rough guess but the result of a survey based on (1) a questioning of the three most recent returnees from Sallee, (2) a study of the petitions received in recent years, and (3) an examination of the merchants who had visited Sallee for the purpose of ransoming captives.

Between 1627 and 1630 attacks upon English shipping by Salleemen were greatly reduced, following the embassy of John Harrison; but at the start of the 1630s, the Sallee pirates returned to prey on English merchantmen, and soon the level of attacks was as high or higher than in the mid-1620s. If losses in the ten or eleven years following the Trinity House estimate were equal to those of the earlier period, then in all between 2400 and 2800 persons were captured by Salleemen. And if manning levels of the ships taken by Sallee were the same as those taken by the pirates of Algiers, then between 120 and 140 ships were lost in addition to those taken by the pirates of Algiers. No precise figures are available for the other pirate ports, but scattered evidence shows that throughout the early 17th century pirates operating out of Tunis, for example, attacked English ships,[1] and in the Commonwealth period the Mediterranean squadron of Admiral Blake made several efforts to redeem captives from Tetuan, Tunis, and Tripoli, as well as Algiers.[2] In all, 500 persons – maybe as many as 1000 – were taken by other Barbary ports.[3]

When pieced together, all this evidence suggests that for the period 1622 to 1642 above 300 ships and around 7000 or more English subjects were taken by the Barbary pirates. As for figures on losses prior to 1622, only rough estimates are available. For example, a deposition in a High Court of Admiralty case, dated 1 January 1612, lists 17 ships from west country ports recently taken captive,[4] and when at Algiers, Mansell himself claimed that he had evidence that 150 ships had been taken in the previous five

---

[1] Ibid., f.5v. (6 March 1609), f.65 v. (15 September 1621); PRO, SP 71/1/f.157.
[2] *The Letters of Robert Blake together with supplementary documents*, ed. J.R. Powell (Navy Records Society, LXXVI), pp. 276, 318.
[3] The ports of the eastern Mediterranean were seldom used as bases for attacking English ships largely because trade in this area was monopolized by the Levant Company, whose ships were strong enough to fend off attacks by the smaller, lightly-built vessels favoured by the pirates. See, R. Davis, *The Rise of the English Shipping Industry: In the Seventeenth and Eighteenth Centuries*, pp. 46, 59.
[4] PRO, HCA 1/47/f.261, 25 January 1612.

years.[1] Even if one does not take these figures at face value, the evidence suggests that losses for the period 1616 to 1622 were substantial and if only at a rate similar to that of the following 20 years came to more than 90 ships and 1800 men.[2]

When all the figures for various ports and periods are put together, English losses to the Barbary pirates come to a staggering total of approximately 400 ships and above 8000 persons. The practical and political effect was much greater than these bare totals suggest, for the losses were heavily concentrated geographically. Almost all the ships taken by the pirates came from London or the south-west ports. This concentration can be seen in Table 4 in the list of losses between 18 May 1639 and 15 January 1640.[3]

Other lists show a similar geographic distribution, though the pattern is even more marked, with Dartmouth, Plymouth, Barnstaple, and Bristol showing proportionately greater losses.[4]

From this evidence, it may also be inferred that merchants and mariners engaged in the southern trades, i.e., those to Biscay, Spain, Portugal, and the Mediterranean suffered most heavily. The lists also indicate that almost all losses were of relatively small, lightly-manned ships, though only rarely do these lists provide explicit information on tonnage. However, crew size may be used as a rough guide to calculate tonnage. Using the closest approximations found in Ralph Davis's study – 6.7 tons per man for ships sailing to Cadiz and Malaga[5] – the average size of the ships taken by the pirates in the above list is 121 tons (slightly less

---

[1] PRO, SP 71/1/f.91: states that ships were first taken in 1609; over 70 English ships were taken between 1609–11; and that 466 were taken in the period 1609–15. PRO, SP 105/147/f.76 states that 100 ships had been taken since 1615 *for which there were records*. PRO, SP 71/1/f.21v indicates that 150 ships had been taken to Algiers in the five years prior to 1621.

[2] While there is no evidence to confirm or refute these claims, it is worth noting that the rate of capture is higher than in the period 1 April 1629 to 2 November 1638, PRO, SP 71/1/f.157, though much less than in the period 1639 to 1641. Also, in assessing these estimates, one must remember that it was only in the 1620s that Sallee became a major base for pirates; until then attacks were restricted to vessels in the Mediterranean, a circumstance that reduced the number of English targets available. The extension of operations beyond the Straits meant that more time was spent by the pirates in transit and therefore less was available for attacking English ships.

[3] HLRO, Main Papers, 5 March 1641. 'Washford' may be Wexford.

[4] PRO, SP 71/1/ff.77, 157, and indicated in the home towns of redeemed captives listed in J. Dunton, *A true journal of the Sally Fleet, with the proceedings of the voyage*, pp. 42–6; and *A Relation of the Whole Proceedings Concerning the Redemption of the Captives in Argier and Tunis . . . Also the letters from Edmond Cason, Agent for the Parliament there*.

[5] Davis, *Rise of the English Shipping Industry*, pp. 58–9.

Table 4
English losses to the Barbary pirates, 18 May 1639–15 January 1640

Port	Ships	Captives
London	21	586
Dover	3	59
Southampton	6	96
Weymouth	2	47
Lyme	1	13
Topsham	2	19
Dartmouth	6	71
Plymouth	3	19
Milbrooke	6+	109
Fowey	4	22
Barnstaple	6	60
Bristol	1	13
Yarmouth	1	14
King's Lynn	1	8
Dungarvan	2	34
Washford	2+	44
Jersey	1	10
Total	68+	1224

than the overall average of approximately 134 tons per ship), much less than the 200 to 500 ton vessels normally employed by the Levant Company.[1]

Estimates of the value of the ships and goods lost are more difficult to determine. Of the 73 ships included in the list covering April 1629 to January 1640, only eight were given a valuation, and these were ships of above-average size. For example, the cargo of the *Success* of London was valued at £9000. None of the other ships exceeded £5000.[2]

Though precise information on the value of English losses cannot be presented, it is possible to provide a rough estimate which will, at least, show the general magnitude of the problem. If

---

[1] In 1633, the Levant Company employed seven ships between 350 and 600 tons; average tonnage was 420 tons: PRO, SP 105/149/f.42v.

[2] PRO, SP 71/1/f.157. Some of the smallest appear to be no more than fishing boats. The *Hearts Desire* of London, however, was valued at 15 000 Rs/8, or over £30 000: SP 71/1/f.77.

each ship was worth £1500 (£1000 for the vessel with furniture and ordnance,[1] plus £500 (at a minimum) for goods and trading capital), and approximately 400 ships were lost, then the minimum cost in terms of ships and goods, exclusive of lost future revenue or replacement costs, was £600 000. However, this is only an estimate based on average values. To this sum must be added some figure for extraordinary losses, such as the *Rebecca* of London which was lost to the pirates in 1640 off Lisbon with £260 000 in silver on board. Thus, for the period under study, English losses in terms of ships and goods alone come to between £850 000 and £900 000.[2]

In addition to losses for ships and cargoes, one must consider the monetary value of the crewmen made captive. To do this, one might use as an appropriate measure the valuations of the market for captives at Algiers or the sums paid when captives were ransomed. As will be shown shortly, the market price for English captives at Algiers was £40, but to this figure would have to be added transportation, collection charges, and profit. A more realistic cost would be about £45 per head, or approximately £360 000 for 8000 captives.[3] Thus, the direct cost for the ships, goods, and captives lost to the pirates in this period amounts to over £1 000 000 and may have been as high as £1 300 000.[4]

Although these totals are only approximations, derived from a number of sources, a measure of the credibility of the figures may be gleaned from scattered sources. For example, in the late 1630s merchants and officials of the western ports petitioned the Crown

---

[1] The best evidence available on ship and shipping costs is found in Davis, *Rise of the English Shipping Industry*, pp. 338–87; a 120-ton ship for the Malaga trade cost £580 for the vessel and £440 to fit out in 1635; a larger ship, e.g. the *Diamond*, 250 tons, had a capital cost of approximately £1990, and £247 was spent to provide guns and powder for her voyage to the Mediterranean. Freight rates varied according to many factors but for an average Mediterranean voyage in the 1620s or 1630s a rate of about £4 per ton appears to be normal. The value of goods is probably on the low side, see below, for example, the figures for losses for the west country ports in the 1630s where ship and cargo averaged £1727, and these were smaller ships than average and probably did not include any ship or cargo of great value.
[2] *CSPV*, 1640–1642, pp. 24, 32, and notes; BL, Add. MS. 11,045, f.101.
[3] This figure is somewhat lower than that found by E.G. Friedman, *Spanish Captives in North Africa in the Early Modern Age*, for redeemed Spanish captives in Barbary. The cost of redemption for the Spaniards was more than £60 per person. Perhaps more Spanish women or young boys were taken and redeemed for as shown below – they brought a higher price.
[4] For the purposes of comparison, this is greater than the prizes taken by English privateers in the Spanish and French wars, 1625–30. Appleby estimates gross English takings at £800 000 to £900 000: J.C. Appleby, 'English Privateering during the Spanish and French Wars, 1625–30' (unpublished Phd thesis, University of Hull, 1983), p. 270.

for help against the pirates and included very precise information on the damage to their towns and trade; they wrote:

> That there are a great number of Turkish Pirates from Argier and especially from Sally in Barbary which of late years have infested both this and the Irish coasts that they have within these last few years taken from your petitioners four score and 7 sail of ships, that their said ships with their ladings were worth £96,700; That they retain in miserable captivity 1,160 able seamen taken in the said ships, besides which almost 2,000 others of his Majesty's subjects taken in other ships; That your humble petitioners the last summer did not dare to trade in foreign parts, as otherwise they would have done; That your petitioners are exceedingly burdened with the wives and children of those captives.[1]

The exact figures in this petition accord well with the total loss figures produced above. For example, the value of each ship and cargo works out to £1727 per vessel; crew size works out to 20.7 per ship as expected for vessels trading on this route; average tonnage comes to 139 tons per vessel. An extrapolation from these figures suggests total losses would amount to £690 800 for 400 ships and cargo; £360 000 for £8000 crewmen or £1 050 800 in all. If one adds the value of the *Rebecca* to this figure, then the total comes to approximately £1 300 000 – or almost exactly that estimated above.

This petition also directs our attention to another cost not yet considered. The petitioners indicated that they had been forced to withdraw from trade because of the pirates. As early as 1612 there were warnings that merchants were deterred from trading because of pirates. In *Trade's Increase*, Robert Keale advised that commerce with the Mediterranean was being spoiled by pirates, and in 1622 piracy was cited as one of the main reasons for economic decay.[2] Five years later, officials of Poole believed that piracy was the chief cause for the decline of shipping in their port, supporting their case by quoting the customs ledgers. The livelihood of the town was further burdened by having to provide relief for 400 distressed widows and orphans, many of whom were

---

[1] PRO, SP 16/536/97.
[2] J.R. [Robert Kayll or Keale], *The Trades Increase*, p.14; HMC 23, *12th Report, App. i, Cowper MSS*, p. 126.

impoverished as a result of 232 men of the town being held in captivity in Barbary.[1] In similar fashion, Weymouth complained of the great charge for poor relief to the wives, widows, and children of inhabitants held captive in Algiers and Sallee.[2]

Some of the complaints about pirates were, no doubt, exaggerated, as was observed by Sir Henry Mervin, when he wrote to the Privy Council:

> it was usual (in these parts) to fancy the Crescent in any colours, as they did last year by the King's ships which were employed for their safety, and fled from them, filling the country with acclamations of the Turks that had chased them.[3]

But there was a real basis to many of the complaints, as private correspondence, especially that between merchants, discloses. For example, on 26 October 1636 Edmond Percivall wrote to his brother in Bristol:

> I do not advise you to send any cattle over whilst the Turks are so busy, least both your agent and cattle should suffer, there having been a multitude of passengers taken this summer. I hear nothing of Mr. Dobbins. Perhaps Mr. Dampire keeps him back, or it may be fear of the Turks.[4]

Town records and histories of the ports of the south-west, such as those of Exeter for example,[5] frequently show piracy as a cause of trade disruption or decline.

There were other hidden costs. In particular, the costs of protection were significant, though it is difficult to quantify. Ships built for the Levant Company were larger and stronger. Construction costs were driven up by the need to use more and costlier timber; outfitting expenses also increased greatly as larger and more numerous guns had to be mounted. And increased protec-

---

[1] PRO, SP 16/51/55, 56.
[2] PRO, SP 16/61/7. The town's losses were put at £26 000.
[3] PRO, SP 16/345/70.
[4] HMC, 63, *Egmont MSS*, vol. I, p. 90. Also see Chapter 8, p. 189 fn. 3.
[5] W.B. Stephens, *Seventeenth-Century Exeter: A study of industrial and commercial development, 1625-1688*, pp. 35, 59.

tion demanded higher manning levels; costly skilled labour, like gunners, had to be employed. Ships engaged in the southern trades regularly carried larger crews for defence. Since the pay and victuals of the crew made up the largest component of the operating costs of a ship,[1] these were greater for ships sailing in pirate-infested waters. In all, the money needed to protect a ship from pirates was significant and protection costs substantial.

Piracy also drove up insurance costs. Because the registers of marine insurance[2] have not survived, little is known about the English insurance market, but from surviving merchants' correspondence and legal documents, it appears a large portion of the goods of ships trading southwards were regularly covered by insurance. For example, on 23 July 1619 London underwriters wrote a policy in the amount of £320 on a cargo of lead, fish, calf skins, and perpetuanoes[3] carried by the *Dove* of Bristol, taken by the Turks shortly thereafter.[4] A few years later the *Diana* of Sandwich was captured by Turks off Bayonne; part of her cargo was insured for £400.[5] In the years 1622 to 1623 John della Barre, an important London merchant, paid, on average, 5% premiums for insurance to Leghorn.[6] In a more dangerous year, 1635, the same merchant paid 12% for insurance to Malaga; by way of comparison, his insurance in the same year for voyages to Virginia (a longer voyage) was only at a rate of 8.5%.[7] A century later, when the threat of piracy had been reduced, the rate in peacetime for cover on London–Leghorn voyages was only 1.5%.[8] While some of the decline in transportation costs may be attributed to increased productivity, several studies suggest that a reduction in

---

[1] Davis, *Rise of the English Shipping Industry*, pp. 338–9.
[2] They were kept from 1574 at least until the 1690s.
[3] A durable woollen textile.
[4] PRO, HCA 1/48/f.287.
[5] PRO, HCA 1/49/f.24.
[6] PRO, HCA 30/635, the della Barre account book: in October 1623 a voyage from the Canaries to London was insured by della Barre at a rate of 4.5%; in June of 1622 the rate for a voyage to Livorno and Genoa was 6%; by way of contrast, in the same period voyages to the Atlantic coast of Spain were insured for little more than 2%.
[7] Davis, *Rise of the English Shipping Industry*, pp. 378–9.
[8] Ibid., pp. 319, 377–9 suggests that insurance rates were halved between the early 17th and early 18th century. He attributes this fall to the clearing of the oceans 'of pirates, and the Moorish corsairs were compelled to grant immunity to English ships' [as the result of the use or threatened use of the Royal Navy]. For more on the deployment of the Royal Navy to further English maritime trade in the Mediterranean in the late 17th century, see S.R. Hornstein, *The Restoration Navy and English Foreign Trade, 1674–1688*, pp. 226, 260–3.

protection costs was the major factor.[1] Declining insurance rates would certainly have contributed to a reduction in transaction costs.

Less obvious were the social costs. Most mariners had relatives in England who depended, either totally or partially, on their income. Testimony of the hardships endured by these captives and their dependants is abundant. Two examples from the borough records of Bodmin, Cornwall highlight the social costs. The first reads, 'Item. given to a poor man that had his tongue cut out by the Turks – 12d'. Another entry reads, 'Item. given a woman, a suckling child and a maid that had a pass from Bristol and had been formerly taken by the Turks – 8d'.[2] Local records contain frequent reference to personal hardship suffered as a result of the pirates. For example, the manor court of Stepney, London contains an account of the case of Jane Beck who had to surrender a copyhold property because her husband William had been taken by pirates.[3]

Because the evidence is incomplete and the cause of hardship often obscured, the social costs of piracy cannot be calculated in a monetary way. Nor is it obvious what measure one might use. But clearly, in addition to those actually taken captive, thousands more suffered as a result of the Barbary pirates. Families suffered a loss of income. For instance, if each of the 8000 mariners earned £20 a year, then approximately £160 000 in income was lost annually. If two-thirds of those captured were never redeemed and spent 12 years of their working life in captivity, their lost wages (£1 279 920) would more than equal the amount for lost shipping and goods. Beyond direct shipping and cargo losses, few of the costs of piracy may be calculated with any precision. Yet from even a cursory examination of the subject, it is obvious that the total cost of piracy for England in the early Stuart period needs to be reckoned in the millions.

In contrast to the evidence on the cost of piracy, that on capture and captivity is richly documented. Judging by the record of ships brought into Algiers, the pirates of the Barbary coast operated all

---

[1] D.C. North, 'Sources of Productivity Change in Ocean Shipping, 1600–1850', *Journal of Political Economy*, LXXXIV (1968), pp. 953–71; G.M. Walton, 'Sources of Productivity Change in American Colonial Shipping, 1675–1775', *Econ Hist Rev*, 2nd series, XX (1967), pp. 67–78.
[2] CRO, Bodmin Borough Accounts, 1635, no. 288; 1637, no. 289. Also Westminster City Archives, E. 23, St Margaret's, Churchwardens' accounts, for similar examples.
[3] BL, Eg. 3006, f.98d. I wish to thank Dr P.E. Croot for this reference.

year round.[1] However, further examination shows that the areas of operations varied during the course of the year. Between November and March, attacks were restricted to the southern seas with most incidents taking place in the Mediterranean or just outside the Straits. Only in the period April to October did the pirates haunt the western approaches or enter the Channel. A few reports survive of Turks in the Thames and Severn estuaries, but these are rare and on investigation it appears that the vessels involved were captained or piloted by renegade Europeans.[2]

In the 1620s and 1630s Turks were reported to be operating from ports in the United Provinces and France. As a part of the agreements struck with the Barbary states, ships of each country were permitted to use the ports of the other. This use was supposed to be restricted to legitimate purposes, but in the mid-1630s French ports were used extensively by the pirates. The English government objected to this and, as discussed later, sent a special embassy to Paris to bring a halt to this practice.[3]

In the course of the 17th century, the type of ship favoured by the pirates changed considerably. Until 1610 or thereabouts, large, oar-driven galleys – the traditional warship of the Mediterranean – were used.[4] However, as the century progressed, use of galleys by the pirates declined and sailing ships, both lateen and square-rigged, came to be employed more frequently. Contemporaries attributed this innovation to Simon Dansker, a northern renegade, who was also said to have taught the pirates how to navigate the Straits and sail the Atlantic where weather made the use of galleys dangerous.

Whatever the source of innovation, by the 1620s the Barbary pirates were using sailing vessels, usually of modest size, i.e., about 80 to 100 tons, and lightly built for speed.[5] The pirates learned to avoid combat with men-of-war or large, 'defensible'

---

[1] PRO, SP 71/1/f.157 indicates that ships were brought into Algiers during every month of the year, though the greatest number occurred between May and November.
[2] Letters of George Lord Carew, p. 62; PRO SP 14/90/24 (included in the October news).
[3] PRO, SP 16/311/24. This subject is dealt with more fully in Chapter 10.
[4] Sometimes these galleys carried as many as 400 men; manpower shortages may have led to their abandonment.
[5] P. Earle, *Corsairs of Malta and Barbary*, pp 58–60. For details on a typical Turkish pirate vessel, see PRO SP 16/328/29 incl. By the late 1650s, the pirates of Algiers were using larger, more heavily armed vessels.

ships such as those employed by the Levant Company.[1] Instead, pirates sought smaller merchantmen and relied on superior speed, stealth, and manpower to catch their prey. The following account of an attack on the *Dolphin* gives an insight into the sort of tactics used by the pirates:

> in the morning watch we had sight of a small sail making from the shore towards us; which drove into our minds some doubt and fear . . . Whereupon our master sent one of our company up the maintop; where he discovered five sail of ships coming up . . . the first booming before the wind . . . Whereupon we immediately made ready our ordnance . . . which being done, we went to prayer, where our master gave us such noble encouragement, that our hearts thirsted to prove success . . . Being within shot of them, our master commanded his gunner to make his level and to shoot; which he did, but missed them all. At which the foremost of them bore up apace, and returned as good as we sent. At about eleven o'clock, they laid us aboard . . . and . . . entered on the larboard quarter . . . but we having a murtherer in the roundhouse, kept the larboard clear . . . but the other ship laid us aboard on the starboard side, and in at quarter they entered . . . with scimitars . . . and other weapons, running to and fro, crying still in the Turkish tongue, 'Yield yourselves! Yield yourselves!' But we, giving them no ear, stood stiffly in our defence, choosing rather to die than to yield, as it is still the nature and condition of all Englishmen; and being thus resolved, some of our men plied our ordnance against them, some playing small shot, some with swords, and half-pike and the like. In the midst of which skirmish our ship was fired . . . the fire being perceived by our enemies to burn outrageously, and thinking that our ship would suddenly be burned to the water; they left us to our fortunes, falling astern from us.[2]

The heroes of the *Dolphin* escaped, but many more were not so lucky. Some were victims of deceit or deception. The crew of the *Supply* of Bristol were captured when 'upon parley [they] were betrayed'. Others in the list of ships brought into Algiers are

---

[1] Davis, *Rise of the English Shipping Industry*, p. 45.
[2] Anon., *A Fight at Sea*, pp. 2–5.

CAPTIVITY AND REDEMPTION

described as 'betrayed', though the form of the betrayal remains unknown.[1]

Craft and guile were also employed by the pirates. For example, from a mariner's deposition in an Admiralty case we learn that:

> upon the 10th day of May . . . 1631, the said ship, following her course towards Cadiz, early in the morning, about break of day, her company espied a ship lying with all her sails struck down . . . the Sally man-of-war, after they espied the said ship, the *William and John*, raised their sails and used all means they could to get wind . . . and lay her aboard.[2]

False colours were also used by the pirates to deceive potential prey. A pamphlet written in 1634 by Nathaniel Knott, a west country mariner, stated that it was impossible to identify a Turk either by the build of the ship or the flag she flew. Sail towards shore (if near a Christian coast) was the best protection because Turks would not follow for fear of being cast away on a hostile coast.[3] In general, this advice may have been sound, but there are many instances of Turkish pirates sailing close to English coasts, and on three occasions they came ashore to take captives. In 1625, Turkish pirates raided Lundy, in 1631 Baltimore, and in 1640 Penzance.[4]

Of these attacks, only the raid on Baltimore was very successful. On 16 June 1631, a party of about 200 Turks and renegades, led by a Dutch turncoat known as Morat Rais, landed at night and carried away 109 men, women, and children.[5] All were brought back to Algiers and sold into slavery. Since then they have become a part of Irish mythology; their fate being celebrated in 1844, for example, by a nationalist poet who wrote:

> The Maid that Bandon gallant sought is chosen for the Dey,
> She's safe – he's dead – she stabbed him in the midst of his

---

[1] PRO, SP 71/1/f.157.
[2] PRO, HCA 13/52/226v.
[3] Knott's pamphlet, dedicated to Archbishop Laud, is in PRO, SP 16/279/106.
[4] National Library of Wales, Wynn of Gaydir MSS, no. 1371, 19 September 1625; PRO, SP 71/1/f.99; SP 16/459/36; *Calendar of State Papers Ireland*, 1625–1632, pp. 621–2.
[5] The best account is H. Barnby, 'The Sack of Baltimore', *Journal of the Cork Historical and Archaeological Society*, LXXIV (1969), pp.101–29. These captives are mentioned frequently in the reports of consul Frizell, e.g., PRO, SP 71/1/ff.124, 135.

Serai; And, when to die a death of fire, that noble maid they bore, She only smiled – O'Driscoll's child – she thought of Baltimore.[1]

The historical record of these events is less dramatic. No dey was killed, at least by an Irish maid, nor were any O'Driscolls taken captive. In fact, the victims were not native Irishmen but Protestant English settlers from the plantation of Thomas Crooke.[2]

A number of captives left narratives, which, when pieced together, provide a full account of the early stages of captivity. First of all, capture did not necessarily bring enslavement. The captain and crew of the *Hopewell* of Rye were set free shortly after being taken in 1620. In a deposition, one of the crew stated that the Turkish captain took pity on them and arranged for the crew to be set adrift in a small boat with enough provisions to reach the Spanish coast.[3] In a similar fashion, several members of the *George Bonaventure* were landed on the coast of Spain.[4] When the pirates took the *Rebecca*, with its cargo of over £260 000 in silver, they were so overjoyed at their good fortune that the surviving crew of the *Rebecca* were set free and given a boat and enough provisions to reach the Spanish coast.[5] Most of the crew of the *Blessing* of London, bound for Alicante in 1619, were as fortunate. Only the cabin boy suffered, being retained by the Turks for 'their Sodomitical use'.[6]

On some occasions, a crew might be able to negotiate their liberty. In 1614, for example, the *Tiger* of Bristol was attacked by an Algerine man-of-war of much greater strength. The crew of the English ship put up such resistance, fighting off the pirates for three hours during which time all but five crew were killed, that in the end an agreement was reached whereby the Turks received the cargo but the ship and crew were allowed to go free.[7] Valour was not always required as the case of the *Phenix*, shows. This 18-gun Bristol ship 'fought not; laden with fish butter, frize bays cloth and other commodities; whose people were set ashore by Lisbon on composition'.[8] Alas nothing more was recorded to illuminate on

[1] Ibid. Barnby, p. 102.
[2] Ibid., pp. 104, 106, 124.
[3] PRO, HCA 1/48/ff.302–3.
[4] PRO, SP 71/1/f.157.
[5] *CSPV*, 1640–1642, pp. 24, 32; BL, Add. MS. 11,045, f.101.
[6] PRO, HCA 1/48/f.295.
[7] PRO, HCA 1/48/ff.22–3.
[8] PRO, SP 71/1/f.157.

the nature of the 'composition', but more is known about the terms made by the *Samson* of London. The master, John Gibbons, 'yielded upon composition which was to save his own liberty with three others he elected'. The other crew members, 38 in all, were sold into slavery after reaching Algiers.[1]

Captivity usually began with an interrogation to determine whether any valuables were hidden on board. The pirates also sought to learn the status and wealth of the prisoners in order to set a sale price or ransom figure. According to James Wadsworth, captivity started in the following way: 'We were carried to the Castle [in Sallee] and there crammed like capons, that we might grow fatter for sale, and being brought to the market were shared amongst them and sold'.[2] More details about the market come from other captives. John Rawlins was brought to Algiers in 1622 where

> the Bashaw had the overseeing of all prisoners . . . who were pesented unto him at their first comming into the harbour; and so he chose one out of every eight, for a present or a fee to himself. The rest were rated by the captains and so sent to the market . . . where, as men sell hackneys in England, we were tossed up and down to see who would give us the most; many came to behold us; sometimes taking us by the hand, sometimes turning us round about, sometimes feeling our brawns and naked arms; and so beholding our prices written in our breasts they bargained for us accordingly; and at last we were all sold.[3]

William Okeley, who was taken in 1639, tells us more about the attitude and interests of his buyers:

> their first policy is to look in the captives' mouths and a good, strong entire set of grinders will advance the price considerably . . . for they know that they who have no teeth, can not eat, can not work . . . The next process is to feel their limbs, as whether

---

[1] Ibid. In 1659 a Dutch captain stated that it was customary for the crew to be freed if the captain would agree to buy back his ship and cargo; until the transaction was completed the captain remained captive: SP 18/202/71.
[2] J. Wadsworth, *The English Spanish Pilgrime, or, a new discoverie of Spanish popery and jesuitical stratagems* (1630 ed.), pp. 39–40.
[3] Anon., *The Famous and Wonderful Recovery of a Ship of Bristol, called the Exchange, from Turkish Pirates of Argier*, p. 5.

there be any fracture, or dislocation in the bones; anything analogical to spavin, or ring-bone, for they will bring down the market wonderfully . . . Age is also considerable . . . they go by general conjectures from the beard, face, or hair . . . But they are very curious in examining the hands; for if they be callous and brawny, they will shrewdly guess that the captives have been inured to labour; if delicate and tender, they will suspect some gentleman or merchant, and then the hopes of good price of redemption makes him saleable.[1]

In 1646, parliament sent Edmund Cason to Algiers to redeem those held captive. His negotiations reveal more about the market process and the price of English captives. Descriptions of the Algiers market indicate that two price figures were used in the sale process. Cason reports that he bought back captives at the 'first price' which was less than the final amount. The first price apparently was something in the nature of a formal offer; the second price included incidentals and was the final amount paid by the buyer.

Cason purchased freedom for 244 captives. Payments ranged from a low of 200 dobles or 43 dollars (for Richard Cockle of Plymouth), up to 1655 dobles or 356¾ dollars (for Elizabeth Alwin of London). The average price was 532 dobles or 114 dollars – about £32 a head. The price paid by Cason, it should be noted, was 'first price', not the usual, higher final price. It should also be kept in mind that the 244 persons redeemed by Cason were probably the cheaper sort, for as he explains:

> I thought to take away the better sort of people first, and the rest afterwards, the which I understood to be the command given me; but it pleased God so to order that I must take away those I could have for cloth and leave the rest till afterwards.[2]

Most contemporary reports suggest that £40 per person was an average rate,[3] though the price of redemption could vary con-

---

[1] W. Okeley, *Eben-ezer; or a small monument of great mercy appearing in the miraculous deliverance of W. Okeley [and others] from . . . slavery* pp. 9–11.
[2] *Relation of Proceedings Concerning the Redemption*, p. 13.
[3] PRO, SP 71/1/f.130 suggests an average ransom cost of £40 per head in 1633. In 1637 Frizell wrote that ransoms cost between 150 to 1600 Rs/8(£30–320): SP 71/1/f.156. In April 1633, when he was negotiating for the release of 83 captives, the average price including various taxes and duties amounted to £58 per person: SP 71/1/f.124.

siderably. On one occasion, Trinity House redeemed 16 captives at less than £9 per head.[1] But at other times the price of redemption came higher. In 1625, William Leg of Milbrooke a captive at Sallee complained about the excessive amount of the ransoms: the smallest was 300 ducats (£112), while as much as 1500 ducats (£562) was being demanded for some captives.[2]

The slave market sale was one of the few experiences that captives had in common; thereafter, life for the captives varied. Those purchased by the local government were sent to the galleys or put to work in the city quarries, on fortifications, or other public building projects. Some captives were used for domestic service or given work in the palace kitchens. Captives sold to private individuals were often put to work in the fields outside the city or employed grinding flour or weaving cloth.[3]

Some captives, those suspected of wealth or possessing a marketable skill, might be bought on speculation, allegedly by resident Jews or Italians. The wealthy were held for ransom, while the skilled were put to work in their trade. Craftsmen could expect to lead a tolerable life in captivity. Often they lodged in their owner's house and dined at the same table. Some were even allowed to retain a part of the money they earned. A lucky few were able to accumulate enough in this way to arrange to buy their own freedom. Even when offered freedom and a return to England, some captives chose to remain in Barbary to carry on their trade as free men.[4]

In general, it appears that young captives were treated with kindness. They were often purchased as a way of honouring Allah: young boys were frequently sent to Alexandria or Constantinople where they might be brought up as good Muslims.[5] Usually these boys or young men were given light duties, for example, many were employed as pages to prosperous men.

There are several documented reports of brutality and attempts

---

[1] Trinity House, Transactions: there are 12 examples between 1609 and 1633 for which a ransom price is given.
[2] *Debates in the House of Commons in 1625*, ed. S.R. Gardiner (Camden Society, New series, VI, 1873), p. 116. In 1658/9 the earl of Inchquin was taken captive and brought to Algiers; £5000 was authorized for his redemption: PRO, SP 71/1/f.496.
[3] F. Knight, *A Relation of Seaven Yeares Slaverie under the Turkes of Argeire, suffered by an English Captive Merchant*, p. 51.
[4] Okeley, *Eben-ezer*, pp. 2,43, states that Robert Lake was staying on voluntarily. Okeley was one of over 60 taken when they were on their way to Providence Island; the company arranged for the ransom of John Symonds.
[5] *Relation of Proceedings Concerning the Redemption*, p. 11; Trinity House, Transactions, f.72, 7 January 1624.

to force conversion. For example, in November 1625 Robert Adams wrote from Sallee:

> Loving and kind father & mother my humble duty remembered to you both praying continually for your health as my own: you may be pleased to understand that I am here in Salley in most miserable captivity under the hands of most cruel tyrants for after I was sold my patron made me work at a mill like a oxen from morning untill night with chains upon my legs of 36 weight a piece. My meat nothing but a little course bread & water; my lodgings in a dungeon under ground where some 150 to 200 of us lay altogether, having no comforts of light but a small candle & being so full of vermin for want of shift & not being allowed time to pick myself that I am almost eaten up by them. And every day beaten to make me turn Turk or come to a ransom for our Master's boy had told my patrons that I was the owner of the ship and you were able to ransom some 40 such as I was which was no sooner known but they forced me to come to a ransom. [730 duckets, i.e., about £350][1]

Although one encounters similar reports from captives of brutal treatment and attempts of forced conversion, other captives swore that 'the Turks compel none to their religion'.[2] Some captives may have devised stories of forced conversion to protect themselves from accusations of apostasy when they were redeemed. Others may have confused the brutalities of slavery with attempts to force conversion. It is also possible that the practice of slave owners may not have been in accord with official religious principles.

An interesting facet of the question of religious tolerance concerns clerics. Several English priests or preachers were taken captive in these years, and one, the Reverend Devereux Spratt, wrote of his experience. He tells of 'being given liberty by the civil authorities to preach the Gospel'.[3] After being ransomed, he remained in Algiers for two years to 'minister to his poor countrymen'. Another captive, William Okeley, confirms Spratt's

---

[1] PRO, SP 71/12/f.107. Adams indicates that he had sent three or four letters prior to that quoted above but had heard nothing.
[2] PRO, HCA 1/47/f.262, reports on forced conversion; E. Kellet, *A Return from Argier: A sermon preached at Minehead the 16. of March 1627, (by H. Byam)*, p. 31, denies use of compulsion.
[3] *Autobiography of the Rev. D. Spratt*, p. 18.

service stating that 'Thrice a week this godly, painful servant of Jesus Christ prayed with us and preached to us the word of God'. Okeley provides more information on the practice of Christianity in Algiers:

> Our meeting place was a cellar which I had hired at some distance from the shop. To our meetings resorted many, and though we met next to the street, yet we never had the least disturbance from the Turks or Moores . . . though such were the circumstances of slavery of many poor Christians that they could not attend.[1]

Another source hints at the freedom some Christians had in Algiers and of the extent of Spratt's pastoral duties. In the parish register of Cartmel is the entry: 'January 5 Anno Dom. 1644. Gyles Park, son of John Holker and Elizabeth Gordon, daughter of Robte. Gordon, Lord Viscount of Kentmeere, married in Algear in Barbary by Mr. Spratte, Minister'. A further entry reads: 'October 21, 1645, Elizabeth, daughter of the said Gyles Park, baptized in Algier in Barbary'.[2]

Something of the living arrangements and social life of the captives can be gleaned from letters and printed accounts. Some captives reported living only on bread and water, but there is no indication whether this was mere exaggeration, a normal practice, or some form of punishment. Others wrote that they received a sufficient amount of coarse black bread each day, cabbage or a local variety of turnip on occasion, and that even meat was sometimes provided.[3]

As for lodgings, James Wadsworth described his this way:

> it was in a dungeon in the market place where they use commonly to lodge their slaves, who repair there every night about eight of the clock, their masters manacling their hands before for fear they should make an insurrection . . . our beds were nothing but rotten straw laid on the ground . . . and our coverlets pieces of old sails . . . about 5 o'clock in the morning the door opened, we repaired to our masters house, and so to our wonted work.[4]

---

[1] Okeley, *Eben-ezer*, pp. 23–4.
[2] R.L. Playfair, *The Scourge of Christendom: Annals of British Relations with Algiers prior to the French Conquest*, p. 61.
[3] Wadsworth, *English Spanish Pilgrime*, p. 29.
[4] Ibid., pp. 41–2.

In several ways these narratives leave us with an imperfect, incomplete and biased view of captivity since they were written by captives who returned to England. All were also by captives who resided in one of the port towns of Barbary. We know nothing of the life of those sent to remote inland parts. It was the common view that a captive had little chance of redemption, if he or she did not remain in one of the main ports.[1]

While a captive remained in one of the major port towns of Barbary, the possibility of release still existed. Captives sent to sea in the galleys or sailing ships of the pirate towns sometimes took the opportunity to escape. On 7 March 1622, for example, 24 English captives overpowered their masters and brought the ship into a friendly port.[2] Another 50 captives gained freedom in 1636 when the ships in which they were serving were defeated by a French fleet.[3]

A daring few even managed to escape from Algiers or Sallee. These escape attempts display all the ingenuity and courage that we have come to expect from escaping prisoners. In one escape, the enterprising captives made keys from plaster casts to unlock the gates of their sleeping quarters. In another escape attempt, five English captives in Algiers secretly made a wooden-framed canvas boat, disassembled it and smuggled it out of the city in laundry bags. On the night of 30 June 1644, they surreptitiously left the city, reassembled the boat, and set sail across the Mediterranean. Six days later the small vessel and its crew reached Majorca.[4]

While some escape accounts appear a little far-fetched, if not fanciful, the story of George Penticost has the ring of truth. It begins:

> There were 15 of us captives agreed with one consent to seize on a Turkish house wherein was a store of ammunition, as muskets, harquebuses, and other weapons, which on the 4th

---

[1] Anon., *The Famous and Wonderful Recovery of a Ship of Bristol*, p. 6.
[2] Ibid., pp. 12–22. PRO, SP 71/1/f.74, dated 21/6/1627, refers to a 'Turkish' pirate ship being brought into Cornwall by the Christian crew after they had overwhelmed their masters. This report states that there were nearly 40 'Turks' leaving in England at the time; about a dozen had been released from prison by Mr Harrison, a Barbary trader and occasional envoy of the Crown, and were living and working in London as tailors (3), shoemakers (2), menders (2), botton maker (1), and solicitor (1).
[3] *CSPV*, 1636–1639, p. 82.
[4] Okeley, *Eben-ezer*, p. 39.

day of July [1640] at eleven of the clock in the forenoon we all met, seized on this house, took these weapons by force of arms, armed ourselves, and entered a boat: but before we got the boat we lost three men in fight so that 12 escaped safe into the boat, put off to sea being under the command of two castles which shot many guns at us, but it please God none hit us; then was manned after us three boats . . . which came off to us and fought with us 5 hours, to the loss of diverse lives and the wounding of three of our men; and about five of the clock in the afternoon of the same day, they gave us arear, then we rowed for Mayorca.[1]

But escape was exceptional. Liberty, if it came at all, usually was a result of negotiations which could take several forms. Some individuals arranged their own release; if they had sufficient credit or their claims of wealth were convincing, local merchants might put up the money necessary for ransom. In 1622, Frenchmen did so for James Wadsworth.[2] If the consul of a European state were resident, he might assist. More frequently, captives relied upon family or friends in England.[3] Merchants trading with Barbary were used to carry letters back and forth. After 23 months in captivity, Captain William Hawkridge was ransomed; his friends and relatives raised £270 for his release.[4] On occasion, shipowners might contribute towards the ransom of the crew. In 1638 the owners of the *Mary* of London offered to contribute £100 for the release of the crew.[5]

Private charity was also available. The will of Sir James Campbell (d.1642) established a trust of £1000 to be used in 'the ransoming of captives who have been taken by Turkish or other Mediterranean pirates'.[6] Lord Craven left a bequest of a similar

---

[1] BL, Sloane MS. 3317/8.
[2] Wadsworth, *English Spanish Pilgrime*, pp. 41–2.
[3] BL, Eg. MS 3006, f. 98d. For example, in August 1642, Jane Beek ransomed her husband through the sale of property.
[4] PRO, SP 71/26/f.5. An unnamed father obtained release to go to England to raise ransom money to redeem himself and his son who remained in captivity: SP 71/1/f.89.
[5] PRO, SP 16/391/95,96.
[6] *DNB*, vol. 3, pp. 727–8; W.K. Jordan, *Philanthropy in England, 1480–1660: A study of the changing pattern of English social aspirations*, p. 239. Sir Henry Marten (1559–1641), Judge of the High Court of Admiralty, left £350 to redeem English captives: B. Levack, *Civil Lawyers in England 1603–41*, p. 252.

nature with £100 per annum available for redemption.[1] Impoverished relatives might seek letters patent to collect funds for redemption: Ralph Matress of the Isle of Thanet was authorized in this way.[2] Help also came from Trinity House, sometimes directly by way of contributions; at other times, assisting indirectly by certifying that a petitioner's relative was captive, thereby enabling charity to be obtained.[3]

Civic or county authorities also aided captives and their families. In 1622, collections in Bristol and the surrounding countryside raised £160 for redemption; 40 people secured their freedom as a result.[4] A few years later, the JPs of Devon raised over £137 'for redemption of twenty captive of these Western parts'.[5] In July 1630, authorization was granted for collection of £4100 to be used for the release of 140 English captives.[6]

Traditionally, the Church had been the primary body concerned with redemption. Before the Reformation, religious orders specialized in this form of charitable work, and, although such orders disappeared in England, the Church continued to be active in assisting redemption.[7] Maritime parishes frequently took up collections to free those held in captivity. In 1628 in Minehead, for example, collections for this purpose were made on three successive Sundays.[8] And during the 17th century, several national collections were authorized. One, in 1624, raised over £2848 of which £150 came from the House of Lords,[9] who saw their role as exemplary:

> And by way of example, the Lords of Parliament are now ready to leade the way by giving in their severall rankes . . . fourty shillings of every member above the degree of a Baron: And

---

[1] W.K. Jordan, *The Charities of Rural England, 1480–1660: The aspirations and the achievements of the Rural Society*, p. 356.
[2] W.A. Bewes, *Church Briefs or royal warrants for collections for charitable objects*, p. 22.
[3] Trinity House, Transactions, f.58v., 19 March 1620, f.59, 28 March 1620, f.65v., 15 September 1621, f.70v., 14 May 1623, f.72, 7 January 1624, f.73–73v., 17 April 1624, f.95v., 24 September 1631.
[4] PRO, SP 16/354/179.
[5] PRO, SP 71/1/f.84; eventually £300 was expended; see also SP 14/173/22.
[6] Birmingham, Coventry Papers, Dv 904, ff.195–8.
[7] J.A. Gari y Siumell, *Historia de la Rendenciones*, *passim*, and for a more modern and accurate treatment of the subject, Friedman, *Spanish Captives*, *passim*. Friedman has evidence that Spanish religious orders redeemed 15 500 captives between 1575–1769, ibid., p. 143.
[8] Kellet, *Return from Argier*, p. 2.
[9] *Lords Journals*, III, p. 738a.

those of the degree of Barons (Lords Spirituall and Temporal) twenty shillings apiece, . . . to be collected for the use above mentioned. And it is further ordered, That absent Lords may not be exempted from this Contribution, but that the Lords that have their proxies deposite the same for them.[1]

Although these acts of charity helped to reduce suffering, such measures were palliative at best. In 1633, the report by a royal commission studying the problem concluded that church briefs could raise only a tiny fraction (one-fortieth by their calculation) of the amount required.[2] This commission also recommended against using royal gifts for this purpose. They favoured a 1% levy on imports and exports with the money being used to redeem captives and suppress piracy.[3]

Despite the noble purpose of these charitable causes, only small amounts were collected. Even then, the money was not used wisely and some may have been misappropriated. In 1632, the English consul in Algiers wrote that

> to this day, not one penny of any collect money gathered in England or Ireland appears; by which the King's Majesty and State are much abused as also the captives kept in thraldom by the collectors sinister means that detaineth the said money to a contrary use.[4]

The Privy Council investigated the consul's accusations, and from the surviving evidence it appears that merchants held the funds for extended periods and used it for their own purposes before employing the money to redeem captives. Even when the money was expended quickly, it was used to buy luxury goods from friends or associates to use in trade for captives or as bribes for officials.[5]

---

[1] Bewes, *Church Briefs*, p. 120.
[2] PRO, SP 71/1/ff.106, 109, 111, 130. These reports are concerned with policy toward the pirates and consider the option of redemption. SP 71/1/f.130 put the cost to free 1000 captives at £40000, or £40 a head.
[3] PRO, SP 71/1/ff.130–132v. Ten years later, parliament enacted such a measure: see Chapter 12.
[4] PRO, SP 71/1/f.119.
[5] PRO, SP 71/12/f.221v., SP 71/12/f.274: in 1626 out of £900 authorized to redeem captives, £260 was paid to the shipowners for transporting the gifts that would be given to officials. SP 71/13/f.46.

Nor were merchants the only ones accused of wrongdoing.[1] James Frizell, English Consul in Algiers for much of this period, was suspected of abusing the trust put in him. One captive wrote to his wife that should she send ransom money to Leghorn, it should not be delivered to the Jewish brokers of Frizell, for they were said to hold the money waiting for the captive to die.[2] In fairness to Frizell and the Jewish brokers, it must be said that there is no evidence to corroborate this charge and there is other evidence to show that they were active in assisting the release of English captives.[3]

Barter arrangements were sometimes used to purchase freedom for those held in Barbary. In 1637, Robert Blake traded cloth for captives, and in 1646, parliament's agent did the same.[4] Also, between 1610 and 1633, John Harrison was sent several times by the Crown to Morocco to redeem English captives. In 1628 he secured the release of approximately 200 persons, though the price he paid was thought by some to be too great.[5] The Chief Judge of the High Court of Admiralty, for example, thought bartering with munitions was a shortsighted measure at the very least, nor did he think it prudent in general to treat with pirates.[6] On another occasion, an English ship with arms for Barbary was seized by a Dutch man-of-war; at other times the Dutch were accused of supplying the pirates with arms.[7]

As well as bringing arms to trade, Harrison took with him several Moors to exchange for English captives. Shortly before he left England, he wrote to the Council that as he was about to collect the Moors from prison, a Mr Barrat came

pretending likewise . . . the same end to transport them to

[1] PRO, PC 2/43/f.430. In 1633/34, after hearing allegations against John Harrison, envoy to Morocco, the Privy Council ordered an examination of how he spent the money assigned to him for the release of captives.
[2] PRO, SP 105/149/ff.9, 256; Privy Council 2/41/f.459.
[3] PRO, SP 71/1/f.135. A Jewish factor in Algiers was responsible for the release of the first captive from Baltimore in 1633.
[4] *Relation of Proceedings Concerning the Redemption*, p. 55. This Robert Blake is not the future Admiral; this Blake was a merchant and later factor of the Barbary Company; he met a sad end being hanged in 1642 after the battle of Edgehill. Prince Rupert found letters in the baggage of the Earl of Essex which revealed that Blake had been spying for the parliamentarians.
[5] BL, Add. MS. 21,993, f.281.
[6] Ibid., ff.281–4. See PRO, SP 16/40/24,25 for the Admiralty opinion.
[7] PRO, HCA 30/864: Robert Woodroof, *William and Elizabeth*, shipped 200 matchlocks, 600 swords, and 300 lances to Barbary. For the Judge of the Admiralty's objection, see SP 16/40/24, 25 November 1626.

Barbary to redeem captives, but indeed had compacted with some London merchants who had a ship in Dartmouth at that time bound for Livorno in Italy to carry from thither only for private benefit, there to be sold as slaves to the great prejudice and utter overthrow of your Majesty's service.[1]

Harrison's commission was not the only one with such provision. In 1635, Robert Blake received a warrant to transport 45 Moors to Barbary for use in bargaining for the release of English captives.[2] Five years later, Sir Henry Vane was writing to Secretary Windebank about using captured pirates to free some of the English subjects being held in Algiers.[3]

One of the most intriguing ideas for an exchange is found in an anonymous letter presented to the king in 1636 as a New Year's gift. In it the writer advised 'that the whores, harlots, & idle lascivious portion of the female sect [sic]' should be exchanged for English male captives so that 'one harlot may redeem half a dozen captives'.[4] Unfortunately, the evidence does not inform us whether this was the standard rate, nor is it possible to discover what Charles I thought of the proposed exchange which valued England's mariners so cheaply and the realm's harlots so highly.[5]

Only the outline of the actual process of redemption can be discovered. Merchants clearly acted as middlemen and agents much of the time. In the early 1620s, when west country officials undertook to redeem captives, they sought the assistance of Nicholas Leate, a member of the Levant Company and the leading trader with Barbary.[6] On a later occasion, when JPs of Devon set about redeeming captives of the county, Nicholas Spaicer, a merchant of Exeter, was employed by them to go to Algiers.[7]

Sometimes merchants advanced money expecting repayment from captives on their return. Merchants papers sometimes include accounts or entries relating to loans for the release of captives. For example, a one-page account of redemption transac-

---

[1] PRO, SP 71/12/f.126v. The Levant Company opposed such a transaction in 1627, fearing ill-effects on the company's trade: SP 105/148/f.174v.
[2] PRO, SP 16/408/118; SP 16/354/179.
[3] PRO, SP 16/467/5, 10 September 1640.
[4] PRO, SP 16/311/9.
[5] PRO, SP 16/332/30 incl. 5: In an examination of John Dunton, it is declared that the pirates especially prized English women, seven of whom were taken in his ship.
[6] PRO, SP 14/173/22.
[7] PRO, SP 71/1/f.84.

tions made by Lewis Hodges, a factor of the London merchant, Richard Hill, survives in the Hill papers in the British Library. As well as giving the cost of redeeming each captive, this account shows that over £2100 credit was extended and that there was almost £1000 in unpaid debts on the books. The Hill account also reveals that in three cases, bonds were taken from friends or relatives to guarantee payment.[1] Redemption was a risky business and repayment was often slow or uncertain. In 1628, the Bishop of Exeter wrote to the Privy Council that Nicholas Spaicer had disbursed over £300 redeeming captives, 'for which he hath received no satisfaction, although there have been money enough collected by the county'.[2] In the same year, Sir Kenelm Digby borrowed £1650 which he used to procure the freedom of 47 captives from Algiers; 20 years later, he was still trying to obtain reimbursement from the government.[3]

Fees and bribes had to be paid at times, as well as the redemption cost. For instance, as part of an agreement he made with Algiers, Cason had to pay a 6% duty on any money brought into the city to redeem captives. He also had to pay a portion of the export duty on each person redeemed as well as 20 pesos per captive to officers for unspecified services. In all, these fees came to about £6 per captive.[4]

At times the purpose of various transaction costs was made explicit. Robert Blake paid 200 ducats (about £95) 'to the officers who took pains to find out the number and whereabouts of the captives', and 400 ducats to one of the emperor's favourites who had four English slaves, 'for that he should not oppose the King's sending them with the rest'.[5] These payments confirm reports that some owners were prepared to evade official agreements. Thomas Sweet describes one such evasion as follows:

> Since our last sent you in September, Master Cason the Parliament's agent and the bashaw here [Algiers] concluded a peace, and it is agreed all English captives (not turned Renegadoes) shall be redeemed . . . which our patron understanding . . . made us over by bill to a Moor in Tunis being a merchant of his acquaintance, the place being under another government,

---

[1] BL, Add. MS. 5489, ff.87v–8.
[2] PRO, SP 71/1/f.84.
[3] Grantham, Buckminster Park, Tellemeade MS, Will Murrey's Papers 4850. I wish to thank C.S.R. Russell for this reference.
[4] *Relation of Proceedings Concerning the Redemption*, p. 12.
[5] PRO., SP 71/1/f.89.

and swore we should not be redeemed . . . unless we could procure . . . £250.[1]

Bribes apparently were an integral part of the negotiation process. During the Interregnum, Robert Brown, the English Consul in Algiers, was authorized to pay out about £200 in bribes to release English captives.[2]

Because redemptions were usually arranged privately, there is no series of documents in public archives which may be used to determine the number of captives who regained their liberty. In the course of this study, the names of a little over 600 individuals who were redeemed have been found.[3] Additionally, there is evidence which confirms that another 600 unnamed captives gained release.[4] This suggests that only a fraction, probably less than one-third, ever gained freedom and returned to England.[5]

The case of a group of 302 Icelandic men, women, and children captured in 1627 may serve as an indicator of the prospects captives might face. Almost nine years after the capture, an agent of Christian IV arrived in Algiers with money to redeem his countrymen, but he reported that only 37 could be found. What became of the other 265 is not known.[6] Admittedly, there are unusual aspects in the case of the Icelandic captives. Their

---

[1] *Carteret's Barbary Voyage of 1638*, ed. P. Penrose, p. 20, indicates that at least four English captives had been concealed by their owners the previous year despite the civic authority's order to turn over all captives to Captain Rainsborough.
[2] PRO, PC 2/55/f.9.
[3] The names of 568 captives are given in *Relation of Proceedings Concerning the Redemption*; Dunton, *Journal of Sally Fleet*; and BL, Add. MS. 5489; and dozens more individuals can be found in the records of Trinity House, the High Court of Admiralty, and State Papers Domestic and Foreign.
[4] Harrison indicated he had released 190 captives, in PRO, SP 71/12/f.248; this was after only one of four embassies he made between 1610 and 1633. Frizell reported he had redeemed 240 and hoped to free 50 or 60 more: see Chapter 10. Kenelm Digby claimed to have freed 80 captives during his voyage: see Chapter 10.
[5] Even if Roe actually redeemed 800 captives, as claimed, this would account for only about one-third of those estimated to have been taken up to that time. Later, in 1632, Frizell wrote that of 708 taken since 1629 only 24 had been redeemed: PRO, SP 71/1/f.119. His reports continued to keep tallies of those taken captive and ransomed. In 1637 he reported that 65 ship and 1524 English subjects had been taken with another ten ships captured (but yet to enter Algiers); of the captives, he related sadly 'there is not of them ransomed 100th persons' and that this had been managed by Mr Henry Draper and his Jewish factors (in Algiers).
[6] There is information on the Icelanders in H. Barnby, 'The Sack of Baltimore', pp. 113, 120–1, whose main sources were Eigil, *Litil Saga*, and *Tyrkjaranid a Islandi*, eyewitness accounts. Sigurdur A. Magnússon, *Northern Sphinx: Iceland and the Icelanders from the Settlement to the Present*, pp. 115–16, states that many were killed, 242 were sent to Algiers, 39 ransomed, and 13 returned.

homeland was more distant from Algiers than was England, and Iceland had no direct Mediterranean trade which might facilitate redemption as England did. The nine-year interval between capture and the arrival of a redemption agent would also have been a factor contributing to the low rate of return. The chances of redemption decreased with time spent in captivity. Yet even if one keeps the differences in mind, the experience of the Icelanders may not have been so different from that of the English captives.[1] Redemption efforts by the English government, for example, were infrequent and took years to organize.

For those fortunate enough to be redeemed, homecoming might not bring joy; in fact it could be rather painful, especially for those believed to have 'turned Turk'. Those found on Turkish men-of-war, for example, risked being tried for piracy.[2] And even if they escaped the rigours of the law, many innocent captives had to endure the wrath of the clergy. Three contemporary sermons demonstrate the ordeal that returnees could expect to undergo.

In 1636 Charles FitzGeffrey preached at Plymouth under the title, 'Compassion towards captives, chiefly towards our Brethren and Country-men who are in miserable bondage in Barbarie'.[3] As the title implies, FitzGeffrey spoke on the nature and need for charity. On the whole he preached consideration and understanding, though a causal link between captivity and sinfulness was at least implied. The plight of the returnees was also used to admonish his listeners, 'O that England may be warned by these sad examples. God can turn Britaine into Barbarie.'

Near the beginning of this sermon, FitzGeffrey criticized the government, albeit gently, for its failure to suppress piracy and free those held in bondage. He also relates in it that an [unnamed] peer had promised 'with tearful eyes . . . to the mournful wives and children of those oppressed captives, that when he returned to Court he would become their advocate unto the Majestie of the King'.

---

[1] In February 1633/4, only about three years after the capture of 109 (89 women and children and 20 men) from Baltimore, Consul Frizell wrote 'near 70 remainith to be redeemed, the rest being dead or turned Turk'. Only one person of this group had been ransomed by that date.
[2] PRO, SP/335/1: 1 November 1636, a report to the Admiralty on the trial at Winchester of Sallee pirates. Four Dutch and English renegades were acquitted, 11 condemned. Minutes of the session are in HCA 1/60/ff.142–144v.
[3] C. FitzGeffrey, *Compassion towards Captives, chiefly towards our Bretheren and Country-men who are in miserable bondage in Barbarie*. The parts quoted are from pp. 6–10.

The humane tone so evident in FitzGeffrey's sermon stands in sharp contrast with the two sermons read at Minehead in 1628. The morning sermon was given by Edward Kellet, who showed no sympathy for those whose faith had slipped while they were in bondage. Kellet's purpose and tone can be gleaned from the following passage which appears at the beginning of his sermon:

> I intend (by God's grace) in a holy servitude, for the good of they soule, and for the terrour of others, to plucke the figgleaves, to take away the excuses, to remove the loose veils and covers, that so you may see and bewaile the monstrousness of your offence; and that others may avoid the like.[1]

Kellet's text is also curiously rich with sexual overtones. Again and again, he told the congregation and his readers about the circumcision of the penitents. And in Kellet's mind, the Prophet's alleged sexual misbehavior loomed large, as can be seen here:

> that Rake-shame of the world . . . the Ravisher of his Mistress . . . the known Adulterer of one Zeid . . . a seducer, a salacious lustful Amoroso [whose] intemperate lasciviousness, was wayted on by infirmities and sicknesses correspondent to his lewdness.

Also in Kellet's view, the Muslim religion possessed 'more insensate fopperies, yea blasphemies' than any other, and he took obvious pleasure in criticizing alleged theological weaknesses or inconsistencies. The only feature he thought worth praising was the Muslim prohibition against alcohol. He warned his parishioners that 'Mohammet taught that every red grape had a devil within it; but some have found the devil in Sack, rather than Claret.'.

When Kellet turned to the sins of the penitents before him, his psychological astuteness and the power of his language becomes evident. In contrast to FitzGeffrey, Kellet began with slashing attacks and venomous accusations regarding the conduct of the captives; these were followed by some lulling remarks, a few phrases which suggested that there might be some mitigating circumstances which could explain the captives' behaviour, but just when the penitents might expect relief, Kellet turned on them

---

[1] Kellet, *Return from Argier*. The quotations given are from pp. 18–35.

with a new ferocity. Their waywardness was condemned, utterly and without exception; martyrdom by the cruellest torture, Kellet thundered, was preferable to the sinful apostasy of those before him.

The harsh, unrelenting attitude of Kellet was not shared by all, as internal evidence in the sermon indicates. At one point Kellet tells a penitent former captive:

> whereas by thy kindred, friends, or acquaintances (in foolish pity hurtful to thy souls) false colours are set on bad cloth; fair painting on a rotten board; and some have risen up in your defence with semblances to make thy sin shew less.

Later in the sermon Kellet returned to this theme warning:

> Let me not be thought, (beloved in the Lord) to be too severe, in aggruatine the Circumstances, of a prostrate Penitent's sinne. I profess, my heart is moved with sorrow, for him: and pity towards him: I grieve with him, who grieveth; I bear part of his burden. And whil'st I strike, I groan, whil'st I reprove, my Bowels earne, and my faint passions melt. But which is better, quaero medicum elegantem, sed sanantem, said the Wise-man of old. As I expect mercy, I would not add weight to the oppressed, nor break the bruized reed. But since in my hearing, such a Fault, was said in effect, to be paid-for too dear, with such a Penance: since too many in this Congregation, out of a Compassion uncharitably-charitable, lessen such an offence: since it is presumed, that Divers present, have run the same course, with the delinquent (though it cannot be proved as yet) and since it may turn to the terror of others hereafter (who of this Maritime town may be taken Captives) I have laboured to cut-out the Cores; to shew the Renouncing of Christ, to be a most heynous, abominable and execrable sin.

The afternoon sermon, by the Reverend Henry Byam, made the same point, though less eloquently. Byam also spoke against Mohammed, and thought him to be the true Antichrist. But what is especially interesting about this sermon is that he too found it necessary to justify the penance and its severity. Precedents from the early Church, ecclesiastical law and learned commentaries on the scripture, and recent authorities (Calvin, for example) were all cited to justify the action of the Church. Yet even with these supports, Byam doubted whether his arguments would convince those present for, as he put it, some 'will cry out against the Churches severity, extreme, excessive severity'. By the end of the sermon, his mood had softened. Spiritual redemption was possible, he advised those before him, but a penitent would need to demonstrate his restored faith by good acts.[1]

Perhaps the evident general dissatisfaction with the way spiritual redemption had gone at Minehead caused John Hall, Calvinist bishop of Exeter, to write to Archbishop Laud for advice on the way to bring penitents back to the Church. Laud later wrote:

> This year, by reason of the return of divers that were captives in Marocco, and having been inhabitants of those western parts, there arose in my lord the Bishop [of Exeter] a doubt, how they, having renounced their Saviour, and become Turks, might be readmitted into the Church of Christ, and under what penitential form. His lordship at his last being in London spake with me about it, and we agreed on a form, which was afterwards drawn up, and approved by the right reverend fathers in God my lords the bishops of London, Ely, and Norwich, and is now settled by your majesty's appointment . . . to remain as a precedent for future times, if there should be any more sad examples of apostasy from the faith.[2]

The service devised by Laud and the bishops began with the delinquent being brought before a bishop's court for committing the crime of apostasy.[3] Following conviction, a notice was made in both the parish church and in the cathedral. Upon submission by a penitent former captive, penance was given which would be supervised by the vicar. The vicar was required to announce in public the nature and form of penance. Next the vicar would confer with the penitent to 'lay open and aggravate the heinous-

---

[1] Kellet, *Return from Argier*, p. 7.
[2] *The Works of Archbishop Laud*, ed. W. Scott and J. Bliss, vol. V, p. 352. The service devised by Laud and the bishops has an importance outside of its relevance to the subject of piracy. Laud, William Juxon (bishop of London), Francis White (bishop of Ely), and Matthew Wren (bishop of Norwich), were all Arminians, and this service is in many ways emblematic of the sort of Church they sought. Throughout the service, the role of the priest is emphasized; for example, the service makes it clear that only through the priest's intercessions and ministrations can the faith of the penitent be restored. And this restoration must be accomplished in a highly ceremonial way.
[3] Ibid., pp. 372–6. The pages contain a printed edition of the service and the parts quoted below are found there. The original in manuscript is in the Lambeth Palace Library.

ness of his sin' to see whether the sinner was truly fit for absolution.

When the penitent was thought ready spiritually, the formal, public process of reconciliation could begin. The ceremony was spread over three weeks. First, the penitent had to stand in the porch of the church on Sunday through all the time of service.[1] The penitent was ordered to present himself 'in a white sheet, and with a white wand in his hand, his head uncovered, his countenance dejected, not taking particular notice of any person that passeth'. In the draft copy, Laud added at this point, 'Order must be taken, that boys and idle people flock not about him'. When the parishioners arrived or departed, the penitent was instructed to fall to his knees and humbly say, ' "Good Christians, remember in your prayers a poor wretched apostate or renegado" '.

On the second Sunday the penitent, dressed as before, was allowed to stand just inside the church door. After the *Te Deum* ended, he would then be brought by a churchwarden to the west end of the font where he was ordered to kneel until the second lesson ended. Then, the penitent was instructed to submit orally and ask for God's mercy.[2]

On the third Sunday, at the beginning of the service, the penitent (still in white robes), was brought into the church and placed in a pew near the priest. Immediately prior to the Apostle's Creed, the priest would speak publicly, putting 'the offender in mind of the foulness of his sin, and stir him up to a serious repentence, advising him that a slight and ordinary sorrow is not enough for so grievous an offence'. The priest then asked the penitent whether he found 'a true and earnest remorse in his soul'. If the response was positive, the sinner was ordered to make the following supplication:

> I do here in the presence of Almighty God, and before you His faithful people, humbly and penitently confess, that I have grievously offended the majesty of God, and deeply wounded my own soul, in that I far yielded to the weakness of my sinful flesh, as that I suffered myself through the cruelty of God's

---

[1] If the church had no porch, Laud and the bishops advised that the penitent should stand outside the front entrance of the church.

[2] Here in the draft, Laud recommended in the margin that when the penitent was reciting a prayer of submission, he should 'smite his breast three times' and then 'in an humble and devout manner, kiss the bottom stone of the font, strike his breast, and presently depart into the church porch'.

enemies to be miscarried to the renouncing of my dear Saviour, and the true Christian religion, wherein I was brought up. I do well know what I have deserved, both at the hands of God and of His Church, for this wicked and graceless act: and now, as I have often betwixt God and my own soul washed this sin with my tears, and craved His merciful forgiveness; so I beseech you all to take knowledge of this my public sorrow and humiliation, and both to pardon and forgive that just offence, which I have herein given to you also.

When this plea was finished, the priest was required to speak to the congregation on the need for forgiveness. Then the priest was 'charitably to embrace him with arms of tender pity and compassion, as a true Christian convert to His Saviour'.

The faithful were then asked to ponder 'the weakness of our frail nature, when it is overpressed with violence and extremity of torments, and both to commiserate his fearful apostacy, and to encourage and comfort him in this happy return to Christ and His Church'. The penitent was then ordered to kneel, facing eastwards again, to recite a lengthy prayer. When this was finished, the priest stood over the penitent and read a passage from the Book of Common Prayer. Then both were directed to kneel, again facing east, with the penitent behind the minister who was required to recite an amended version of the Collect that forms part of the Visitation of the Sick service. Finally, the priest was instructed to physically raise up the penitent, take away the white sheet and wand, and welcome him back into the fold. The penitent would then be advised of his special need to lead a righteous life. At the next communion-day, the penitent would at last be permitted to receive the sacrament, thus completing his reconciliation to God and Church.

Viewed simply as a rite of religious passage, the service is exemplary. The sinner is made aware of the gravity of his sin, and the priest and Church are elevated to a critical role in the reconciliation of man to god. In ceremonial terms, it is rich in symbolism and certainly replete enough with ritual to satisfy Laud. Certainly, it shows how seriously Laud took the matter.[1] His annotations reveal, he made time to study the draft carefully and alter it where he felt the need.

---

[1] He was extremely busy at the time for he was Lord Treasurer as well as Archbishop of Canterbury.

As a practical matter, the service was quite unworkable, and there is no evidence that this grand Laudian scheme was ever implemented. That common seamen were expected to learn and recite the lengthy prayers illustrates how unrealistic these Laudian clerics were. Memorizing the 'neck verse' was often too much for the common man of the day, even when his life depended upon its recitation. Moreover, the earlier experience at Minehead suggests that maritime communities were unlikely to inflict upon friends and relatives the humiliation and ordeal implicit in this service. The experience of Minehead is instructive; it suggests that the people of the maritime parishes preferred to take back wayward members quietly and without ceremony. Their compassion may have been strengthened by an appreciation that they too might be seized by the Turks, carried to Barbary, and sold into miserable slavery.

These displays of compassion toward captives and resistance to the harsh measures of the Church may also be taken as evidence of how much at risk to pirates people of the maritime communities believed themselves to be. Implicit in their response is the assumption that they too might be taken by the pirates and forced to 'turn Turk'. The costs of piracy, both in social and economic terms, were all too familiar to the maritime people of England. They knew full well that the costs were great, great enough to put pressure on the government, too great for the government to ignore.

Part 3
POLITICS, APPEASEMENT, SHIP MONEY AND THE SALLEE EXPEDITION

8
DIPLOMATIC INITIATIVE: SIR THOMAS ROE'S EMBASSY

The order recalling Mansell's fleet signified neither a loss of interest nor will on the part of the English government to find a solution to the chronic problems of the Barbary pirates. In fact, while Mansell was still operating in the Mediterranean, the government was seeking other means to secure the release of English captives and bring an end to the depredations of the pirates. Originally, it will be recalled, the government intended to keep a fleet in the Mediterranean for two full years, but by the autumn of 1621 this no longer seemed possible. The expedition was working out to be more costly than anticipated and the money needed to finance it was proving difficult to collect. The problems of supply and the poor condition of Mansell's ships forecast further difficulty and even greater expense. Finally, there was the growing commitment of resources to aid the Palatinate.[1] All of these factors made it unlikely that a fresh fleet could be dispatched and that the government would be able to continue pursuing a policy of suppressing the pirates.

Alternative courses open to the government were few, however. Economic sanctions against the pirate states could achieve little because trade with Algiers and Tunis was insignificant and on balance to England's advantage; in any case, other European

---

[1] In the autumn of 1621, the Hapsburg forces had moved into the Lower Palatinate, further dispossessing Frederick, the son-in-law of James I. So desperate was the situation, that Ambassador Digby pawned his own silver to raise some money to pay for troops and stave off the defeat of Frederick. A few days later, James I borrowed £30 000 from City merchants at short notice for the same purpose. Also, parliament was unexpectedly recalled with the aim of raising a large sum to support armed forces on the Continent. The government estimated the cost of recovering the Palatinate at £900 000.

traders would supply the Barbary states with essential commodities. If trade with Turkey were cut off, England's Mediterranean trade would suffer heavily, but the pirates of Algiers would not cease to attack English ships.

Thus, with both the use of force and sanctions ruled out, the government's only hope rested in some sort of diplomatic solution. At one time in 1621, direct negotiations with Algiers were contemplated. Sir Thomas Glover, former ambassador to Constantinople, was appointed consul to Algiers, an unusually senior figure for such a minor post.[1] In the event, he did not take up the appointment. Instead, diplomatic efforts were directed towards Constantinople. Taking advantage of a complaint by the Levant Company, the Crown recalled Ambassador Sir John Eyre, who had been resident in Turkey for little more than a year, and appointed in his place Sir Thomas Roe.

Few other men in England possessed the ability and experience needed for this assignment. Roe had both. He was one of the most widely travelled men of his day. As a young man he had been involved in the Guiana plantation scheme, and not just as an investor: he visited the settlement and even ventured up the Amazon some 400 miles.[2] In these years Roe acquired a personal knowledge of the trade of the Indies and Spain, and his writings demonstrate a sound grasp of international trade and politics in general. Not long after returning to England he was appointed to undertake an embassy to the court of the Great Mogul of India, where he acquired an understanding of oriental ways and displayed considerable political skill. His letters and writings also reveal a keen and observant mind and wide-ranging interests, including art, science, and classical antiquity. He was a shrewd observer of European politics and for much of his life acted as an unofficial adviser to Elizabeth of Bohemia, daughter of James I, whom Roe knew well as a young man and whose cause he championed for most of his life, even though his good advice was all too often ignored by her and her husband, the impetuous Frederick, Prince of the Palatinate and one-time King of Bohemia.

Roe was a fine and prolific correspondent and thousands of his letters have survived including many revealing ones from his

---

[1] A.C. Wood, *A History of the Levant Company*, p. 84.
[2] M.J. Brown, *Itinerant Ambassador: The Life of Sir Thomas Roe*, and M. Strachan, *Sir Thomas Roe:, 1581–1644: a life*, covers Roe's life and career extremely well; *DNB*, vol. 17, pp. 89–93, provides a good, concise account of his activities.

embassy to Constantinople.[1] Though the tasks given to Roe were exceedingly difficult and his career did not advance smoothly, never in his letters are there signs of bitterness nor morosity. He appears a born optimist, but not unrealistically so. In fact, he had the rare gift of seeing the world much as it is; consequently he was seldom surprised by events, and, unlike Gondomar, personal vanity did not distort his reports. In negotiations, Roe frequently was shrewd and cunning, well able to match the intrigues of opposing courtiers or diplomats, yet he was not a devious schemer. Quite to the contrary, he was a man of undoubted moral strength and generosity of spirit, earning the sobriquet of 'Honest' Tom Roe – a quality associated with few, if any, politically active men in early Stuart England.[2]

The post at Constantinople was an especially difficult one because the ambassador was required to serve two masters. The choice of ambassador rested with the Levant Company, whose council elected Roe on 31 July 1621 to fill the post.[3] The ambassador's salary was paid by the company, not the Crown. In addition to his salary, he received a grant of £500 a year from the Sultan, a perquisite granted to all ambassadors to the Court. Thus, the ambassador was a company man, and his instructions made it clear that one of his main functions was the protection of English merchants and the furtherance of the commercial interests of the company that maintained him.

But the right of appointment did not rest entirely with the company nor were the duties of the ambassador solely commercial. Although it was not expressed in writing, the Crown retained an interest in the choice of ambassador and from the very first appointment had been active in the selection process, usually by confirming or vetoing the company's nominee.[4] To the Crown, the ambassador was primarily a political agent whose chief function was the furtherance of royal foreign policy. Since late Elizabethan times, the main tenet of the Crown's eastern policy had been the balancing of Turkish power against Hapsburg dominance.

---

[1] Most of his official correspondence for this embassy is in PRO, State Papers Foreign, Turkey (SP 97), but many letters have been published in *The Negotiations of Sir T. Roe in his embassy to the Ottoman Porte, from the Year 1621 to 1628 inclusive*.
[2] Brown, *Itinerant Ambassador*, p. 43; also, for comment on Roe's character, see Anthony Wood, *Athenae Oxonienses*, ed. P. Bliss, vol. III, col. 113.
[3] Wood, *Levant Company*, p. 6.
[4] Ibid., p. 87.

At times, as during periods of Roe's tenure, English commercial and political interests inclined toward divergent courses. However, in the summer of 1621 when Roe was appointed, the interests of the Levant Company and the Crown had converged. Both parties had come to favour a policy of negotiation with the Turkish Sultan to find a solution to the problem of the Barbary pirates. If successful, this policy would bring political and commercial benefits. In recent years the company had employed only strong, well-armed ships, and thus suffered little directly from the pirates. Nevertheless, the company's interests were threatened indirectly. Action against the pirate states might be seen in Constantinople as an affront to the sovereignty and authority of the Sultan. As a consequence, reprisals against the company might be expected. The company's factors and factories in Turkey were highly vulnerable to seizure. But in the long-term the company would lose even more if excluded from all trade with the Ottoman empire.

Mansell's fleet had done little to reduce piracy; if anything, the pirates had been stirred up, and almost directly following the departure of the fleet, English merchant ships began to suffer again.[1] With so much at risk, the company favoured an agreement with the pirates, but James would not allow his government to treat directly with the pirates. According to the Venetian ambassador in London, company officials then applied pressure on the government. If negotiations were not undertaken, they would (it was implied) be forced to abandon trade completely, an act which would adversely affect the government's foreign policy.[2]

James was initially reluctant because he believed his honour and reputation would be diminished if he were to treat with the pirates directly: as he saw it, he would then be treating thieves as equals. Yet the problem could not be ignored, and however much the king might wish to reduce the pirates by force – the most honourable course – it was no longer feasible. Nor did James want to risk antagonizing the Turks because the friendship of the Sultan might be used to put pressure on the Hapsburgs to restore the Palatinate. Therefore, negotiations with the Sultan remained the only practical course for the king to follow.

This convergence of interests resulted in the company and the Crown agreeing to send a new embassy to Constantinople specifi-

---

[1] PRO, SP 14/123/46.
[2] *CSPV*, 1621–1632, pp. 170–1.

cally to try to persuade the Sultan to restrain the subjects of his Barbary dependencies from piracy against English ships. On 9 September 1621, Secretary Calvert sent Roe written instructions to guide his embassy. These instructions are worth looking at closely for two reasons. First, they state in unambiguous terms the objectives of the embassy, and second, they provide documentary evidence on the dualism which attended the ambassador and governed his functions. The instructions read:

> For in all other matters concerning our merchants, their trade in the Levant, we doubt not but you will have that care which becomes you, in anything that may appertain to the welfare of their persons and goods, referring you for all particular informations and directions unto the Levant Company, either at this time, or hereafter, as they shall have occasion to write you: only we must remember you of that, which, without doubt, doth most concern the good of their trade, and toucheth us not a little in honour, the suppression of those insolencies committed upon our subjects and goods, by the pirates of Algiers and Tunis, against whom we have so often heretofore complained in that port, but have found no redress: You shall therefore let the Grand Signior now know, that howbeit we have been forced, out of necessity, to set forth of late a royal fleet, for the security of our merchants' trade in the Mediterranean Sea against that wicked crew, whose actions, we know, he, in justice, will not avow; yet we do so much rely upon his friendship, which we have ever been careful to preserve, by all good offices on our part, as that he will take present order therein himself to cut off those common enemies, and their harbours and receivers within his dominions, that the commerce between our subjects may be safe and free, as in times past it hath been, which is the only means to continue amity betwixt us; and in this point you are to deal very effectually and roundly, as your discretion shall seem meet.[1]

Five years later when justifying his actions, Roe would write that he had been guided and encouraged throughout his embassy by these royal 'particular and precise instructions'.[2]

---

[1] Roe, *Negotiations*, p. 4. These instructions show the importance attached to the suppression of piracy by the Crown.
[2] Ibid., p. 573.

The exact date of Roe's departure has not been discovered, but by the middle of November he was at Malaga from whence he wrote to Calvert a precocious appreciation of the central issue underlying his forthcoming negotiations. He reported that since Mansell's departure the seas had been infested with pirates. At that time over 70 pirate ships were operating between Sicily and the North Cape. It had become so dangerous, he told Calvert, he feared for his wife's safety and thought that his ship would be lucky if it managed to avoid capture after leaving the Spanish coast. 'They have taken near forty vessels of his majesty's subjects', the ambassador wrote; 'those who had any goods they have carried away; some others they have scourged with blows, and disgraceful, barbarous usage, such as I am loath and ashamed to mention'.[1]

The growing strength of the pirates, Roe surmised, was a reflection of the Sultan's loss of control over his Barbary dependencies, which in turn was a sign of the decline of Turkish power. But in this state of affairs, Roe could see no advantage to England. The Sultan needed the Barbary pirates because they might provide him with a powerful naval force in times of war. In this letter, and the next one from Messina, dated 7 December, Roe developed this theme:

I was bold to write to Mr. Secretary Calvert from Malaga, of the great increase of pirates in these seas and of the dangers of the merchant, with mine own thoughts, if his majesty have any further purpose to attempt their destruction, which is both honourable and necessary, if these trades or the other to the south of the North Cape, be of any consequence to his Majesty's kingdoms. If they be suffered to increase, they will brave the armies of the kings at sea in a few years, and attempt even the coasts shores with peril; and because they carry the name of thieves, they are yet condemned or neglected: but they will become a dangerous enemy when they shall rob with fleets, and therefore would be in time considered. The Spaniards now make great offers to continue the contract, though their performance be slow, and their own estate chiefly interest; yet besides the danger and ruin of the merchants, it is considerable that this army increasing, is at the obedience of the Grand Signior, the common enemy, who hath no strength but galleys.[2]

[1] PRO, SP 97/8/ff.74–75v.
[2] Roe, *Negotiations*, pp. 8–9; PRO, SP 97/8/ff.74–5.

Three months later (and after he had acquired firsthand knowledge) Roe sent Buckingham an assessment of the Sultan's fleet which included only galleys, less than a hundred in number and these were in a poor state and discipline was lacking.[1] The head of the Sultan's navy made no effort to conceal Turkish naval weakness, admitting to Roe that for any major naval operation the Sultan would find it necessary to depend on the fleets of the pirate states. In view of this dependence, Roe believed it unlikely that the sort of formal protestations or declarations he was instructed to make would be sufficient to restrain the pirates.

Given the circumstances, normal diplomatic measures were not likely to produce the desired effects. Roe also realized that any worthwhile solution would not come cheaply. A permanent solution would require the commitment of substantial naval forces and unified action by the princes of Christendom. Roe hoped that another fleet (with Spanish backing) could be sent.[2] In terms of tactics, Roe's views differed little from the designs of Mansell. The fleet should expect 'to ride before the town [Algiers], when the weather will give leave; and stand off to sea, and return at every opportunity, [when] in two years time they [the pirates] will be worn out and dispersed, besides opportunities of fire, and such other as shall in time be offered'.[3] In fact, throughout his embassy, Roe believed that any true and lasting solution would require the destruction of the pirate fleets and the reduction of their bases. Echoing Cato, he wrote the following to Calvert in January 1622:

My last was directed to your honour from Zant . . . whereby I have at last discharged my conscience to inform your honour of the misery and danger of the merchant in the seas; and the times have come about to the same thing, the place only changed, as Rome once did; and we ought in every occasion, to

---

[1] Roe, *Negotiations*, p. 27, 9 March 1622, from Constantinople.
[2] As Roe saw it, Mansell had failed because of inadequate supplies and insufficient support from Spain. Any new fleet should consist of an equal number of ships from England and Spain. They should be double-manned and captained only by men 'that have used the Levant'. Provisions should be accumulated beforehand and lodged in one or two storehouses, specially built on the Spanish coast, for the use of the fleet. To keep the fleet at sea for extended periods, a feat Mansell had found difficult, one or two supply ships would be provided to shuttle back and forth between storehouses and fleet. PRO, SP 97/8/ff.74–75v; Roe, *Negotiations*, pp. 4–6.
[3] PRO, SP 97/8/ff.74–75v.

cry out, *Memento Carthaginem*, for either they must be suppressed, or these trades deserted.[1]

He had grasped one of the essential features of the problem. As he explained:

> It is a true word, receivers make thieves; and if they had not so many traders with them from the Christian coasts, they would be soon unable for want of munition, and more for the lack of vent. They are supplied, and traffic freely with Ligorno in Italy, and in Provence are succored from Morteque, Marseilles, La Ciotat, Talon, Santropes, Antiquas principally, but generally from one of the petty ports: yea, some of the ports of Provence have contracted with them for all the fish they can take from our Newfoundland-men . . . to our great damage.[2]

To end the support which the pirates received from European merchants upon whom they were dependent for many goods, Roe advised James to obtain from the King of France and the princes of Italy prohibitions preventing their subjects from aiding the pirates. If his suasive powers were not enough, James should threaten them. And if that did not work, the king should authorize English ships to make prize of Italian and French ships with goods taken from English vessels.

Finally, as an immediate and more practicable measure, Roe sought permission to move the Sultan by threatening to bring an end to trade between the two states, if action against the pirates were not taken. Roe was well aware that 'our Levant and Turkey companies may mislike this as prejudicial to their trades' but concluded that 'yet I know it is better to have none at all with the infidels, than such as we now drive on the conditions' then pertaining. If a remedy were not provided quickly, Roe asked that he be permitted to inform the Sultan that the king of England might be compelled to 'wink at any subjects that shall do the like spoil upon any of his [the Sultan's] subjects in the Red Sea'.[3]

The English government's response to Roe's proposals was written by Calvert on 11 April 1622. After commenting on the merits of the ambassador's proposals which though valued and thought 'the surest remedy', he went on to say:

[1] PRO, SP 97/8/f.107–107v.
[2] PRO, SP 97/8/ff.74–75v.
[3] Ibid.

But we are so distracted here with a multiplicity of other businesses, which take up nights and days incessantly without rest, as, though that business be of great consequence as almost any other can be, yet I do not see hours of leisure for it. Besides, to deal plainly with you, who knows well in what condition you left us, for means to do any great exploit at sea, I must needs tell your lordship that his Majesty's exchequer is not yet able to furnish any considerable part of the charge to so great an enterprise. On the other side, the merchants are earnest suitors to come to some treaty with those of Algiers: but that his Majesty, will not harken unto, taking it to be a dishonour unto him, as indeed it is (though the Hollanders have done it of late) especially now the first contact made betwixt him and the king of Spain, when Sir Robert Mansell was set forth with his fleet, for three years, being not fully expired; however, for want of timely provision of victual, and fresh supply of new ships, the fleet was forced to come home before the expiration of the term.[1]

This letter of Calvert clearly removed any possibility that the first and fundamental part of Roe's proposal might receive royal favour.

Roe's other master, the Levant Company, was of two minds over which course to follow. Some merchants favoured the ambassador's recall and the abandonment of all trade: the company's resources, they argued, should then be directed towards privateering in the Red Sea. Others suggested that the company should continue to trade but set out ships only in convoys, a measure employed in earlier, troubled days, and one that would come to be adopted with success in the summer months of 1622. Though it would bring security to the great ships and crews of the Levant Company, this measure would do nothing to protect the small, vulnerable ships from the west country. Nor would it help secure the release of his majesty's subjects in captivity, then believed to amount to between 800 to 1000.

Thus, by the middle of 1622, Roe had come to see that any remedy to the problem could only come from his personal diplomatic efforts. He had also come to believe that the problem was more important than had been perceived, as he indicated to James on 7/17 March:

---

[1] PRO, SP 97/8/ff.140–142v.

I have been very vehement against the increase of the pirates, whose dangers, not only as thieves, but as armed and strong enemies, I better understand, then I could think of, at distance in England; and I am of the opinion, there is nothing of more consequence considerable in the Christian commonwealth, then their growth; for, as in the declination of the papacy, the jesuits rose as new engineers and counsellors to support the imminent ruin of the tyranny of Rome; so I find, that these last locusts are increasing, to be a bulwark and guard for the falling estate of the Turkish Empire, which is so weakened in power and corrupted in government and discipline, that it is upheld now more by opinion and reputation, then by any true and real greatness.[1]

On 9 March, the ambassador had his first interview with the Grand Vizier, chief agent of the Sultan. Roe spoke with unusual boldness for an ambassador, and there was no ambiguity in his message. The Grand Vizier was told that the king of England expected action against the pirates and amends to his subjects. Promises, Roe warned, would not be enough: if redress did not come, he was empowered to break off all commercial and diplomatic relations. And if this did not produce results, Roe told the Grand Vizier it was his duty to inform the Sultan that:

> in regard of the rovers, your Majesty must either send an army to defend them [the merchants] which would be troublesome neighbours; or else ruin and beat down the towns that harboured and received them; or finally give letters of marque to your Majesty's oppressed subjects, to right themselves upon all the friends and abettors their villainy.[2]

The Grand Vizier replied that the Sultan looked upon the English as his true friends and hoped their friendship would continue and prosper. If a few subjects of the Sultan had acted wrongly against English subjects, then every power of the state would be used to bring the wrongdoers to justice and prevent new cases of malfeasance. To bring this policy into practice, he proposed a messenger (accompanied by an English official) be sent to Algiers and Tunis with express commands to reaffirm the peace and end unlawful seizure of English ships and crews. Roe immedi-

---

[1] PRO, SP 97/8/ff.129–30.
[2] PRO, SP 97/8/f.118.

ately replied that this was not enough. He suggested that they include a provision stating that if the Sultan's commands were not scrupulously honoured, all the ports within the Ottoman empire would be closed to ships from the state that had violated the peace. Unless this measure were included, doubt must remain whether, as Roe put it, 'the emperor dealeth sincerely with your Majesty'.[1]

Whether Roe really believed that the Sultan would agree to his demand is uncertain: he was asking more than a sovereign ruler might reasonably be expected to accept but by making such a strong demand, the ambassador underlined the seriousness with which his government viewed the problem. Roe's stance also showed that he and the government he represented were not going to be fobbed off with weak, half-measures. This interpretation is given some credence by the fact that he did not break off the discussion when the Grand Vizier indicated that they could not accept his amendments. After Roe had spoken and the Vizier had given his reply, discussion of the matter was dropped, and the two men spent the rest of the interview talking about Polish-Turkish relations.

Although Roe thought the proposal of sending a joint delegation to the pirate towns inadequate, this is exactly the course that the ambassador would follow. In April and largely at his own expense, Roe outfitted a galley to carry a Turkish representative of the Sultan and an English observer to Algiers and Tunis. On 28 April, he informed James of his undertaking with the following explanation:

> Among the rest I have procured the emperor to bind himself to your majesty for those of Tunis and Algiers, that they observe the peace of this empire with the subjects of your majesty; but because in my last I wrote diffidently of the hopes of that business, both here, and of the observance there, your majesty will pardon me if I recant to our advantage; not that I am confident of the faith of these infidels, but that contending against my opinion, I have obtained more than expected, and such by the circumstances give me some belief, that they are real here; having your majesty's order to do somewhat therein, and instructions from the Levant Company left to discretion; and lastly, foreseeing the great damage our trades were subject

[1] PRO, SP 97/8/ff.119v–120.

to their robberies, I have chosen to make some trial, then leave it at the worst.[1]

The unexpectedly favourable terms mentioned by Roe included the promise that all English captives would be released and that no more English ships would be seized, if an English consul were appointed and maintained at Algiers and free and open trading between England and Algiers was established.[2]

It was June before London's response to the proposed agreement arrived. Calvert signified disapproval:

> As for the intimation you give of some likelihood to make some peace with the pirates, I cannot give you warrant from his Majesty for such a treaty; neither do I observe . . . that you much incline to any such counsel.[3]

At approximately the same time, the Lords of the Council advised Roe only to make a strong protest and warn the Sultan that his majesty would be compelled to seek redress against Turkish subjects in the Levant and Red Seas if English subjects held captive were not released and attacks on English shipping not ended.[4] What Roe thought of the Council's reply to his proposals, we do not know. He may have been disappointed in not being allowed to proceed to a treaty. He had seen the proposal as a trial, and his success in Constantinople, at least, made him optimistic, though Roe remained cautious, as always, about whether Algiers and Tunis would conform in fact or for long.

Initially, the mission got off to a good start. George Vernon, the English observer, and the Turkish official appointed by the Sultan arrived in Tunis and received a generally favourable response. The town's officials released money and goods confiscated from Nicholas Leate, the leading Barbary trader, an action which Roe interpreted as a sign that the viceroy sincerely wished to conclude a real accord, but Roe's optimism was qualified for he added that he would 'not be a surety for knaves'.[5] After leaving Tunis, Vernon and the Sultan's representative travelled to Algiers. Here the delegation received a very different response. Soon after

---

[1] PRO, SP 97/8/ff.149v–50.
[2] Ibid.
[3] Roe, *Negotiations*, pp. 60–1, 24 June 1622.
[4] PRO, SP 97/8/f.176, 6 June 1622.
[5] PRO, SP 97/9/ff.13–14v, 25 January 1623.

presenting themselves, the Sultan's representative was accused of being an imposter and the commands brought were claimed to be forgeries which had been obtained by bribing some court official. The Sultan's delegate refuted the charge and demanded obedience, but town officials ignored him. They would obey only those orders from the Sultan which they had heard with their own ears. Moreover, the delegation was informed that Algiers intended to send a commission to Constantinople to inform the Sultan of their grievances against the English.[1]

If disappointed with the turn of events at Algiers, Roe wasted no time on regrets but took action to forestall the commission from the pirate ports. On 25 January he advised the Privy Council that:

> I am not sorry that an end was not made at Algiers; for here I doubt not to bind them to harder conditions and in faster chains than upon their own dunghill. As yet we have not met, but I have prepared their welcome, and procured them a round admonition at their first audience.

Then, more calmly, Roe went on to explain in a passage that shows his strong practical and political sense:

> The viziers pretend to be constant, and promise to settle all in security. I believe they will deal sincerely; for they are not desirous to enforce his majesty's fleet to join with Spain, nor see them in those seas.

Next he indicated that in his view any agreement with the pirate states was likely to be transitory at best. Of the pending agreement, he wrote:

> how long it will endure, I dare not undertake: for though I am confident, that I shall lay all the authority of this port upon their shoulders, yet they are a kind of depending skirt of this empire, and not in absolute obedience. And lastly I know not by what other trade so many idle villains, nourished in theft, can live. Therefore, my conclusion is, that the surest way were fire and sword; which I do not think difficult, but for the charge and

---

[1] Ibid. In fact a commission of twelve men, ten from Algiers and two from Tunis, was sent to Constantinople.

distance; yet seeing I am desperate for so honourable and secure a remedy, I will apply this I have begun, with your honour's command, to the best use; at least to take breath, if not to a perfect cure.[1]

This passage of Roe's letter strikes at the essence of the problem. The pirate states were not in fact subordinate to Constantinople. Any agreement would be short-lived because piracy was of great economic importance to these states and the oligarchies controlling them. Only a prolonged naval campaign against the pirate fleets and bases could bring about a true and lasting solution to the problem of piracy; however, Roe also realized that such an operation would be expensive and difficult for England to mount because of the distances involved. In the meantime, he had to deal with circumstances as he found them, which, in this case, was the arrival in Constantinople of a delegation from Algiers.

Following their arrival, several months were spent in negotiation before any agreement was reached.[2] In a fairly short time the two sides were able to agree to form an accord over the issue of captives held by each side. In return for the release of 40 Algerian prisoners held in England, the commissioners promised Roe that all English captives would be released to an official English consul as soon as he took up residence. Their insistence on the establishment of a proper consulate in Algiers before English prisoners were released caused Roe much difficulty. In the first place, he was not empowered to establish or appoint consuls at will. Secondly, he realized that this clause could be used to delay the implementation of the agreement. Even if Roe were able to persuade his government in London to establish a consulate in Algiers, much time would pass before someone could be appointed and take up his post there. In the end, Roe was able to get the wording of the agreement altered to read that the English nation would be granted the *privilege* of establishing a consulate in Algiers, and the appointed consul would oversee matters such as the release of captives and the trading activities of the king's subjects. Having succeeded in making the appointment of a consul a Crown privilege, rather than an obligation, Roe then recommended to the Lords of the Council that an official be appointed, not only to

[1] Ibid.
[2] The following discussion of the negotiations and agreement is based on PRO, SP 97/8/ff.149–50; SP 97/9/ff.74–5.

monitor the agreement but to advance English trading interests which might be expected to expand.

The agreement for the release of prisoners was only a first step in the negotiations. The contentious issue of contraband goods had to be settled. The delegation from Algiers insisted that Roe agree that ships of either nation would not carry arms and goods of any nation hostile to the other. Such an agreement, however, would be very much to England's disadvantage for England had substantial foreign trade, whereas Algiers had very little. Much of England's trade was carried on with states, such as Spain, which were considered hostile to Algiers. Commercial interests in England would never accept a prohibition of this sort. After much wrangling, Roe was able to get a compromise agreement which provided that neither state would be *prohibited* from carrying goods of any nation hostile to the other, though these goods would be considered lawful prize.

The terms of this agreement satisfied neither side entirely, though each gained something by the accord. Roe believed enough had been gained to justify ratification by his government. An acceptable basis for the release of English captives had been arranged, and procuring their freedom this way would be much less expensive than sending another expedition. If the settlement were honoured, it would protect English ships from future attacks as long as they carried no goods of a nation hostile to Algiers or Tunis. Merchantmen trading with Spain or some of the Italian states might still be at some risk, though they would be no worse off than before, while merchant ships carrying goods of nations friendly to Algiers would gain from the agreement since they would no longer be at risk. The agreement was not entirely satisfactory because English ships might become the subject of stop and search tactics, and there was also room for disagreement over what might constitute contraband goods. But as Roe appreciated, this agreement would bring a measure of relief and some degree of protection – and at very little cost to England.

The agreement was probably the best that could have been obtained under the circumstances. English influence and bargaining power were limited. Mansell's expedition had shown the potential of English naval power, but it had also shown how difficult it was to use this power effectively. The mere presence or potential of the fleet may have influenced the Turks to make some concessions, but its lack of any major success meant that England could not dictate terms.

The immediate response to Roe's agreement in England was not favourable. According to Chamberlain, James was greatly dissatisfied with the terms and prepared to disown his ambassador's work.[1] Reportedly, the Spanish ambassador was encouraging James against ratifying the agreement,[2] but it is more likely, as Calvert had observed earlier, that the king was reluctant to come to an agreement with those whom he considered little more than common thieves.

The government may also have been influenced by members of the Levant Company. They were concerned about the clause which allowed the goods of a hostile state to be considered a legitimate prize. The company was also concerned about the authority of the ambassador to make a treaty on his own. An underlying concern here was the fear that the company might incur financial liabilities as the result of the agreement. The company informed the Privy Council that Roe had undertaken the business without an express order from them. The Privy Council was informed that the Levant Company was not responsible for any costs arising from the agreement, and these, in any case, should be carried largely by the Spanish Company.[3]

For months no action was taken to confirm or repudiate the agreement. But by early June the increasing number of attacks on English ships and the consequent mounting level of complaints by merchants forced the government to act at last. As Calvert explained to Roe on 6 June:

> The great losses our merchants have lately received by the pirates of Algiers and Tunis, whereof there hath been so many complaints, have made your service the more acceptable unto his majesty, and the lords of the privy council, in endeavouring by the means and power of the grand signior to free our merchants from the future danger and spoil of those wicked people, and, to reform divers of his majesty's subjects taken prisoner by them. In the performance whereof, as soon as I understood that you had disbursed some moneys, I acquainted their lordships with it, who have given directions, that the

---

[1] PRO, SP 14/148/81.
[2] *CSPV*, 1623–1625, pp. 94–5, 107. As can be seen by the outcome of this episode, this was another case where the alleged influence of the Spanish ambassador came to nothing.
[3] PRO, SP 105/109/f.60. The Levant Company claimed that the Spanish Company gained the most by the settlement and, therefore, they should pay the greatest portion of any costs resulting from the agreement.

Levant merchants, and the rest of the English traders into the South-seas, shall presently take order amongst themselves for the raising of so much money as will satisfy your demands; and what power shall be wanting in them to effect the same, their lordships will supply; I shall be careful to see performed.[1]

As was the case so often in early Stuart England, the collection of money – even to pay for a worthy project – proved difficult. The proposed voluntary accord among merchants' groups could not be achieved for their interests varied greatly. In April 1623, Roe would write:

Concerning Tunis and Algiers, because I have written in general to the Lords, I will be bold to refer your honour to your part therein; only beseeching you, that so good a work, now almost perfect, may not perish for want on our parts, who complain, and yet do nothing; least I say to the merchants (whose slowness I know) *I have piped, but yee danced not*.[2]

Soon after this letter arrived in England, James came around to approving the agreement made by Roe, and steps were taken to implement the accord.[3] A merchant with much experience in the Levant, James Frizell, was appointed consul in Algiers.[4] He arrived in Algiers early in 1624, but contrary to the declarations of the officials, they made no attempt to bring the accord to a 'public conclusion'.[5] It would be many months before Frizell was able to report that the agreement had been implemented.

To some extent, the delay seems to have been the work of the Dutch consul, resident in Algiers. Reports of his alleged interference and misdeeds were sent to Roe who complained of them to Carleton, the English ambassador to the Hague. Carleton put pressure on the Dutch government to restrain its agent.[6] It is interesting to note that Roe took the matter directly to Carleton, and that Carleton, as he explained to Roe, had a quiet word with Dutch officials, thereby avoiding any advertisement of the affair in England where it might have been used to disrupt Anglo-Dutch relations. As a result of Carleton's complaint, the Dutch consul

---
[1] Roe, *Negotiations*, p. 160.
[2] Ibid., p. 143.
[3] PRO, SP 103/1/f.71.
[4] Wood, *Levant Company*, pp. 62–3; Roe, *Negotiations*, p. 574; PRO, SP 105/109/f.60. Frizell had been a factor in Algiers in 1613: SP 105/147 f.135v.
[5] PRO, SP 105/109/f.60. His letter is dated 20 March.
[6] PRO, SP 97/10/f.42; Roe, *Negotiations*, p. 256.

was recalled, and Frizell was able to proceed without further Dutch interference.

The difficulty experienced by Roe and Frizell in implementing the accord cannot be attributed solely to the machinations of the Dutch consul. This period witnessed a recrudescence of pirate activity in general.[1] Not only were English ships attacked at this time, but Venetian and French vessels were seized. Even Dutch merchants suffered losses, though relations between Algiers and the United Provinces were generally good. On one occasion in this period a Dutch ship was captured while riding in the harbour of Scanderoon. This attack shows the pirates of Algiers had scant respect for the Grand Signior, an attitude that was made even more patent when the pirates went on to sack the town.[2]

Since almost all the maritime nations of Christendom were suffering at this time, the Christian ambassadors in Constantinople came together to make a joint approach in the hope that their combined voice would have more effect. According to the Venetian ambassador, they agreed to seek 'the exemplary punishment of some ministers' in the hope that this measure would be more effective than the Sultan issuing more orders. However, these common efforts came to little. Despite letters and proclamations against the pirates, little was done and, as the Venetian observed, 'all the ports of this empire receive pirates, share their booty and provide them with the means of disposing of it, and without such help they could not remain long at sea'.[3] Though all suffered from the pirates, the Christian states found it difficult to agree on a course of action. Each state preferred to pursue short-term, national self-interests. This attitude was made explicit by Roe when writing to Carleton on 24 November 1624. It is an astonishing letter for Roe was well aware that the pirates posed a common threat and also of the impossibility of solving the problem if individual states acted alone. Yet without the slightest hesitation, he indicates that he was prepared to do exactly that. In this letter, Roe pulls aside the veil and reveals the sort of underlying attitude which made the problem of the Barbary pirates so intractable in the 17th century:

> Your lordship will give me leave to consider the propositions you mention in your last, made by Mons. d'Espesse to the

---
[1] PRO, SP 97/10/ff.24–5.
[2] Roe, *Negotiations*, p. 243.
[3] *CSPV*, 1623–1625, p. 246.

States, to enter the same accord of peace with Algiers, or to draw them to join in a war; in my opinion both are impossible. It seems not to me honourable for the French king to descend in peace to the Dutch treaty; that is, to join the pirates to make war, or to take any spoil, any foot of christian land; in which, necessity may excuse the Dutch, but nothing could defend the honour of a great prince to make such a contract with thieves; and without it he cannot enter into the Dutch agreement. On the other side, to draw the Dutch to break their peace, is untimely; they have then no place to water in the Levant, but only Zant; I mean their merchants using the bottom; and it is a kind of concession, that the French king is not able to trade in these seas, without their help. I fall upon this business, because I have made a peace lately, by a new bashaw, and commands procured by me: I have advice, that it is lately proclaimed and accepted; and it a little concerns us, to leave the French for a prey: cormorants and wolves must have some food, else they will seize on anything.[1]

Few letters of this period bring together so succinctly or define so clearly the place of honour and princely reputation, religious bonds, state necessity, and the devil-take-the-hindmost attitude that characterized international relations.

Roe wasted no time in reaching a bilateral accord with Murad IV, the new Sultan. It was virtually a restatement of the first agreement. English captives would be released with compensation of the owners; English subjects would be afforded protection and good treatment when in Algiers and Tunis; the ships of England and Algiers would treat each other in a friendly manner; an English consul, whose appointment was desired, would when present administer the exchange of prisoners; the seizure of the goods of states hostile to the other would not be considered a breach of the peace. What distinguished this accord was the way it was supported. The new Sultan was induced to replace the Bashaws in Algiers and Tunis with men more responsible to Constantinople who were more likely to see that the accord was enforced. Roe informed James that he had been present when the new viceroy was given his orders from the Grand Vizier. The official was told that he would pay with his head if the peace was broken by an Algerian attack on an English ship.[2]

[1] PRO, SP 97/10f.159–159v.
[2] PRO, SP 97/10/f.107.

Roe had now done all he could. As he explained to James, everything he wanted had been granted 'except only in the punishment of the bashaws, who have money to fine for their heads, and I none, but to maintain my own'.[1] Though optimistic, Roe remained cautious, as usual, about the lasting nature of the settlement. On 4 September, he wrote to the Council:

> What the success will be, I dare not promise; your lordships will be pleased to expect it from the consul of Algiers, whom I have ordered to give you account: but my opinion is, that it will be performed at first, and that the Grand Signior's commands will be accepted, and the peace proclaimed: for the Bashaw hath given here such satisfaction, that I cannot doubt him; and the soldiery are weary of the smart encounters they meet with our good shipping; and the rumours of our fleet of war at sea will make them desirous to have no quarrel with us.[2]

There was a natural inclination in Algiers to engage in piracy and this inclination would have to be countered. Roe was not so foolish to rely on the words or the goodwill of the Sultan or the Grand Vizier, as he explained:

> There is only one circumstance wanting, which I have no power to undertake; the bashaws of these two ports have their great profit by their shares of prizes, and that hath made them so backward to obey, and make peace to their loss.

However, he went on to explain he had made what provisions he could. He had not sufficient funds to buy off the many armadors, captains, and crews whose profit or livelihood was derived from piracy. The benefits of trade with England might be stressed, but they were not great enough to act as a substitute. Instead, Roe decided to concentrate all his influence on a couple of powerful officials. Roe outlined his strategy to the Council as follows:

> but I have procured them [the bashaws] to take any: so if it might be supplied by some feeling, (which is the best argument

[1] PRO, SP 97/10/f.90–90v.
[2] PRO, SP 97/10/f.111–111v.

in Turkey) that is, 1,000 dollars a year allowed me, to give in present to the bassa at the end of every year, that we have experience that he had kept the peace, and not otherwise.

By paying what amounted to a couple of bribes of only 1000 dollars a year, Roe informed the Council, shipping losses amounting to 100 000 dollars a year might be saved.[1] At first the peace was kept, and not long after his arrival, Frizell was able to secure the release of 240 captives.[2] As Frizell explained to Roe on 2 December 1625, he expected Algerian officials would continue to honour the accord as long as payment of the bribes continued.[3]

But without a regular source of funds to support the agreement, Roe's best efforts would be undermined. By August of the same year Frizell had spent 6000 dollars assisting prisoners to return home, but when he sought compensation, the authorities in England were reluctant to pay.[4] The Levant Company refused to contribute, declaring that the consul had acted without their authority. In November, the Privy Council began looking for other sources. The Lord President decided that money collected in a church brief could be used to meet Frizell's expenses. The search for money took time, and, in the meantime, Frizell could not redeem more captives for want of money. Frizell had to rely on credit, but at least one bill of exchange, drawn on Mr Leate, was refused, and Frizell was threatened with imprisonment.[5] At other times Roe provided money from his own funds to redeem captives, though he would also have great difficulty in getting reimbursed.[6]

As predicted by Roe, the settlement was not a lasting one. With some exaggeration it might be claimed that for three years the pirates of Algiers and Tunis did not take captive a single English ship.[7] However, by September 1626, the peace was at an end, and Algiers was in open rebellion against the wishes of the Sultan.[8] Any agreement with pirate states would necessarily be

[1] Ibid. He proposed to the Council that they get the Levant Company to raise the money to pay the bashaw.
[2] PRO, SP 71/1/f.91. According to Frizell he was able to release most captives at that time; he paid £3000 in 'head money'.
[3] PRO, SP 105/109/f.60.
[4] PRO, SP 71/1/f.91; SP 105/109/ff.60–1.
[5] PRO, SP 105/48/f.130.
[6] PRO, SP 97/13/ff.88, 202.
[7] PRO, SP 105/109/f.58.
[8] PRO, SP 97/12/f.192v. Tunis remained in obedience.

fragile, as Roe had perceived. In January 1623, even before an accord had been agreed, Roe foresaw how it might end:

> The greatest difficulty will rest in taking of the wind, and speaking together, when they meet with any of our stout ships; for these being men of war, stand upon terms: honest men, well assured in a good quarrel, will not bear up; but, as their custom is, they will hold their own, and not come under any man's lee; but shoot, and begin first: which will breed a new quarrel and breach, which these fellows will always seek under some fair pretence.[1]

All too easily and unintentionally the accord might be breached. A single incident could set off a cycle of retaliation that would lead to the conditions of virtual open warfare such as had prevailed in the years leading up to Roe's embassy. The taking of an Algerian ship by the Cadiz fleet was one such incident and the sort of pretence that pirate interests in Algiers had been looking for to end the peace.[2]

The peace that Roe's skilful diplomacy had brought lasted less than three years. Its short duration may be one reason why it has been largely forgotten or dismissed. The historian, A.C. Wood, thought it of little import and suggested that 'neither the agreement of 1623 nor the presence of these consuls made any difference to the conduct of the corsairs'.[3] Roe himself had no illusions about its permanence, though he thought an agreement might have come sooner and lasted longer had he been given greater support.

In any assessment of this episode, it must be remembered that Roe's agreement applied only to Algiers and Tunis. It did not apply to the Moroccan port of Sallee. As Frizell and others noted at the time, those who did not wish to be bound by the agreement could operate from Sallee, which many did, so much so that Sallee became the main source of piracy against English ships and merchants in the mid to late 1620s.[4]

Those trading to the eastern Mediterranean gained a brief but welcome respite, but since almost all of this trade was carried on

---

[1] PRO, SP 97/9/ff.13–14v.
[2] PRO, SP 97/12/f.192v. This is how Roe saw it according to his letter of 7 September 1626.
[3] Wood, *Levant Company*, p. 62.
[4] PRO, SP 105/109/f.61.

by the Levant Company, whose ships were strong and sailed in convoy, these benefits can be exaggerated. As the Venetian ambassador commented:

> I may add that during my stay here I have not heard much complaint from the merchants about the pirates, with whom, although the English have no formal treaty like the Dutch, I fancy there exists an understanding not to molest each other, the inference being reasonable as the company alone trades with certain marts in the Levant and within the Strait, forming at stated seasons their fleet of 12 or 15 ships, more or less, prepared to resist and defend themselves.[1]

Indeed, the security which the Levant Company's ships enjoyed as the result of the use of strong ships and convoys helps explain why the company did little to support the accord or the efforts of Roe and Frizell to see that it was maintained.

Thus the benefits for which Roe laboured appear to have had little effect on the operations of either the great Turkey merchants or the mariners who would suffer at the hands of the Salleemen. Seen in this light, Wood's dismissal might be justified. Such assessments, however, do not take into consideration the benefits English captives received as a result of the work by the ambassador and the consul. Exactly how many captives gained freedom as a consequence of the agreement is open to some question. In September 1626, Roe stated that most of the captives had been released,[2] and by November he felt confident enough to inform the Council that:

> [Frizell] hath not complained to me of any prize brought in, in 20 months; and hath written me, that almost all the slaves have been released, to above the number of 800.[3]

Frizell's letter has not survived, and thus it is impossible to verify the figure of above 800 mentioned by Roe. In letters going back to the beginning of his embassy, Roe often used the figure of 800 when referring to the number of English subjects in captivity. On hearing from Frizell that almost all those held captive had been

[1] *CSPV*, 1626–1628, p. 312. The Venetian ambassador's comment about the English in the Levant is in a letter dated 6 August 1627.
[2] PRO, SP 97/12/f.192v.
[3] Roe, *Negotiations*, p. 573.

released, Roe may have assumed that approximately 800 had been released.

The validity of Roe's figures are in some doubt because of two letters written by Frizell. On 12 February 1624/5, he wrote that he had released 240 captives,[1] and later, on 4 August 1626, that there were still 50 or 60 held captive[2] From these two comments, it is possible to infer that no more than 300 captives in all were released, though this assumes that Frizell's comments in these letters refer to all captives released from the time of his arrival in Algiers up until 12 February. It may be that he was only referring to a group of captives released in the last few months. Whatever the true figure, there can be no doubt that at the very minimum 240 captives and perhaps as many as 800 persons gained freedom as a consequence of Roe's embassy.

We do not know how much Roe and Frizell spent in freeing the captives. It appears that only a few thousand pounds were spent, ten thousand pounds at most. If over 800 captives were freed, then Roe's diplomacy was extremely cost effective; if only 240 captives were redeemed, the government still would have paid out no more than the going rate for English captives. In comparison to Mansell's expedition, Roe's diplomatic efforts achieved much. If only 240 were released, this is still eight times as many as Mansell was able to free and they were released at a fraction of the cost.[3]

Roe's success was very much a personal achievement. At crucial stages, he had taken the initiative, going beyond his instructions, to push forward negotiations, often in the face of opposition in London and Algiers. He understood both how little control the Sultan had over Algiers and Tunis and how slight was the power of England to influence events in this part of the world. Yet by skill and shrewdness, specifically by focusing his limited funds and influence, Roe had managed to force through an accord which was to the honour of king James and his subjects' benefit.

Throughout the negotiations, a sharp realism infused Roe's diplomacy, and it was this quality which made success possible. From beginning to end, he understood that only the united force of the Christian maritime powers could achieve a lasting solution. But with the Thirty Years War raging about him, Roe did not need years of diplomatic experience to see that the divisions within

[1] PRO, SP 71/1/f.45.
[2] PRO, SP 71/1/f.64.
[3] See above, Chapter 7, Mansell's expedition cost at least £64 000 or over £1000 per captive.

Christendom cut too deeply for a united front to be established against the pirate enemy. He was also painfully aware that the English government lacked the will and resources to pursue a strategy of naval blockade on its own for as long as was required. Roe's hand was a weak one, yet he played it brilliantly and served his masters well (with little appreciation), much better than they deserved.[1]

---

[1] It is both ironical and coincidental that on the return voyage Roe's ship was attacked by pirates off Malta and that the ship, the *Sampson*, was commanded by William Rainsborough, who, as explained in Chapter 10, came to play a major role in English efforts to suppress pirates: Brown, *Itinerant Ambassador*, pp. 165–6; M. Strachan, '*Sampson's* Fight with Maltese Galleys 1628', *MM*, LV (1969), pp. 281–9.

9
PIRACY, PARLIAMENT AND PERSONAL RULE

In the reign of Elizabeth I, relations between England and Morocco had been amicable; however, as the 17th century progressed, this relationship changed. The port of Sallee grew increasingly independent of the authority of the king of Morocco, especially after the influx of thousands of Moriscos,[1] and by the 1620s had become a major base for pirates. The multitude of complaints and letters sent to the king and Council during the latter half of the decade attest to the rise of Sallee as a pirate base. The wives and mothers of captives followed the king and Council about importuning them so frequently and vigorously for relief that eventually orders were given to keep them away.[2] Complaints about the pirates were also addressed to parliament which met with unusual frequency in the 1620s.

Although Sir Robert Phelips commented upon Mansell's unfortunate expedition in March 1624, the first substantial discussion of piracy did not occur until 5 July 1625.[3] The issue came up when Sir Walter Earle was speaking on tonnage and poundage.[4]

---

[1] The Moriscos were Spanish Moors expelled from Spain; most settled in Morocco.
[2] PRO, SP 71/1/f.492: 'These poor women that follow the King are many of them in great misery and want and likewise those in the western parts . . .'. At one point Charles I, who succeeded his father in March 1625, was forced back inside when besieged by a throng of imploring relatives of the captives. In 1633 the Privy Council issued an order for wives of captives not to importune the Council any more. PRO, PC 2/43/f.551.
[3] *Journals of the House of Commons* (hereafter *Commons Journals*), I, p. 724.
[4] S.R. Gardiner, *History of England: From the Accession of James I to the Outbreak of the Civil War, 1603–1642*, V, p. 364. At least since the reign of Henry VI, these duties on imports and exports had been granted to the monarch for life by his first parliament.

However, the Crown was claiming additional duties[1] which Parliament had not specifically authorized, and MPs, like Earle, simply wished to limit tonnage and poundage for a year.[2]

Earle sat for the maritime county of Dorsetshire, one of those worst affected by piracy.[3] He did not talk in abstract terms about constitutional rights, but when speaking of tonnage and poundage reminded the House that these duties had been granted specifically to enable the Crown to guard the seas. But the seas, he observed, were not secure; to the contrary, so great was the failure of the navy royal in providing security, he claimed, that now 'Turkish pirates come into our seas and take our ships at our doors'.[4] In the past few weeks alone, Earle continued, several English ships had been taken off the Scilly Isles.

These claims were neither contrived nor exaggerated, and the particular depredations of which he spoke are documented. Though MPs in general may not have known, the government was by then well aware how the west country was suffering from pirate attacks. On 18 April, Sir James Bagg had written to the Lord High Admiral, Buckingham, about the loss of several Cornish ships in recent weeks and that the Turkish pirates were becoming so bold, he claimed, that they now plucked victims from the mouths of English harbours.[5] On the same day, the mayor of Plymouth informed the Council that Sallee men-of-war were spoiling English ships all along the coast.[6] At approximately the same time, John Trewinard, deputy searcher at St Ives, wrote to Secretary Conway that Salleemen were taking ships only to make slaves of the crew and that recently they had taken 18 out of one English ship and 16 from another.[7] At the end of April, John Godolphin wrote to the governor of the Scilly Isles that two Salleemen, one, of 32 guns, were cruising about and that reportedly 20 other pirate ships were

---

[1] Preternated customs, as they were called.
[2] C.S.R. Russell, *Parliaments and English Politics 1621–1629* pp. 227–9. They wished to limit the king's right to these duties until a new law could be drafted and passed which would settle the questions of constitutional rights raised by the recent impositions.
[3] Earle had also sat for Weymouth and Melcombe Regis, one of the ports that suffered most from pirates.
[4] *Commons Journals*, I, p. 803.
[5] PRO, SP 16/1/69, 94, describe acts of piracy in preceding months in harbour mouths and off the Scilly Isles.
[6] PRO, SP 16/2/36 and inclosure. Also on 7 May. The mayor also sent the examination of William Court, recently released from captivity by pirates: SP 16/1/68, inclosures, contains two examinations.
[7] PRO, SP I1/2/33. He reported that 30 ships were out to sea by Sallee.

coming to rove about the western parts of England.[1] In May, the mayor of Weymouth and Melcombe Regis warned the Council about the harm being done by the Sallee pirates. So fearful were the people of these parts, the mayor explained, that ships were no longer putting to sea because of the danger.[2] Other reports speak of the lamentable outcries of wives, widows and children of sailors taken captive. Examinations of captives recently freed were sent to the Council so that the sufferings of the west country mariners might be known to their lordships and the intelligence they possessed about the pirate fleets passed on to the Admiralty.[3]

The political implications of these reports were quickly perceived. Buckingham was warned that diverse west country towns had written to their burgesses complaining of the daily oppression they suffered by the Sallee pirates. Bagg advised the Lord High Admiral that royal warships should be sent out. Just to be certain that Buckingham didn't miss the point, he added that the ships should be sent immediately so that the remedy might appear to precede the complaints.[4] Long before this advice was received, however, Buckingham had written to Sir Francis Stewart, commander of a naval squadron, passing on the reports about the presence of Turkish pirates.[5] Stewart was ordered to take the *Lion, Rainbow,* and as many other ships as were ready to clear the coast of these pirates.[6]

However, neither Buckingham's orders nor Stewart's actions stopped MPs from complaining about Sallee pirates on the coasts. Alderman Whitson of Bristol registered his concern and John Rolle, a merchant, gave evidence of the great harm being done.[7] The sufferings of the king's west country subjects at the hands of the pirates were described in a letter by William Legg that was read to the House. He told how his ship[8] had been taken and the

[1] PRO, SP 16/1/94.
[2] PRO, SP 16/2/75. SP 16/4/9, examination of David Cockburn, states that 600 captives were held in Sallee.
[3] PRO, SP 16/5/23, 24 incl.; also SP 16/4/9. They indicated that Salleemen were infesting the coast much more than Algerines or pirates of Tunis had ever done.
[4] PRO, SP 16/5/6. Bagg informed Buckingham that 20 Salleemen were on the coast and that they had taken two ships worth £5000 in the previous week off the Lizard.
[5] It should be noted that Buckingham wrote to Stewert eight days before Earle brought up the matter in the House.
[6] PRO, SP 16/3/97, 27 June 1625. It was added that Stewert should not allow his ships to be led on a long chase by the pirates so that his squadron would not get too distant to join the Cadiz fleet when it was formed at Plymouth.
[7] *Commons Journals*, I, pp. 814, 820.
[8] It was from Milbrook.

crew sold into slavery in Sallee where they had been tormented. The House was told that captives had had their ears cut off and been forced to eat them; others were burned and starved and forced to turn Turk. Eighteen ships had recently been brought into Sallee, the MPs were informed, and the pirates were demanding as much as £600 a head in ransom money, and even the meanest soul had to find £120 to purchase freedom. The Commons also heard the testimony of Robert Dollinge who swore that 14 pirate ships from Sallee were operating off Land's End and that they had already taken four ships but a few days ago, including one of 100 tons from Plymouth.[1]

Many of these incidents can be confirmed. The historical record includes evidence on the suffering of captives but it does not suggest that there were multitudes of mutilated mariners roaming the west country.[2] No 17th-century Captain Jenkins presented himself to stir up the House; nor was one needed. The reports were gruesome and credible enough, and even if every horrible detail were not accepted, the reports as a whole were apparently believed.[3] Whatever the intent, these complaints provided a reason for limiting the grant of tonnage and poundage. They confirmed that the seas were not being guarded and by implication the competence of Buckingham, the Lord High Admiral, was brought into question. His defenders claimed that the Duke was working to remedy matters and had already dispatched a fleet to clear the coasts.[4] Though such speeches may have satisfied the House, some such as Sir Francis Stewart found the whole debate ludicrous:

> I am much grieved that the Western gents and merchants should inform your grace that I have given them no help since my coming hither for the securing of these coasts. If their

---

[1] *Debates in the House of Commons in 1625*, ed. S.R. Gardiner, pp. 116–17. A letter by John Barker of Bristol was also read, describing the great spoil done in the two weeks before 9 August 1625. A ship of Milbrook worth £9000 was reported taken. PRO, SP 16/2/36 incl., confirms the capture.
[2] In CRO, Bodmin Borough Accounts, 1635, no. 288, there is an entry for a man who had his tongue cut out by pirates.
[3] No speaker or piece of evidence was challenged.
[4] *Debates in the Commons*, ed. Gardiner, p. 117. Sir Robert Mansell chipped in that this was a matter for the Council of War (of which he was a member) and that they 'would undertake to redress it, or else answer it with their lives'. Alas, no diarist informs us whether these words by the leader of the Algiers expedition gave comfort, nor is there any evidence that his brother councillors received his ultimatum appreciatively.

complaints were just ... I should judge myself fitter for Wapping then to command the meanest ship in the fleet ... In lieu of those gents and merchants complaints who came up to parliament I protested them with a humble petition that they would have procured an act that we might have fair winds at pleasure to perform their service, but I doubted that they would hardly find any precedent for it.[1]

His pique is understandable for adverse winds did hamper his efforts.[2]

In the parliament of 1628 the questions about Buckingham's stewardship of the navy were much sharper than the earlier, gentle debate over tonnage and poundage. One of the major complaints in the impeachment charges brought against the duke was his failure to guard the Narrow Seas.[3] Vivid accounts of the damage and the suffering caused by the pirates gave emotional force and substance to the charge and were used in the attack on Buckingham. Sir Walter Earle claimed that he had 'a certificate of 80 and odd ships taken by four Turkish pirates that were masters of the Channel at Swalley for four months together'.[4] He was followed in the debate by Sir Robert Mansell, who declared that 'from east to west nothing is so much neglected totally as the seas'.[5] In defence of Buckingham, Edward Nicholas, Secretary to the Admiralty, could only say that six ships were then at sea, though 30 more would be needed to deal effectively with the problem.[6] Characteristically, Sir Robert Phelips pointed out the obvious, 'This now being visible to every man's sense, let us resolve that trade is decayed and that this decay is come from a loss upon the seas'.[7] From the rather scanty accounts of the parliament's proceedings, it appears that the speeches were largely catalogues of complaint and devoid of any dispassionate analysis of the cause or nature of England's naval weakness. Buckingham was to blame and his removal was the only remedy put forward.

[1] PRO, SP 16/5/49.
[2] His orders also inhibited his actions and explain why he did not chase the pirates but let them get away.
[3] *Journals of the House of Lords*, III, pp. 619–24; for a full discussion, see C.C.G. Tite, *Impeachment and Parliamentary Judicature in Early Stuart England*, pp. 190–202.
[4] *Commons Debates 1628*, ed. M.F. Keeler, M.J. Cole, W.R. Bidwell, IV: 28 May–26 June 1628, p. 202.
[5] Ibid., pp. 202–3.
[6] Ibid., p. 203.
[7] Ibid., p. 203.

The role of Buckingham as Lord High Admiral has been reconsidered by Roger Lockyer and A.P. McGowan.[1] As a result of their studies, it seems clear that Buckingham brought a new energy to the office of Lord High Admiral. However, it also appears that this new interest in the navy and the expansion of the service was more in the nature of a short-term expedient than as the consequence of a grand strategic vision. There is also evidence, albeit circumstantial, that the build-up of the navy under Buckingham came as a response to a growth of naval power abroad rather than from a reforming impulse of the Lord High Admiral.[2] Whatever the impulse, new and considerable efforts were made to guard the maritime commerce of England during the mid- to late-1620s.[3] First, instructions to naval captains in these years provide evidence that the defence of English seaborne trade was a major concern. These instructions show how frequently the Admiralty deployed warships to clear the coasts of pirates or to waft merchantmen through dangerous areas.[4] Secondly, a special commission was created in 1627 to look into the state of the navy.[5] In some ways the work of this commission was similar to that of earlier investigating committees in that the commissioners were concerned with defects and malfeasance in the navy. But the discussions dealt with weightier matters than inefficiency and corruption; much of the discussion of the commissioners was focused on the strategic role of the navy. The root of the problem was strategic in nature: England was faced with two distinct and very different threats.

---

[1] R. Lockyer, *Buckingham: The life and political career of George Villiers, first Duke of Buckingham 1592–1628*, pp.48–50, 76, 301–4, 341–5, and especially 359–67; A.P. McGowan, 'The Royal Navy under the First Duke of Buckingham, Lord High Admiral 1618–1628', (unpublished PhD thesis, University of London, 1967), p. 270. Much of the actual work and effort of reform is attributed to the commissioners. More recently, K.R. Andrews has examined the Caroline navy in *Ships, Money, and Politics, seafaring and naval enterprise in the reign of Charles I*. The first half of this work is very useful, though the latter half appears derivative and is less convincing.
[2] For example, the Spanish rebuilding programme was underway in 1617, a year before Buckingham became Lord High Admiral. Like that of the United Provinces, it was brought on by the approach of war. These years mark the first phase of the great naval race of the 17th century.
[3] See, for examples, PRO, SP 16/157/11,17,18, for attempts in September 1625.
[4] PRO, SP 16/157/ff.11–11v, 14v, 15, 16–16v, 17v, 18–18v, 20, 21, 23–23v, 25–25v, 26v, 32v, 34, 35v, 53v, 56, 59, 155 (Naval Instructions 1625–8).
[5] PRO, SP 16/41/45,93, subjects to be examined by the commissioners and their names.

The most immediate threat came from the Dunkirk privateers and the Barbary pirates. They posed a serious threat and in the long run might damage English seaborne commerce sufficiently to weaken the realm and make it prey to stronger powers, as Coke and Roe noted.[1] The Dunkirkers and pirates were a threat only to merchantmen since they employed lightly-constructed ships of less than 200 tons designed for speed. The large, heavy warships of the Royal Navy were strong enough to defend themselves against such vessels but were too slow to chase and catch such vessels.

To meet the threat posed by the Dunkirkers and pirates, the special commission examined several proposals. Sir Sackville Trevor's proposal followed traditional lines. He recommended the setting out of a fleet of 20 ships of between 300 and 600 tons plus two pinnaces of 80 tons each. Based on a charge of 20s per man per month (28 days) for 3000 men for 13 months, the cost of such a fleet was put at £78 000. Later, this charge was reduced to £43 280 by limiting operations to nine months and cutting the number of men to 2020. Seven ships of 300 tons would be hired at £60 per ton per month and nine ships of 200 tons at a rate of £40 per ton per month, exclusive of all charges for munitions.[2]

A far more comprehensive and original proposal was put forward by Captain Richard Gifford on 15 February 1627. In it the various threats were defined and appropriate responses recommended.[3] Gifford proposed the creation of a fleet of 30 ships of between 300 and 400 tons and ten pinnaces of between 80 and 100 tons. The estimated cost of building this fleet, based on a charge of £4 per ton, was put at £55 000.[4]

Some members of the commission, principally Lord Harvey and Sir Henry Wainwaring, objected immediately to Gifford's idea of building small warships. They argued that ships of 400 tons or less would be of little service and that only those of 600 tons or more were worth building. Gifford replied by noting that the larger 300 to 400-ton ships used by the Dunkirk and Ostend privateers were employed chiefly between Spain and the West Indies, and only occasionally did they take English merchantmen. The real damage to English shipping was done by ships of only 80 to 150 tons. These

---

[1] PRO, SP 16/269/51; T. Roe, *Negotiations of Sir T. Roe in his embassy to the Ottoman Porte, from the year 1621 to 1628 inclusive*, pp. 8–9.
[2] PRO, SP 16/54/12,13.
[3] For example, so that 'the Dunkirk[ers might be] suppressed, [and] the Turks and Moors and all pirates [be made] not so hardy as now they are . . .'.
[4] PRO, SP 16/54/9. Another copy with minor differences in SP 16/54/11.

shallow-draft vessels were able to operate in shoal areas and coastal waters. Lightly constructed and clean of line, such ships were nimble and speedy. Such ships were not very threatening if operating alone, but by operating in packs their combined strength was sufficient to overpower much larger and better armed ships.[1] The traditional, large English man-of-war of 600 tons or thereabouts was of little use against such ships, Gifford told the commission. English men-of-war were well suited for defending the realm against an invasion fleet but of little use in protecting trade against attacks by pirates and privateers. He advised the commission that:

> England was never so well provided of good shipping as now it is, and therefore the less need to build suddenly any great ships, but for offence never so weak or ill, they are of strength suficient to defend, but none doth sail well, and therefore no way good to offend.[2]

Only by building light, swift ships of approximately the same size as (but stronger and better-armed than) those of the Dunkirkers and Turks would it be possible to counter this threat. In Gifford's view, ships of 200 tons plus would best serve England's needs. Moreover, he argued, two ships of 300 to 400 tons would cost less to build than one of 600 tons, and two ships would be of more use operationally since they could operate separately and thereby secure two areas at the same time.[3]

Though the whole of Gifford's programme was not adopted, his recommendation of smaller, lighter ships was taken up by the navy. The special commission ordered master shipwrights to meet and submit plans for 'a perfect mould for Narrow Seas ships'. They wished these vessels to be 'good sailors' with a length to beam ratio of greater than three and for ships to be of between 200 and 400 tons.[4] On 6 March the shipwrights responded, producing plans for what they described as a nimble and strong ship. They envisioned a 28-gun warship of 339 tons with a length to beam ratio of 2.69 and a beam to depth ratio of 2.04.[5] Extreme conservativism characterized the shipwrights' proposed design.

[1] PRO, SP 16/54/46. Evidence of capture supports Gifford's judgement.
[2] Ibid.
[3] Ibid.
[4] PRO, SP 16/54/24. A ship of 300 tons was thought best by the commission.
[5] PRO, SP 16/56/56.

The proportions are typical of a galleon of the late Elizabethan period – simply scaled down. The hull form and dimensions suggest that a warship of this design would have possessed neither the speed nor nimbleness sought by the commission.[1]

Evidently the commissioners were not satisfied, for the shipwrights' design was quickly put aside. Instead, authorization was given for construction of ten smaller ships which would be known as the *Lion's Whelps*. Each measured 185 tons and had a length to beam ratio of 2.48 and beam to depth ratio of 2.78. From these particulars, it is clear that they too would not possess great speed, though their shallow draught would make them useful for operations in shoal or coastal waters. Built at a total cost of approximately £9 per ton, the *Whelps* proved more expensive than anticipated.[2] Despite their shortcomings, the *Whelps* served the navy well over the next decade. The large number of ships built to this design allowed the Crown to maintain an extensive naval presence in many seas which otherwise would not have been covered. The mere presence of such warships was often sufficient to deter privateers or pirates or compel them to move on to unprotected areas.

If the Dunkirkers and pirates had been the only source of trouble for the navy, then its maritime strategy and fleet-building programme would have been fairly straightforward and not very costly. But as well as being menaced by the small, swift ships of the privateers and pirates, England faced the more remote but more serious threat posed by the battle fleets of the major powers.

In the early 17th century many Englishmen wrongly assumed that Spanish naval power ended with the Armada catastrophe.[3] In fact, by the 1590s the *Armada del Mar Oceano* had been rebuilt

[1] T. Glasgow, jr, 'The Shape of the Ships that Defeated the Spanish Armada', *MM*, L (1964), pp. 177–87, provides the mean dimensions for galleons. For a further discussion of ship characteristics, see below, Chapter 11.
[2] M. Oppenheim, *A History of the Administration of the Royal Navy and of Merchant Shipping in Relation to the Navy*, pp. 254–5, gives the dimensions; PRO, SP 16/58/25, the building contract; SP 16/96/56, the total cost; SP 16/365/17, cost of ordnance: these ships were hurriedly built with 'sappy timber' and not very successful, SP 16/121/41 and 365/17. This sum was exclusive of ordnance which came to £5216 13s 4d.
[3] For example, Sir Edward Coke believed the Spanish virtually defenceless; however, J.C. Appleby, 'English Privateering during the Spanish and French Wars, 1625–30' (Unpublished PhD thesis, University of Hull, 1983), p. 270 shows the falsity of the claim. Unfortunately, some historians have accepted the view that Spanish naval power ended with the Armada. For historical opinion, see R.A. Stradling, 'Catastrophe and Recovery: the Defeat of Spain, 1639–43', *History*,

and strengthened, and again in the 1620s the fleet was extensively modernized.[1] Some measure of the Spanish naval strength in the 1630s may be seen in the number of ships Philip IV was able to send to Bahia in 1638. His fleet included 30 galleons and 20 other major warships: at this time, the English government possessed only about 40 warships in all.[2] Also, with the implementation of Olivares' 'northern' strategy, the naval threat posed by the Hapsburgs took on a new and ominous dimension, for Olivares was attempting to create a fleet in northern waters which could operate from secure bases.[3] Potentially, this threat was as great or greater than that which faced the Elizabethans. Until the destruction of Oquendo's armada in 1639 by the Dutch, Spain remained a great naval power with a fleet of warships greater in number than that possessed by England.[4] English naval planners in the 20s and 30s had to include provisions to counter the Spanish threat.

But Spain was not the only potential enemy with which England's naval planners were concerned. Dutch maritime power had increased dramatically since the late 16th century and by the early 17th century was the greatest in the world.[5] Relations between the English and Dutch had also deteriorated in this period. No longer did the Dutch act as a grateful protectorate.[6] From very early in the reign of James I, certainly by the end of the 1620s,

---

LXIV (1979), p. 205. For an appreciation of the Spanish threat for the whole of this period, see the same author's important study, *The Armada of Flanders, Spanish Maritime Policy and European War 1568–1668.*

[1] I.A.A. Thompson, *War and Government in Hapsburg Spain 1560–1620*, pp. 197–200, 304–6.

[2] AGS, Guerra Antigua, legajo 1308.

[3] J. Alcalá-Zamora y Queipo de Llano, *España, Flandes y el mar del Norte (1618–39): La última ofensiva Europea de los Austrias Madrileños, passim.* Also, see R.A. Stradling, 'The Spanish Dunkirkers, 1621–48: a record of plunder and destruction', *Tijdschrift voor Geschiedenis* XCIII (1980), pp. 541–58 and also the later and more comprehensive, *The Armada of Flanders: Spanish Maritime Policy and European War, 1558–1668.*

[4] On the strength of Spain, see R.A. Stradling, *Europe and the Decline of Spain: A Study of the Spanish System 1580–1720*, pp. 60–7; idem, 'Catastrophe and Recovery, 1639–43', pp. 205–19. Spain built 16 galleons in 1622–3: Thompson, *War and Government*, p. 306, and between 1634–8, a further 28 galleons were added, 12 of which were 800 tons or more: C. Fernández Duro, *Armada Española*, IV, pp. 440, 442.

[5] PRO, SP 84/149/ff.65–80 shows that the Dutch admiralties possessed a combined fleet of 98 men-of-war, roughly three times the number of England.

[6] C. Reed, *Lord Burghley and Queen Elizabeth*, p. 544, shows that the Lord Treasurer recognized the Dutch threat as early as 1596. I wish to thank Professor C.S.R. Russell for this reference.

diverging political interests and colonial and commercial conflict had become manifest.[1] The special embassies of 1610, 1613, 1618, 1622–3, 1624, 1627, 1628, and 1636 attest to the increasingly bitter relations between the two states. Many English writers in this period vented their fear, frustration, and jealousy of the Dutch.[2] While it might be possible to dismiss some of these anti-Dutch tirades as the work of Spanish sympathizers, the genuineness of English antipathy becomes evident when even notoriously anti-Spanish men like Raleigh were inveighing against the Dutch, and especially against their growing 'command and mastery of the seas'.[3] Within the government, even a man of Puritan sympathies like Sir Robert Heath thought it necessary to advise that the honour, safety, and profit of both king and kingdom needed protection from the Dutch threat. He wrote:

> In our safety we suffer if our shipping be not maintained, and right to the Narrow Seas not preserved, for in former ages our strength at sea preserved our peace at home, and made it abroad, and the same reasons remain now, and we find our nearest neighbours, the Hollanders, take too much boldness out of the opinion of their strength at sea and of our security.[4]

By the late 1630s the clash of political and commercial interests made naval warfare between the two states a real possibility and necessitated a strengthening of the navy.[5]

France also began to look threatening, for under Richelieu measures were taken to rebuild the French navy, first by hiring foreign ships, but later by constructing warships in French yards. By early 1631 this build-up had been so successful that the French Channel fleet of sizeable ships was larger in number than the

---

[1] G. Edmundson, *Anglo-Dutch Rivalry during the First Half of the Seventeenth Century*, passim.

[2] One of the most intriguing expressions of this awareness of the Dutch threat, especially when one thinks of 1667, is found in Coke's warning of 1619 to stop the Dutch from entering the Medway since their fleet is less than 10 hours away with a good wind, *Cal. Clarendon Papers*, I, p. 16.

[3] W. Raleigh, 'Observations touching Trade and Commerce with the Hollanders and Other Nations'; '. . . wherein is proved that our sea and land commodities serve to enrich and strengthen other countries against our own', in *The Works of Sir Walter Raleigh, Kt.*, VIII, pp. 351–76.

[4] PRO, SP 16/229/102. Attacks on English ships in the 1630s by Dutch vessels are listed in SP 84/150/ff.189–190v.

[5] For a contemporary account of Dutch threats, see PRO, SP 16/269/51.

English navy (39 to 38).[1] The French threat became even greater in the 1630s when, as Secretary Coke noted with trepidation, it appeared that the 'French and Dutch may join fleets to impeach his Majesty's dominion in these seas'.[2]

These threats to English sovereignty and interests were potentially so great that any reasonably prudent monarch or council would be compelled to concentrate limited naval resources on building and maintaining a battle fleet of large, defensible ships. Indeed, even though Gifford advocated the creation of a fleet of small, swift, offensive ships to counter pirates and privateers, he realized that England needed a fleet of warships of 600 tons or more for 'any service to the great danger of England's safety'.[3]

To many contemporary critics, and indeed some later observers, the nature and dimensions of this strategic dilemma were not appreciated. They tended to see the inability of the navy to guard the seas largely as a consequence of corruption by the naval administration of the Duke of Buckingham or other Crown officials. Malpractice, misappropriation, and waste, and general inefficiency were alleged and investigated by special commissions,[4] and though the commissions' work lends substance to the charge of corruption, no study – either then or since – confirms whether these irregularities were common at the time, or, more importantly, different from those of preceding or later naval administrations.

The question of corruption is a vexing one in part because it depends so much on definition and perspective.[5] The development of the Royal Navy was not one of smooth steady progress. There were periods of rapid expansion to meet foreign threats, as under Henry VIII and Elizabeth, only to be followed by periods under Mary and James when the need to keep a battle fleet at peak

---

[1] E.H. Jenkins, *A History of the French Navy: From its beginnings to the present day*, pp. 15–21. More recent and detailed information on the French navy can be found in the numerous articles and guides to French naval papers by Etienne Taillemite, and Philippe Le Masson: J.P. Cooper, 'Sea-Power', pp. 230–1. For the strength of the French channel fleet, see PRO, SP 78/101/f.146.

[2] PRO, SP 16/328/37. Coke was obviously very concerned about Dutch-French naval collusion as is evident in his correspondence with William Boswell, ambassador to the Hague, for example, SP 84/149/ff.34,98, 100v, 112–116.

[3] PRO, SP 16/54/9.

[4] PRO, SP 16/42/17,19,25–7,38,40–1,47–8.

[5] For more on this point, see J. Hurstfield, *Freedom, Corruption and Government in Elizabethan England*, pp. 137–62.

strength and efficiency was difficult to justify.[1] Decline and decay in these periods was inevitable. It is also by no means clear whether the naval administration of the Stuarts was scrutinized because its deficiencies were so patent, or whether it attracted scrutiny because of the important role of the navy at the time. Furthermore, it may be argued that what is taken to be 'corruption' may not signify decline but rather a rational, though unofficial, process of governmental reorganization, an alternative form of tax collection and salary system.[2] This last view, however, was not one likely to find support in the parliaments of the 1620s.

But while parliament was considering the failure of the Crown and Lord High Admiral to secure the seas, government officials were making new efforts to protect seaborne commerce and to alleviate the sufferings of those assaulted by pirates. Except when shipping was needed for special expeditions, such as those to Cadiz, La Rochelle, and Isle de Rhé, Royal Navy vessels were regularly ordered to use 'all the means you are able to annoy or apprehend all Pirates, Turks, [and] Dunkirkers' or 'scour the said seas and to clear them from Pirates'.[3] Additionally, the use of letters of marque as a means of combating the pirates was examined, though this remedy was not favoured by some. The Levant Company, for example, thought that it would lead to retaliation against their ships and factories in Turkey.[4]

Diplomacy also continued to play a part in the Crown's programme to protect seaborne commerce. The success of Roe's embassy may have encouraged Charles I to try a similar approach in dealing with the pirates of Sallee. A commission was given to John Harrison, a royal servant of long standing, to go to Sallee and treat with the pirates. However, almost immediately there was an outcry against Harrison's embassy. Henry Marten, Chief Judge of the High Court of Admiralty, opposed Harrison's commission,

---

[1] Oppenheim, *Administration of the Royal Navy*, pp. 44–183; also T. Glasgow, jr, 'The Navy in Philip and Mary's War, 1557–1558', *MM*, LIII (1967), 321.
[2] See A.J. Heidenheimer, *Political Corruption: Readings in comparative analysis*, but especially the essay by J.S. Nye, 'Corruption and political development: A cost-benefit analysis'. J. de Vries, 'Is There an Economics of Decline?', *Journal of Economic History*, XXXVIII (1978), pp. 256–8, has some useful comments on this question. This point is developed in G.E. Aylmer, *The King's Servants: The Civil Service of Charles I, 1625–1642*, pp. 178–81, 246.
[3] PRO, SP 16/157/20,21,97.
[4] PRO, SP 105/149/f.61v. HCA 25/224, a register of commissions for reprisal and marque, shows that between 12 February 1626 and 26 April 1627, ten commissions of reprisal to take pirates were issued.

and his reasons are interesting for the light they shed on how Sallee was perceived. He wrote:

> Yesterday Captain Harrison was with me and showed me his commission under the great seal, by which he hath power to go and treat with the King, Princes, and States of Barbary, of which Sallee is one. Now his commission under the great seal is not only contrary to the declaration made by the Lords of the Council last Monday concerning Sallee, viz. That they were but a base company of pirates, but also overthrows the very foundation of all means that otherwise might have conduced to justify the taking of the goods in the *Blue Dove*, & the rest of that kind: for with pirates there is no treaty nor consideration. But in this commission there are things to be observed, which conclude them to be no pirates.
> 1. That we treat and make a league with them.
> 2. We term their spoils and depredations but acts of hostility.
> 3. We establish traffic, trade, and commerce with them.
> 4. And lastly we furnish them with arms and great ordnance.
> Now upon these premises, how we can bar the subjects of the States from trade and commerce with them, or blame them for that which we seek ourselves, or justify our proceedings upon our former supposed grounds, I know not. The commission in my opinion might have been more cautiously framed, and yet the same thing acted which now is intended for Sallee, since it doth so please his Majesty, as I will more at large tomorrow (God willing) declare unto his Grace, if it be not too late. Hereof I thought good to advertise to you, and tomorrow I purpose to attend my Lord Admiral at court, and signify to his Grace, that if this commission goes forward, his Sallee hopes in my understanding will be utterly desperate. And so I take my leave and rest.[1]

What happened following Marten's meeting with Buckingham remains obscure, though it is known that Harrison's embassy was delayed. Possibly, Marten's objections were met, at least in part, by redrafting the commission along the lines suggested by the Chief Judge of the Admiralty.[2]

---

[1] PRO, SP 16/40/24.
[2] Harrison's commissions were enrolled under the great seal on the Treaty Rolls, the appropriate one of which does not survive. I wish to thank Dr D.L. Thomas of the PRO for his efforts to find the commissions.

In the event, Harrison did go to Sallee where he was able to free between 200 and 260 English captives with the help of some Moriscos.[1] In return for their help, Harrison provided the Moriscos with 14 bronze guns and powder and shot.[2] His success was repeated the following year on a smaller scale by Sir Kenelm Digby, who secured the release of 80 more captives from Barbary.[3] However, the work of Harrison and Digby, like that of Roe, was short-lived. By the beginning of the 1630s, Sallee pirates were again operating on the coasts of England, seizing ships and men with, if anything, greater vigour. Evidence in English archives suggests that this resurgence was sparked off by an incident involving a London ship, the *William and John*, of which John Maddocke was master.[4] According to one account, this ship took a Sallee vessel off Cape St Vincent in April 1631 and brought its crew to Cadiz where they were sold. In retaliation, it was alleged, Sallee men-of-war began seizing English ships and goods and selling the crews into slavery. Among those claiming losses was Sir William Courteen, the great London merchant, who brought an action in the High Court of Admiralty against Maddocke to recover damages. However, a very different account emerges from the testimony of the crew of the *William and John*. According to them, the incident began early in the morning on 10 May when they saw a ship lying with all her sails struck down. Moments later this vessel, a Sallee man-of-war, raised her sails and began to chase the *William and John*. Though outnumbered, the crew of the *William and John* fought off the pirates and overwhelmed their attacker. The crew also testified that their prisoners were examined by the Spanish at Cadiz and that the Moors confessed that prior to sailing the governor of Sallee told them they might take all English ships they met and make prize of them and their crews.[5]

Although the crewmen of the *William and John* were obviously biased, some of the undisputed facts appear to support their account. First, it is highly unlikely that a ship of 20 men would attempt to take one with a crew of 50. Maddocke would have known that a Salleeman would carry a larger crew. Second, both

---

[1] According to Harrison, the Moors under the government of Mully Sidans were the cause of all the trouble. The English captives were brought back on the *Rainbow* and two other ships.
[2] PRO, SP 71/12/f.125. HCA 13/52/f.200v states that 260 were freed.
[3] PRO, SP 71/1/f.106, 22 March 1628.
[4] PRO, HCA 13/52/ff.200–28.
[5] PRO, HCA 13/52/ff.227v–228v.

parties to the dispute agreed that the Sallee man-of-war was 'a great deal swifter' and had the wind of the *William and John* when the action began. It seems improbable, therefore, that the English ship could have attacked the Salleeman. Finally, there is independent evidence in a letter between two English Leghorn merchants which states that the pirates of Sallee were already active before the incident involving the *William and John* took place.[1]

Whatever the truth, from early 1631 onward English ships were frequently attacked and their crews sold into slavery. As a consequence, relatives of the captives began to petition the king for redress.[2] As in earlier epidemics of piracy, the west country maritime community suffered most heavily. Petitions were sent to the king praying for assistance. These were passed on to Sir Sidney Montague, Master of Requests, who on the king's instruction, wrote to Sir Thomas Roe, Sir Paul Pindar, Sir Kenelm Digby, and Alderman Garraway, requiring them to make a special investigation into (1) the best means to redeem those held captive and (2) how the pirates' attacks might be stopped.[3]

This committee went about its task with a thoroughness that suggests the Caroline government's use of extra-governmental *ad hoc* advisory bodies was as efficient as it was expedient. The committee met in London with representatives of the western ports who gave evidence on the nature and extent of the piracy. Members of Trinity House were called to give expert advice on shipping and trade in the Mediterranean.[4] At the end of these hearings, the committee produced a report notable for its clarity and sophistication in setting out the possible courses open to the government and the advantages and disadvantages of each option.[5]

The committee rejected redemption as a viable or desirable course of action. Approximately 1000 persons were then being held, and at the going rate of £40 a person, redemption would cost at least £40 000. It was impossible, the committee concluded, to raise a sum of this magnitude by a national brief. They cited the experience of an earlier attempt to raise money by a national brief

[1] PRO, SP 46/88/f.67.
[2] PRO, HCA 30/841: John Vicarie, writing from Sallee on 15/5/1633, states that 'of late here hath been taken a great many captains, both of English, French, and Spanish so that this place hath not peace with any nation'.
[3] PRO, SP 71/1/f.100.
[4] Trinity House, Court minute book, f. 85. Also PRO, SP 16/379/111.
[5] The following discussion of this report is based on PRO, SP 71/1/ff.130–132, the quotations given are taken from this source.

when two years had been needed to collect a twentieth of the amount. Only the Crown had the means to provide such a large sum, but were Charles to make a grant from his coffers, they concluded, 'it would encourage the enemy, and make him more eager in the chase when he shall find that the Bodies of your Majesty's subjects become so good merchandise'.[1] Only three courses were likely to yield a positive result: treaty, war, or trade embargo. Proceeding by treaty was quickly dismissed for they believed it would not be observed: 'The Grand Signor has given sundry Capitulations, Stipulations, Promises, such as no greater can be required . . . But not one Article has been well and truly observed'. As for the second option, the committee declared:

> What can be done by war made on the Pirates alone has been tried at great charge without effect, their ships are light, always clean and fitted as well to fly as to fight, so they can (except surprised in a strait) choose their Party.

On further consideration, however, they concluded that 'much may be done upon them by maintaining 3 squadrons of 8 good ships for 3 years', but the cost of implementing such a course would come to £50 000 or more per year. Moreover, the committee concluded that this course was hazardous and the likelihood of success remote; therefore they declined to recommend it. Even if it were likely to lead to success, they did not know how the cost could be met, unless the king were to lend some royal warships, 'and that all the Maritime Cities, Towns and Counties will contribute in such a measure'. Realistically, however, they were forced to conclude that, 'we have no ground to hope or expect'. This last remark certainly reflects the experience of the inadequate support for Mansell's expedition and can be taken as a general commentary on the traditional funding system for naval expeditions.

Having dismissed the first two options, the committee could only recommend a policy based on a trade embargo. Although the committee described this course as an embargo – and the withdrawal of trade was a central element of it – their proposal was more than just a passive measure. In many ways it might be better to describe their recommendation as a *guerre de course*, and a

---

[1] According to Roe's later account, ransom costs were based on figures provided by James Frizell, consul at Algiers: SP 16/379/111.

rather ruthless one at that. Not only were English merchants to break off trade with Turkey, letters of reprisal were to be issued. All commerce with Constantinople would then be attacked until the city was brought to starvation. According to Roe, a fleet of eight ships would be sent 'to range all the coast of Barbary, and to land among the villages and places of least strength and opposition, and to make prisoners of all men, women, and children fit for sale'.[1]

While an embargo appeared to be the best of the three possible courses, it was also open to criticism. First, the king's customs might be diminished; second, trade might suffer, especially the cloth trade; and third, it might prove difficult to re-establish England's trading position when peace was finally secured. The committee, however, went on to suggest how these objections could be overcome. Since the customs were contracted, the Crown would receive the usual amount, no matter how much or little was collected. Any losses that the farmers of the customs might incur could be compensated from the percentage which the Admiralty received from prize goods. They also believed that the cloth trade need not necessarily suffer: demand would remain and could be met by sending cloth to other ports, such as Leghorn and Ragusa, where it could be sold to intermediaries trading with the Turks. Finally, the committee suggested that the Turks' desire to end the trade war would be so great that they would agree to re-establish trade on conditions favourable to English merchants.

Despite the thoroughness of the analysis and the unambiguous nature of the recommendation, nothing came of the work of the committee. From the general record it appears that interest in the subject melted away and the report was quietly forgotten. However, by chance we now know what happened to this report and the reasons for its seemingly quiet demise.

Four years after the committee submitted its report, another attempt to suppress piracy was initiated. The new committee began its work by reviewing previous efforts. Because they could not find any copies of the report that had been sent to the king in 1632, they wrote to Roe. In reply, Roe indicated that he had destroyed his copy in disgust. However, he went on to reconstruct the essence of the report and also to explain what had happened after it was submitted.[2]

[1] PRO, SP 16/379/111.
[2] Ibid. Additionally, there is a less detailed account in SP 71/1/ff.100–101v.

According to Roe the report was read to the King and Council and then approved. But then,

> upon some suggestion mentioned by my Lord Treasurer, the Earl of Portland, that it was fit to be recommitted *ab integro* to the first referees, and to add to them the present farmers, and other Aldermen, and Merchants of the Levant Company, to consult anew of other ways, supposing that this course was uncertain in the event, but certain to interrupt the trade and abate the customs, a new reference, and the number increased.

When the enlarged committee met, all the evidence was reviewed and they 'resolved that their first answer was full, and . . . that they would neither add nor recede from it'. Only the customs farmers objected saying that they risked losses if this policy were adopted. In reply, Roe indicates that he said that they should accept the offer of reprisals as recompense or give up their farm to others who would accept these terms. The farmers answered that Roe did not understand such matters. Anyone who undertook the farm on such terms would be crushed by the burden. Whereupon, Aldermen Garraway, Freeman, Clothero, Abdy, and Sir Morris Abbot silenced the farmers saying that they would take up the proposition. As a result of this conference, a general return was made. But this was found 'not pleasing to the Lords of the Council, and thus the business fell, and the deputies of the West Country departed', ending the matter as far as Roe was concerned.[1]

Although the course recommended by the committee was not pursued, it appears that the Council continued to seek a solution. The evidence on this is scanty coming mainly from the Privy Council registers which do not provide much detail. The registers indicate that in May 1633 a committee of councillors was formed to look into the matter of pirates.[2] There is also a brief entry for 14 June, that preparations for the sending of a fleet were begun.[3] Evidence from the Court of Aldermen show that in late June

[1] PRO, SP 16/379/111.
[2] PRO, PC 2/42/ff.550–551, 10 April 1633, report discussed, Committee to meet; ibid., f.573 report read and turned over to Secretary Coke to deal with; PC 2/43/f.25, Committee about Pirates: Lord Privy Seal, Earl of Dorset, Viscount Holland, Lord Cottington, Lord Newburgh, and Secretary Windebank; PC 2/43/f.25, petition received from western ports, Committee to examine.
[3] PRO, PC 2/43/f.46, order giving deputies of western ports and London power to treat; PC 2/43/ff.94, 96–97, 149 after conference a fleet to be prepared.

orders were received for them to attend the Privy Council concerning matters touching the suppression of pirates.[1] A more substantial indication of the government's intention is found in the minutes of the Levant Company dated 15 July. Included is a report of a meeting of the Privy Council attended by members of the company. It states that the king intended to send ships against the pirates of Algiers and Tunis, 'and that their lordships did not send for those merchants to consult of the way or means to effect this business or to hear reasons or arguments against it, but to make known unto them his Majesty's pleasure which was . . . that twelve ships should be set out'. The report further states that the king would furnish some ships to accompany them, and that a charge of £40 000 for the adventure had been computed. One-fifth of this sum was to be borne by the 'Western Traders' and the outports. The rest was to be carried by London, 'to all which was added that if the merchants would not consent and find a way to raise the money, that then his Majesty would'.[2] The substance and tone of this report suggests that the government was (and had been) in favour of setting out an expedition, but that the merchants and others had not been enthusiastic over furnishing ships or financing a fleet. The minutes of the Levant Company go on to indicate the company's intention to petition to avoid payment.

Thus, after two years' effort, a sound and well-prepared policy once again foundered on finance. From the surviving evidence it appears that all parties agreed on the need to suppress the pirates, but this shared interest diminished when it came time to pay the charge. The weaknesses of a voluntary approach to financing public policy had been made explicit in the 'levy' for Mansell's expedition. A decade later there was no cause to believe that this system of finance would work any better. Certainly, Roe's committee had no confidence in such an approach. Those hurt by the pirates could not afford to contribute to the cost of protection, while those such as the Levant Company who could afford to contribute, saw no need. In these discussions there is little evidence of a sense of common interest or mutual dependence.

For all its careful arguments, the report of Roe's committee was founded on a delusion. Implicit in Roe's report of 1632 was a belief or delusion that important policy objectives could be achieved at

[1] CLRO, Repertory, vol. 47, f.265, Aldermen appointed to meet; ibid., vol. 47, ff.269–269v, 271–271v, committee appointed to attend Privy Council.
[2] PRO, SP 105/149/f.37, 15 July 1633. Debate over the measure was postponed: SP 105/149/f.38, 18 July 1633.

little or no cost, a belief quite common in the period and underlying, for example, the foreign policy debates of the 1620s. In a world where war was an ever-present reality and force the common currency of relations (and growing in cost), there was a desire in England, at least, to think that use of force somehow could be made to pay for itself.[1]

---

[1] PRO, SP 71/1/f.132. This same attitude is expressed in the foreign policy debate in the 1621 parliament: Russell, *Parliaments and English Politics*, pp. 125–42, and again in the proposals of Sir Dudley Digges in 1624 for a self-financing navy: Cambridge University Library, MS. Dd. 12–20, ff.129–32. This delusion was given encouragement by Piet Heyn's seizure of the New Spain fleet in 1628, the exception that proves the rule.

10
PIRACY AND THE ORIGINS OF CAROLINE SHIP MONEY

Like the members of Roe's committee discussed in the preceding chapter, at times Charles I appears to have been seduced by similar dreams of a world without costs. However, frequently the king's executive responsibilities forced him to face the harsh realities of the world in which the resources of his realm were often too slender to support the desires of his subjects or his government. England was not a great power like France, Spain, or even the United Provinces. The royal purse was inadequate and the country unwilling to build and maintain the sort of navy that included powerful warships able to stand up to the men-of-war of the continental naval powers and smaller, faster vessels fit to protect trade against pirates and privateers. By the early 1630s, if not earlier, it was evident that action against pirates and privateers as well as defence of sovereignty and national interests required the navy to be expanded greatly.

Expansion to the scale required would be expensive, too costly to be met by traditional means of naval finance. Roe's committee, it will be recalled, had estimated that action against the Barbary pirates alone would cost no less than £50 000 a year. In 1633, Trinity House provided the government with another costing for an expedition against Algiers. Their estimates were for a relatively small fleet of only eight men-of-war and two pinnaces; nevertheless, wages and victuals were estimated at £49 440 per annum.[1] The Trinity House figures were estimates for operations and did not include cost figures for building, arming and fitting out of a fleet, or for support services such as dockyards and administration.

[1] Trinity House, Court minutes 1626 to 1635, f.87. 22 March 1633.

The expense of protecting trade against depredations of the Barbary pirates was great enough to overwhelm traditional means of naval finance. Had the threat from piracy not existed, it would still have been necessary to evolve some new means of naval finance like Ship Money.

The relative weakness of the English state also limited the government's foreign policy options.[1] Moreover, a propensity on the part of many of the political nation to delude themselves about England's strength and influence abroad also distorted foreign policy. The vacillations, uncertainties, and apparent opportunism of early Stuart diplomacy have been attributed by some historians to the moral weakness of James I and Charles I, rather than the relative impoverishment of the state and the realities of power. Policy-making has been perceived as a matter of personal proclivity rather than a process that reflected and sprang from real forces. Professor Edmundson, on the other hand, has astutely observed that it was a 'constant fear of imminent bankruptcy' which compelled [the early Stuart monarchs] 'to be shifty in their dealings with foreign powers'.[2]

Charles I has been commonly portrayed as an increasingly isolated monarch surrounded by sycophants, yet there is much evidence in letters or formal communications addressed to him that the king was not put off by sharp, even critical, plain-spoken language.[3] For example, Sir John Coke presented Charles I with a memorial deeply critical of Crown policy. In this document, Coke analysed both the naval and foreign policy requirements of the realm in sharp relief and anticipated major policy developments for the next few years. This memorial is undated but was probably written in late 1633 or early 1634, at the latest, that is shortly after the Council tried and failed to procure from London merchants funds for an expedition against the pirates.

Included in Coke's memorial is a frank survey of the decline of English power and a catalogue of the abuse and disrespect given to king and country by foreigners.[4] Coke signalled his intent in an opening statement that refutes the charge of sycophancy:

---

[1] An example of the way the problem of piracy was related to other concerns of state may be seen below in the discussion of Anglo-French relations in 1635–6.
[2] G. Edmundson, *Anglo-Dutch Rivalry during the First Half of the Seventeenth Century*, p. 5.
[3] For example, Hopton's letter to Windebank, 28 March/7 April 1634, printed in *State Papers collected by Edward, Earl of Clarendon, commencing 1621*, I, p. 80.
[4] The following discussion is based on Coke's memorial in PRO, SP 16/269/51.

> Pleasing things are fittest for the ears of a Prince. But it is both the duty and safety of a Secretary to represent to his master the truth in all affairs how distasteful soever . . . yet (I know not how) the world is possessed, that our ancient reputation & respect is not only cried down, but we submit ourselves to wrongs & indignities in all places which are not to be endured.

The king is then informed of some of the wrongs and indignities suffered by English subjects abroad and on the high seas:

> I have in my hand a relation of our sufferings at Constantinople under the Great Turk: when your Ambassador was questioned, his house (which had ever been a sanctuary) was searched, his arms taken away: your merchants arrested, imprisoned and ransomed without colour of justice: your ships burnt, & your seamen made slaves. . . . Against which barbarous proceedings the company doth so complain that they are at a stand to relinquish that trade & seek redress by other means, there being no hope of reparation at their hands. Besides at Tunis and Algiers, it is lamentable to consider how many are kept in slavery, & how many turn Turk. So at Sally & Morocco when the favour of England was their greatest ambition, now the spoils of our people are their greatest wealth.

Other paragraphs describe insults and injuries perpetrated by Venice, France, Spain, the Spanish Netherlands, the United Provinces, Denmark, Sweden, Poland, the Holy Roman Empire, and Russia. The memorial ends by declaring:

> Thus as briefly as I could I have reported to your Majesty & your sworn councillors only, what usage your subjects do find on all coasts. It remaineth, that I humbly pray your Majesty that with the grave advice of my Lords, you will consider of such speedy and powerful means to redeem us from this contumely and contempt. Further I presume not, save only to put you in mind of Mr. Hopton's good advice: That there is no hope left of obtaining justice, but by doing it yourself, which requireth the present reinforcing of your guards, to recover your undoubted right of sovereignty in all your seas.

The reputation of the state and the rights of English subjects abroad would only be restored when the Ship Money fleets were created.[1]

The motivation behind Ship Money has never been adequately explained.[2] As outlined above, the threat of the Barbary pirates was a major factor. This threat and its resolution were intricately entwined with other threats to the state. To judge the relative contributions of each, it is first necessary to disentangle Ship Money from the context in which it was placed by Gardiner in his seminal *History of England*.[3]

Gardiner's account is factually accurate, but underlying his interpretation are several presumptions about Charles I and royal diplomacy.[4] These presumptions led Gardiner to emphasize some aspects of Caroline policy while ignoring others. However, if they are removed or altered, then many of Gardiner's conclusions must also be put aside. In the remainder of this chapter, the origins of Caroline Ship Money are re-examined and an alternative explanation offered.

As with so many of the developments of the 1620s and 1630s, historians have tended to relate them to the constitutional conflict that followed rather than to the problems of foreign policy, naval strategy, and finance that preceded the first Ship Money writs. Gardiner was correct in seeing that Ship Money should be placed in a foreign policy context, but he was predisposed to see

[1] On 29 September 1635, Sir Kenelm Digby wrote to Coke of the beneficial effect that the Ship Money fleet was already having on England's reputation, implying that Coke had much to do with the naval revival and the means by which it was brought about: HMC 23, *12th Report, App. ii, Cowper MSS*, p. 95. Ibid., p. 70, a paper by Coke of October 1634 for the first Ship Money writ, calls for a fleet for six months' service. The gravity of the memorial leads me to conclude that Coke did not see Ship Money as a temporary solution since he did not see its cause as temporary. This interpretation is given support by notes of a slightly later date by Nicholas who saw Ship Money as a proposition continuing yearly: PRO, SP 16/535/74.
[2] Recently, both K.R. Andrews, *Ships, Money, and Politics, seafaring and naval enterprise in the reign of Charles I*, pp. 128–83 and A. Thrush, 'Naval finance and the origins and development of ship money', ed. M. Fissel, *War and Government in Britain, 1598–1650*, pp. 133–62, have written pieces relating to Ship Money; both used my PhD thesis extensively during the formative stages in their work. On at least five different occasions, Thrush read my thesis before writing his article. Chapters 6, 7 and 8 of Andrew's book cover much the same ground as Chapters 7 to 12 of my thesis, though his interpretations are at times at variance with mine. Curiously, neither author has credited my work in text, footnotes, or bibliography.
[3] S.R. Gardiner, *History of England: From the Accession of James I to the Outbreak of the Civil War, 1603–1642*, VII, pp. 342–91.
[4] Gardiner's own extreme Protestant religious views appear to have coloured his perceptions of Caroline diplomatic and political activity.

international politics in a very selective and dogmatic way. Gardiner assumed that (1) there was a correct foreign policy for England in the 1620s and 1630s, but (2) that neither James nor Charles pursued this policy, i.e., the furtherance of the Protestant cause and unequivocal support for the Dutch. Interestingly, Gardiner's view closely mirrors advice which Roe presented to Lord Holland, and many of Gardiner's opinions were derived almost verbatim from Roe's memorial.[1] Since the foreign policy of Charles I did not conform to his ideal, Gardiner found royal policy unacceptable or irrational.[2] This presumption about Caroline foreign policy mistakenly led Gardiner to portray Ship Money as part of a grand intrigue of Charles I in which English naval and military forces would join with those of Catholic Spain for an attack on the Protestant Dutch. As evidence of this intention, Gardiner cites the secret negotiations that led to and followed Cottington's treaty.[3]

A particular feature of Gardiner's account, is the way in which royal diplomacy is presented in moralistic terms. Charles I is criticised for duplicity, rebuked for carrying on secret negotiations with Catholic powers, and for acting behind the backs of his councillors.[4] For example, Gardiner presents Coke's memorial as a put-up job, commissioned by Charles to fool the Council into supporting the creation of the Ship Money fleets. No evidence is ever offered to support this claim.[5] Throughout this section of his history, Gardiner portrays Charles I as a Machiavellian character, though Whiggish standards are used to judge the king. Gardiner seems incapable of appreciating that early Stuart monarchs were forced through weakness, as Edmundson has put it, 'to work for the achievement of their ends by the purposes of a devious diplomacy rather than risk the costly charges of an appeal to arms'.[6]

---

[1] PRO, SP 16/218/29 and inclosure.
[2] Gardiner, *History of England*, VII, pp. 169–70, 352.
[3] Ibid., pp. 354, 357, 366–9.
[4] Ibid., pp. 169–70, 371, 381–2.
[5] Ibid., pp. 356–7.
[6] Edmundson, *Anglo-Dutch Rivalry*, p. 5. A thoughtful criticism of Gardiner is found in R. G. Usher, *A Critical Study of the Historical Method of Samuel Rawson Gardiner with an Excursus on the Historical Conception of the Puritan Revolution from Clarendon to Gardiner*. Usher recognized that inconsistency was a mark of Gardiner's work (pp. 28–40); this critique is also effective in revealing the hidden assumptions of Gardiner's study, such as his belief in the role of England as a Puritan nation (pp. 56–62); he is also perceptive on Gardiner's treatment of Gondomar and James (pp. 16–18).

Though Gardiner's account has an apparent coherence, there are inconsistencies in the argument. For example, he writes that in November 1633 'so weak was Charles at sea that he had proposed to Necolade [the Spanish ambassador] that Spanish warships be sent to protect the fishery against the Dutch', while only two months later (and two pages on in Gardiner's text), the strength of the Royal Navy was so great that Charles felt confident in offering 'to lend twenty or thirty vessels to the King of Spain'.[1]

Gardiner also applies a double standard when treating Charles I and royal foreign policy. It was reprehensible for Charles to intrigue or take part in secret negotiations, yet quite acceptable for Richelieu or the Dutch to do the same.[2] Charles is criticized by Gardiner for being devious, but only selectively when it suits his purposes. It was inconceivable to Gardiner that Charles might attempt to manipulate Weston, Cottington, or the Spanish as he did honest Protestants, the anti-Spanish faction, the French or the Dutch.[3]

Gardiner applied a double standard in another sense. Whenever the Spanish or Dutch made promises in the course of secret negotiations (such as those by the Spanish over the restoration of the Palatinate) it is inferred that these were simply manoeuvres. But when Charles I tells the Spanish in secret, for example, that he is willing to lend his fleet, or, if given money, he will build a fleet for use against the Dutch, these declarations are taken as the true intention of the king. Gardiner could not conceive that the king's statements might be ploys or manoeuvres, diplomatic means and not declarations of royal ends.

If one abandons the Procustian bed into which Caroline foreign policy was placed by Gardiner and examines what actually happened, then the royal foreign policy and the origins of Ship Money appear quite different. It is important to note what actually took place and what never occured. Though agreement with Spain included a secret clause calling for the dismemberment of the Dutch territories, the English government made no attempt to implement it.[4] It is difficult to believe there was no occasion

---

[1] Gardiner, *History of England*, VII, pp. 349, 351.
[2] Ibid., pp. 205–6, 380–1.
[3] For example, Gardiner quotes a letter by Windebank, then declares that it represents a true exposition of Charles's intentions: *History of England*, VII, pp. 351–2.
[4] AGS, Estado, legajo 2520; also a copy in *Clarendon State Papers*, I, pp. 109, 112.

between 1630 and 1640 when this provision of the treaty might not have been put into effect, if the king had been in earnest. If his actions are a guide, then Charles never intended to join with Spain in the dismemberment of the United Provinces. Knowledgeable contemporaries had reached this conclusion; for example, as early as March 1634, Olivares had concluded that the English monarch had never intended using his fleet in conjunction with the Spanish against the Dutch.[1] It should also be recalled that Charles never joined the Dutch or French against the Hapsburgs, despite holding lengthy, and, at times, secret negotiations with both parties on such an alliance.

What weight should one put on these negotiations? Do they really signify royal intent? Should we see them as examples of the failure of Caroline diplomacy? The apparent lack of success and the frequent changes in policy were seen by Gardiner as evidence of a 'constitutional infirmity of purpose' on the part of the Stuart monarchs.[2] However, these negotiations may just as easily be seen not as separate fruitless attempts to achieve particular, declared ends, but rather as a series of manoeuvres necessary to support a policy based on national self-interest and independence.[3]

England gained more by neutrality. Of course, at times it was necessary or useful to lead on one side or the other into believing that England would become a belligerent. Commitment to one side could be risky; a second rank power like England could be reduced to client status as happened to Sweden which effectively became a client of France as a result of an alliance. Gardiner failed to recognize this risk, nor did he see the benefits that flowed to England from the foreign policy of Charles I. Indeed, he believed Charles had no real policy nor even an understanding of the basis on which one might be made.[4]

When Caroline diplomacy is examined in terms of interest of state, it appears remarkably consistent and realistic. The relative economic and military weakness of England led Charles I to

---

[1] AGS, Estado, legajo 2520, consulta 30 March 1634. Olivares went even further stating that Charles would not have assisted the Spanish with a fleet even if he had been given all the money he requested.
[2] The phrase is Edmundson's, *Anglo-Dutch Rivalry*, p. 5, but his target is Gardiner. For an expression of this view, see Gardiner, *History of England*, VII, pp. 169–70.
[3] The Venetian ambassador anticipated that English foreign policy would follow this line: *CSPV*, 1603–1607, p. 516.
[4] Gardiner *History of England*, VII, p. 169.

pursue a foreign policy based on the principle of balance of power. This expression may seem anachronistic but it was used frequently at the time. For example, Sir Kenelm Digby believed that with the Ship Money fleet, 'our master will have a power to keep the balance even'.[1] Nor was this approach novel to the Stuarts. It was a traditional theme of English policy, as Sir John Coke explained when he wrote to his son:

> The wisdom of this State under our late blessed Queen balanced our neighbour potent kings in France by our religious interest in the protestants of that Church, and in Spain by other diversions and by keeping correspondence with Turkey and Barbary; whereby not only our peace and trade grew great in those parts, but we had a ready means to keep that king in alarm upon his own coasts and to supply our fleets for all attempts against Spain, the Islands, or the West Indies.[2]

A policy based on the principle of balancing the power of greater states had to be pursued actively; of necessity it would demand shifts in position, secrecy, and deception. Much of the diplomatic manoeuvring that seemed so dishonest and futile to Gardiner can now be seen as attempts to contain and entangle the great powers, while keeping England from becoming too heavily committed to one side. A policy based on these lines was even, at one time, recommended by Roe, who – typically – cast it in a vivid metaphor, observing that the great powers of Europe were interested only in gratifying their own ambitions and, therefore, they were 'best employed like millstones to grind themselves thin'.[3]

For strategic and economic reasons, the focus of English foreign policy was traditionally the Low Countries, and the diplomacy of Charles toward this area was neither wayward nor contradictory, but rational and consistent. Charles sought to secure the Flanders pocket from domination by any of the major powers: Spain, France, or the United Provinces. Naturally, this policy took

---

[1] *HMC, 12th Report, App. ii, Cowper MSS*, p. 95. Arundel used a similar phrase to Aston in 1637, PRO, SP 16/362/56, '. . . that our nation shall hold that ancient just attribute, the balance . . .'. I owe this reference to Professor Russell.
[2] HMC, 23, *12th Report, App. ii, Cowper MSS*, pp. 296–7. A similar view of this principle of English foreign policy may be seen in a letter from Roe to Windebank, 8 January 1634, in PRO, SP 16/258/29.
[3] PRO, SP 16/218/29 and inclosure, for Roe's views on European states.

different forms to meet changing circumstances. Despite secret talks and promises of support for the Spanish interests, Olivares was certain these were but ploys and that Charles really was just conniving for the creation of a Flanders independent of foreign control but under English protection.[1] The establishment of an English protectorate across the Channel would satisfy fundamental English security needs by preventing any strong foreign power from occupying this traditional launchpad for invasion. It would also secure the Flemish ports and England's important continental trade. Although Gardiner believed that any commercial benefits resulting from the Caroline policy of armed neutrality were at best unworthy, contemporaries, such as Weston and Wentworth, appreciated the wisdom of this policy.[2] Only recently, as a result of the work of Harland Taylor and J.S. Kepler, has it been established how much England gained from this policy.[3]

But peace and profit did not come freely; they needed to be 'advanced' and 'preserved carefully', as Sir Robert Heath advised:

> For our safety, this being an island . . . lies in our walls, which is our shipping, and [there is a need] thereby to maintain the King's undoubted right of Lord of the Narrow Seas . . . To let our neighbour Kingdoms know, not by words but by actions that we are resolved to maintain the ancient honour of our nation and also that we will not take any occasion before it be offered, *nemo nos impune lacessit*, we shall make our peace assured, when we are prepared for war.[4]

Heath was by no means alone in appreciating how much the realm was endangered by the maritime power of the great continental

---

[1] AGS, Estado, legajos 2520, 2574.
[2] *The Earl of Strafford's Letters and Dispatches*, ed. W. Knowler, II, p. 59: 31 March 1637, Wentworth to the king. For Gardiner's contemptuous view of Weston's policy of peace and material prosperity, see *History of England*, VII, p. 208. Also, M.V.C. Alexander, *Charles I's Lord Treasurer: Sir Richard Weston, Earl of Portland (1577–1635)*, pp. 127, 217.
[3] H. Taylor, 'Trade, Neutrality, and the "English Road", 1630–48', *Econ Hist Rev*, 2nd ser., XXV (1972), pp. 236–60; J.S. Kepler, 'Fiscal Aspects of the English Carrying Trade during the Thirty Years War', *Econ Hist Rev*, 2nd ser., XXV (1972), pp. 261–83, and idem., *The Exchange of Christendom: The International Entrepôt at Dover, 1622–51*, pp. 36–55, 105–15.
[4] PRO, SP 16/229/102. The document has been improperly dated by the PRO; though its arguments apply, perhaps even more to the 1630s, it appears to have been composed about 1622 for it contains a reference to Mansell's fleet.

states. The memory of the Armada was still fresh, and the danger of Spain was evident to many.[1] Zealous Protestants were especially fearful of Spain as an agent of the counter-Reformation. This danger was not entirely imaginary, though it was exaggerated and given more prominence than the equally great threats posed by the French and Dutch.

Both the French and the Dutch would challenge English sovereignty and attempt to dominate the Narrow Seas. Because their ports were close to England, both states could threaten England more easily than Spain. They also possessed greater means to carry out that threat: both states had become maritime powers very recently, too recently for their strength to be widely appreciated in England.[2] The war with Spain had concealed the increasing power of both the Dutch naval and merchant marine.[3] By the second decade of the 17th century, however, the Dutch threat was becoming manifest.[4] Dutch domination of the fishing industry, competition in the cloth trade, and control of most of Europe's maritime trade and shipping threatened English economic and political interests, as writers as early as Raleigh, Gentleman, Mun, and Monson acknowledged.[5] Though it was not published until the early 1630s, Seldon's *Mare Clausum* was written, as its author tells us, much earlier – under James I – and was directed against the encroaching power and insolence of the Dutch.[6] The war against Spain tended to obscure this challenge,

---

[1] Not only was there the memory of the Armada, the flotilla of privateers based in the channel ports of the Spanish Netherlands represented a major threat to English seaborne commerce. For a full appreciation of this threat, see R.A. Stradling's important study, The Armada of Flanders, Spanish Maritime Policy and European War, 1568–1668.
[2] The only detailed estimates of Dutch naval strength that I have seen are those in the State Papers that were requested by Coke: PRO, SP 84/149/ff.34, 65–80, 98, 112–16. In 1631 there were 98 men-of-war in the fleet; in 1634 another 30 were being built; these figures do not include company ships or privateers.
[3] C.R. Boxer, *The Dutch Seaborne Empire 1606–1800*, pp. 76–7; J.P. Cooper, 'Sea Power', p. 227; and for a contemporary view, that of Nicolo Molin, *CSPV*, 1603–1607, p. 522.
[4] PRO, SP 84/149/ff.65–80. As Heath explained, the Dutch threat grew 'out of their strength at sea and our insecurity'. PRO, SP 16/229/102.
[5] W. Raleigh, 'Observations touching Trade and Commerce with the Hollanders and Other Nations, in *The Works of Sir Walter Raleigh, Kt.*'; T. Gentleman, *England's way to win wealth, and employ ships and mariners*; T. Mun, *England's Treasure by Foreign Trade: Or, the balance of our foreign trade is the rule of our treasure*; *Sir William Monson's Naval Tracts*, ed. M. Oppenheim, III, pp. 212–18, 220–2, 225–31.
[6] It appears that Coke was the force behind its publication: HMC 23, *12th Report, App. ii, Cowper MSS*, p. 90.

but after the peace, Dutch maritime power began to threaten English interests and the claims of Stuart monarchs to sovereignty in the Narrow Seas.

In the long run, however, France presented a more serious threat. France was a richer state, better endowed to sustain war, and the least vulnerable of the great powers. France had Channel ports, and a French invasion fleet could be on the English coast in less than a day. For almost two centuries, France had been the traditional enemy of England.[1] In the 16th century, England fought France for control of the Narrow Seas, but in the late Elizabethan period and during the first part of the reign of James I, France was racked by religious and political strife. The Hapsburg threat brought England and France together in these years, but by the early 1620s, all this changed.[2] By the beginning of the 1630s Richelieu had built up the French navy until it was equal – in size at least – with that of England. This development was in itself cause enough to make an English monarch anxious, but it was made more alarming because of the growing closeness of the French and the Dutch.[3] By 1636 the Franco/Dutch relationship had developed to such an extent that Sir John Coke warned Aston that he thought the French and Dutch would join their fleets 'to impeach his Majesty's dominion in these seas'.[4]

Faced with such serious threats, Stuart foreign policy – that of playing off and balancing the continental powers – was eminently sensible. But for this policy to succeed, a strong navy and merchant marine would be needed to underwrite it, as advisers such as Heath put it.[5] The problem was not a new one; maritime insecurity and the decay of shipping had been obvious for decades. From time to time, various solutions were proposed. For example,

---

[1] *CSPV*, 1603–1607, p. 517. The ambassador describes the two countries as 'bitter enemies'.
[2] Lord Danvers expected the French to seize the Channel Islands: PRO, SP 15/42/62; Sir Philip Carteret feared similar action: SP 16/533/108; and Lord Goring warned Coke that Richelieu intended to seek revenge for the Ile de Rhé: HMC 23, *12th Report, App. ii, Cowper MSS*, p. 18. On 11 March 1634, Windebank informed Coke of the great preparations the French were making; in response the English fleet had been put to sea in great haste: ibid., p. 49.
[3] As time passed, the relationship was not one of equals: increasingly the Dutch came to depend on French support.
[4] PRO, SP 16/328/37.
[5] Gardiner, *History of England*, VIII, p. 269. When introducing the subject of the 1636 levy, even Gardiner agreed that there was a necessity for a powerful fleet and that the traditional means of financing the navy were no longer adequate.

in 1626 a scheme was put forward to finance the navy by means of a special excise.[1] But the most common proposal over the years was based on an extension of the ancient duty of Ship Money. Such a proposal had been made in 1603, and even adopted, albeit briefly, in 1628.[2]

As the need for a strong fleet became more apparent in the early 1630s, a solution to the conundrum of naval finance became more urgent. Attempts to set out a fleet by voluntary means had not met with success: in the summer of 1633 efforts to finance an expedition against the pirates by traditional means had shown that the port towns and merchant companies could no more be relied upon than in 1621 when the Algiers expedition was being financed.[3] By the beginning of 1634, the Crown had resolved to find another way to pay for the ships that were so clearly needed.[4]

According to Gardiner, Charles was seeking funds to set out a fleet for a purpose quite different to that envisaged by Coke and others. Gardiner implies that Coke was 'hoodwinked' into being the unwitting instrument of the king, and that Charles intended to use the fleet in conjunction with a Spanish armada for a joint attack on the United Provinces.[5] However, on close examination, Gardiner's evidence for this claim appears slight, and even that which might seem to support his contention is open to interpretation. No evidence was adduced by Gardiner to support his assertion that Coke was hoodwinked.[6] There is evidence, however, which shows that Coke truly believed the threats

---

[1] PRO, SP 16/43/1. The writer recommends an excise which has the advantage of providing a continual supply of money being paid in small amounts, rather than a subsidy which is only occasional and requires large amounts of money at short notice.
[2] R.J.W. Swales, 'The Ship Money Levy of 1628', *BIHR*, L (1977), pp. 164–76.
[3] The Ship Money levy of 20 October 1634 at first took the traditional form and called for ships to be provided by the maritime nation; with the exception of London, the port towns could not provide suitable ships, and, therefore, the charge was soon transformed to provide funds which might be used for the setting forth of suitable ships by the Crown.
[4] PRO, SP16/269/51; *Cal. Clarendon Papers*, I, p. 247. Many observers like Hopton, Coke, and Kenelm Digby perceived the need.
[5] Gardiner, *History of England*, VII, p. 357. It is just as likely that Coke 'hoodwinked' the king, and more probable that he recognized the same dangers.
[6] PRO, SP 16/269/51. Although it is by no means certain, it seems likely that he reached this conclusion from reading the endorsement on a copy of Coke's memorial. This states that the paper was the 'Sum of a declaration made by his Majesty's command at the Council Board'. However, all this really tells us is that the memorial was read to the Council at the king's command. It does not indicate that the memorial was written at the king's command, nor does it explain why Charles wished the Council to hear Coke's memorial or why Coke wrote it. The

described in his memorial were both real and grave. If Coke actually believed the threats were real, it seems reasonable that he might submit to the king a paper on the subject.[1] Though more expansive, Coke's memorial was also not very different in character or substance from other advisory pieces, such as that earlier advice by Heath referred to above. If statesmen such as Heath and Coke saw matters this way, why not also the king?

Moreover, evidence on the supposed secret use of the English fleet in alliance with the Spanish against the Dutch is ambiguous. Charles did conduct secret negotiations with the Spanish, but he had similar secret negotiations with other states over the years. The king did not inform the whole Council of these negotiations. Both secrecy and selective disclosure had long been a characteristic of Tudor and Stuart monarchy.[2] In fact, there was nothing unusual about the king informing only Windebank, Portland, and Cottington about his secret negotiations with the Spanish.[3] Though Gardiner relies on Windebank's statement about the royal aims of these negotiations, there is no reason to believe Windebank's view of Charles's intentions. Nor should we be surprised that Windebank would believe the negotiations he was conducting were in earnest or that he believed what the king told him: presumably Charles would not have done this if he expected his secretary would not believe him. Significantly, the Spanish ambassador who had a greater need to ascertain the king's true intentions had not the slightest doubt that Charles was disin-

king may have thought it a useful ploy to deceive the Council, as Gardiner suggests, or he may have wished it read to the Council because he genuinely believed the view put forward by Coke and wanted his councillors to share his perception. We can never know which motive lay behind the king's direction, but in one sense the interpretation put forward here seems more likely. The endorsement appears to have been written later, probably in January 1668/9 for it declares that it was shown to the king by Lord Arlington. There is no evidence of precisely when the memorial was written, but since the beginning of 1634 an interest in English rights to the Narrow Seas, and abuses thereof, had been developing: SP 16/259/17.

[1] Coke's correspondence contains frequent reference to the dangers of the French, the Dutch, and the pirates. When the problem of pirates came before the Privy Council, Coke was the one who was invariably ordered to take the matter in hand, e.g., PRO, PC 2/42/f.573, 17 April 1633. Evidently, those who knew him well thought he would be interested in this sort of intelligence; see for example, Sir Kenelm Digby's letter, *HMC* 23, *12th Report, App. ii, Cowper MSS*, pp. 94–5.

[2] Though full consultation may have been normal, accepted practice for 19th-century cabinet government, as in Gardiner's day, it was not in the period of which he wrote, as his own work so amply demonstrates.

[3] Being pro-Spanish, they would be inclined to believe this tale and keep it a secret, whereas other more anti-Spanish members of the council might have leaked the information to the Dutch.

genuous when discussing joint Anglo-Spanish projects like this one.

The Anglo-Spanish articles of agreement did include a plan to keep open the Flanders ports, but keeping open the Flemish ports was in the interest of both states, though for different reasons. England did not become a Spanish poodle, nor Spain an English one, because they held this objective in common. Some of the secret clauses of Cottington's treaty were revived, but nothing was ever done to implement the clause encompassing a partition of the Netherlands. Charles might wish to tantalize the Spanish with such offers, but the Spanish had long recognized the need to discount such offers.[1]

A better measure of the king's intentions may be found in his use of the money received from the Ship Money levies. Although a small portion of the Ship Money account was used to cover ordinary naval expenditures, most of the money was spent building new ships, restoring older vessels, and setting out fleets. Two pinnaces were constructed specifically for an expedition against the Barbary pirates, but the other new ships were large men-of-war. The building of men-of-war suggests that the primary purpose of the fleet was defence. Certainly, by Gifford's criteria, Charles was not attempting to build a fleet for offensive action against the Dutch.[2] A fleet of commerce-raiding vessels would have been cheaper to build and more effective against the Dutch.

Finally, the Ship Money writs themselves explain the purpose of the fleets. The writs follow very closely the line put forward by Coke; in the first writ the king declared:

> We are given to understand that certain thieves, pirates, and robbers of the sea, as well as Turks, enemies of the Christian name, as others, being gathered together, wickedly taking by force and spoiling the ships and goods and merchandises, not only of our subjects, but also of subjects of our friends in the sea which hath been accustomed anciently to be defended by the English nation, and the same at their pleasure carried away, delivering the men in the same into miserable captivity; and forasmuch as we see them daily preparing all manner of shipping further to molest our merchants and to grieve the kingdom, unless remedy be not sooner applied, and their

---

[1] AGS, Estado, legajo 2520, 20/30 March; PRO, SP 16/239/71.
[2] M. Oppenheim, *A History of the Administration of the Royal Navy and of Merchant Shipping in Relation to the Navy*, pp. 254–5.

endeavours be not more manly met withal; also the dangers considered which in these times of war do hand over our heads, that it behoveth us and our subjects to hasten the defence of the sea and kingdom with all expedition or speed that we can; we willing by the help of God chiefly to provide for the defence of the kingdom, safeguard of the seas, security of our subjects, safe conduct of ships and merchandises to our kingdom of England coming, and from the same kingdom to foreign parts passing.[1]

Ambassador Necolade, who had been deeply involved in the negotiations, believed that the king's intentions were more authentically represented in the words of the Ship Money writs than the whispers made by the king and the unsupported promises of the secret agreement.[2]

Subsequent developments appear to support the Spanish ambassador's suspicions. The Ship Money fleets were employed very much as set out in the writs.[3] They were used to guard and establish sovereignty in the Narrow Seas, protect English commerces, especially in the Narrow Seas, and to suppress pirates.[4] For example, Northumberland was ordered in 1636 to pursue all pirates 'that the subject in these parts may have knowledge of his Majesty's care of them and find the benefit of his fleet at sea'.[5] The purpose of keeping a fleet at sea may have eluded some observers for no battles were fought nor were many pirates captured. Others, like Sir Kenelm Digby, understood that the fleets were serving a useful purpose; to Coke, he wrote:

that though my Lord of Lindsey do no more than sail up and

---

[1] *Historical collections of private passages of State, . . . beginning 1618 . . . to . . . 1648*, comp. J. Rushworth, II, p. 257.
[2] AGS, Estado, legajo 2520, Necolade to Philip IV, 21 November 1634.
[3] The instructions given to the fleet in 1635 are an indication of its purpose: HMC 23, *12th Report, App. ii, Cowper MSS*, p. 104, contains Coke's draft for that year. There is a certain irony in noting that the Ship Money fleet was eventually used most successfully not by the Crown but by Cromwell and in blockading the Flemish ports, a campaign in which even the *Sovereign of the Seas* could find a useful role: see Stradling, *The Armada of Flanders*, p. 148.
[4] PRO, SP 16/299/29, PRO, SP 16/157/143–149, Instructions; BL, Northumberland MSS, M-285, 30 August 1636. According to Nicholas, the fleet in 1635 was to be employed (1) against the Turks in the Straits, (2) protecting English fishing, (3) securing trade against freebooters, and (4) exerting sovereignty against the French and Hollanders: SP 16/285/84.
[5] Northumberland MSS, M-285, 30 August 1636.

down, yet the very setting of our best fleet out to sea is the greatest service that I believe hath been done the king these many years.[1]

The Ship Money fleets were built for two purposes: first, they were created to protect England from the great powers, and, second, they were raised to reduce the threats posed by the pirates.[2] In 1635 reports began to reach London that the Turks were operating from French ports.[3] On 22 October, James Howell informed Wentworth that there were now 25 Turkish men-of-war off the west of England, and that they had offered their services to the French.[4] A few months later, Pennington wrote to Secretary Coke that:

> William Fenner speaks the news of a peace between the French King and the Turkish pirates of Sallee, and that Peter de Shallad, the French Admiral for that employment, had given them tickets for coming into these parts.[5]

In March, Howell again wrote to the Lord Deputy about Turkish pirates using French ports, and in August of the same year Laud confirmed that 'The Mischief, which the most Christian Turks did about Plymouth is most true'.[6] He went on to complain that:

> The Pillage of the Turks upon this coast is most insufferable, and to have our Subjects thus ravished from us, and after to be from Rochelle driven overland in Chains to Marseilles, all this under the Sun, is a most infamous Usage of a Christian King, by him suffered that wears Most-Christian in his title, that I think was ever heard of. Surely I am of opinion, if this be passed over in Silence, the Shipping Business will not only be much

---

[1] HMC 23, *12th Report, App. ii, Cowper MSS*, p. 95.
[2] Even the East India Company (whose ships were strong and sailed in convoy) started to fear the Turks at this time: India Office Library, Court Book XIV, f.122. Intended action against the pirates was postponed in 1635 because supplies had not been organized: PRO, SP 16/285/84.
[3] PRO, SP 16/293/15. On 2 July 1635, Vice Admiral Monson ordered the *James* to get intelligence on Turkish pirates at Ushant, Brest, Conquet. Mr Hailes of the *James* was ordered to be speedy so that the Earl of Lindsey could take the likeliest course to destroy the pirates.
[4] *Strafford's Letters*, I, p. 474.
[5] PRO, SP 16/312/24. C. de la Roncière, *Histoire de la Marine Française*, IV, pp. 689–92, describes the French mission which freed 303 French captives.
[6] *Strafford's Letters*, II, p. 24.

blackened by it, but the Sovereignty of the Narrow Seas become an empty title, and all our Trade in fine utterly lost.[1]

To prevent the further use of French ports by the Turks, the Earl of Leicester was instructed in early 1636 to raise the matter and 'demand speedy order for redress' when he spoke to the French ministers.[2] Leicester carried out his instructions, but in writing of his representation he added:

> But if you did see in what confusion many of their affairs are, and how negligent some of their ministers are, who love their pleasures more than their Master's business, you would not wonder that there is no great expedition.[3]

In fact, it was not until early 1637 that an agreement was reached 'wherein . . . they shall neither admit any men-of-war of Barbary, or other Turkish pirates to have access into their harbours, nor remain there, but to join with us in making war upon them'.[4]

Direct action against the pirates of Sallee had been considered since 23 April 1636, when Nicholas noted that the Lords of the Admiralty were about to consider a course of action against the pirates.[5] Salleemen were operating near the Isle of Lundy in the Bristol Channel in March, and as many as 36 men-of-war were expected on the English coasts before the year was out.[6] In June, Giles Penn of Bristol spoke to Cottington about the danger of the pirates and was told that his relation would be brought before the Council.[7]

In early July the ports of the west country were so fearful of pirates that they banded together in an attempt to get redress.[8]

---

[1] Ibid., p. 25.
[2] PRO, SP 78/101/ff.33v–34. Leicester was sent as an extraordinary ambassador; the ordinary ambassador was Viscount Scudamore. The combination was not a happy one. In one of his letters to Scudamore, Secretary Coke wrote: 'I receive weekly letters from the Earl of Leicester and yourself; and therefore find it strange that neither by his nor yours I can give an account to his Majesty that your counsels and endeavours do concur in the great business of the treaty': SP 78/102/f.209–209v.
[3] PRO, SP 78/103/f.30.
[4] *Strafford's Letters*, II, p. 50.
[5] PRO, SP 16/319/30.
[6] PRO, SP 16/316/52, and inclosure, examination of Christopher Pige.
[7] PRO, SP 16/327/69.
[8] *Weymouth Corporation: Descriptive catalogue of the charters, minute books, and other documents of the borough of Weymouth and Melcombe Regis*, comp. H.J. Moule, pp. 178–9, contains an edited account of Crewkerne's report, on which the following description is based.

As well as petitioning the king, they sent John Crewkerne to the Court where he found the king attended by only four of his Council. He presented the west country petitions to Secretary Coke, but it was a fortnight before he received an answer. In the interval, the Court moved to Woodstock where Crewkerne repaired and 'upon Sunday before the Sermon, the Lords sitting, I preferred your petition' to them. The next day Charles gave Crewkerne an audience. After some discussion, Crewkerne was told that he could report to the western towns that a fleet would be sent down their way at the first fair wind. On hearing this, so Crewkerne reported, he boldly told the king and Council that such a measure would only treat the symptom, not cure the disease. A privy councillor replied that 'his Majesty would not be dictated by us'. However, as Crewkerne goes on to relate, Laud intervened:

> My Lord Archbishop at that time gave exceeding[ly] good words and at the delivering of my petition did protest (striking his hands upon his breast) that whilst he had breath in his body he would do his utmost endeavour to advance so necessary and consequential a business.

This description of Archbishop Laud's concern in the suppression of pirates tallies with other evidence regarding his special interest in this secular matter.[1] As noted above, he was greatly angered to learn that the French had given support, even ports, to the Turkish pirates. Also, it will be recalled, he took a personal interest in drawing up the form of the service for redeemed captives.

Following the Woodstock meeting, Crewkerne advised his masters to petition the king again when the Court had settled at Hampton Court. As a result of his meeting with Charles and his Council, Crewkerne was convinced that the government were in earnest and that something useful would be done soon.[2] His assessment was correct: shortly thereafter, three or four ships were sent down to Land's End to scour the seas around Cornwall for pirates, and later, in the autumn, the government took the first definite steps to send an expedition against Sallee to rout out the pirates.

---

[1] Juxon, Bishop of London and Lord Treasurer was another lord spiritual who expressed much concern with the damage pirates were doing.
[2] *Weymouth Corporation: Descriptive Catalogue.*

11
THE SALLEE EXPEDITION OF 1637

It is difficult to pinpoint with a high degree of exactitude the beginning of the expedition against the pirates of Sallee. Only a few years after the Sallee pirates began to prey on the English coast, Sir Francis Stewart reached the conclusion that an expedition against the town was necessary. On 16 August 1625, he wrote:

> these piceroones I say will ever be hankering upon our coast, and the State will find it both chargeable and difficult to clear it or secure the Newfoundland fishermen from them unless it be directly resolved to sack Sallee; a sure way, if easy to be performed, as some report it is, that are lately come thence; in the meantime . . . your Grace [Buckingham] must expect many complaints.[1]

And later, in the 1630s, there were numerous meetings, petitions, and proposals concerned with reducing the problem of the Sallee pirates by the application of naval force. And as related in the previous chapter, an expedition against Sallee was being mooted by the autumn of 1636. A few months earlier, Giles Penn had proposed an expedition to various government officials, but it was not until autumn that the government officially resolved to send a fleet against the Sallee pirates.[2] On 14 November, Edward Nicholas noted that an order would be given at the next meeting of

---
[1] PRO, SP 16/5/49.
[2] PRO, SP 16/327/69. Penn was a Bristol merchant, father of the Commonwealth Admiral William Penn, trading to Barbary: *DNB*, vol. 15, p. 753.

the Admiralty with regard to what ships would be appointed for action against the Turks of Sallee.[1] A week later, a conference was arranged with the officers of the navy and Trinity House representatives to discuss the choice of ships for this expedition. At this time, the Admiralty contemplated a small force consisting of only two large men-of-war, the *Leopard*, the *Bonaventure*, two *Whelps*, and two frigates.[2]

Within a week, Nicholas noted that the victualling of the ships was under way and that the king was being informed which ships were thought most fit for employment against Sallee and for how long they were to be victualled.[3] Charles I took a personal interest in this project as is evident from a marginal note added to the Admiralty's paper in the king's handwriting. He suggested that Rainsborough and Penn were to be employed as commanders of the enterprise and that they were expected to offer their opinions concerning particular aspects of the proposed expedition and ships.[4]

The Rainsborough referred to in the king's note was William (1587–1642), the son of Thomas, a mariner of Wapping and father of Col. Thomas Rainsborough, who in the Civil War became famous as the foremost military leader of the Leveller cause.[5] We do not know why Charles I recommended Rainsborough to command the fleet, but it would appear that his name was put forward by Lord High Admiral Northumberland[6] under whom Rainsborough had served that year as captain of the *Triumph*, flagship of the Summer Guard.[7]

Rainsborough, in any case, was an obvious and worthy choice for his ability had been demonstrated during a long career. He was an experienced and knowledgeable seaman who probably had sailed as a boy and young man with his father who successfully

---

[1] PRO, SP 16/335/60.
[2] PRO, SP 16/336/31. For Trinity House certificate, see SP 16/337/30, inclosure.
[3] PRO, SP 16/336/56. Note by Nicholas dated 28 November 1636.
[4] PRO, SP 16/336/57.
[5] For the career of William Rainsborough, see *DNB*, vol. 16, pp. 616–17; also W.R. Chaplin, 'William Rainsborough (1587–1642) and his Associates of the Trinity House', *MM*, XXXI (1945), pp. 178–97; H.F. Waters, *Genealogical Gleanings in England*, I, pp. 162–8.
[6] M.F. Keeler, *The Long Parliament 1640–1641: A Biographical Study of its Members*, p. 320. A few years later, Rainsborough was elected to the Long Parliament with the help of the Bence family from East Anglia and Northumberland.
[7] *DNB*, vol. 16, pp. 616–17. In 1636, he had been chosen by Northumberland to command the Admiral's flagship: PRO, SP 16/314/111.

captained and part-owned a number of ships which traded chiefly to the Mediterranean. William acquired more experience on voyages to the Mediterranean; an entry in the Levant Company records for 1618 mentions William Rainsborough as captain of a company ship which had done 'good service against the pirates'.[1] For this service he was offered a reward of £25 by the company; however, in a display of the sagacity that would in the long run bring him great wealth and advancement, he declined the money and requested instead membership in the company.[2]

In 1620, Rainsborough was again in the Mediterranean sailing to Constantinople as captain of the company ship *Castle* and in 1625 he commanded another Levant ship, the *Sampson*. The following year Rainsborough was requested by Secretary Conway to take on board a Levant-bound ship, the trunks of Sir Thomas Phillips who had been appointed to go to Constantinople as ambassador. As related in an earlier chapter, Rainsborough brought Sir Thomas Roe, the returning ambassador, back with him from Constantinople. It was during this voyage when in command of the *Sampson* that he achieved recognition for successfully defending his ship against four pirate vessels off Malta.[3] In later years he may have sailed to New England, for ships which he owned were involved in colonial voyages and three of his children settled in Massachusetts.[4]

By 1625 Rainsborough had been elected an Elder Brother of Trinity House, and from the early 1630s his acknowledged maritime experience led him to be appointed to several committees concerned with efficiency and management of the navy.[5] By 1635 he was in royal service and in that year was named captain of the royal man-of-war, *Merhonour*, flagship of the Earl of Lindsey. In the following year he held a similar command on the *Triumph*, his last posting before being named as Admiral of the Sallee expedition.

---

[1] PRO, SP 105/148/f.59.
[2] Twenty years later he would display the same shrewdness and practicality when he declined a knighthood offered by Charles I and requested instead a gold medal worth £300.
[3] PRO, SP 105/110/f.119, for the *Castle*; M. Strachan, '*Sampson*'s Fight with Maltese Galleys, 1628', *MM*, LV (1969), pp. 281–9.
[4] See Waters, *Genealogical Gleanings*, I, pp. 164–8, for connections with the New England colony.
[5] According to the *DNB*, Rainsborough was a member of committees appointed to look into the manning of the navy (1632), Chatham Chest (1635), defects of the navy (1636), and timber frauds (1638). PRO, SP 16/285/59, 314/111.

Rainsborough did not receive notice of his appointment until 4 December when he informed Nicholas that he was at that time too ill to come up to London, though he was eager to get started. In the meantime, he informed Nicholas, he had written to the Earl of Northumberland and Viscount Conway of his desire to prosecute the business.[1] By the second week in December, preparations were moving ahead as can be seen from the following summary by Lords of the Admiralty:

(1) The fleet was to be made ready by the middle of February or the beginning of March;
(2) The king had approved of the advice of Trinity House;
(3) Rainsborough was hastening to prepare the royal ships *Leopard* and *Antelope*; he planned to take into service two merchants ships, the *Hercules* and the *Angel*, and was making a contract with their owners to hire them at the rate of £3 per man;
(4) Their Lordships wished two pinnaces to be built and had requested the Treasurer of the Navy to draw up contracts with the builders.[2]

The advice rendered by Trinity House (referred to in point 2 above) made three main points. First, these experts stated that four ships and two pinnaces would probably be sufficient for the expedition; they recommended taking the royal ships *Leopard* and *Bonaventure*, along with two merchantmen, the *Hercules* and *Angel*. Second, they signified that it was important for all ships to be available by the middle of February or beginning of March because this was the time when the pirates set forth their ships to intercept the returning English Newfoundland fleet. Third, the Trinity House officials recommended that each ship be provisioned with six months' victuals and that a further three months' supply should be sent subsequently so that the fleet might lie on the Moroccan coast until early October.[3]

Specifications for the two pinnaces were soon submitted for approval. According to the proposed design these vessels would measure 90 feet on the keel and be 25 or 26 feet in breadth, and

---

[1] PRO, SP 16/337/8, from Southwold; on 5 December Nicholas indicates Admiralty would give warrant for setting out of ships for Sallee.
[2] PRO, 16/337/30.
[3] PRO, SP 16/337/30, enclosure I: they recommended four ships and two pinnaces to be sent out by March to protect Newfoundland ships.

each was designed to carry 14 pieces of ordnance. In addition to sails, these specially built ships were to be equipped with 15 or 16 banks of oars to a side. It was expected that both could be made ready by the last day of February.[1] In the event it would be the third week in March before both of the pinnaces were launched.[2] Part of the delay may have resulted from uncertainty about the optimum size of these ships. On 19 December, Nicholas noted that Charles had told the Admiralty officials that he wanted them to build eight ships of no more than 60 tons, and that two of these should be employed in the expedition to Sallee.[3] In the end only two pinnaces were actually built, and they were a good deal larger than the king wished: the *Expedition* and *Providence*, measured 301 and 304 tons respectively.[4] They were unusual ships,[5] perhaps the most distinctive of the early Stuart navy, yet little is known of their design. The *Expedition* and *Providence* measured 90 × 26 × 9.8/9.9 ft. The length to beam ratio was 3.46.[6] From the dimensions, two observations may be made about these ships and the purpose for which they were designed.[7] First, the hull form indicates that speed and shallow water operations were the main design objectives. Their long, thin hulls would permit them to sail quickly, unlike the other royal ships; therefore, they would be fast enough to catch the speedy vessels favoured by the pirates. Second, the draught measurement shows that they were intended to work close in to shore and would be able to prevent the small,

---

[1] PRO, SP 16/337/30, enclosure II, for details of the proposed ships.
[2] PRO, SP 16/350/31, 18 March 1637, and SP 16/350/50, 21 March 1637.
[3] PRO, SP 16/337/70.
[4] M. Oppenheim, *A History of the Administration of the Royal Navy and of Merchant Shipping in Relation to the Navy*, p. 255. The tonnage is by builders' measurement.
[5] T. Glasgow, jr, 'The Shape of the Ships that Defeated the Spanish Armada', *MM*, L (1964), pp. 178–86. The typical English warship of the period was a three-masted vessel with two gun decks in a short, broad, deep hull. For example, the *Leopard*, Rainsborough's flagship, built in 1634, measured 95 ft on the keel, 33 ft in breadth, and 12.4 ft in depth. The length to beam ratio (2.87) was in the middle of the range for Tudor and Stuart warships (2.80–3.00) and her stated armament of 34 guns and tonnage of 516 builder's measurement were about average.
[6] Oppenheim, *Administration of the Royal Navy*, pp. 254–5.
[7] The speed of a ship is determined by the amount of propulsive power available less the resistance produced by friction and wave-making. The amount of resistance produced by friction is proportional to the wetted area of the hull and its form: a fine entry, considerable mid-section rise, and a sharp stern resulted in ships with less wetted area and therefore greater speed potential. Wave-making resistance is largely a function of the speed length ratio: a long, narrow hull will reduce wave-making resistance and increase speed: see H.I. Chapelle, *The Search for Speed under Sail, 1700–1855*, pp. 28–9, 42–6.

light pirate vessels from sneaking into or out of port, as had happened when Mansell's ships attempted to blockade Algiers. If becalmed, they could be rowed or manoeuvred against the wind to gain tactical advantage or catch up a better-placed foe. And experience would show that these ships were good sailors as well.

But in addition to being fast and nimble, the *Expedition* and *Providence* were large enough to support a relatively heavy armament. Initial plans called for them to carry 14 guns, but more cannon were mounted before they departed.[1] In any case, as equipped in 1637 they were sufficiently well-armed to defend themselves against the type of ship normally employed by the Sallee pirates. If they encountered a stronger vessel, their speed and manoeuvrability would allow them to break off the action; and it was expected that they would operate in company with the *Leopard* and *Antelope*, both exceptionally strong and well-armed warships.

While the pinnaces were being built, other preparations went ahead, even though Rainsborough's ill health did not allow him to get up to London until 21 December.[2] From Nicholas we learn that the Admiralty had resolved the problem of what to do about Giles Penn who had been considered initially for a position of command. Penn had also been one of the prime movers of the business and had spent considerable time, effort, and money helping to project the expedition.[3] For example, that very month he submitted a ten-point memorandum on the subject of the expedition.[4] By early January, Penn had been told that he would not go on the expedition. He expressed disappointment and stated that he had spent £100 promoting action against the Sallee pirates only to see others preferred – adding sourly that preparations were moving far too slowly and it would now be impossible for the fleet

---

[1] The design specification called for 14, but on 24 April it was reported that the captains of the pinnaces desired two short minions, or saker drakes, in addition to the guns already aboard: PRO, SP 16/354/70. Later in their career, they would carry as many as 30 guns each.
[2] PRO, SP 16/337/76.
[3] PRO, SP 16/337/76; SP 16/343/45; SP 16/327/69.
[4] PRO, SP 16/338/51. In it he recommended the following: (1) the fleet should have a pinnace with it; (2) the Dunkirk pinnace would be most suitable; (3) only fit seamen should be taken and enough shirts and jackets should be provided to clothe the poorest sort; (4) two ships should carry shallops instead of long boats for they would be more suitable for reconnaissance; (5) good provisions, including cider, should be provided, and they should take along good surgeons, physicians, and devines; (6) experienced Bristol seamen should be impressed; (7) Moorish prisoners should be taken for use in exchange; (8) advantage should be taken of

to get there by the recommended time.[1] A week later, he was again seeking compensation, though now he was looking for employment as an ambassador to Morocco for which, he claimed, he was well qualified by reason of his knowledge of the land and fluency in the language spoken there. As for his expenses (which by this time had been reduced to £50), he suggested these be taken out of the money collected for redemption of captives in years past.[2]

By late December 1636, preparations for the expedition had become public knowledge. The day after Christmas, the Venetian ambassador sent off a report about the intended expedition.[3] On 9 January, the *Leopard* and *Antelope* were ready to sail but for a lack of victuals which were expected daily.[4] A week later, William Russell, Treasurer of the navy, told Nicholas that the fleet was almost ready and should set sail by the middle of the following month.[5] By this time Rainsborough was actively overseeing preparations. The builder of one of the two pinnaces, Robert Tranckmore, was accused of using rotten timber, and Phineas Pett, Master Shipwright, and Rainsborough went to investigate. Rainsborough reported that the timber was 'somewhat faulty' but that Tranckmore was replacing it.[6]

On 15 January, Rainsborough submitted a memorial concerning the ships that were to go on the expedition. He intended to sail as Admiral in the *Leopard*, George Carteret would be Vice-Admiral in the *Antelope*, Brian Harrison would captain the *Hercules*, George Hatch would command the *Great Neptune*, and Thomas White and Edmund Seamen would be in charge of the two pinnaces.[7] All of Rainsborough's nominees were accepted. All

civil strife in Sallee; (9) the fleet should sail by 20 January, if they went later all the pirate ships would be at sea and the English fleet would accomplish little; (10) lastly, he requested that he be named commander of the expedition since he was the first 'mentioner' of the business; and he also requested appointment as surveyor of goods taken in reprisal.

[1] PRO, SP 16/343/45.
[2] PRO, SP 16/343/86. All his requests, however, were in the end rejected. It should be noted that Penn praised the naval skills of those selected for the expedition; his criticism was that they lacked experience in Barbary.
[3] *CSPV*, 1636–1639, p. 116.
[4] PRO, SP 16/343/62. Kenrick Edisbury, the Surveyor of the navy, also advised Nicholas that the captains were to be appointed shortly, but that the timber selected for the pinnaces was bad.
[5] PRO, SP 16/343/84. Warrants needed to be issued so that the charter party agreements for the hired ships could be settled.
[6] PRO, SP 16/343/87.
[7] PRO, SP 16/344/17.

were experienced seamen, except Carteret,[1] and all were Londoners, old friends of Rainsborough, men he knew and trusted.[2] The rest of Rainsborough's memorial is routine; in it he did, however, recommend that the maximum permissible amount of gunpowder be carried and that each ship should be supplied with 40 additional pistols or carbines. This provision suggests that Rainsborough expected a long blockade and close combat.

The expedition received a setback towards the end of January, when the *Great Neptune* broke her cables during a storm and was driven aground near Woolwich.[3] Pett and some of the other shipwrights inspected the damage and reported to Nicholas that she had several defective beams and would require much repair work to make her serviceable. It was recommended that the Admiralty appoint another ship in her stead. Nicholas was informed on 28 January that the *Prosperous* and the *Mary*, two merchant ships of ten taken up for service that year, were closest to being ready for sea duty and so might be chosen for the Sallee expedition. It was also suggested that another royal ship, the *Dreadnought* or the *St Dennis* might be included.

As the English fleet prepared to depart, efforts were begun to get assistance from Spain. On 16 January, a letter was sent to Sir Walter Aston, the English ambassador in Madrid, requesting him to obtain permission for the English warships to use Spanish ports and for them to be provisioned from Spanish stores, if necessary.[4] The English government also hoped to get the Spanish to provide some galleys to assist Rainsborough. At the beginning of February, Aston received the letter and immediately submitted his government's request,[5] but by 1 April he had heard nothing and advised Whitehall that:

I am of the opinion that they have entertained some jealousies

---

[1] Though a man of considerable naval experience, Carteret was an outsider, and he was also the only one, as events showed, who would act behind Rainsborough's back. PRO, SP 16/363/99. On 10 July, Sir John Pennington wrote to Nicholas that he had heard from friends in London that they had received covert letters from Carteret, who stated that Rainsborough's reports were not correct.

[2] D.E. Kennedy, 'Naval Captains at the Outbreak of the English Civil War', *MM*, XLVI (1960), pp. 184–5.

[3] R.A. Preston, ' "To Outsail the Dutch" ', *MM*, XXXVI (1950), p. 335, describes the history of this ship; PRO, SP 16/345/27, describes its loss.

[4] This account of the English side of the negotiations is based on a reading of the letters of Sir Walter Aston covering the relevant period: BL, Add. MS. 36,450.

[5] BL, Add. MS. 36,450, f.119. By 18 March, Aston had learned little, though he pressed the ministers almost daily; he was told that they were working on the matter and would have a reply for him shortly.

of his Majesty's demand and suspect he had other designs than what he pretended.[1]

Aston's suspicions were to some degree justified. In early March the Council of State considered the English request and their opinions were recorded in a *consulta* dated 5 March.[2] There was little substantive division in the Council, though members differed on particulars. The Duque de Albuquerque was in favour of allowing English ships to use Spanish ports, as long as no more than six were allowed in Spanish waters at one time. He viewed the request for Spanish galleys with less favour believing these ships were needed for service on the French and Italian coasts. The Marques de Santa Cruz thought the English king's request for port facilities should be met in order that Spanish ships might enjoy the same right in England. The English fleet should be treated courteously in his view, though he added that they should be watched carefully as well. He wondered whether the English might have some other design in sending the fleet at this time. He also recommended that the English ships should use Gibraltar since that port was easy for Spanish forces to defend. He felt that the galleys should be provided, when available, though he believed they were not fit for service in the seas off Sallee but could go to Mamora, if need be. Don Carlos Coloma was of the opinion that they could not deny the English port facilities and also expressed an interest in obtaining reciprocal arrangements. He recommended that they speak to the English ambassador '*con mucha franqueza*' (very frankly) about how inconvenient it was at that time to release galleys from their present service for reasons that were very apparent. Like Santa Cruz, he was suspicious of the aims of the English fleet, and thought it should be treated with caution and circumspection. Finally, the Duque de Villahermosa said that he was concerned about the coming of the English warships. He reminded the Council of the advice that had been received by the *consejo de Portugal* which included information about English merchants supplying the pirate ports of Morocco and of the agreements between England and Morocco. He also thought that all Spanish galleys would be needed for operations in the Mediterranean.

[1] Ibid., f.126–126v.
[2] AGS, Estado, legajo 2521, contains the *consulta* and related letters, including Aston's follow-up letter of 21 March 1637.

As a result, as Aston informed Secretary Coke on 25 April:

> your lords I presume will observe how they avoided answering to the point of assistance in their first paper & being prest to it by my reply I have in a manner forced thus much now from them, but truth is, their occasions are so great & their sea provisions so short considering the French armada that lies upon them in these parts that I believe they will have so much to do in their own business that they will be unable to give us that aid which is desired.[1]

Aston's assessment was essentially correct, though the Spanish government did send notices to the port towns requiring officials to assist the English fleet, and, eventually, a few Spanish galleys were sent to Morocco, though not as far as Sallee.

By early February, English preparations were well advanced. Last minute provisions were coming in for the fleet, and Nicholas was demanding 'orders to be given speedily' to satisfy the fleet's needs.[2] His notes for the 9th tell us that the Admiralty was preparing instructions for Rainsborough.[3] These were issued on the 17th and consisted of only five main charges:

> (1) 'First and above all things you shall provide that God be duly served twice every day in his Majesty's said ship, and by every ships company under your charge according to the usual prayers & liturgy of the Church of England'.
> (2) Second he was called upon to take the ships (named) under his command and 'repair in a straight course to Sallee, & there to employ yourself with industry & courage principally for suppressing of Turkish pirates, & redeeming of his Majesty's subjects, whom they have taken'.
> (3) If any pirate ships were encountered he was 'to do your best to apprehend or sink them'.

---

[1] BL, Add. MS. 36,450, ff.127v–128. In this period Spain was at war with France, with much of the naval operation taking place in the Mediterranean where galleys would be useful.
[2] PRO, SP 16/346/36,71. It is interesting to observe that Nicholas asked whether iron cannon, which were considerably cheaper than brass, might be used for the pinnaces. SP 16/354/106 indicates that eight refined iron culverin drakes and four ordinary semi-culverins were supplied along with 16 brass cannon.
[3] PRO, SP 16/346/71.

(4) All pirates who were taken were to be brought back to England and put in jail, 'where they are to be received & safely kept & to have trial according to the law, as the keepers will answer the contrary at their peril'. All ships and goods taken from the pirates were to be preserved and care taken 'that no part thereof be spoiled, wasted or embezzled, spiking down the hatches and holds & sending them by some honest men into some of his Majesty's ports or harbours for his Majesty's use advertising us thereof'.

(5) 'You are from time to time to send us notice of all your actions & proceedings, and to advertise us of all such certain intelligence as you shall learn fit to be made known unto us or the States, together with the names of the parties from whom, or by what means, you receive the said'.[1]

The brevity and directness of these instructions stand in contrast with those issued to Mansell. From the wording, it also appears that some of the lessons of Mansell's expedition had been learned. The objective was clearly stated: Rainsborough was instructed to sail directly to Sallee and stay there until he had achieved the desired ends. The fruitless patrols and sweeps that had characterized much of Mansell's operation were not authorized. Also, the sort of problems relating to captives and prizes which arose during the Algiers expedition were anticipated and resolved in the instructions given to Rainsborough.

After receiving his instructions, Rainsborough prepared to leave his Wapping home to board ship. By 20 February, he was ready to go to sea but had still not heard from Carteret to whom he wrote promising to save a place for him while the fleet remained in the Thames or even while it was in the Downs.[2] On 21 February, Rainsborough boarded the *Leopard* at Tilbury ready to depart but found it still lacking some sails and other minor items.[3] Three days later, Rainsborough's ships at last weighed anchor and sailed round to the Downs where they waited for the *Antelope* and

---

[1] PRO, SP 16/347/32. The instructions were initialled by the Earl of Lindsey, Sir Henry Vane, Sir John Coke, and Sir Francis Windebank.
[2] PRO, SP 16/347/63. By the 23 February Rainsborough was requesting Nicholas to replace Carteret if he did not appear shortly: ibid. 348/8.
[3] Rainsborough started his journal on 21 February 1637 when he boarded the *Leopard*: PRO, SP 16/369/72. John Dunton's account of the expedition, *A true journal of the Sally Fleet, with the proceedings of the voyage*, indicates that he boarded the *Leopard* at Chatham on 26 January. The *Antelope* was short of crew when Rainsborough went to sea.

Captain Carteret to appear. On 1 March Rainsborough wrote to the Admiralty that he was exceedingly anxious to set out for Sallee, even though his fleet was incomplete.[1] Fortunately, the *Antelope* appeared the next day, though there was still no sign of Carteret.[2] After waiting two more days in vain, Rainsborough gave order for the fleet to set sail for Sallee.[3]

At 6 p.m. on the 6th the fleet, minus the *Antelope* which was left to await Carteret, left English waters and headed southwards. According to the journal of the expedition made by Rainsborough, the voyage to Morocco was largely uneventful.[4] On 12 March the fleet was hit by a gale which snapped the main mast of the *Hercules*. The rest of the fleet remained with the stricken ship through the night and rendered what assistance they could the next day. Rainsborough then ordered the *Hercules* to make her way to the nearest major port to get a new mast rigged, after which it was expected that she would join the rest of the fleet at Sallee.

On the 20th, as they approached Cape St Vincent, the *Antelope*, with Carteret aboard, came into sight and soon caught up. Though still not at full strength, Rainsborough's fleet sailed on to Sallee arriving there on the 24 March. To his surprise, Rainsborough discovered that his ships were not the only English vessels anchored in the roadstead. Two merchantmen were there: one belonging to Mr Courteen and the other to the heirs of Mr Woodruff, who had died at Sallee a few days earlier.[5] Rainsborough immediately ordered both ships to depart, but on being informed that each had merchants ashore, he gave them an additional day to retrieve those individuals still ashore. From these merchants, he learned that most of the English captives of the town had been transported recently to Algiers and Tunis, and that there were probably no more than 250 captives remaining in Sallee.

On the 25th March, Rainsborough started proceedings with a

[1] PRO, SP 16/369/72.
[2] PRO, SP 16/349/34. Just before he left, Rainsborough penned a note for Carteret in which he signified that he was exasperated by Carteret's non-appearance and that he had risked his reputation and the success of the expedition tarrying for him. He intended to set forth with an easy sail and hope Carteret in the *Antelope* would catch him up at Falmouth or finally in the road at Sallee, if it came to that.
[3] PRO, SP 16/349/4. They convoyed a ship, the *Grace*, carrying munitions to Falmouth.
[4] PRO, SP 16/369/72. Rainsborough waited off Falmouth until the *Grace* was safely in harbour. His journal entries for 7–11 March give only wind direction, course, and latitude.
[5] Ibid., entry for 24 March 1637.

letter to the governor, but received no answer.[1] The next day he launched a boat, but as it was heading toward shore, six small vessels from the new town came out and attacked it, though eventually they were driven off by cannon fire from the English men-of-war. During the next three weeks, Rainsborough kept his small fleet riding as close as possible to the harbour entrance. On three occasions, ships of the town tried to get into or out of the harbour; Rainsborough's vessels gave chase but never succeeded in intercepting the fast, shallow-draft pirate vessels which hugged the shoreline to avoid the English warships which drew too much water to get in close or were too slow to catch them.

On 18 April the *Hercules* arrived from Lisbon where she had gone for repairs. On that day Rainsborough sent Aston one of the few letters that he wrote during the expedition. In it he thanked the ambassador for obtaining port facilities for the *Hercules*. He went on to say that he found the governor of Sallee (a Morisco) 'puffed up with his luck in thieving', and quite unwilling to release any English captives. Rainsborough also explained that he had arrived just in time, for the pirates had prepared a fleet of 40 to 50 vessels, of which about 20 were large enough to carry between 12 and 20 cannon.[2] Most of these vessels had been trapped by the English fleet which Rainsborough kept riding within shooting distance of the town. To make the blockade completely effective, however, Rainsborough told Aston he would need Spanish galleys or the two pinnaces (which were expected to arrive shortly). Only when he had shallow-draught vessels with oars, would he be able to cut off the town by manoeuvring close to shore or against the wind if necessary.[3]

Through March, April, and May, Rainsborough had to make do with the forces available.[4] On 27 April an action characteristic of this phase of the operations took place. On that day, the English fleet was attempting to blockade Sallee as tightly as possible when the pirates set out some ships. According to Rainsborough's journal:

The wind at the West: I sent 7 boats to watch into the shore,

---

[1] PRO, SP 16/354/28. Rainsborough described his reception to Aston in a letter dated 18 April 1637. See also SP 16/369/72, journal entries for this period.
[2] PRO, SP 16/354/28.
[3] Ibid. This point is emphasized again in his letter to Sir Henry Vane dated 9 May 1637: PRO, SP 16/355/161.
[4] PRO, SP 16/369/72. *Providence* came in on 10 June and the *Expedition* on 11 June 1637.

there came out 2 carvels, our boats fought with them 3 hours but could not take them, they killed my coxen and shot 8 more but I hope all save one of them will recover.[1]

Attempts were made in this period to destroy the trapped pirate ships both by gunfire and by sending in a fire-ship, though neither method was terribly successful.[2] The use of the fire-ship was reminiscent of Mansell's attempt at Algiers, and as in that earlier English attempt, the townsmen were alerted in time and came out and put out the fire before it had achieved much. One English sailor was taken prisoner during the action. Although Rainsborough's tactics produced no dramatic results, the continuous presence of the fleet began to have an effect on the morale of the town after a couple of months.[3]

The port of Sallee was in fact made up of two towns lying either side of the Bou Regreg river.[4] The old town was situated on the south side of the river, while to the north a new settlement had been created by the influx of thousands of Morisco refugees from Spain. The two communities were quite different; the older one had long maintained good relations with England, while the newer community supported the assaults on Christian shipping and was less obedient to the Emperor of Morocco. For much of the 17th century, the interests of the two sections were in conflict. In fact, when Rainsborough arrived, the two sections of the town were quarrelling, a situation he hoped to use to his advantage.[5] The first hint of a break came on 21 April when a Moor from the old town came out to Rainsborough's ship with some intelligence and offers of alliance. Eight days later, Rainsborough felt confident enough about the good intentions of the old town to send in one of his boats to reconnoitre the scene. They returned a day later with news that some of the food supplies of the new town had been burned. Following discussions with officials of the old town, Rainsborough then sent one of his gunners ashore to make a

[1] Ibid., entry for 27 April 1637.
[2] The English warships could not get close enough to bring their cannon to bear on the pirate ships at their anchorage in the river; see illustration no. 3: plan of Sallee which shows the depths of the roadstead.
[3] PRO, SP 16/369/72. On 21 April a representative from Old Sallee came aboard with the offer of an alliance.
[4] R. Coindreau, *Les Corsaires de Salé*, pp. 44–55. A contemporary plan of the town is shown in illustration no. 3.
[5] Rainsborough's journal entry for 24 March reads 'also that the two towns have a war one with another': PRO, SP 16/369/72.

reconnaissance of the defences of the new town. He returned with a representative of the Saint, the leader of the old town. That evening the two sides met to draft an agreement, though it would take a week before the Saint's representative could get it confirmed.[1]

But even before it had been formally settled, this alliance began to bear fruit. Cannon from the ships were brought ashore and mounted on specially-fashioned carriages for use on land from positions near or in the old town.[2] A protective trench was also dug so that more English cannon could be brought safely to a position close to the enemy. Rainsborough then sent sailors ashore to act as infantry. Within a few days, a partially complete blockade was transformed into a tight siege. Over the next month, Rainsborough's forces tightened their grip on the new town and shore-based cannon fire began hitting enemy targets both in the town and river. In this way, 13 pirate ships in the harbour and river were smashed to pieces.[3]

While all this was going on, Rainsborough detached a couple of ships to range upon the coast in search of pirate ships, using intelligence gained from sources in the old town.[4] In June, the English pinnaces arrived to further strengthen the blockade and coastal raids: these operations were extremely successful; four more pirate ships were destroyed, including the 22-gun 'Admiral' of the Sallee fleet which was caught by the *Hercules* and the *Mary* in the roadstead at Fedally.[5] Two other pirate ships were taken prize in these actions; one of these was subsequently taken up by Rainsborough's men to serve in the blockading squadron.

Through June and early July, the blockade and siege continued. The new town was by then completely cut off both from the land side and from the sea. Several neutral ships approached the roadstead, but Rainsborough would permit none to enter. One of these was the *Neptune*, a Dutch ship from Amsterdam. Her master protested and somewhat limply proclaimed that his ship's cargo of gunpowder was really intended for Santa Cruz and not the new town. Not only did Rainsborough brush aside the protest, he

---

[1] In his letter of 9 May Rainsborough informed Vane of his agreement: PRO, SP 16/355/161. The terms are printed in Dunton, *Journal of the Sally Fleet*, p. E 2–3, and there is a copy in Coke's papers: HMC, 23, *12th Report, App. ii, Cowper MSS*, p. 158.
[2] PRO, SP 16/369/72, 3 May 1637.
[3] Ibid., 4 May, 1, 3, 7 June 1637.
[4] Ibid., 10 May 1637.
[5] Ibid., 5 May 1637.

ordered the removal of 40 barrels (from a cargo of 51) of powder for use by his fleet.[1]

By late July, Rainsborough had intelligence that resistance in the new town was starting to crumble. Food was becoming scarce in the town, and, as a consequence, factional fighting had broken out. Earlier in April, Rainsborough learned that a very militant faction had seized power and deposed the governor and sent him in chains to the emperor of Morocco.[2] At the end of July, the old governor returned (suitably chastened by the emperor) along with Robert Blake, an English merchant who claimed to farm the customs for the emperor. Together, Blake and the old governor entered the town on 27 July to try to arrange for a surrender and the release of all English captives. The next day the new town surrendered to the representative of the emperor, and within a few days over 300 captives were released and returned to the English fleet with the help of Robert Blake.[3]

In early August, Rainsborough dispatched the *Antelope*, *Hercules*, *Providence* and *Expedition* for the coast of Spain to look for pirates from Algiers and to protect the English ships which sailed that way in the vintage time.[4] Carteret was dispatched for Cadiz on the 8th where he remained from the 15th to the 21st, taking on water and ballast. From Cadiz, he wrote to Northumberland that he would be sailing directly for England, unless he heard that Algerian pirates were about.[5] Two weeks later, Carteret, the four ships, and the hundreds of released captives were back in England.[6]

Rainsborough stayed on at Sallee. His small fleet was reinforced by the arrival of the *Mary Rose* and *Roebuck*.[7] These two ships had been sent out in early July when it was uncertain how long

---

[1] Ibid., 25 June 1637.
[2] Ibid., 22 June 1637; Dunton, *Journal of the Sally Fleet*, p. 10.
[3] PRO, SP 16/369/72. Thirteen were released on 19 June, 40 on 31 July, 180 on 1 August, 73 on 2 August. For the names, see SP 71/13/ff.29–35.
[4] PRO, SP 16/365/44. Ever mindful of his mission, Rainsborough instructed Carteret not to allow more than one ship at a time to put into a Spanish port.
[5] PRO, SP 16/366/12. From this letter it would appear that Carteret did not follow Rainsborough's instructions very closely. He appears more intent on returning to England than catching pirates.
[6] PRO, SP 16/368/3. On 20 September *Hercules* reported in Falmouth; on 23 September Sir John Pennington reported from the Downs that all four ships had returned. *Antelope* and *Hercules* had but five days' victuals on board, but the pinnaces were victualled for two months more, another indication that Carteret was not anxious to chase pirates off Spain, as instructed.
[7] PRO, SP 16/369/72, 12 August 1637.

Rainsborough would need to maintain the blockade. They came with two months' supplies, arriving on 12 August, too late to take part in the blockade; nevertheless, their arrival was appreciated because provisions were much needed by the fleet at that time.[1] The release of the captives meant Rainsborough had to use much of his initial supply of victuals to feed the 340 former captives who joined his fleet.

On the 20th of August, Rainsborough left Sallee and sailed to Safi where he put ashore Mr Blake, his lieutenant, and one of his sons.[2] After coming ashore at Safi, they made their way to Fez to see the emperor of Morocco to try to arrange for a general settlement and the release of any other English captives held within the emperor's domain. The English fleet remained in Safi until 21 September, when Mr Blake and the rest of the party returned with an emissary from the emperor.[3] After everyone was on board and a gift of horses for Charles I had been safely stowed, the fleet set sail for England. Within two weeks they had reached Land's End; soon thereafter some of the former captives were landed at Torbay; on 7 October, Rainsborough's four ships were in the Downs once again. Five days later, Rainsborough left his flagship at Porchester, and a day later his ships crossed the chain (the protective barrier), signifying an official end to the voyage.[4]

Unlike Mansell, who had slipped into port so quietly that his arrival went largely unrecorded, the return of Rainsborough's fleet set in motion a great public triumph. Much of the ceremony in the following weeks centred around the newly-released captives and the ambassador from the emperor of Morocco who had accompanied Rainsborough back to England. The arrival and reception of the ambassador were extraordinary events and the occasion for much comment. The best published account includes the following description:

---

[1] The correspondence regarding the sending out of the resupply ships is in PRO, SP 16/363/48,59. Consideration was given to sending more ships to reinforce Rainsborough, but Northumberland advised that such a move would be of no purpose, the ships arriving too late to affect events: SP 16/365/18.
[2] Although it is not certain, it is probable that the son referred to was Thomas Rainsborough, the future Leveller. His presence at the blockade and siege of Sallee may explain his later success in the Civil War in which he gained fame for his successful siege operations. The elder son, William, is found residing in New England shortly after this date.
[3] PRO, SP 16/369/72. Blake and company returned on 16 September, the horses were loaded on the 18th.
[4] Ibid., entries for 5–13 October 1637.

Thursday, the nineteenth of October, when by his Majesty' command and appointment, Sir John Finnet, Knight Master of Ceremonies, was sent down to Gravesend, to conduct the ambassador to London . . . They had no sooner taken their barges, and were launched, but an expression of <u>love</u> and <u>welcome</u> flew in thundering manner our [sic] of the mouths of great ordnance from both the blockhouses of Gravesend and on the Essex side, and the tide being reasonable calm, they pleasantly passed to Woolwich, where they saw his Majesty's new great ship (the Eighth Wonder of the World) with pleasing and much contenting admiration. After which they passed to Greenwich, where they landed and stayed at the Rose and Crown four hours . . . So they took barges at Greenwich, almost an hour before night, with their trumphets sounding before them all the way: and after an hour's rowing they landed at the Tower, where they were attended by thousands, and ten thousands of spectators, and welcomed and conveyed with his Majesty's coach, and at least one hundred coaches more, and the chiefest of Citizens and Barbary Merchants bravely mounted on hourseback, all richly apparelled, every man having a chain of gold about him; with the sheriffes and aldermen of London in scarlet gowns, with an abundance of torches and lights, that though it were night, yet the streets were almost as light as day. And in this brave way, the ambassador and his associate, Mr. Blake, were accompanied from Tower-wharf to their lodgings . . . at the house that was Sir Martin Lumley's.[1]

Three weeks later another parade was organized to accompany the ambassador's progress to Whitehall for an audience with King Charles. The description of this procession is too lengthy to include here, but some sense of the magnificence and pageantry of the event may be perceived from a brief description of just a few of the 16 orders of march which made up the parade. In the first order were the Earl of Shrewsbury and 12 other aristocrats. In the sixth order rode seven trumpeters who sounded all the way. They were followed by 'four horses [gifts to the king from the ambassador] with very rich saddles embroidered with gold, the stirrups of

---

[1] Anon., *The Arrivall and Intertainments of the Embassador Alkaid Jaurer Ben Abdella*, pp. 7–9. This reception stands in marked contrast to that accorded to the Moroccan embassy that came in 1628: J. Finett, *Finetti Philoxenis: som choice observations of Sir J.F., . . . touching . . . forren ambassadors in England*, p. 225.

two of them being massie gold and the bridles embroidered suitably with golden bosses, [these] were led along by four black Moors in red liveries'. Next came the newly-released captives, 'cloathed all anew by the Alkaid'. The 11th order included 'twelve gentlemen of the Privy Chamber to his Majesty of Great Britain, on brave horses with footcloths, riding'.[1]

On the way through the City, the procession passed through Temple Bar where they were attended by the trained bands (400 men in all) and saluted with a thunderous volley. In this way the ambassador and his company were brought to court. Here they were greeted by the Yeoman of the Guard and numerous gentlemen and nobles who saluted the ambassador and conducted him to the king. After seeing the ambassador in the Banqueting House, the king went to the park where 'the horses with four hawks, and the former captives' had been assembled for the king to view them. The ambassador waited upon the king there, and the former captives were brought near 'for his Majesty to see them'. Shortly thereafter, the Moroccan ambassador returned to his residence in Wood Street accompanied by another torchlight parade.

Of these events the Venetian ambassador observed:

> The excessive honours accorded to the Moroccan ambassador, to the general amazement, both at his entry and audience, have induced me to observe carefully their aims, and I think it my duty to send an exact report. Besides a numerous ascort of aldermen and merchants, on horseback, he was accompanied at both functions by an earl, at the king's express command, with all the circumstances of coaches and other things used with all extraordinary ambassadors of kings and with the ordinary ambassadors of France and Spain, and not usual with others.[2]

The Venetian goes on to conclude that all these formalities were really just an attempt to slight him and the republic which he represented. Apart from the egocentric nature of the observations, the ambassador was quite right in his appreciation. The honours were excessive. Morocco was not a France or Spain, and the ambassador, Jaurer Ben Abdella, was not a man of noble birth or a great officer of state.[3] He was Portuguese by birth, a eunuch

---

[1] Anon., *Arrivall and Intertainments*, pp. 12–15.
[2] *CSPV*, 1636–1639, pp. 322–3.
[3] *The Earl of Strafford's Letters and Dispatches*, ed. W. Knowler, II, p. 129.

in the emperor's household. And there is evidence to support the Venetian ambassador's conclusion that the reception of the Moroccan ambassador had been carefully organized, though not for the reason that he suggested. First, a spectacle of such magnitude required co-ordination, forethought and preparation. Second, as indicated above, certain officials were present 'at the King's express command', evidence that the matter had been taken up at the highest level of government, though to what end we may only speculate.

The excessive honours given to the Moroccan ambassador fitted in with the main foreign policy objectives of the government at the time. We know much about the Crown's objectives from a letter by Sir John Coke to his son.[1] The beginning of this letter has been quoted earlier,[2] but the remainder, though less generally significant, is useful in helping to elucidate the treatment of the Moroccan embassy:

> The wisdom of this State under our late blessed Queen balanced our neighbour potent kings in France and Spain by our religious interest in the protestants of that Church, and in Spain by other diversions and keeping correspondence with Turkey and Barbary; whereby, not only our peace and trade grew great in those parts, but we had also ready means to keep that king in alarm upon his own coasts and to supply our own fleets for all attempts against Spain, the Islands, or the West Indies. How these counsels have changed in . . . Spain by the long abusive treaty whereof this kingdom hath been very sensible, though some still apt to oppose all counsels that seem to tend to the prejudice of that crown; as by the confident

[1] HMC 23, *12th Report, App. ii, Cowper MSS*, pp. 296–7. Coke's letter was written in 1641 and arose from a charge that years earlier he had wrongfully stayed a ship bound for Barbary. In answering this charge, he put the incident in the context of the larger aims of English foreign policy for this part of the world which he stated explicitly.

[2] See above, Chapter 10 for a discussion of the motivations behind English foreign policy. Also, see S.L. Adams, 'Foreign Policy and the Parliaments of 1621 and 1624', in the useful collection, *Faction and Parliament: Essays on Early Stuart History*, ed. K. Sharpe. Perhaps because Adams has studied the writings of men of strong religious beliefs, he sees different motivations to English foreign policy than presented here and as expressed by Coke and other royal policy-makers. Other historians of this period play down religious motivations in foreign policy; J.I. Israel, for example, writes, 'Only someone totally ignorant of their policies . . . could imagine that sympathy for the Protestant cause played any part in their policy making': *Times Literary Supplement*, no. 4285, 17 May 1985, p. 552.

complaint against the Barbary Company may be made to appear, who have been made the instruments for the overthrow thereof. . . . All men can remember what we suffered by the pirates of Algiers, Sallee, and Morocco, and the many letters and instructions written by other secretaries and by myself and sent by divers agents sufficiently testify how we laboured to redeem our captives, and to renew the ancient correspondence in those parts, which by the troubles in that kingdom could come to no good issue till the king of Morocco, hoping by His Majesty's favour to settle his distressed affairs, sent a solemn assambage[?] to treat on such articles as might conduce to the common good. . . . And their Lordships' pleasure was that . . . I should prepare articles . . . and the ambassador, consenting to all our demands, required for his master but this one article, that His Majesty trading freely with all his people should not permit his subjects to trade with that King's rebels.[1]

By treating the Moroccan envoy as an equal of the Spanish ambassador, the government intended to flatter the Moroccan official, and remind the Spanish representative that Spain had a vulnerable flank. The government also intended for the Spanish to not take English friendship lightly and to consider that they perhaps might have been more forward with offers to assist the English fleet.

Seen in this way, it also appears unlikely that the Moroccan ambassador and entourage were taken to admire 'the king's new great ship' simply by chance. This ship, the *Sovereign of the Seas*, was an impressive sight. She was probably the largest and most heavily armed warship the world had ever seen: she was the first three-deck man-of-war, and the first vessel to carry over 100 large cannon.[2] In comparison, the *Leopard* (the largest of Rainsborough's warships) was but one-third of the size and strength of the king's new ship. Charles had been personally responsible for ordering a ship of such enormous size and great strength. The *Sovereign of the Seas*, as her name indicates, was meant to symbolize the naval power of the king of England. This warship was also lavishly decorated with five huge, ornate lanterns and extensive carving and much giltwork. The decorations alone cost

---

[1] HMC, 23, *12th Report, App. ii, Cowper MSS*, pp. 296–7.
[2] T. Heywood, *A Description of his Majesties royall and most stately ship called the Sovereign of the Seas, built at Woolwich in Kent 1637*, pp. 45–6, gives the dimensions.

£6691 or more than the total amount spent in building an entire warship like the *Leopard*.[1] Though our sources do not say why the entourage was shown the *Sovereign of the Seas*, the government would have been hard put to find a more pointed way of displaying (to both the Moroccans and the Spanish) the naval power and resources of England.

These processions were also meant to impress the people of London. They were a dramatic and visible way of highlighting one of the government's few unalloyed accomplishments. The four-hour delay at the Rose and Crown, encouraged by Sir John Finett, the royal Master of Ceremonies, was a way of turning the journey into a torchlight spectacle. It is difficult to imagine a more effective means of informing the populace of the good use to which the Ship Money levies were being put. Contemporaries appreciated the connection.[2] For example, on 23 October, Lord Conway wrote to Thomas Wentworth the following:

> There is an ambassador come from the King of Morocco, and is received with great pomp, and if there can be a means found, I believe it shall be assisted, the reason of all is the Shipping Money.[3]

A month later, Wentworth replied to a similar comment by Archbishop Laud with these words:

> This action of Sally I assure you is so full of honour, that it will bring great content to the subject and should, me thinks, help much towards the ready and cheerful payment of Shipping Monies.[4]

Although Wentworth may have been overly optimistic about the effect of the government's triumph on the collection of Ship

---

[1] PRO, SP 16/378/32, gives a breakdown of the costs which came to £33 846 5s 4d exclusive of the armament, for which an additional £24 753 8s 8d was spent: SP 16/374/30; SP 16/387/87. The cost of a warship like the *Leopard* was between £5500 and £6500: Oppenheim, *Administration of the Royal Navy*, p. 260.
[2] These developments should be seen in the context of Hampden's case which was challenging the Crown's right to levy Ship Money.
[3] *Strafford's Letters*, II, p. 124. For further comment on the relationship between the suppression of piracy and Ship Money, see PRO, SP 16/369/8.
[4] *Strafford's Letters*, II, p. 138. As another example, Burlamachi reported to Secretary Windebank on 31 August 1640 that the taking of two Turks would bring great contentment and the ready payment of Ship Money, as he had learnt from a letter from Plymouth: PRO, SP 16/465/61.

Money, his comment, and those of others, show that government officials believed there was a connection between the successful expedition and Ship Money. More importantly, they wanted the populace to believe that Ship Money was being put to good use. The effect of this propaganda effort is not easily measured, but it may safely be said that on this occasion, at least, the message of the government was seen by tens of thousands of Londoners. They were shown how the government's policies were working in a way likely to impress and create a lasting memory. In a similar fashion, the populace of the ports of the west country learned of the good use to which Ship Money was being put by the 300 or more captives that were freed and sent home.

Propaganda use of the Sallee expedition was not directed solely at commoners. The court was also educated on the beneficial consequences of Ship Money. For example, the twelfth-night masque of 1637, *Britannia Triumphans*,[1] by Inigo Jones and William Davenant, had a naval theme. The subject of this masque was Britanocles, 'the glory of the Western world [who] hath by his wisdom, valour, and piety, not only vindicated his own, but far distant seas, infested with Pirates, and reduced the land (by his example) to a real knowledge of all good Arts and Sciences'.[2] The virtues of the monarch figure were celebrated in these words:

> How hath thy wisdom rais'd this isle?
> Or thee, by what new title shall we call
> Since it were lessening of thy style,
> If we should name thee natures Admiral
>
> So well o're seas doth Reign,
> Reducing what was wild before,
> That fairest Sea-Nymphs leave the troubled main
> and haste to visit him on shore.[3]

A courtier would have been exceedingly dim not to recognize a similarity between Britanocles and Charles I: both were great powers on the sea and the scourge of pirates.

---

[1] I. Jones and W. Davenant, *Britannia Triumphans: A Masque, Presented at White Hall by the Kings Majestie and his Lords, on Sunday after Twelfth-night 1637*. The political uses of Caroline court drama have been explored recently in several papers by Kevin Sharpe.
[2] Ibid., p. 2.
[3] Ibid., pp. 22, 25.

The successful consequences of the expedition were also evident to many in another way. From the west country came reports that the coasts were free of pirates while the fleet was abroad.[1] Yet in spite of the obvious success achieved by Rainsborough, historians have paid very little attention to the fleet or its accomplishments. Gardiner, for example, dismissed the expedition in a few lines: he thought Rainsborough's actions were largely 'ineffectual', and as for the release of the captives, he attributed this entirely to the fortuitous outbreak of civil war in Sallee.[2] Even naval historians have also largely ignored the expedition. For example, in 297 pages of text on the early Stuart navy, C.D. Penn limited his reference to the expedition to a ten-line footnote.[3] Even Oppenheim devoted no more than a page and a half to the subject, though in fairness to him, it must be said that the expedition is only tangential to the subject of his book. Moreover, his comments show an awareness that Rainsborough had accomplished much. He writes of 'the bulldog grip' maintained by the fleet while 'riding on a dangerous lee shore' which was exposed to 'the heavy Atlantic swell'.[4]

Admittedly, the Sallee expedition was not on the same scale as other Stuart expeditions like those sent against Cadiz, Isle de Rhé, or La Rochelle. But unlike these (or Mansell's expedition) or indeed any English naval enterprise from Cadiz in 1596 until Porto Farina in 1655, the Sallee expedition was completely successful and for this reason alone deserves to be wider known. An examination of the factors that contributed to Rainsborough's success at Sallee also may shed light on the reasons for failure so normally characteristic of Stuart naval operations.

First, the Sallee expedition was essentially a unilateral naval operation. A last-minute attempt was made to procure a couple of Spanish galleys, and port facilities were desired and used on two occasions.[5] In neither case, however, would their absence have altered the outcome of the expedition. The Spanish galleys might

---

[1] PRO, SP 16/364/16. Captain Stradling reported that the coasts had been free from all Turks or pirates that summer. The Council made this point also when sending out Ship Money writs in October 1637: SP 16/369/18.
[2] S.R. Gardiner, *History of England: From the Accession of James I to the Outbreak of the Civil War, 1603–1642*, VIII, p. 270.
[3] C.D. Penn, *The Navy under the Early Stuarts, and its Influence on English History*, p. 251 n.
[4] Oppenheim, *Administration of the Royal Navy*, pp. 277–8.
[5] The repair of the *Hercules* and the refreshment of Carteret's homeward-bound ships.

have proved useful had they been available when Rainsborough arrived at Sallee. However, unlike Mansell's Algiers expedition, operations were never based on the assumption that they would be available. If the pinnaces had been completed on time or arrived earlier, they would have made the Spanish galleys entirely superfluous. One consequence of this unilateral approach was the ability to avoid possible, indeed probable, delay while delicate points were negotiated in Madrid or London. Rainsborough's fleet sailed when ready; it did not have to await a diplomatic agreement.

The size and composition of the force also contributed to its success. With other expeditions, 'the more, the better' seems to have been the rule. Rainsborough, in contrast, sailed with the absolute minimum number of ships to do the job. The *Leopard* and *Antelope* provided just enough strength to defend the small fleet against the strongest pirate force the fleet was likely to encounter. The decision to build two pinnaces shows an early recognition of the sort of vessels that were needed to make the blockade work. The design and construction of the *Expedition* and *Providence* suggest that some of the lessons of Mansell's expedition had been learned. A blockade could not have been maintained without shallow-draft warships, nor could any enemy port in this region be closed economically without oar-driven vessels. Rarely in naval history up to that time had ships been built for (and properly employed in) a specific naval operation, an indication of the forethought behind the success of the expedition.

The strict economy of force that characterized Rainsborough's fleet had several beneficial effects on operations. The small number of ships made command and control by Rainsborough much easier. There was no need for time-consuming or factious councils of war. With the exception of Carteret, all the captains were well known to the commander and appear to have obeyed his orders without question.[1]

More importantly, the compact nature of the force reduced the sort of supply problems that all too often hampered Stuart naval expeditions. In contrast with Mansell's expedition, for example, the record of Rainsborough's expedition contains none of the usual complaints about deficient munitions, rotten food, bad beer, or leaky and unserviceable ships. There are some references to an occasional shortage here or a minor deficiency there, but these occur almost entirely in the preparation phase and appear to have

[1] PRO, SP 16/363/99.

been remedied by the time the fleet sailed.[1] The only evidence of any real shortage during the expedition took place in early July, when the water allowance was reduced to four-fifths of the normal amount for about two weeks until additional supplies could be brought from Mamora.[2]

The ability to keep a fleet operational and in good condition on a distant station for almost eight months is a sign of the growing competence of the naval administration of the early Stuart government. While the importance and effectiveness of Rainsborough's expedition should not be overstated, the level of competence displayed at Sallee makes the apparently sudden competence of the Interregnum navy appear less miraculous. Viewed from this perspective, the great fleets of the Commonwealth and Protectorate can be seen as having evolved from, and owing much to, the Ship Money fleets of Charles I.

The expedition to Sallee and its success were very much bound up with Ship Money. The outrages of the Sallee pirates acted as an impetus for the revival of English naval power in the 1630s, and, as shown here, the success at Sallee was used by the government as a justification for Ship Money. It need only be noted here that the large naval budget made possible by the Ship Money levies resulted in the development of a royal fleet that was substantially stronger, better equipped and better trained. Good ships in good condition were available for the expedition without stripping the rest of the navy; and, as shown above, the fleet never wanted for the right equipment or enough supplies. The experience of preparing the Ship Money fleets in the preceding years may also account for the efficiency of the naval administration in setting out and supporting the Sallee fleet. Until the administration of the navy in the 1630s finds a worthy historian, this conclusion must remain tentative. Although only evidence relating to the Sallee expedition has been studied for this book, the records examined show that naval administrators – in particular Northumberland and Nicholas – took decisions that contributed to the success of the expedition.[3]

Rainsborough's contributions in planning and preparing the expedition were crucial, and in many instances the chances of

---

[1] PRO, SP 16/349/37. Captain Harrison of the *Hercules* reported that his ship was short of crew shortly before he left.
[2] PRO, SP 16/369/72, entries for 29 June, 10 and 15 July, 1637.
[3] Lesser, unnamed, officials may have actually performed the work, but the letters authorizing or reporting work completed are addressed to or signed by these men.

success were greatly increased by his determination and resourcefulness when in command. He was willing to bring the king's ships dangerously close in to shore to bombard the fortifications of the town, for example, and this made the blockade as tight as possible. His letters were few and his journal pithy in the extreme, yet from them one can learn something about his character. In particular, they show his ability to concentrate on essentials and that 'bulldog' spirit, discerned by Oppenheim, also comes through. The brevity and matter-of-factness of his journal entries give the impression of a business-like approach. Rainsborough was clearly perturbed by the delay of Carteret, the lateness of the pinnaces, and the lack of the Spanish galleys, but his anxiety and anger always seem controlled and was never an excuse for inaction. Though steady and reliable, Rainsborough displayed considerable resourcefulness and boldness. For instance, he was willing to set out for Sallee even though his fleet was at less strength than planned, and he was prepared to make an alliance for which he had no express warrant. His deployment of the ships' cannon and crew on land suggest a flexibility of mind and lack of timidity, two essential characteristics for a successful commander.

The success of Rainsborough at Sallee was generally recognized at the time.[1] King Charles thought he had accomplished enough to offer Rainsborough a knighthood as a sign of appreciation.[2] In the following year, Rainsborough was further rewarded with command of the *Sovereign of the Seas*, the pride of the Caroline navy.[3] In that year he also submitted a proposal for an expedition to Algiers. As might be expected, his plan closely followed the concept that had proved successful at Sallee, though it was on a larger scale. He wished a fleet of ten ships and six pinnaces to be sent to blockade the harbour of Algiers for a period of up to three years.[4] Based on his experience at Sallee, he estimated the cost of such an expedition to run to £100 000.[5] This sum was far greater than had been expended on the Sallee expedition, though it is not possible to provide a precise figure for

---

[1] *Strafford's Letters*, II, p. 129. See Waters, *Genealogical Gleanings*, I, pp. 116–17, for verse by Waller celebrating Rainsborough's triumph.
[2] Instead, Rainsborough received a gold medal worth £300; this was in addition to £500 which he earned in salary for the expedition.
[3] PRO, SP 16/379/116. He was the highest paid captain, receiving 10s a day.
[4] By the end of that period, Rainsborough submitted, the trade would have been destroyed and their ships become worm-eaten and unserviceable.
[5] PRO, SP 16/379/87. Although not specifically stated in the document, this figure presumably refers to the annual cost.

the cost of the 1637 expedition. Accounts for various expenditures survive, but many are of limited use. For example, a sum of £2399 16s was spent on cannon for the pinnaces, but since these ships were to have many years' service, only a proportion of this charge is attributable to the Sallee expedition.[1] However, by using the figures prepared by Trinity House as a basis for costing an expedition, it is estimated that wages and victuals for eight months' service for the 990 men that went with Rainsborough amounted to about £27 720. The building of the pinnaces and fitting-out costs would add another £7000. Thus, as a rough estimate, the total cost of the expedition must have been nearly £40 000.[2]

If measured in terms of the number of captives released, the cost of the expedition appears rather high, for each captive was freed at a cost of about £118 per head, or more than twice the rate for redemption by peaceful means. In terms of expenditure, the expedition was a more expensive way of freeing captives than earlier diplomatic efforts like those of Roe or Harrison. However, such a comparison is misleading. First, it is not certain that negotiations with the pirates of Sallee would have obtained anything or as much as Rainsborough achieved. Roe was able to use the influence of the Grand Signior on the governors of Algiers. There was no similar influence to use against the rulers of Sallee. When Harrison went to Sallee, the emperor of Morocco still exerted an influence over the town of Sallee, but in 1637, as we have seen, the emperor was dependent on English arms to influence the local government. Second, such a comparison does not include an amount for those saved from captivity by the blockade, nor does it include the deterrent effect of such action. Roe's efforts may have encouraged the pirates of Algiers to come back for more. In contrast, Rainsborough prevented the pirates from setting out a powerful fleet of 22 ships in 1637 and thus saved many from captivity. Because of his actions, the coasts of England

---

[1] PRO, SP 16/354/106. Other charges appear more definite. Charges for powder and shot added up to £1194. PRO, SP 16/347/35.
[2] Trinity House, Court minutes 1626 to 1645, f.87: the charge for wages and victuals was £3 10s a month per man. The fleet was at sea for approximately eight months, so the bill for this item would be £27 720. Building costs/depreciation and fitting out would have come to at least £7000, and munitions were approximately £1200. Thus, an approximate sum of £36 000 was spent on the expedition, though this is a minimum figure and probably does not include all expenses in preparing the fleet or for such costs as the replacement mast for the *Hercules* or incidentals like Rainsborough's reward.

were free of Sallee pirates that year, and though the pirates would become active again by the end of the decade, they were never as great a threat to English shipping as they had been.[1]

If one may judge by the actions of English governments in the years that followed the Sallee expedition, then one has to conclude that they were convinced that the policy of sending a fleet to deal with the pirates was the correct one. Almost immediately after Rainsborough returned, planning began for a similar type of expedition against Algiers.[2] Even politicians opposed to Crown policy in general, did not question its approach in dealing with the pirates; when parliament returned, legislation was drawn up to provide for the suppression of piracy and the redemption of captives on a permanent basis.

---

[1] PRO, SP 16/364/16. It is interesting to note that the merchants thought that the price of the 300+ redeemed was approximately £10 000. Rainsborough believed that if he had not arrived in time, pirates would have taken 500 more captive.

[2] Before the planning and preparations could be completed, the outbreak of the Bishops' War and then the political crisis that followed it put an end to the government's programme.

12
EPILOGUE AND CONCLUSION

Following the success of Rainsborough's expedition against Sallee, the concern of the government turned to the pirates of Algiers. The plan of attack proposed by Rainsborough[1] was thought promising, but the high cost of the expedition made authorization problematic, especially after the outbreak of the First Bishops' War which strained the government's finances to breaking point. It was not until early 1640 that an expedition against Algiers came to be considered seriously again. The revival of interest was not a consequence of an improvement in the government's finances. If anything, the government's financial position had deteriorated with the growing costs of the war and the decline in receipts of Ship Money. Renewed interest for an expedition against the Barbary pirates was brought on by two unrelated developments.

First, there was a resurgence in the number of attacks by pirates, especially those from Algiers. Credible reports indicate that a fleet of upwards of 80 Algerian men-of-war was operating off the Atlantic coast of Spain, and as many as ten pirate ships were lying off the Scilly Isles and Cornwall in 1640.[2] Shipping losses to

[1] See above, Chapter 11.
[2] *CSPV*, 1640–1642, p. 24, 9 March 1640. PRO SP 16/457/68 describes attacks by Turkish pirates on a Plymouth ship coming from Virginia. SP 16/457/93 consists of a report from the Mayor of Exeter who states that the western parts and their trade are endangered by the Turks who have four great men-of-war plying off Mousehole Point. SP 16/459/8, a letter from the Deputy-Lieutenant of Cornwall, advises of the difficulty he has had in pressing men; he reports that the people complain of the harm done on the coast by the Turks who have taken away people from Looe, Penzance, and other places; 60 men-of-war were reported abroad, and the fishermen were too frightened to put to sea; all along the coasts the people were forced to keep continual watches. SP 16/459/36: Edmund Rossingham reported in

pirates reached an all-time high between 10 May 1639 and 15 January 1640, when more than 68 ships and 1222 mariners were taken captive.[1] The magnitude of these loss figures becomes apparent when they are compared to the losses suffered between 1 April 1629 and 2 November 1638 when a total of 73 ships and 1473 persons were taken by the pirates of Algiers.[2] It was not just the increasing number of ships and men being lost that was causing concern at this time. As indicated earlier,[3] at the beginning of 1640 the Algerines seized the *Rebecca* of London with a cargo of over £260 000 in silver being brought to England for minting and transhipment to Flanders.[4] So great was the loss of the *Rebecca* that the news of her capture caused the pound sterling to slump as bankers, especially the Dutch, withdrew funds fearing more losses in the future.[5] The 1630s had been a boom time for English shipping, and much of this business had been won by providing more security rather than lower freight costs. English neutrality in the Thirty Years' War, the government's strong action against pirates, and the use of 'defensible' ships made international merchants keen to use English vessels. As a result, a large trading surplus was being earned from shipping. But the loss of a large vessel like the *Rebecca* to pirates put into question the advantage English shipping was thought to possess. So dangerous were the pirates of Algiers becoming that even the Levant Company, which hitherto had believed the strength of their ships sufficient security, now began to petition the Crown for protection.[6]

The second development bringing renewed interest in an expedition against Algiers was the return of parliament after an absence of almost 12 years. When parliament met, the issue of piracy was brought up almost exclusively by government speakers in the course of defending government policy. For example, Lord Keeper Finch raised the matter when he spoke on 21 April 1640, defending the Ship Money levy. He stated that the king had not intended to issue writs that year but had been compelled to do so for three 'weighty' considerations. First, the Scots' invasion

his newsletter that 'those roguish Turkish pirates which lie upon our Western coast have taken from the shore about Penzance, near St. Michael's Point, 60 men, women, and children'.
[1] HLRO, Main Papers, 5 March 1641.
[2] PRO SP 71/1/ff.157–157v.
[3] See Chapter 7.
[4] BL, Add. MS. 11,045, f.101.
[5] Ibid., f.109.
[6] *CSPV*, 1640–1642, p. 172.

created a need for additional shipping. Second, a fleet was required to protect the kingdom and its trade from those 'neighbouring powers' that were setting out great fleets to gain dominion over the seas. And thirdly, Ship Money was needed because 'those of Algiers were going to have 60 ships to sea to infest our merchants trading into the Straits'. To emphasize the seriousness of the pirate threat to English commerce, Finch added 'that lately a ship had been taken by them called the *Rebecca* valued at £260 000'.[1]

The dissolution of the Short Parliament prevented any action against the pirates, but when the next parliament met again, piracy received new and vigorous attention by the legislature. Interest this time came not from the Crown's spokesmen but from country members who were responding to complaints and petitions by their constituents. On 24 September 1640, citizens of London petitioned for redress of grievances, and a chief concern was that notwithstanding pressing and unusual impositions upon merchants and the levying of Ship-Money they were suffering greatly as a result of ships and goods lost to pirates.[2]

Not until 10 December did the Commons take its first, formal step to deal with the problem of piracy; on that day a committee was set up by the House to discover the best means for redress. Appointed to this committee were Sir Henry Vane, Sir Thomas Roe, John Pym, Captain William Rainsborough, Richard King, Robert Jenner, John Moore, John Potts, and MPs who represented London or the outports. Most of those appointed to the committee had shipping or commercial interests or had been involved previously with attempts to formulate or execute a policy to suppress or appease pirates.[3] Two days later, the House asked Vane and Rainsborough to inform the king of the latest intelligence which showed that ten pirate vessels or more were infesting the coasts of the west country. They were also ordered to ask Charles to send out two royal warships then in the Downs to scour

---

[1] *Proceedings of the Short Parliament of 1640*, ed. E.S. Cope and W.H. Coates (Camden Soc., 4th ser., XIX), p. 67, gives several versions of the speech by Finch, and in one version the loss was reported as £200 000.
[2] PRO SP 16/468/29.
[3] *Commons Journals*, II, p. 48. Also, *The Journal of Simonds D'Ewes from the Beginning of the Long Parliament to the Opening of the Trial of the Earl of Strafford*, ed. W. Notestein, p. 134. For the interests of the members of the committee, see M.F. Keeler, *The Long Parliament, 1640–1641: A Biographical Study of its Members*, pp. 232, 240, 277.

the coasts of Cornwall and Devon.[1] On 17 December, Vane reported to the House that they had spoken with the king who had ordered two ships sent to the west country as requested.[2]

In the weeks that followed, plans were drawn up for a major expedition against Algiers. On 27 January 1641, Trinity House reported on propositions regarding: (1) the suppressing of pirates of Algiers and Tunis, (2) the releasing of 3000 held captive, and (3) the settling of firm trade with the Turks. Some of their recommendations were similar to those of previous reports, but several were new. First, the naval strength of the 'Turks' had increased recently, they reported, and consequently a larger and stronger English naval force would be needed. Second, they thought the option of withdrawing trade, as previously proposed by Roe's committee, was now impractical. Many months would be needed to organize such a withdrawal, and the Turks would get wind of the plan and seize all English merchants and their goods. Third, if trade were cut off voluntarily, the Venetians and French would fill the gap and English merchants would never be able to get back their share. They concluded that sending an expedition was the only solution. In their considered opinion the fleet should consist of three squadrons: one would operate outside the Straits, a second would patrol inside the Straits, and the third (to include pinnaces like the *Expedition* and *Providence*) would ride before Algiers to effect a tight blockade of the port. These squadrons would have to be replaced by fresh ships every nine months. The cost of this fleet for 18 months, the minimum thought necessary, was put at £170 960.[3]

On 1 March 1641, the House met again to consider the problem of piracy. Speaking for the committee, Mr King informed MPs that they had reached the following conclusions:[4]

(1) Between 4000 and 5000 of the king's subjects were currently being held captive in Algiers and Tunis.
(2) They had reliable intelligence that 60 pirate ships were ready to set sail and that 30 of these ships were bound for English coasts.

---

[1] *Commons Journals, II*, p. 50.
[2] Notestein, *Journal of Simonds D'Ewes*, p. 164.
[3] BL, Northumberland MSS, M-286, Trinity House Report, 27 January 1640. It was recommended that all squadrons be prepared to return at short notice if foreign invasion threatened, an indication of the seriousness with which the threats of invasion were considered at the time.
[4] Notestein, *Journal of Simonds D'Ewes*, pp. 418–19.

(3) Six royal warships (2nd, 3rd, and 4th rate vessels) should be sent out to guard the western ports and seas.

(4) All merchants should be free and encouraged to make prize of Turkish pirate vessels.

(5) A policy of ransoming captives was thought unfit since it only encouraged more losses and cowardliness on the part of English mariners.

(6) A conference with the Lords should be arranged so that joint action on the matter might be taken.

In the week that followed, the report of the committee was debated before being sent back to committee for further consideration.[1] The next day the House was told that the king was ready and willing to set out royal ships as requested, but could do so only if he were provided with money.[2] Members were informed that, as a sign of their goodwill and forwardness, both Charles and his Lord High Admiral had agreed to forego all rightful prize money due them for any pirate ships that would be taken.[3] In the next week, the House debated the subject again and eventually decided to see if the funding problem could be overcome with the assistance of the Treasurer and Victualler of the navy.[4] The need for immediate action against the pirates was reinforced on the 15th of March when a petition in the name of James Frizell and others was introduced to the House. The former consul at Algiers and the other signatories swore that since 1628 the pirates of Algiers had taken 131 ships and made 2555 of his majesty's subjects captive.[5]

Five days later, a bill for the relief of captives and the suppression of the pirates of Algiers and Tunis was read for the first time. On 3 April this bill was given a second reading and then sent to committee. Three weeks later the bill was again brought before the House, given a third reading and passed. At the beginning of May the bill was sent to the Lords.[6]

---

[1] *Commons Journals*, II, p. 95; Notestein, *Journal of Simonds D'Ewes*, pp. 447–50. One of the points the House wished the committee to consider was whether the problem of piracy could be dealt with by using fewer ships than had been recommended.
[2] *Commons Journals*, II, p. 97; Notestein, *Journal of Simonds D'Ewes*, p. 450.
[3] Notestein, *Journal of Simonds D'Ewes*, p. 450.
[4] Ibid., p. 471.
[5] Ibid., p. 492. These numbers are almost exactly the same as those on a list sent by Mr Ramsey who wrote that 131 ships and 2554 persons had been taken: BL, Northumberland MSS, M-286, April 1641.
[6] *Commons Journals*, 11, pp. 108, 115, 130–1.

For reasons which are not entirely clear, the Lords did not act immediately on the bill. The Venetian ambassador was of the opinion that the Lower House had acted primarily to satisfy the merchants of the Levant Company, an interest which may not have been shared by the Lords. That same day, 5 July, the ambassador reported that plans were being made to set out 20 ships to secure trade and that it was expected that this fleet would more than pay for itself from prize money. However, he added that those with experience in the matter did not think this feasible and were fearful that the English captains would attack shipping almost indiscriminately and even take friendly ships, as they had done in the past under the pretence that all ships which they seized were going to Barbary or carrying pirate goods.[1]

Whatever the cause, the Commons' bill was returned by the Lords. Following the recess, however, the Commons took up the matter again, and the bill was given a first reading on 30 October 1641. A few days later it was read a second time and then sent to the committee. In the 27 November meeting, Mr King reported on the bill and showed the House the amendments recommended by his committee. These were added and the bill was returned to the committee a second time.[2] The political crisis of the autumn of 1641 was probably responsible for the delay suffered by this piece of legislation which had been signified by the House as an important bill of great 'public concernment'.[3] However, part of the delay may have been due to genuine doubts some members had over the bill itself. When the bill was debated before the House for the third reading, Simonds D'Ewes, for example, expressed concern that, if passed, the bill might be taken as a precedent. In any case, he went on in words that showed how little the views of some had changed since the 1620s, parliament had already given the king in tonnage and poundage a source of revenue for the guarding of the seas.[4] Despite these objections, the bill was read a third time, engrossed, and sent to the House of Lords.[5] There the bill was given a first reading on 4 December, a second reading two days later, and a final reading on the 11th. Royal assent was given on 15 January 1642, and ten days later

---

[1] *CSPV*, 1640–1642, p. 172.
[2] *The Journal of Sir Simonds D'Ewes: From the First Recess of the Long Parliament to the Withdrawal of King Charles from London*, ed. W.H. Coates, pp. 54, 69, 203.
[3] A. Fletcher, *The Outbreak of the English Civil War*, pp. 158–67.
[4] Coates, *Journal of Sir Simonds D'Ewes*, p. 227, 3 December.
[5] Ibid.

executors were appointed to see that the provisions of the Act were carried out.[1]

The Act itself was a straightforward measure, so much so that it is easy to overlook its significance. Its very simplicity belies the way in which it overcame with an Alexandrian decisiveness the fundamental impediment that had long frustrated any effective action against the pirates. In this Act, which runs to less than a page, two new principles were introduced: (1) finance was put on a long-term basis, and (2) the tax burden was apportioned more fairly and with greater political discretion.

From as early as the discussions of 1617, it was realized that maintaining a naval force to blockade the pirate ports for several years was the only really effective way of destroying their power. However, to maintain a naval force on the Barbary coast for years required a reliable source of funds, in addition to normal revenues, but none was created until 1642. With the Act of 1642 (6 Car. I, c. 24, 25), a way of financing long-term operations against the pirates was at last found.[2] Though the Act initially covered funding for only three years, its duration was extended regularly during the Interregnum.[3] Finance on a continuous basis also meant that collection was spread over time and that the ratepayers were never shocked by the demand for immediate payment of a large sum, as had happened with occasional levies, such as that for Mansell's expedition.

The Act also settled the long-standing problem of spreading the burden of taxation more fairly. No attempt was made to use or develop the ancient approach embodied in Ship Money. The weaknesses of this approach were all too apparent by 1642. Mariners and overseas merchants benefited directly from the suppression of pirates, but could not bear the full cost of protection on their own. Attempts to spread the burden to those who benefited indirectly had done little but put the government in an impossible position. Central government could not spread the burden fairly, even on a county basis, nor decide satisfactorily how to proportion cost with benefit at a local level. The Act of 1642

---

[1] *Lords Journals*, IV, pp. 462–3, 470, 516, 571. The Lords committee appointed to oversee the Act consisted of the Lord High Admiral, Pembroke, Warwick, Juxon, Winton, Rochester, Spencer, Kymbolton, and Brooke.
[2] *Statutes of the Realm*, V (1819), pp. 134–5.
[3] *Commons Journals*, VIII, pp. 216–17. Even though the rate was reduced, almost £70 000 was collected; however, because of the Civil War all but £11 109 was diverted to cover general naval expenditure.

removed the onus of apportionment from the government. By arranging that money for use against the pirates was raised indirectly from a 1% duty on all goods imported and exported, the cost of protection was spread widely and payment effectively concealed. Consumers paid nothing directly; only the customs farmers had to pay duty. In a sense almost all producers and consumers contributed, as in fairness they might since all benefited from maritime security, but because the tax was indirect, the burden was not apparent nor seen as a grievance by the political nation.

This measure was a significant step forward, not so much for what it accomplished, but for the way it pointed towards a solution to the problem of piracy. The final resolution of the problem was not to come for over a century and a half, but the basis for it was foreseen in the debate and Act of the early 1640s. In the end, the problem of the Barbary pirates was resolved only when the great European powers were able to organize and finance overwhelming naval and military force to destroy the bases on which the pirates depended. In the early 17th century, no European state, certainly not England, possessed sufficient naval superiority, military force, and financial strength to overcome the pirates for more than a brief period. The power of the pirates was too great at the time to be countered by any single European state, and national interests prevented full co-operation between them.

The magnitude of the losses suffered by England alone suggests the size of the problem. Approximately 400 ships and 8000 people were taken captive in the period studied. Losses simply in terms of ships, goods, and men exceeded £1 000 000 or roughly double the losses England sustained in the wars against Spain and France between 1624 and 1630; moreover, the latter losses were largely offset by prizes taken by English ships, a compensation hardly available against the pirates.[1] The problem posed by the pirates, of course, had significance beyond mere numbers. At an individual level, thousands of families, especially in the south-west, were cruelly torn apart and the prosperity and livelihood of communities in these parts severely disturbed. But one of the main consequences of the pirate danger was political. The pirates posed a political threat to the Crown. Their assaults in the Narrow Seas –

---

[1] J.S. Kepler, 'The Value of Ships Gained and Lost by the English Shipping Industry during the Wars with Spain and France, 1624–1630', *MM*, LIX (1973), pp. 218–19.

even on occasion in the rivers and creeks of the realm – underlined the inadequacy and impotence of royal government. To the Stuart monarchs, as much as to Philip III, the pirates were, in Digby's phrase, a thorn in the foot: not a fatal affliction, but painful and incapacitating, and difficult to eliminate. The inability of Stuart monarchs to guard the seas and protect their subjects was revealed by the attacks of the pirates. This failure led in turn, as the debates of the parliaments of the 1620s and early 1640s show, to a reluctance to provide tonnage and poundage and Ship Money.

The danger of the pirates was not simply a problem of national political interest. At its most basic level, the pirate scourge was an expression of the old and deep-rooted struggle between Christendom and the Islamic world. Increasingly in the 17th century, however, piracy lost its religious character and became a commercial activity for the Barbary states. This business depended upon competition and conflict between the Christian states. Mansell was satisfied with protecting English shipping only, and Roe's willingness to sacrifice the French make it evident that even he was interested primarily in protecting English ships, goods, and men. Piracy in this period exposed the conflicting interests of the Christian states, fed their fears and suspicions (largely unwarranted as has been shown) and furthered pursuit of selfish political and economic goals. At the same time, it has been shown that even in the years leading up to and including the Thirty Years' War, common interests and grander visions existed and a surprising degree of co-operation could be achieved.

This study has focused on the reponses of the Stuart government to the problem of pirates. For policy-makers of the early 17th century, the pirates posed many problems; official plans to suppress pirates were clearly not a ploy or a cover, as many contemporaries and some historians aver. What has also become clear is the extent to which the government was influenced by and acted in response to local complaints, whether from its own agents, petitions from individuals or local groups, or delegations from official or mercantile bodies. The west country suffered most heavily, and it was often the complaints of officials from these parts that were responsible for action being initiated. The governments of James I and Charles I were sympathetic and tried to provide redress. Frequently, the Crown and Privy Council sought the advice of interested and knowledgeable parties outside the formal structure of government. For example, on many occasions, Trinity House was asked to provide expert advice or make detailed submissions, and these reports were often used as a basis for government policy.

In developing policies to deal with the problem of pirates, officials and advisors displayed a high degree of bureaucratic sophistication. For example, the paper of Roe's committee – with its statement of the options available to the Crown and the advantages and disadvantages of each option – might serve as a model in a course on public administration of the form in which advice should be presented to decision-makers. In looking at the way Stuart governments dealt with piracy, it has become evident that even the failures were rarely failures of conception. For instance, almost all the strategic and tactical difficulties that Mansell's expedition would encounter were discussed in the Privy Council meetings in 1617, and the government did not believe that its policy of diplomacy would have more than a short-term effect. The difficulties experienced by government were largely those of execution, and this deficiency highlights a main limitation of early Stuart government. The fiscal arrangements, as exemplified by the levy to finance Mansell's expedition, or later the Ship Money levies, were inadequate because they were based on outdated, medieval concepts and experience. The financial difficulties of the central government were made worse by government's failure to provide guidance below the county level, a delinquency that encouraged factiousness and delayed payments.

Administrative inadequacy in the navy is also apparent, especially in the arrangements for the supply of Mansell's fleet. To a degree, this weakness may be traced to a reliance on outmoded procedures and organization. Historically, the navy was active for only a few weeks a year, and the bulk of the fleet taken up from trade. Operations had been largely confined to the Narrow Seas or, at most, to occasional, short duration raids on the coast of Spain. As a result, the fleet operations rested on a system of logistics and command and control procedures derived from an earlier period and these were inadequate for distant water, long duration expeditions. Action against the pirates involved sending large fleets to the Mediterranean for periods of a year or more. The demands put on the naval administration by the pirate threat encouraged a higher degree of competency in planning and controlling fleet operations. The administrative competency needed for the expeditions against pirates did not come quickly; it evolved gradually and was becoming evident in this period, though it would not be fully established until later.

Both the pirate threat of the early 17th century and the changing nature of naval operations were at the same time integral to and symptomatic of broader developments involving the transformation of seaborne commerce and naval warfare. As long-distance trade expanded, so too did piracy cease to be a local activity or problem. The growth of England's Atlantic and Mediterranean trade brought in its train attacks on English ships by the Barbary pirates. In similar and related fashion, the navies of the great maritime nations grew from little more than occasional, coastal defence forces into permanent fleets of specially-built warships capable of mounting and sustaining blue-water operations.

The progress of this transformation was neither rapid nor consistent, as the Whig historians have suggested; but in the story of the response of the English government to the problem of piracy in the early 17th century, one can see signs of evolutionary change. For example, the 1642 Act dealing with the suppression of pirates may be seen as the culmination of a learning process and a clear step forward. And when compared to Mansell's venture, the Sallee expedition serves as evidence of a growing power and competence in the navy. Though it would be many decades before the English government came to possess the naval power and financial and logistical resources needed to end piracy,[1] it was in fact under the early Stuarts that the first, formative steps were taken to fulfill James I's promise of 'bringing peace to the seas'.[2]

---

[1] For information on the use in the late 17th century of a much stronger Royal Navy to protect English seaborne trade in the Mediterranean, see S.R. Hornstein's fine study, *The Restoration Navy and English Foreign Trade, 1674–1688.*
[2] PRO, SP 14/90/136.

SOURCES AND BIBLIOGRAPHY

Primary sources: manuscripts

Algemeen Rijksarchief, The Hague

Almiraliteitsarchieven – 954 Journal of William de Zoete (Haultain)

Archivo General de Simancas, Spain

Sección de Estado: legajos 711, 845, 1881, 2038, 2520, 2521, 2574, 2596, 2850.

Sección Guerra Antiqua: legajos 808, 873, 1308.

Berkshire Record Office, Reading

Trumbull MSS: Alph. VII

Bodleian Library, Oxford

Ashmolean MSS: 824/XV

British Library, London

Additional MSS: 5489; 5500; 11,045; 17,677, vol. I, Correspondence from Archives of the United Provinces; 21,993; 36,444 Aston Papers, vol. I, 36,445 Aston Papers, vol. II, 36,450 Aston Papers, vol. VII.

Cotton MSS: Julius F. 111.

Harleian MSS: 1580, 1581, 6383.

Northumberland MSS: M-285; M-286.

Sloane MSS: 3317.

Stowe MSS: 365.

Cambridge University Library
MS. Dd. 12–20: Diary of Bulstrode Whitelocke

Cornwall Record Office, Truro
Bodmin Borough Accounts, nos. 288–9

Corporation of London Record Office
Repertory, vol. 47

House of Lords Record Office
Main Papers

India Office Library, London
Court Book, XIV

Kent Archives Office, Maidstone
Sackville Knole MSS (U 269), Cranfield Papers

National Library of Wales, Bangor
Wynn of Gwydir MSS

Public Record Office, London
High Court of Admiralty

HCA 1   Oyer and Terminer Records, 1535–1834
HCA 13   Prize Court, Examinations, etc., 1536–1826
HCA 14   Prize Court, Exemplifications, 1541–1768

HCA 25   Letters of Marque, bonds, 1549–1815
HCA 30   Prize Court, Miscellanea, 1531–1888

Privy Council

PC 2   Registers, 1540–1920.

Public Record Office

PRO 31/12 MSS   Transcripts, Spanish Archives, Gondomar, 1594–1672.

State Papers

SP 12   State Papers Domestic, Elizabeth I
SP 14   State Papers Domestic, James I
SP 15   State Papers Domestic, Addenda Edward VI to James I
SP 16   State Papers Domestic, Charles I
SP 18   State Papers Domestic, Interregnum
SP 46   State Papers Domestic, Supplementary
SP 71   State Papers Foreign, Barbary States
SP 78   State Papers Foreign, France
SP 80   State Papers Foreign, Germany (Empire) and Hungary
SP 84   State Papers Foreign, Holland
SP 94   State Papers Foreign, Spain
SP 97   State Papers Foreign, Turkey
SP 99   State Papers Foreign, Venice
SP 103   Treaty Papers, 1577 to 1780
SP 105   State Papers Foreign, Foreign Ministers (in England)

Descriptive List of Exchequer, Queen's Remembrancer, Port Books (1960).

Trinity House, London

Court Minute Books

Transactions

Westminster City Archives

E. 23 St Margaret's parish records

Yale Center for Parliamentary History
Transcript of Diary of Sir William Spring

Primary sources: published

Acts of the Privy Council of England, 11 vols. (1921–40).
The Arrivall and Intertainments of the Embassador Alkaid Jaurer Ben Abdella (1637).
Blake, Robert: *The Letters of Robert Blake together with supplementary documents*, ed. J.R. Powell (Navy Records Society, LXXVI, 1937).
Button, John: *Algiers Voyage [in a Journall or Briefe Repatary of all occurents hapning in the fleet of ships sent out by the King his most excellent Maiestie, as well against the Pirates of Algiers, as others; the whole body consisting of 18 ships]* (1621).
Cabala, Sive Scrinia Sacra: Mysteries of State and Government, in Letters of Illustrious Persons, and Great Ministers of State, As well Foreign as Domestick, In the Reigns of King Henry the Eighth, Queen Elizabeth, King James, and King Charles (3rd edn. 1691).
Calendar of the Clarendon State Papers in the Bodleian Library, vol. I 1623–1649, ed. O. Ogle and W.H. Bliss (1872).
Calendar of State Papers Ireland, Reign of Charles I.
Calendar of State Papers Venetian.
Carew, Sir George: 'A relation of the State of France with the Character of Henry IV and the principal persons of that Court', *An Historical View of the Negotiations between the Courts of England, France and Brussels, 1592–1617*, ed. Thomas Birch (1749) *Letters from George Lord Carew to Sir Thomas Roe, ambassador to the court of the Great Mogul, 1615–1617*, ed. J. Maclean (Camden Society, Old Series, LXXVI, 1860).
Carleton, Sir Dudley: *Letters from and to Sir Dudley Carleton, Knt., during his Embassy in Holland, from January 1615/16, to December 1620* (2nd edn. 1775).
Carteret's Barbary Voyage of 1638, ed. P. Penrose (Philadelphia 1929).
Commons Debates, 1628, IV, ed. M.F. Keeler, M.J. Cole, W.R. Bidwell (1978).
Dan, Pierre: *Histoire de Barbarie et de ses corsaires* (Paris 1637).
Debates in the House of Commons in 1625, ed. S.R. Gardiner (Camden Society, New series, VI, 1873).

SOURCES AND BIBLIOGRAPHY 281

D'Ewes, Simonds: *The Journal of Simonds D'Ewes from the Beginning of the Long Parliament to the Opening of the Trial of the Earl of Strafford*, ed. W. Notestein (New Haven 1923) *The Journal of Sir Simonds D'Ewes: From the First Recess of the Long Parliament to the Withdrawal of King Charles from London*, ed. W.H. Coates (New Haven 1942).

Documentos Inéditos para la Historia de España, 13 vols. (Madrid 1936–57).

Dunton, John: *A true journal of the Sally Fleet, with the proceedings of the voyage* (London 1637).

The Famous and Wonderful Recovery of a Ship of Bristol, called the Exchange, from Turkish Pirates of Argier (1622).

A Fight at Sea (London 1617).

Finett, Sir John: *Finetti Philoxenis: som choice observations of Sir J.F., . . . touching . . . forren ambassadors in England* (1656).

FitzGeffrey, Charles: *Compassion towards Captives, chiefly towards our Bretheren and Country-men who are in miserable bondage in Barbarie* (Oxford 1637).

Gentleman, T.: *England's way to win wealth, and employ ships and mariners* (1614).

Heywood, T.: *A Description of his Majesties royall and most stately ship called the Sovereign of the Seas, built at Woolwich in Kent 1637* (1637).

Historical collections of private passages of State, . . . beginning . . . 1618, . . . to 1648, comp. by J. Rushworth, 8 vols. (2nd edn. 1721–2).

Historical Manuscripts commission 7, *8th Report*, vol. III, Manchester MSS.

Historical Manuscripts Commission 8, *9th Report, App.*, MSS of Corporation of Plymouth.

Historical Manuscripts Commission 9, *MSS of Marquess of Salisbury*, part XXI (1970).

Historical Manuscripts Commission 23, *12th Report, App. i–iii, Cowper MSS* (Cal. of Coke Papers).

Historical Manuscripts Commission 63, *Egmont MSS*, 2 vols. (Perceval family papers).

I. or J.R.: *The Trades Increase* (1615).

James I: *Lusus Regius, being Poems and other Pieces by King James I*, ed. R.S. Rait (1902).

New Poems of James I of England, ed. Allen W. Westcott (New York 1911).

Jones, Inigo, and William Davenant: *Britannia Triumphans: A*

Masque, Presented at White Hall by the Kings Majestie and his Lords, on the Sunday after Twelfth-night. 1637 (1637).
Journals of the House of Commons.
Journals of the House of Lords.
Kellet, Edward: *A Return from Argier: A sermon preached at Minehead, the 16 of March 1627, (by H. Byam)* (1628).
Knight, Francis: *A Relation of Seaven Yeares Slaverie under the Turkes of Argeire, suffered by an English Captive Merchant* (1640).
Laud William: *The Works of Archbishop Laud* (New York 1975, reprint of 1847–60 edn., ed. W. Scott and J. Bliss).
Middleton, Thomas: *A Game At Chess*, ed. J.W. Harper (1966).
Mun, T.: *England's Treasure by Foreign Trade: Or, the balance of our foreign trade is the rule of our treasure* (1644).
Oglander, Sir John: *A Royalist's Notebook: The Commonplace Book of Sir John Oglander, Kt., of Nunwell*, ed. F. Bamford (1936).
Okeley, William: *Eben-ezer; or a small monument of great mercy appearing in the miraculous divererance of W. Okeley [and others] from . . . slavery* (2nd edn. 1684).
Proceedings of the Short Parliament of 1640, ed. E.S. Cope and W.H. Coates (Camden Society, 4th series, XIX, 1977).
Raleigh, Sir Walter: 'Observations touching Trade and Commerce with the Hollanders and Other Nations', *The Works of Sir Walter Raleigh, Kt.*, 8 vols. (Oxford 1829).
Records Relating to the Society of Merchant Venturers of the City of Bristol in the Seventeenth Century, ed. P. McGrath (Bristol Record Society, XVII, 1952).
A Relation of the Whole Proceedings Concerning the Redemption of the Captives in Argier and Tunis . . . Also the letters from Edmond Cason, Agent for the Parliament there (1647).
[Robinson, Henry]: *Libertas or Reliefe to the English Captives in Algier* (1642).
Roe, Sir Thomas: *The Negotiations of Sir T. Roe in his embassy to the Ottoman Porte, from the Year 1621 to 1628 inclusive* (1740).
Sir William Monson's Naval Tracts, ed. M. Oppenheim, vol. III (Navy Records Society, 1913).
Spratt Devereux: *Autobiography of the Rev. D. Spratt, who died at Mitchelstown, Co. Cork, 1688*, ed. T.A.B. Spratt (1886).
State Papers collected by Edward, Earl of Clarendon, commencing 1621, 3 vols. (1767–86).
Statutes of the Realm, 11 vols. (1810–28).

Strafford, Earl of: *The Earl of Strafford's Letters and Dispatches*, ed. W. Knowler, 2 vols. (1739).
Stuart Royal Proclamations, ed. J.F. Larkin and P.L. Hughes, 2 vols. (1973–83).
Wadsworth, James: *The English Spanish Pilgrime, or, a new discoverie of Spanish popery and jesuitical strategems* (1630 edn.).
Weymouth Corporation: Descriptive catalogue of the charters, minute books, and other documents of the borough of Weymouth and Melcombe Regis, comp. by H.J. Moule (1883).

Secondary works: unpublished theses

Appleby, J.C., 'English Privateering during the Spanish and French Wars, 1625–30' (PhD thesis, University of Hull, 1983).
Hurd, D.G.E., 'Some Aspects of the Attempts of the Government to Suppress Piracy During the Reign of Elizabeth I' (MA thesis, University of London, 1961).
McGowan, A.P. 'The Royal Navy under the First Duke of Buckingham, Lord High Admiral 1618–1628 (PhD thesis, University of London, 1967).
Moore, R.O., 'Some Aspects of the Origin and Nature of English Piracy, 1603–25' (PhD thesis, University of Virginia, 1960).
Senior, C.M, 'An Investigation of the Activities and Importance of English Pirates 1603–40' (PhD thesis, University of Bristol, 1973).
Williams, P.L. 'The Court and Councils of Philip III of Spain' (PhD thesis, University of London, 2 vols., 1973).

Secondary works: published

Adams, S.L. 'Foreign Policy and the Parliaments of 1621 and 1624', in *Faction and Parliament: Essays on Early Stuart History*, ed. K. Sharpe (Oxford 1978), pp. 139–71.
Alcalá-Zamora y Queipo de Llano, J.: *España, Flandes y el mar del Norte (1618–39): La última ofensiva Europea de los Austrias Madrileños* (Barcelona 1975).
Alexander, M.V.C., *Charles I's Lord Treasurer: Sir Richard Weston, Earl of Portland (1577–1635)* (1975).

Alvarez, M.F., *Charles V: Elected Emperor and Hereditary Ruler* (English edn. 1975).
Anderson, R.A., 'The *Providence* and *Expedition*', *The Mariner's Mirror*, XXXI (1945), p. 234.
Andrews, K.R., *Ships, Money, and Politics, seafaring and naval enterprise in the reign of Charles I* (Cambridge 1991).
Ashton, R., *The City and the Court 1603–1643* (Cambridge 1979).
Aylmer, G.E., 'Attempts at Administrative Reform, 1625–40', *English Historical Review*, LXXII (1957), pp. 229–59.
—— *The King's Servants: The Civil Service of Charles I, 1625–1642* (1974 edn.).
Barnby, H., 'The Sack of Baltimore', *Journal of the Cork Historical and Archaeological Society*, LXXIV (1969), pp. 101–29.
Bewes, W.A., *Church Briefs or royal warrants for collections for charitable objects* (1896).
Bono, S., *I Corsari barbareschi* (Turin 1964).
Boxer, C.R., *The Dutch Seaborne Empire 1600–1800* (1973 edn.).
Braudel, F., *The Mediterranean: And the Mediterranean World in the Age of Philip II*, 2 vols. (1972–3).
Brightwell, P., 'The Spanish Origins of the Thirty Years' War', *European Studies Review*, IX (1979), pp. 409–31.
—— 'The Spanish System and the Twelve Years' Truce', *English Historical Review*, LXXXIX (1974), pp. 270–92.
Brown, J.M., 'Scottish Politics 1567–1625', in *The Reign of James VI and I*, ed. A.G.R. Smith (1973), pp. 22–39.
Brown, K., 'An Urban View of Moroccan History, Salé 1000–1800', *Hespéris Tamuda*, XII (1971), pp. 46–63.
Brown, M.J, *Itinerant Ambassador: The Life of Sir Thomas Roe* (Lexington, University Press of Kentucky, 1970).
Carter, C.H., 'Gondomar: Ambassador to James I', *The Historical Journal*, VII (1964), pp. 189–208.
—— *The Secret Diplomacy of the Hapsburgs* (1964).
Chapelle, H.I., *The Search for Speed under Sail, 1700–1855* (1968).
Chaplin, W.R., 'William Rainsborough (1587–1642) and his Associates of the Trinity House', *The Mariner's Mirror*, XXXI (1945), pp. 178–97.
Clark, G.T., *Some Account of Sir Robert Mansell, Kt., Vice Admiral of England, . . . and of Admiral Sir Thomas Button, Kt.* (Dowlais 1883).
Coindreau, R., *Les Corsaires de Salé* (Paris 1948).

Cooper, J.P., 'Sea-Power', in *New Cambridge Modern History*, IV, *The Decline of Spain and the Thirty Years War*, ed. J.P. Cooper (Cambridge 1970), pp. 226–38.

Corbett, J.S., *England in the Mediterranean: A Study of the Rise and Influence of British Power within the Straits, 1603–1713*, 2 vols. (2nd edn. 1917).

———— 'The Teaching of Naval and Military History', *History*, I (1916–17), pp. 12–19.

Davies, C.S.L., 'The Administration of the Royal Navy under Henry VIII: the Origins of the Navy Board', *English Historical Review*, LXXX (1965), pp. 268–88.

Davis, R., 'England and the Mediterranean, 1570–1670', in *Studies in the Economic History of Tudor and Stuart England*, ed. F.J. Fisher (Cambridge 1961), pp. 117–37.

———— *The Rise of the English Shipping Industry: In the Seventeenth and Eighteenth Centuries* (Newton Abbot 1972 edn.).

Denucé, J., *L'Afrique au XVIe siècle et la commerce anversois, (Collection de documents pour l'histoire du commerce, vol. II)*, 3 vols. (Paris 1934–38).

Devoulx, A., 'La marine de la Regence d'Alger', *Revue Africaine*, XIII (1869), pp. 384–420.

Dictionary of National Biography, ed. Sir Leslie Stephen and Sir Sidney Lee, vols. I–XXII, 1917–22.

Donaldson, G., *Scotland: James V to James VII* (1965).

Earle, P., *Corsairs of Malta and Barbary* (1970).

Edmundson, G., *Anglo-Dutch Rivalry during the First Half of the Seventeenth Century* (Oxford 1911).

Elliott, J.H., *Imperial Spain, 1469–1716* (1963).

Fernández Duro, C., *Armada Española*, 9 vols. (Madrid 1895–1903).

Fisher, G., *The Barbary Legend: Trade and Piracy in North Africa, 1415–1830* (Oxford 1957).

Fletcher, A., *The Outbreak of the English Civil War* (1981).

Friedman, E.G., *Spanish Captives in North Africa in the Early Modern Age* (Madison, 1983).

Gardiner, S.R., *History of England: From the Accession of James I to the Outbreak of the Civil War, 1603–1642*, 10 vols. (1895–99 edn.).

Gari y Suimell, J.A., *Historia de la Rendenciones* (Cadiz 1873).

Glasgow, T., jr, 'The Navy in Philip and Mary's War, 1557–1558', *The Mariner's Mirror*, LIII (1967), pp. 321–42.

───── 'The Shape of the Ships that Defeated the Spanish Armada', *The Mariner's Mirror*, L (1964), pp. 177–98.

Gordon, M.D., 'The Collection of Ship-Money in the Reign of Charles I', *Transactions of the Royal Historical Society*, 3rd series, IV (1910), pp. 141–62.

Grammont, H.D., 'La Course, l'esclavage et la rédemption à Alger', *Revue Historique*, XXV–XXVI (1884–5), pp. 1–25.

Guilmartin, J.F., jr, *Gunpowder and Galleys: Changing Technology and Mediterranean Warfare at Sea in the Sixteenth Century* (Cambridge 1974).

Harris, G.G., *The Trinity House of Deptford, 1514–1660* (1969).

Heidenheimer, A.J., *Political Corruption: Readings in comparative analysis* (1970).

Hess, A.C., 'The Battle of Lepanto and its Place in Mediterranean History', *Past and Present*, no. 57 (1972), pp. 53–73.

───── *The Forgotten Frontier: A History of the Sixteenth-Century Ibero-African Frontier* (Chicago 1978).

Hornstein, S.R., *The Restoration Navy and English Foreign Trade, 1674–1688* (1991).

Howard, M., *The British Way in Warfare: A Reappraisal* (1975).

───── *War in European History* (Oxford 1976).

Hurstfield, J., *Freedom, Corruption and Government in Elizabethan England* (1973).

Israel, J.I., 'A Conflict of Empires: Spain and the Netherlands 1618–1648', *Past and Present*, no. 76 (1977), pp. 34–74.

───── *The Dutch Republic and the Hispanic World 1606–1661* (Oxford, 1982).

───── Review in *Times Literary Supplement*, no. 4285, 17 May 1985, p. 552.

Jenkins, E.H., *A History of the French Navy: From its beginnings to the present day* (1973).

Jordan, W.K., *The Charities of Rural England, 1480–1660: The aspirations and the achievements of the Rural Society* (1961).

───── *Philanthropy in England, 1480–1660: A study of the changing pattern of English social aspirations* (1959).

Keeler, M.F., *The Long Parliament, 1640–1641: A Biographical Study of its Members* (Philadelphia 1954).

Kennedy, D.E., 'Naval Captains at the Outbreak of the English Civil War', *The Mariner's Mirror*, XLVI (1960), pp. 181–98.

Kennedy, P., *Strategy and Diplomacy: Eight Studies* (1983).

Kepler, J.S., *The Exchange of Christendom: The International Entrepôt at Dover, 1622–51* (Leicester 1976).

────── 'Fiscal Aspects of the English Carrying Trade during the Thirty Years War', *Economic History Review*, 2nd series, XXV (1972), pp. 261–83.

────── 'The Value of Ships Gained and Lost by the English Shipping Industry during the Wars with Spain and France, 1624–1630', *The Mariner's Mirror*, LIX (1973), pp. 218–21.

Kossman, E.H., 'The Low Countries', *The Cambridge Modern History*, IV, *The Decline of Spain and the Thirty Years War*, ed. J.P. Cooper (Cambridge 1970), pp. 359–84.

Lamont, W. (ed.), *The Tudors and Stuarts* (1976).

Lane, F.C., *Venice and History: The Collected Papers of Frederic C. Lane* (Baltimore 1966).

Lane-Poole, S., *The Barbary Corsairs* (1884).

Levack, B., *Civil Lawyers in England 1603–41* (Oxford 1973).

Lewis, B., 'Corsairs in Iceland', *Revue de l'Occident musulman et de la Mediterranée*, XV–XVI (1973), p.139–44.

Lockyer, R., *Buckingham: The life and political career of George Villiers, first Duke of Buckingham 1592–1628* (1981).

McGowan, A.P., *The Jacobean Commissions of Inquiry, 1608 and 1618* (1971).

McGrath, P.V., 'The Merchant Venturers and Bristol in the Early Seventeenth Century', *The Mariner's Mirror*, XXXVI (1950), pp. 69–80.

Magnússon, S.A., *Northern Sphinx: Iceland and the Icelanders from the Settlement to the Present* (Reykjavik 1977).

Mantran, R., 'L'Evolution des relations entre la Tunisie et l'Empire Ottoman du XVIe au XIXe siècle', *Les Cahiers de Tunisie*, VII (1959).

Marcus, G.S., *A Naval History of England*, vol. I, *The Formative Centuries (to 1793)*, (1961).

Mattingly, G., *Renaissance Diplomacy* (1955).

Miller, E., 'The Economic Policies of Governments: France and England', in *Cambridge Economic History of Europe*, III, ed. M.M. Postan, E.E. Rich, E. Miller (Cambridge 1963), pp. 290–338.

Miller E. and J. Hatcher, *Medieval England: Rural Society and Economic Change, 1086–1348* (1978).

Molloy, C., *De jure maritimo et navali: or, a treatise of affairs maritime and of commerce* (2nd edn. 1682).

Montmorency, J.E.G. de, 'Piracy and the Barbary Corsairs', *Law Quarterly Review*, XXXV (1919), pp. 133–42.

Newark, P., *The Crimson Book of Pirates* (1978).
North, D.C., 'Sources of Productivity Change in Ocean Shipping, 1600–1850', *Journal of Political Economy*, LXXXIV (1968), pp. 953–71.
North, D.C. and R.P. Thomas, *The Rise of the Western World* (Cambridge 1973).
Nye, J.S., 'Corruption and political development: A cost-benefit analysis', in A.J. Heidenheimer, ed., *Political Corruption. Readings in comparative analysis* (1970), pp. 564–79.
Oppenheim, M., *A History of the Administration of the Royal Navy and of Merchant Shipping in Relation to the Navy* (1896).
Ortiz, A.D., *The Golden Age of Spain, 1516–1659* (1971).
Parker, G., *The Army of Flanders and the Spanish Road, 1567–1659: The Logistics of Spanish Victory and Defeat in the Low Countries' Wars* (Cambridge 1972).
────── *The Dutch Revolt* (1977).
────── 'New Light on an Old Theme: Spain and the Netherlands 1550–1650', *European History Quarterly* (formerly *European Studies Review*), XV (1985), pp. 219–36.
Peck, L.L., 'Problems in Jacobean Administration: Was Henry Howard, Earl of Northampton, A Reformer?', *The Historical Journal*, XIX (1976), pp. 831–58.
Penn, C.D., *The Navy under the Early Stuarts and its Influence on English History* (1970 edn.).
Pignon, J., 'Un Document inédit sur la Tunisie au debut du XVIIe', *Les Cahiers de Tunisie*, IX (1961).
────── 'La Milice des janissaires de Tunis au Temps des Deys, 1590–1630', *Les Cahiers de Tunisie*, IV (1956).
Playfair, R.L., *The Scourge of Christendom: Annals of British Relations with Algiers prior to the French Conquest* (1884).
Postan, M.M., *Medieval Trade and Finance* (Cambridge 1973).
'The *Providence* and *Expedition*', *The Mariner's Mirror*, XXXI (1945), p. 234.
Preston, R.A., 'To Outsail the Dutch', *Mariner's Mirror*, XXXVI (1950), pp. 322–36.
The Quarterly Review, no. 408, July 1906, pp. 1–25.
Reed, C., *Lord Burghley and Queen Elizabeth* (1960).
Reed, C.G., 'Transactions Costs and Differential Growth: Seventeenth Century Western Europe', *Journal of Economic History*, XXXIII (1973), pp. 177–90.
Roncière, C. de la, *Histoire de la Marine Française*, 6 vols. (Paris 1899–1932).

Russell, C.S.R., *The Crisis of Parliaments: English History 1509–1660* (Oxford 1971).
—— *Parliaments and English Politics 1621–1629* (Oxford 1979).
Saul, A., 'Great Yarmouth and the Hundred Years War in the Fourteenth Century', *Bulletin of the Institute of Historical Research*, LII (1979), pp. 105–15.
Schurman, D.M., *Julian S. Corbett, 1854–1922* (1981).
Senior, C.M., *A Nation of Pirates: English Piracy in its Heyday* (Newton Abbot 1976).
Smit, J.W., 'The Netherlands and Europe in the Seventeenth and Eighteenth Centuries', in *Britain and the Netherlands in Europe and Asia*, ed. J.S. Bromley and E.H. Kossmann (1968), pp. 13–36.
Smith, A.G.R., 'Crown, Parliament and Finance: the Great Contract of 1610', in *The English Commonwealth 1547–1640: Essays in politics and society presented to Joel Hurstfield*, ed. P. Clark, A.G.R. Smith, N. Tyacke (Leicester 1979), pp. 111–27.
Smith, A. H., 'Militia Rates and Militia Statutes 1558–1663', *The English Commonwealth, 1547–1640: Essays In politics and society presented to Joel Hurstfield*, ed. P. Clark, A.G.R. Smith, N. Tyacke (Leicester 1979), pp. 93–110.
Steensgaard, N., *The Asian Trade Revolution of the Seventeenth Century, the East India Companies, and the Decline of the Caravan Trade* (Chicago 1973).
Stephens, W.B., *Seventeenth-Century Exeter: A study of industrial and commercial development, 1625–1688* (Exeter 1958).
Strachan, M., '*Sampson*'s Fight with Maltese Galleys, 1628', *The Mariner's Mirror*, LV (1969), pp. 281–9.
—— *Sir Thomas Roe:, 1581–1644: a life* (Salisbury, 1989)
Stradling, R.A., 'The Spanish Dunkirkers, 1621–48: a record of plunder and destruction', *Tijdschrift voor Geschiedenis* XCIII (1980), pp. 541–58.
—— 'Catastrophe and Recovery: the Defeat of Spain, 1639–43', *History*, LXIV (1979), p. 205–19.
—— *The Armada of Flanders, Spanish Maritime Policy and European War, 1568–1668* (Cambridge 1992).
—— *Europe and the Decline of Spain: A Study of the Spanish System, 1580–1720* (1981).
—— 'Seventeenth Century Spain: Decline or Survival?', *European Studies Review*, IX (1979), pp. 157–94.
Supple, B.E., *Commercial Crisis and Change in England, 1600–*

1642: A study in the instability of a mercantile economy (Cambridge 1959).
Swales, R.J.W., 'The Ship Money Levy of 1628', *Bulletin of the Institute of Historical Research*, L (1977), pp. 164–76.
Taylor, A.H., 'Carrack into Galleon', *The Mariner's Mirror*, XXXVI (1950), pp. 144–51.
——— 'Galleon into Ship of the Line, I', *The Mariner's Mirror*, XLIV (1958), pp. 267–85.
——— 'Galleon into Ship of the Line, II', *The Mariner's Mirror*, XLV (1959), pp. 14–24.
——— 'Galleon into Ship of the Line, III', *The Mariner's Mirror*, XLV (1959), pp. 100–14.
Taylor, H., 'Trade, Neutrality, and the "English Road", 1630–48', *Economic History Review*, 2nd series, XXV (1972), pp. 236–60.
Tenenti, A., *Naufrages, corsaires et assurances maritimes à Venise (1592–1609)* (Paris 1959).
——— *Piracy and the Decline of Venice 1580–1615* (English edn. 1967).
Tex, J. den, *Oldenbarnevelt*, 2 vols. (English edn., Cambridge 1973).
Thirsk, J. (ed.), *The Agricultural History of England and Wales, IV, 1500–1640* (Cambridge 1967).
Thompson, I.A.A., *War and Government in Hapsburg Spain 1560–1620* (1976).
Thrush, A., 'Naval finance and the origins and development of ship money', in *War and Government in Britain, 1598–1650*, ed. M. Fissel (Manchester 1991), pp. 133–62.
Tite, C.C.G., *Impeachment and Parliamentary Judicature in Early Stuart England* (1974).
Usher, R.G., *A Critical Study of the Historical Method of Samuel Rawson Gardiner with an Excursus on the Historical Conception of the Puritan, Revolution from Clarendon to Gardiner* (Washington 1915).
Vries, J. de, *The Economy of Europe in an Age of Crisis 1600–1750* (Cambridge 1976).
——— 'Is There an Economics of Decline?', *Journal of Economic History*, XXXVIII (1978), pp. 256–8.
Walton, G.M., 'Sources of Productivity Change in American Colonial Shipping, 1675–1775', *Economic History Review*, 2nd series, XX (1967), pp. 67–78.
Waters, H.F., *Genealogical Gleanings in England*, 2 vols. (Boston 1901).

Willan, T.S., *Studies in Elizabethan Foreign Trade* (Manchester 1959).
Williams, N., *The Sea Dogs* (1975).
Willson, D.H., *King James VI and I* (1956).
Wilson, C., *The Dutch Republic: And the Civilisation of the Seventeenth Century* (New York 1968).
Wolf, J.B., *The Barbary Coast: Algiers under the Turks, 1500–1830* (New York 1979).
Wood, A.C., *A History of the Levant Company* (1964 edn.).
Wood, A., *Athenae Oxonienses*, ed. P. Bliss, 4 vols. (1813–1820 edn.).

INDEX

Abbot, George 22
Abbot, Sir Morris 17, 23, 133, 216
Abdy, Alderman 17, 216
Adams, Robert 154, 154n1
Admiralty, the 100n3, 115, 119, 120, 123, 128, 164n2, 238, 242, 246, 248
— High Court of 212
— — Chief Judge of 160
— Lords of 235, 240
Aegean archipelago, 'Arches' 12, 18
Albuquerque, Duque de 245
Aldeburgh 37
Alexandria 18, 153
Algiers (Argier) 11–13, 16, 24–26, 44, 46–48, 51, 56–58, 64, 71, 72, 77, 83, 86, 87, 90, 92, 95–97, 117, 137–9, 144, 147–9, 151, 152, 154, 155, 161, 163, 179, 182–5, 185n1, 186–9, 191, 194, 196, 242, 248, 250, 269
— Bashaw of 87–90, 151, 162, 191, 192, 264
— Bay of 116
— Doana of 88–90
— English consul in 14, 90, 137
— expedition to 77–135 *passim*, 214, 219, 263, 265, 266, 275, 276
— Dutch consul in 189, 190
— Grand Signor (Signior) of 89, 116, 177, 178, 190, 192, 214, 264
— harbour of 92–94, 98, 122, 123, 134, 263
— pirates from 2, 7, 8, 17–20, 46, 50, 51, 107, 138, 139, 143, 174, 177, 188, 190, 193, 217, 221, 257, 264, 266, 267, 269, 270
— representative of Levant Company 137
Aliaga, Father 64
Alicante 87, 92, 95, 96, 99, 118, 119, 150
Alline, Richard 89n1
Alwin, Elizabeth 152
Amazon, river 174
Amboyna, massacre of 57
Anaya, Don Diego Brocharo de 73
Andalusia 15
Andrewes, Lancelot 22
— William 23
Andrews, K.R. 203
Antiquas 180
Argall, Samuel 83
Arlington, Lord 230n6
Aroztegui, Martin de 63, 64, 98
Arundel, Thomas, Earl of 22, 226n1
Aston, Sir Walter 72, 72n8, 73, 73n1, 95–99, 101, 103n3, 116, 120–21, 124, 126, 127, 229, 244, 244nn4 and 5, 245, 246, 249

INDEX

Atlantic Ocean 15, 19, 56, 59, 83, 147
Azores 15, 33
— Santa Maria 2

Backhouse, Rowland 23
Bacon, Sir Francis 22
Bagg, Sir James 199, 200, 200n4
Bahia 207
Baltimore 149, 164n1
Barbary 33, 144, 170
— pirates from 2, 65, 114, 115, 138–40, 146, 147, 176, 178, 222, 232, 273
Barbary Company 21n2, 23, 257
Barcelona 118
Barker, John 201n1
Barnstaple 30, 34, 38, 40, 41, 140, 141
Barrat, Mr 160
Bateman, Robert 23
Bayonne 144
Beaumaris 37, 38n2
Beck, Jane 146, 157n3
— William 146
Bell, Robert 23
Ben Abdella, Jaurer, Moroccan ambassador 253–8
Berwick 31
Biscay 140
Blake, Mr 253, 253n3, 254
— Robert, parliament's agent at Algiers 160, 160n5, 161, 162, 252
— — Admiral 139
Bodmin 146
Boston 31
Boswell, William 209n2
Bou Reg, river 250
Brest 234n3
Bristol 30, 32, 35, 40, 140, 141, 146
Brooke, Sir Fulke Greville, Lord 22, 272n1
Brown, Robert 163
Buckingham, George, Marquess of, previously Earl of, Lord High Admiral 22, 69, 71, 73, 74, 79n2, 83, 95–97, 101, 103n3, 110, 114, 116, 120, 123, 124, 125, 128, 130–2, 179, 199, 200, 200nn4 and 5, 201–3, 209, 211
Burghley, Lord, Lord Treasurer 207n6
Burlamachi, Philip 133, 258n4
Burroughs, Captain 47
Button, John 86, 86n3, 105
— Sir Thomas, Rear Admiral 82, 82nn1 and 2, 87, 92
Byam, Henry, Reverend 166–7

Cadiz 73n1, 77, 87, 95, 96, 100n4, 106, 124, 127, 132, 140, 210, 252, 260
— Veedor General of 134
Calvert, Sir George, Secretary of State 101, 103, 104, 120, 130, 177–81, 184, 188
Campbell, Sir James 157
Canaries, the 15, 145n6
Cape Gabba 56
Cape Ortega, 'North Cape' 115, 178
Cape Pasaro 56
Cape St Vincent, 'South Cape' 56, 115, 212, 248
Cape Spartivento, 'Sparta Venta' 107, 117–19
Cardiff 31
Carew, George, Lord 19
— Sir George, 'A relation of the State of France . . .' 63n1
Caribbean 49
Carleton, Dudley 44–47, 47nn4 and 5, 48, 50, 53–58, 72, 106, 127, 189, 190
Carlisle 31
Carnarvon 37, 38n2
Caron, Noel 52
Cartagena 99, 118, 119, 125
Carteret, George 243, 244, 244n1, 247, 248, 248n1, 252, 252nn1 and 6, 261, 263
— Sir Philip 229n2
Cartmel 155
Cason, Edmund 152, 162
Cave, Eusabey 83
Cephalonia 119
Chamberlain, John 103, 104, 106, 188

INDEX

Channel, the, 'the Narrow Seas' 77, 147, 202, 208, 229, 273
Channel Islands 229n1
Charles I, king, previously Prince of Wales 2, 22, 81n7, 121, 161, 198n2, 210, 215, 216, 219, 220, 222–5, 225n1, 226, 227, 230, 230n6, 231, 232, 236, 238, 240, 241, 245, 253, 254, 257, 259, 263, 268
Charles V, emperor 48, 106, 116, 117
Chatham 83, 247n3
Chester 31, 37, 38, 39n4
Chidley, John 83
Christian IV, king of Denmark, agent of 163
Cinque Ports 31, 35
Clarke, Sir George S. 110
Clothero, Alderman 216
Cockburn, David 200n2
Cockle, Richard 152
Coke, Sir Edward 121, 206n3
— Sir John, Secretary of State 105–7, 204, 209, 209n2, 216n2, 220, 221, 222n1, 223, 226, 228nn2 and 6, 229, 229n2, 230nn4 and 6, 231, 231n1, 232, 232n3, 234, 235n2, 236, 246, 247n1, 256, 256nn1 and 2
Colchester 31, 38
Colmar, Abraham 23
Coloma, Don Carlos 245
Commission to investigate navy (1608) 78
Commons, House of 136n3, 200, 201, 268, 269–71
Conquet 234
Constantinople 117, 153, 175, 176, 184, 215, 239
— English ambassador at 16, 18, 117, 221
— Grand Vizier of 182, 183, 191, 192
— Sultan of 12, 16–18, 20, 175–80, 182, 183, 192, 196
Conway, Sir Edward, Viscount, Secretary of State 102, 199, 239, 240, 258

Corbett, Sir Julian 54, 107–20, 122
— — *England in the Mediterranean* 108, 110, 112
Cornwall 236, 266, 269
— Deputy-Lieutenant of 266
Cottington, Sir Francis, Lord 19, 67, 72, 72n1, 100n5, 121, 216, 224, 231, 235
Counter-Remonstrants 49, 50
Court, William 199n6
Courteen, Mr 248
Cranfield, Lionel, Lord 84, 101, 103, 104, 120, 125, 130, 132
Craven, Lord 157
Crewkerne, John 235n8, 236
Cromwell, Oliver 233n3
Crooke, Thomas 150
Cyprus 12

Dampire, Mr 144
Dansker, Simon, pirate 13, 14n1, 147
Danvers, Lord 108, 110, 229n2
Dartmouth 30, 37, 38, 39n4, 140, 141, 161
Davenant, William, with Inigo Jones, *Britannia Triumphans* 259
Davis, Ralph 140
Delbridge, Mr 136n3
della Barre, John 145, 145n6
Deptford 83
Devon 269
— JPs of 158, 161
D'Ewes, Simonds 271
Digby, Sir John, Lord 3, 22, 22n6, 26, 45, 45n1, 53, 53n6, 60, 63, 64, 67, 69–71, 74, 101, 103, 108, 109, 120, 274
— Sir Kenelm 162, 162n4, 212, 213, 222n1, 226, 230n4, 231n1, 233
Digges, Sir Dudley 218n1
Dike, John 23
Dobbins, Mr 144
Dollinge, Robert 201
Dorchester, merchant adventurers of 36
Dorset, Earl of 216

INDEX

Dover 141
Downs, the 84–86, 247, 252n6, 253, 268
Draper, Henry 163
Dungarvan 141
Dunkirk, privateers from 44, 204, 210
Duppa, John 119
Dutch East India Company 49
— ships of 102

Earle, Sir Walter 198, 199, 200n5, 202
East India Company 16, 21n2, 23, 30, 234n2
Eastland Company 23, 30, 36, 38
Edinburgh 22
Edisbury, Kenrick 243n4
Edmondes, Sir Clement 34, 39n5
Edmundson, G., Professor 220, 223
Elizabeth of Bohemia, princess 80, 174
Emperor, the 103
England 114
— pirates from 9
— western ports of 19
— — mayors of 21
Espesse, Monsieur d' 190
Essex, Earl of 160
Exchequer, the 31, 33, 181
Exeter 22, 30, 33, 34, 37, 38, 38n3, 40, 41
— mayor of 266n2
Eyre, Sir John 174

Falmouth 248nn3 and 4, 252n6
Fearne, Sir John 83, 83n2
Fedally 251
Fenner, William 234
Fenton, John, Lord 22
Finch, Lord Keeper 267, 268n1
Finnet, Sir John 254, 258
Fitz Geffrey, Charles 164–5
Flanders 50
— ports of 232
Flanders Company 23
Ford, 'an ordinary sailor' 90, 90n3, 91
Fowey 39n4, 141

France 33, 36, 37
— ambassador of 229n1, 255
— King of 180, 191
— navy of 208–9
— ports of 147
Frederick, Prince of the Palatinate 80, 102, 103, 173n1
Freeman, Alderman 216
French Company 23, 30
Frizell, James 88, 88n2, 89, 90, 90n1, 152n3, 160, 161, 163nn4 and 5, 164n1, 189, 190, 193, 193n2, 194–6, 214n1, 270

Gardiner, S.R. 223–7, 229n5, 230, 230n6, 260
— — History of England 222
Garrat, William 89n1
Garraway, Mr, Alderman 17, 213, 216
Genoa 50, 117–19, 145n6
— ships of 24
Gentleman, T. 228
Germany 33, 50, 57
— High Seas Fleet of 111
Gibbons, John 151
Gibraltar 86, 91, 97, 100n3, 126, 245
— Straits of, 'the Narrow Seas' 14, 15, 17, 20n1, 35, 56, 65, 68, 83, 91, 100n3, 102, 103, 103n3, 109, 147, 269
Gifford, pirate 13
— Richard, Captain 89n1, 204, 205, 209, 232
Glover, Sir Thomas 174
Godolphin, John 199
Gondomar, Don Diego Sarmiento de Acuña, conde de 61–63, 67, 68, 73, 74, 74n2, 79n1, 83, 100, 101, 114, 175
Gorges, Sir Ferdinando 21–23
Goring, Lord 229n2
Granada 13, 15
Gravesend 254
Green, Lawrence 23
Greenway, Mr 23
Greenwich 254
Greville, Sir Fulke see Brooke, Lord

INDEX

Hall, John, bishop of Exeter 162, 167
— Richard 23
Hammersly, Hugh 23
Hampton, Sir John 83
Hampton Court 236
Hardford, Humphrey 23
Harris, Christopher 83
Harrison, Brian, Captain 243, 262n1
— John, Captain 139, 160, 161, 210, 211, 211n2, 212, 264
— Mr, a Barbary trader 156
Harvey, Lord 204
Harwood, Sir Edward 47, 56
Hatch, George 243
Hawkins, Sir Richard, Vice Admiral 81, 81nn1 and 5, 82, 87, 123, 128, 130
Hawkridge, William, Captain 157
Heath, Sir Robert 102, 208, 227, 228n4, 229, 231
Henry VIII, king 29
Heydon, Sir John 78n1
Heyn, Piet 218
Hill, Richard 162
Hodges, Lewis 162
Holland 49
Holland, Viscount 216, 223
Hopton, Mr 221, 230
Hornachos, in Extremadura, Spain 13n5
Howard, Michael 113
Howell, James 234
Hughes, Thomas, Captain 83, 93
Hull 30

Iceland 164
Inchquin, earl of 153n2
India, Great Mogul of 174
Indies 174
Infantado, Don Juan Hurtado de Mendoza, Duke of 64
Ipswich 31, 34, 38, 41
Ireland 13, 19, 77, 114
Italy 35
— princes of 180

James I, king 1, 3, 7–9, 22, 23, 26, 29, 30, 67, 67n3, 87, 89, 103, 104, 114, 121, 125, 129, 131, 132, 173n1, 181, 183, 188, 191, 192, 196, 220, 223, 276
— — attitude towards pirates 7–20
— — diplomacy against pirates 44, 45, 45n1, 48, 52, 53, 53n6, 54–59, 60–74, 176, 180, 188
— — diplomatic negotiations with Spain 43–44, 60–74 *passim*
— — diplomatic negotiations with the United Provinces 43–59 *passim*
— — *Lepanto* 10–11
James, Edward 17, 23
Jenner, Robert 268
Jersey 141
John of Austria, Don 11
Jones, Inigo, with William Davenat, *Britannia Triumphans* 259
Juxon, William, bishop of London 167n2, 236n1, 272

Keale, Robert, *The Trade's Increase* 143
Kellet, Edward 165–6
Kepler, J.S. 227
Kerby, Jeffrey 23
King, Richard 268, 269, 271
King's Lynn 31, 141
Knott, Nathaniel 149
Kymbolton, Lord 272n1

La Ciotat 180
Lake, Robert 153n4
— Sir Thomas 22, 29, 44, 45, 45n1
Land's End 201, 236, 253
Lane, F.C., professor 3
La Rochelle 210, 234, 260
Laud, William, archbishop of Canterbury 167, 167n2, 168, 168n2, 169, 236, 258
Leate, Nicholas 17, 23, 39n5, 133, 138n3, 161, 184, 193
Leg, William 153, 200
Leghorn (Ligorno, Livorno) 94n5, 145, 145n6, 161, 180
Leicester, Earl of 235, 235n2

Lennox, Ludovic, Duke of 22
Lepanto, battle of 11
Lerma, Duque de 74
Levant, the 12, 18, 36, 184, 191, 195
Levant Company 16, 18, 18n4, 20, 21n2, 23, 30, 36, 39, 90n3, 141, 141n1, 144, 148, 161n1, 174–7, 180, 181, 183, 188, 188n3, 193, 193n1, 195, 210, 216, 217, 239, 267, 271
— ships of 15
Lincoln 22
Lindsey, Earl of 233, 234n3, 239, 247n1
Lisbon 249
Liverpool 37, 39n4
Lockyer, Roger 203
London 23, 32, 53, 84, 101, 117, 135, 141, 145n6, 242, 254
— citizens of 254, 258, 268
— City of 23, 24, 30, 255
— Court of Aldermen 216
— merchant strangers of 36
— ships of 19
— Temple Bar 255
— Wapping Pier 9
— Wood Street 255
Looe 266n2
Lord High Admiral 9, 19; see also Buckingham, Marquess of; Northumberland, Earl of; Nottingham, Earl of
Lord Privy Seal 216n2
Lords, House of 158, 270, 271
Love, Sir Thomas 82
Lowestoft 37
Low Countries 8, 56n3, 57, 226; see also Netherlands
Lumley, Sir Martin 254
Lundy, Isle of 149, 235
Lyme Regis 31, 33, 34, 37, 38, 40, 141

Madrid 45, 60, 73, 101, 119
McGowan, A.P. 203
Maddocke, John 212
Mahan, A.T. 111
Mainwaring, Sir Arthur 82, 82n3
Majorca 91, 92, 98, 99, 156

— viceroy of 98
Mainwaring, Sir Arthur 82, 82n3
— Sir Henry 109, 204
Malaga 19, 87, 91, 92, 95, 125, 126, 140, 145, 178
Malta 197
Mamora 138, 245, 262
Mannique, Don Juan de Aya la 98
Mansell, Sir Robert 73, 74, 74n2, 77–135 *passim*, 139, 173, 179n2, 181, 201n4, 202, 274
— — wife of 121, 124
Marseilles 180, 234
Marten, Henry, Chief Judge of the High Court of Admiralty 210, 211
Massachusetts 239
Matress, Ralph 158
Maurice of Nassau 44, 47, 48, 50, 54, 55
May, W.J., Captain 110
Mediterranean Sea 18, 19, 46, 51, 54, 55, 57, 59, 74, 83–85, 99, 102, 106, 114, 118, 132, 140, 147, 156, 213, 245
Melcombe Regis 31
Mellin, William 89n1
Merchant Adventurers 30, 32, 35, 36
Mervin, Sir Henry 144
Messina 109, 178
Messia, Don Augustin 64
Mexia, Agustin 72n7
Middleton, Thomas, *A Game At Chess* 79
Milbrooke 141, 200n8, 201n1
Milford Haven 31
Minehead 158, 165, 167, 170
Moncado, Hugh 106
Monson, Sir William 106–7, 113, 228, 234
— — *The ill-managed Enterprise upon Algiers . . .* 106
Montague, Sir Sidney 213
Moore, John 268
Morocco (Marocco) 160, 167, 221, 243, 245, 246
— Emperor (king) of 11, 250, 252, 257, 258, 264

INDEX

— pirates of 257
Morteque 180
Mousehole Point 266n2
Mun, Thomas 23, 228
Murad IV, Sultan of Constantinople 191
Muscovy Company 23, 30, 36

Naunton, Sir Robert 53, 56–59
Navy, Royal 29, 67, 111, 145n6, 208, 209, 224, 275, 276
— Treasurer of 270
Necolade, Spanish ambassador 224, 231, 233
Netherlands 33, 49; *see also* Low Countries
Newburgh, Lord 216
Newcastle 31, 41
New England 239
Newfoundland 37
Newfoundland fishermen 237
Nicholas, Edward 138n4, 202, 222n1, 233n4, 235, 237, 238, 240, 240n1, 241–3, 243n4, 244, 246, 246n2, 247, 262
North Africa, pirates from 10
Northumberland, Earl of, Lord High Admiral 238, 238n7, 240, 252, 262, 270, 272n1
Norway 33
Nottingham, Charles Howard, Earl of, Lord High Admiral 9, 19, 61, 77, 79

Oglander, Sir John 9n3
Okeley, William 151, 153n4, 154
Oldenbarnevelt, Jan van 44, 46–48, 74
Olivares, Conde Duque de 207, 225, 225n1, 227
Oppenheim, M.A. 260, 263
Orford 37
Ostend, privateers from 204
Osuna, duke of 50

Palatinate, Lower 173n1
Palmer, Sir Henry 82
Paris 147
Park, Elizabeth 155
— Giles 155

Parliament 2, 136n3, 152, 199, 202, 218n1, 268, 271
Parma, Prince of 49
Pembroke, Philip, Earl of 272
— William, Earl of 22
Penn, C.D. 260
— Giles, Captain 92, 138n4, 235, 237, 237n1, 238, 242–3, 243n2
Pennington, Sir John 83, 234, 244n1, 252n6
Penticost, George 156
Penzance 149, 266n2
Percivall, Edmond 144
Petitions to suppress piracy 16n6, 17, 21, 26
Pett, Phineas 243, 244
Phelips, Sir Robert 107, 198, 202
Philip III, king of Spain 19, 24, 25, 45, 58, 60, 65–67, 73, 74, 85, 104, 115, 274
Philip IV, king of Spain 181, 207, 224
Phillip, Sir Thomas 239
Pige, Christopher 235n6
Pindar, Sir Paul 18–20, 20n1, 213
Pitt, William 112
Plymouth 30, 33, 34, 38, 39, 39n4, 86n5, 140, 141, 164, 234, 258n4, 266
— mayor of 199, 199n6
Poole 31, 37–39, 41, 143
Porchester 253
Porter, Thomas 83
Portland, Richard Weston, Earl of 216, 224, 227, 231
Portugal 33, 114, 140
— *consejo de* 245
Potts, John 268
Privy Chamber, gentlemen of 255
Privy Council 7, 16n5, 21, 22, 29–31, 34–40, 54, 58, 60, 61, 69, 100, 102, 103, 118, 119, 133, 138, 144, 159, 162, 185, 188, 192, 193, 193n1, 195, 198, 198n2, 199, 200, 216, 217, 223, 230n6, 231n1, 235, 236, 260n1, 274, 275
Proclamations:
against Pirates (1609) 10

concerning Warlike ships at Sea (1603) 10
for revocation of Mariners (1605) 10
for the search and apprehension of certaine Pirates (1604) 10
— (1606) 10
prohibiting merchants trading . . . (1608) 17
revoking letters of marque (1604) 16
to represse all Piracies (1604) 10
with certaine Ordinances (1605) 10
Providence Island 151
Pym, John 268

Rainsborough, Thomas 253n2
— William, Captain 82, 163n1, 197n1, 238–53 *passim*, 260–3, 263nn1–4, 264, 265, 265n2, 268
— William, son of William 253n2
Rais, Morat 149
Raleigh, Sir Walter 67, 67n3, 83n2, 208, 228
Ramsay, Mr 270
Rawlins, John 151
Raymond, George 83
Red Sea 181, 184
Remonstrants 49, 59
Rhé, Isle de 210, 260
Rice, Mr 95
Richelieu, Cardinal 224, 229, 229n2
Riviera, the 118
Robinson, Henry 136n3
Rochester, Earl of 272n1
Roe, Sir Thomas 19, 106, 106n2, 138n2, 163n5, 204, 212, 213, 214n1, 215–17, 223, 226nn2 and 3, 239, 264, 268, 269, 274
— — embassy of 173–97 *passim*
Rolle, John 200
Roper, Captain 88–91, 95
Rossington, Edmund 266n2
Rupert, prince 160n4
Russell, William, Treasurer of the Navy 240, 243

Safi 138, 253
St Tropez (Santropes) 180
Salisbury, Earl of 15
Sallee (Sally) 11, 12, 13n5, 138, 138n3, 139, 140n2, 144, 154, 194, 198, 211, 212, 221, 245, 261, 276
— armadors of 136n3
— castle of 151
— expedition to 236–53 *passim*, 258, 260–5, 276
— governor of 212, 249, 252, 264
— harbour of 251
— pirates of 138, 143, 164n2, 210, 234, 235, 237, 257, 265
— Saint of 251
Salter, Sir Nicholas 32
Sandys, Sir Edwin 63, 121
Santa Cruz 251
Santa Cruz, Marques de 245
San Thomé 67
Sardinia 35
Savoy 50
Schurman, Donald 113
Scilly Isles 199, 199n5, 266
Scotland 7
Scudamore, Viscount 235n2
Seamen, Edmund 243
Selden, John, *Mare Clausum* 228
Severn, river 147
Seville 15
Shallard, Peter de 234
Sherley, Anthony, *Political Power in the Whole World* 63n1
Sherwin, Mr 23
Ship Money 27–28, 31, 41, 220–36 *passim*, 258, 258nn2–4, 259, 259, 260n1, 267, 268, 272, 274, 275
Ships:
 Angel 240
 Antelope 82, 91, 95, 129, 240, 242, 243, 247, 247n3, 248, 252, 252n6, 261
 Barbary 83
 Blessing of London 150
 Blue Dove 211
 Bonaventure 238
 Castle 239
 Centurion 83

INDEX

Worcester, Edward, Earl of 22
Wotton, Sir Henry 68, 109n3
Wren, Matthew, bishop of Norwich 167
Wright, Robert 23

Yarmouth 31, 37, 141
Yeomen of the Guard 255

Zante (Zant) 103, 119, 179, 191
Zeeland 49
Zoete, William de 84n4
Zouch, Lord 35
Zúñiga, Don Baltasar de 64, 64n1

INDEX

Constant Reformation 82, 95, 129
Convertine 82, 82n4, 129
Diamond 142
Diana of Sandwich 145
Dolphin 148
Dove of Bristol 145
Dreadnought 99, 100n3, 244
Expedition 241, 242, 249n4, 252, 261, 269
Falcon of London 138n3
George Bonaventure 150
Golden Phoenix 83, 92
Goodwill 87
Grace 248n3 and 4
Great Neptune 243, 244
Hearts Desire of London 138n3, 141n2
Hercules 83, 94, 240, 243, 248, 249, 251, 252, 252n6, 260n5, 262n1, 264n2
Hopewell of Rye 150
Leopard 238, 240, 241n5, 242, 243, 247, 247n3, 257, 258n1, 261
Lion (*Lyon*) 80, 82, 95, 96, 129, 200
Marigold (*Marygold*) 83, 95
Marmaduke 83
Mary 244, 251
Mary of London 157
Mary Rose 252
Merchant Bonaventura (*Bonaventure*) 83, 94
Mercury 91
Merhonour (*Mer-Honour*) 77, 239
Neptune 83
Neptune of Amsterdam 251
Phenix of Bristol 150
Primrose 83, 95
Prosperous 244
Providence 241, 242, 249n, 252, 261, 269
Rainbow 82, 95, 129, 200, 212n1
Rebecca of London 142, 143, 150, 267
Resistance 78
Restore 83, 95

Roebuck 252
St Dennis 244
Sampson 197n1, 239
Samson of London 151
Samuel 83
Sovereign of the Seas 3, 233n3, 254, 257, 263
Spy 91
Star 83n2
Successe of London 141
Supply of Bristol 148
Tiger of Bristol 150
Triumph 238
Vanguard 82, 95, 129, 132
Victory 99, 100n3
William and Elizabeth 161
William and John of London 149, 212, 213
Zouch Phoenix 83, 95
Shrewsbury, Earl of 254
Sicily 35, 178
Sidans, Mully 212
Simonds, Thomas 23
Slaney, Humphrey 23
Smith, Sir Thomas 21, 21n2
South America 49
Southampton 31, 35, 41, 141
Southampton, Earl of 61, 61n3, 63, 77, 121
Southwold 240n1
Spaicer, Nicholas 161, 162
Spain 33, 36, 54, 65, 78, 114, 117, 119, 140, 174, 256, 266
— ambassador of 10, 188, 231, 255, 257
— *Armada del Mar Oceano* 206
— Council of State 63, 67, 118, 245
— Council of War 19, 64–67, 98, 99, 128
— English embassy in 124
— General of the Armada 134
— *Infanta* of 22
— Minister of War 127
— navy of 65–71, 206–7
— Veedor General of 97
Spanish Company 23, 30, 36, 39, 40, 188, 188n3
Spanish Netherlands 50
Spencer, Lord 272n1

INDEX

Spinola, Ambroglio 56, 58
Spratt, Devereux, Reverend 136n3, 154, 155
Squibb, Captain 87, 88
Stepney 146
Stewart, Sir Francis 200, 200n5 and 6, 201, 237
Stone, William 23
Suffolk, Thomas, Earl of 22
Swales, R.J.W. 28
Symonds, John 153n4

Talon 180
Tanfield, Sir Francis 83
Taunton, merchants of 38
Taylor, Hartland 227
Tetuan 89n1, 92, 139
Thames, river 20, 80, 84, 147, 247
Tilbury 247
Tipton, John 13n7
Topsham 141
Torremolinos 95
Totnes 37, 39n4
Tranckmore, Robert 243
Trevor, Sir Sackville 204
Trewinard, John 199
Trinity House 16, 23, 30, 33, 84n1, 128, 138, 153, 213, 219, 238, 240, 264, 269, 274
Tripoli, 11, 13, 138, 139
— pirates from 19
Tunis 11–13, 44, 138, 138n3, 139, 182, 183–5, 185n1, 187, 189, 191, 194, 248, 269
— Bashaw of 191, 192
— pirates from 17–19, 24, 118, 177, 188, 193, 217, 221, 269, 270
Turkey 193
— admiral of 20
Turkey Company 180
United Provinces, navy of 207–9
— ports of 147
— States General of 85
Ushant 234n3

Vane, Sir Henry 161, 247n1, 249n3, 251n1, 268, 269
Venice 50, 68, 71
Verney, pirate 13
— Gazettes of 108
Vernon, George 184
Vicarie, John 213n2
Vienna 103
Villahermosa, Duque de 245
Virginia 145

Wadsworth, James 151, 155, 157
Waller, Edmund 263n1
Ward, pirate 13
Warwick, Earl of 272n1
Washford 2
Wentworth, Thomas, Lord Deputy 227, 234, 258
West Indies 204, 256
Weston, Richard see Portland, Earl of
Weymouth 31, 33, 34, 36–40, 141, 144
Weymouth and Melcombe Regis, mayor of 200
Whitby, Mr 136n3
White, Francis, bishop of Ely 167n2
— Thomas 243
Whitehall 254
— Banqueting House 255
Whitson, alderman of Bristol 200
Wiche, Richard 23
Willson, D.H. 9
Winchester 164n2
— bishop of 272n1
Windebank, Sir Francis, Secretary of State 161, 216n2, 224n3, 226n2, 231, 247n1, 258n4
Winwood, Sir Ralph 22n6, 29, 44, 46–49
Wolstenholme, Sir John 32
Wollestone, Mr 23
Wood, A.C. 194, 195
— William, son of 138
Woodbridge 39, 41
Woodroof, Robert 160n7
Woodruff, Mr, heirs of 248
Woodstock 236
Woolwich 244, 254
Wootton, Edward, Lord 22

— ambassador of 9, 176, 195, 195n1, 225, 243, 255, 256, 271